Mabel Walker Willebrandt

Mabel Walker Willebrandt, Assistant Attorney General of the United States 1921–1929.

Mabel
Walker Willebrandt

A STUDY OF POWER, LOYALTY, AND LAW

Dorothy M. Brown

THE UNIVERSITY OF TENNESSEE PRESS

KNOXVILLE

2p

Library of Congress Cataloging in Publication Data

Brown, Dorothy M. (Dorothy Marie), 1932–
  Mabel Walker Willebrandt: a study of power, loyalty,
and law.

  Bibliography: p.
  Includes index.
  1. Willebrandt, Mabel Walker, 1889–   . 2. Lawyers
—United States—Biography. I. Title.
KF373.W4656B76 1984   349.73'092'4 [B]   83-6651
ISBN 0-87049-402-3   347.300924 [B]
ISBN 0-87049-403-1 (pbk.)

To my parents

Contents

	Prologue	xi
	Acknowledgments	xv
1.	Frontier Beginning	3
2.	California: Professional and Progressive	27
3.	The Justice Department: Prohibition	49
4.	The Justice Department: Prisons, Taxes, the Judgeship	81
5.	Extending Family and Profession	117
6.	Political Campaigns in the 1920s	149
7.	Private Practice, Private Life	179
8.	Hollywood and the Red Scare	229
	Notes	265
	Bibliography	307
	Index	323

Illustrations

(Unless otherwise noted, all photographs reproduced
by courtesy of Dorothy Van Dyke.)

Mabel Walker Willebrandt,
Assistant Attorney General — *Frontispiece*
An early formal portrait — 7
Family and neighbors, Lucerne, Missouri — 7
The Buckley Bank, 1909 — 17
The Buckley basketball team, 1909 — 18
Mabel Walker at twenty — 18
The first home of Mabel and Arthur Willebrandt — 20
The view from the sanatorium home — 20
Lazy days in Arizona, 1910 — 21
Arthur Willebrandt and David Walker — 23
"Queen Superior" surveying the world — 24
Willebrandt and students at Lincoln Park
Elementary School, 1913 — 31
Fred Horowitz, Willebrandt, and John Shepherd
at graduation, 1916 — 35
Myrtle and David Walker, early 1920s — 44
Willebrandt at the Department of Justice
(courtesy of the Library of Congress) — 52
Cartoon of the frustration of prohibition
enforcement, by T. E. Powers — 52
Cartoon by Kessler, 1924 — 59
Willebrandt in typical office attire — 60
Coolidge and Willebrandt, 1924 — 113
Willebrandt and Dorothy — 125
The "baby cabinet" with its lone woman member — 144
Talburt's rendition of public reaction to
Willebrandt's campaigning — 162

Addressing a friendly crowd at Temple City, 1928   170
Broadcasting in the final days of the 1928
    campaign (courtesy of the Library of Congress)   170
Arriving in Boston in regulation flying suit   191
Willebrandt and Amelia Earhart, 1930   193
Willebrandt, Earhart, and a delegation promoting
    aviation   193
A mid-career portrait of Willebrandt   199
Willebrandt and Jacqueline Cochran at a banquet   220
Myrtle and David Walker, 1930   223
Walker Fields   225
Willebrandt, Dorothy, and the Walkers
    at the farm, 1937   225
Christmas at the farm, 1937   227
Backyard cookout with Hollywood clients
    and friends   232
Willebrandt speaking at Nome, Alaska, 1946   247
Willebrandt in the 1950s   254

Prologue

If Mabel had worn trousers, she could have been President.

JUDGE JOHN J. SIRICA
Washington, D.C., July 1978

*I*N 1928, Mabel Walker Willebrandt was the most famous and controversial woman in America. During her arduous, loyal campaigning for Republican presidential candidate Herbert Hoover, the "First Legal Lady of the Land" earned the added titles of "Prohibition Portia," the "Deborah of the Drys," and "Mrs. Firebrand." Syndicated columnist Frank Kent called her "the most notorious woman in America." Friend and foe could agree with the assessment of *Collier's* political commentator: "No other woman has ever had so much influence upon a Presidential campaign as Mrs. Willebrandt has had upon this one."[1]

For Willebrandt, 1928 was the most difficult of seven demanding, challenging years as assistant attorney general of the United States. The highest ranking woman in the federal government, with responsibility for prohibition cases, federal income tax litigation, and the federal prison system, she argued more cases before the U.S. Supreme Court than all but three of her contemporaries. In both prohibition and tax cases, her arguments set the basic interpretations of the scope of the new Sixteenth and Eighteenth amendments to the Constitution. Her initiative and drive won major expansion and reform of the moribund federal prison system.

These accomplishments only capped her meteoric career. Born in a Kansas sod dugout in 1889, Willebrandt lived the nomadic frontier life of her teacher-printer-farmer parents. Her formal schooling began when she was thirteen; four years later, at seventeen, she was teaching in the rural schools in Michigan. Within the next five years, she married, nursed her ailing husband back to health in Arizona, earned a bachelor's degree at Tempe Normal School, and moved to California, where she was appointed an elementary school principal. While still a principal, she sent both herself and her husband through the University of Southern California law school. In 1916, she became the first assistant police court defender in Los Angeles, representing more than 2,000 women in the next two years. Simultaneously, she launched her private practice, began establishing a network of women professionals, and became active in Republican politics and in lobbying for women's issues before the California legislature. Meanwhile she faced the disintegration of her marriage and coped with an increasing hearing disability. In 1921, at thirty-two, recommended by most of the bench and bar of Southern California, she was appointed an assistant attorney general of the United States.

In 1928, Willebrandt's life stood in ruins, ravaged by the political aftermath of the bitter, divisive Smith-Hoover campaign. Frustrated, though far from defeated, Willebrandt resigned her appointment in May 1929. Leaving public office and power, she began a new life, pioneering in the emerging fields of aviation and radio law. An expert in federal regulations and taxes, she represented major industries, from the California grape growers to Metro-Goldwyn-Mayer. The Screen Directors Guild of America was her client for twenty years. In the 1950s, her work with the guild and her own concern for individual freedom and opportunity brought her again into public and political controversy as America agonized through its second big Red Scare.

Clearly, the assertion that women in American politics "have been virtually invisible," did not apply to Mabel Walker Willebrandt. More accurately, she has all but disappeared. Partially, she wielded the eraser herself, vowing as she left Washington to avoid politics and ordering her mother to destroy the correspondence that detailed her successful and traumatic years as assistant attorney general.[2] In 1928, the *New York Times* carried more than seventy-five stories on Willebrandt; the last story that appeared there until her obituary in April, 1963, was in 1935. Similarly, she vanished from the major new histories of the 1920s and is frequently nowhere to be found in the new surveys in women's history. Even in Sophonisba Breckinridge's early analysis, *Women in the Twentieth Century*, Willebrandt is barely mentioned. Only in studies on prohibition and on prison reform is her work acknowledged. Her life had so neatly broken in two that those who shared the second half knew little of her Washington career. The screen directors knew that she had "done something," but saw her only as one of the best lawyers in the country. Even her friend and neighbor, aviator Jacqueline Cochran, raised the question: "Why are you writing about Mabel Walker Willebrandt?"[3]

The answer is obvious. Willebrandt lived one of the most important and interesting lives in twentieth-century America. In the traditional terms of power and influence, she is matched by only one other woman, Eleanor Roosevelt. In the area of legal history, she made major contributions in tax and air law. Not only was she a redoubtable campaigner, she led in coordinating one of the most effective women's lobbies to found the first federal prison for women. Her life provides a case study for women's history as she met major challenges in identity and autonomy.

In 1928, she was in the fight of her life, a life that began on the tumultuous Kansas frontier.

Acknowledgments

*T*HIS biography is the result of the convergence of two factors: the dedication of Willebrandt's daughter, Dorothy Van Dyke, and a research assignment. In their meticulous and painstaking development of the list of 442 women to be included in *Notable American Women: The Modern Period*, editors Barbara Sicherman and Carol Hurd Green sought nominations from professionals throughout the country. Invariably, Mabel Walker Willebrandt was high on the list of notable lawyers. Since I had completed some research on bootlegging and the "wet" history of Maryland in the 1920s, they assigned her article to me. The research problem became obvious immediately. The first half of Willebrandt's life was fairly well chronicled in magazine and newspaper articles. Beyond 1931, the trail was cold. Following the lead in the *Los Angeles Times'* obituary, which noted that friends might send contributions to the Wheaton College scholarship fund, I was finally able to locate her daughter in Cannon Beach, Oregon.

Dorothy Willebrandt Van Dyke had carefully preserved a small collection of her mother's letters and family correspondence. She had written to several biographers trying to interest them in her mother's story. Always the answer was the same. Since most of the letters were dated before 1932, sources posed a problem. Relatively rich for the public years, sources for the private years were meager: records of court cases, briefs, transcripts of federal regulatory hearings, correspondence in the collected papers of her friends, and the shared memories of professional colleagues and friends.

Invaluable to me were interviews with Willebrandt's University of Southern California law school colleagues Myra Dell Collins, Judge May Lahey, and Fred Horowitz; Walter Taylor, of Fruit Industries; her Washington colleagues Judge John J. Sirica, the Honorable Erwin N. Griswold, Judge Fay Bentley, and Louise Foster; international and air law expert Margaret Lambie; screen directors Frank Capra, Al Rogell, Joseph Youngerman; writer Virginia Kellogg Mortensen;

xv

aviator Jacqueline Cochran; her friends and proteges Mary and Calvin Claggett, Dr. Mary Ellen Collins, and Rose d'Amore; and finally, her foster sister Minnie Wells and her daughter Mabel Wells. Former Phi Delta Delta national president Judge Edith M. Atkinson, Fruit Industries executive Captain H.C. Williams, and Willebrandt's friend Mrs. Jan Norduyn wrote to me, sharing their recollections. Dorothy Van Dyke, her husband, Hendrick, and Grace Knoeller, Willebrandt's best friend, and Paula Knoeller Gore, her friend and for a time her secretary, have generously given their knowledge and insights to this biography. Grace Knoeller was particularly helpful in contacting friends and colleagues of Mrs. Willebrandt. Without Mrs. Van Dyke and the Knoellers no biography would have been possible.

Helpful in providing access to their materials were special collections librarians and staffs at the Bancroft Library, University of California, Berkeley; the Research Library, the University of California, Berkeley; the Research Library, the University of California at Los Angeles; the Doheny Library at the University of Southern California; the University of Alaska, Fairbanks; Baker Library, Dartmouth College; the Schlesinger Library, Radcliffe College; the American Film Institute; the University of West Virginia; the Ohio State Historical Society; Western Reserve Historical Society; the Los Angeles County Law Library; the librarians of the *Los Angeles Times*, the Los Angeles *Herald-Examiner*, and the *Kansas City Star*, the American Bar Association; the archivists of Park College, Arizona State University, the University of Southern California, and the city of Los Angeles; the office of the Superintendent of Schools, South Pasadena, California; the Herbert Hoover Presidential Library, West Branch, Iowa; the Hoover Institution, Stanford University; the Franklin D. Roosevelt, Harry S. Truman, and Dwight D. Eisenhower presidential libraries. Every Washington researcher appreciates the professionalism of the staffs of the Manuscript Division of the Library of Congress and of the National Archives. The archivists of the judicial section of the National Archives, who screen all material before releasing it to researchers, were particularly patient and efficient. The Willebrandt letters culled from these sources have been quoted frequently throughout, preserving not only the strength and verve of her style, but also her shorthand spelling and delight in multiple exclamation points.

The biography has been appreciably strengthened by the suggestions of William H. Harbaugh of the University of Virginia, Carol

Hurd Green of Boston College, and Rev. Joseph T. Durkin, S.J., of Georgetown University. Mark Wilkinson of the University of Michigan helped to track down information on the Buckley bank, and Claudine Schweber-Koren shared her knowledge of Mary Belle Harris and the early years of the Federal Industrial Institution for Women at Alderson. The staff at Alderson provided access to that facility and to the manuscript of the Alderson saga. Barbara Gersten was helpful in her comments on legal points. Ann Kelly, Mary McBride, Patricia Byrd Kelly, and Margaret Steinhagen made suggestions from their perspectives in social work, education, and child rearing. Sister Bridget Marie, S.S.N.D., has helped with her sound advice and meticulous reading of drafts. Jean Parlett, Elizabeth McKeown, Josephine Trueschler, and Janet Doehlert, read, questioned, and commented on aspects of the manuscript. David Hagan contributed his photographic skills. Georgetown University supported this research with summer grants. Correspondence and typing was aided by Constance Holden and Anne Martone. The final version was typed by Mary Dyer, for years the "grandmother" of the Georgetown Graduate School and eagle-eyed searcher for correct citations and form. Joanne Ainsworth of the Guilford Group was a meticulous, long-suffering, but always encouraging copyeditor. Her efforts have markedly improved the work. Dick O'Keefe shared his considerable skills in compiling the index. The steady interest and encouragement of acquisitions editor Mavis Bryant and the care of senior editor Katherine Holloway in shepherding the manuscript through the final stages are much appreciated. All errors of omission and commission are, of course, my own.

DOROTHY M. BROWN
Georgetown University

August 1983

Mabel Walker Willebrandt

CHAPTER ONE

Frontier Beginning

The other day at my farm we were clearing out the apple cellar. In it lay a pile of seed potatoes. They were stored in a dark corner against a stone wall. Most of the left-overs were dormant or had a few pale sprouts shriveled, after a few inches growth, for lack of sunshine. But I was challenged by one. It had put down roots and had thrust up a purposeful stem. Curious, I followed the line of its unerring search for light. The frail sprout led to the top of the old stone wall along its length to the opposite southern side through, to my amazement, a crack in the window frame! Still unbelieving, I went outside, and there found beautiful normal foliage on a plant whose stem had traveled more than twelve feet to glimpse a far horizon and feel the sun. What strange impulse of life and growth pushed it on and up?

People are like that. Some are fixed by the environment of traditions surrounding their lives. Others with questing spirit seek a wider view.

MABEL WALKER WILLEBRANDT
Address at the Amelia Earhart Memorial,
New York, November 1939

*H*ER mother wanted to call her Pansy Elvera. The name fit the large violet-blue eyes blinking in the morning sunlight. Yet before the birth of this eagerly awaited baby, her mother had looked out across the waving blue stem grass and prayed that God, who seemed so present in the immensity of the prairie sky, would use this new life for service. The baby was born on May 23, 1889, in a sod dugout on the rough plain of southwest Kansas.[1] She was named Mabel Elizabeth Walker—a name more suited to one who would always face the challenge of the pioneer.

Pioneer ancestors ranged on both sides of the family. Her maternal great-great-grandmother was born on the Atlantic crossing and named for the ship, *Dolly*, bringing her family from Germany in the last years of the eighteenth century. Later settling with her family in Cattaraugus County, New York, she met and married a neighboring farmer of German descent, John Harwick. The pioneer impetus continued westward as their daughter Susan, a school teacher, journeyed with her young husband, John Alton, and their children on a wagon train to establish a homestead in Hancock County, Illinois. One of their young daughters, Cordelia, married Thomas P. Eaton, a farmer of Welsh descent who had also migrated from New York. By the outbreak of the Civil War, the young Eatons had moved to Putnam County, Missouri, and had begun homesteading on the rough, rolling grasslands. Thomas, as did all of the Eatons and Altons who were of age, volunteered to serve in the Union army. Before he left with the Seventh Missouri Cavalry volunteers, their daughter Myrtle, Mabel's mother, was born.[2]

Myrtle Eaton grew up helping with the farm chores and then, as had her grandmother, earned her teaching credentials and won a job in the county schools. As one of the county directors remembered, "She wanted a school and we wanted a teacher. Her teaching was highly satisfactory, well-worth the price we paid her."[3] In March 1887, at the age of twenty-six, she left by stage for the booming Kansas frontier, near Woodsdale in Stevens County, to join her brother Cyrus and to try to stake a claim of her own. She joined those single women who made up a "noteworthy proportion" of the settlers on the Kansas prairie. They were "plucky and staunch" and, "if at all inclined toward matrimony were not left to bloom alone and unseen."[4]

She arrived in turbulent times. The year before, the harsh winter of 1886 had felled 80 percent of the southwest Kansas herds. One settler reported that it would have been possible to walk along the right-of-way of the Atchison, Topeka & Santa Fe Railroad on the carcasses of cattle and never touch foot to ground. While the killing winter hastened the retreat of the cattlemen before the influx of land-hungry settlers, 1887 marked the beginning of the dry seasons that ruined the dreams of the homesteaders.[5]

Myrtle Eaton's first year in Kansas was a disastrous one. Only half of the corn and wheat crop could be harvested. One settler remembered: "Week after week the hot burning sun glared down from a cloudless steel-blue sky. The dread hot winds blew in from the south. Day after day they continued. All fodder, small grain and corn, was cut short. This scorching summer was followed by the great blizzard of 1888.[6]

The hard year of 1888 was never forgotten by Myrtle for another reason as well—the brutal murder of her brother in the haystack massacre. The killing resulted from the heated war to win the county seat. Hugoton, a small town to the south of Woodsdale, had triumphed in the first round, but if Woodsdale or another rival town, Vorhees, could successfully lure a railroad line, the county seat might be won away from Hugoton. To arm for an anticipated fight, both Hugoton and Woodsdale imported gunmen "of unsavory reputation" as their new town marshals.

At one turbulent meeting of representatives of the three towns, the argument over railroad routes degenerated into a bare-knuckles and pistol-whipping fight between the sheriff of Woodsdale and Sam Robinson, Hugoton's new marshal. In retaliation for the severe beating of their sheriff, Woodsdale issued a warrant for Robinson's arrest. After two abortive chases, a Woodsdale posse, joined by Cyrus Eaton, set out on the trail again. The next morning they woke at their campsite in a hay meadow to find themselves surrounded by a Hugoton posse led by Robinson. Disarmed and helpless, they were lined up and gunned down. One survivor, left for dead, rode north; Myrtle learned that her brother had been massacred on July 26, 1888.[7] For the next thirty years she sought justice for the killing.

The tragedy was coupled with a new beginning, for two months earlier, Myrtle Eaton had married David W. Walker, a young printer and teacher from Hugoton. Together they would try to prove up a claim.

The Walkers had emigrated from Wurtemburg, Germany. David's grandfather was the only one of four brothers to survive Napoleon's retreat from Moscow. At the Battle of Waterloo, he was cut down by a saber blow to the head but was able to rise with the survivors though the "dead and wounded were seven men deep."[8] In 1845, his son, John C. Walker, displaying some of the family courage and tenacity, sailed for America and bought a farm in Indiana County, Pennsylvania. Two years later John married another German pioneer, Katherine Synder from Hessen. At the end of the Civil War, with a family of nine children to support, the Walkers left for the cheap land and southern climate of Tennessee. They settled on a farm near Tullahoma and attempted to join a community of decidedly unfriendly southern sympathizers. Experienced in making brick, John Walker offered to build a school with the aid and obviously for the benefit of his sons.[9] When completed it was dubbed the "Yankee Tabernacle" by neighbors who registered their dislike of the newcomers by firing bullets into the door. Though only eight when the school was finished, David reported growing "to manhood there, with scarcely any education, as school advantages were very poor." He did manage to study on his own and at twenty-two was accomplished enough to earn a certificate for teaching the first grade in the Bedford County schools. He taught for ten months before moving with his family to a new farm near the lumber town of Traverse City, Michigan. Here he earned a teaching certificate good for the first eight grades but again taught for only a few months before deciding to move on in what would be a Walker pattern.

At twenty-three, David Walker headed west to join his three older brothers homesteading in Kingman County, Kansas. Within a year he was in charge of the Murdoch School and cited by the county school superintendent as "one of the very best teachers" of the county, "a wide awake man."[10] During this time, he traveled the surrounding countryside searching for a claim of his own, and in 1886, "left with a newspaper outfit on his hands," he began a small paper in Stevens County. To have a sure income he taught school in Hugoton.[11] Two years later he married Myrtle Eaton.

Apparently, the marriage was a case of opposites attracting. Mabel later depicted her parents as viewing life from entirely different angles. Her mother, with a deeply religious spirit, could always "discover some good," "an element of romance or a hidden ideal," even in the thick Missouri mud. Her father, on the other hand, was "as a rule practical in his ideas. His judgments proved more sure, perhaps, because the very quality of his thought was slower."[12] Both were hardy, adaptable, determined survivors. They would need all of these qualities in the next thirty years of a nomadic life of farming, teaching, and editing.

Mabel was born in the 1889 Kansas spring that rivaled the disastrous growing season of 1887. The wheat dried in the fields; by July the winds curled the corn. A settler described "the tiring wind [that] blew steadily from the south, weary day after weary day, cooking the garden plants and even the stunted weeds that grew in the fields. . . ."[13] As David later explained, "life was too short to stay there and wait for the country to prove itself worth the sacrificial price of staying there."[14] In August, they moved back to the "wife's folks" in Missouri. Their covered wagon heading east joined a major exodus. In the next three years of short rainfall, one half of the settlers abandoned

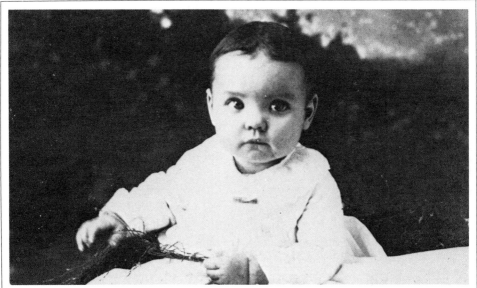

An early formal portrait of Mabel Walker posed on a bale of Missouri hay. *Below,* family and neighbors on the boardwalk in front of the combined offices of the *Lucerne Standard* and post office. From left, Tom and Cordelia Eaton; neighbors Jimmy and Emma Boland (standing); Myrtle, Mabel, and David Walker.

their claims in western Kansas. Twenty towns were left without a single inhabitant. Woodsdale, bypassed by the railroad, joined the casualties.[15]

The Walkers settled in the small town of Lucerne in Putnam County, Missouri. David carried a letter from a Kansas judge attesting that he was a man of "sterling integrity, of unblemished character, of excellent business capacity, of good social and moral standing, a true blue republican."[16] His character and probably the Eatons' long history in the community won him a position as postmaster. With Myrtle, he launched a newspaper, the *Lucerne Standard*, a challenging undertaking in a town with two hundred inhabitants that already boasted the rival *Lucerne Bee*. Office and home shared a two-story clapboard structure that opened on a sturdy boardwalk joining the *Standard* to the other town enterprises—restaurant, dry goods and feed store, grist mill, and lumberyard. At the end of the street was the depot of the Chicago, Milwaukee & St. Paul Railroad. Mabel's earliest memories were of playing on the floor amid the tangy odor and wet-harness smell of set-up type.[17] By 1892, perhaps in response to declining business at the *Standard*, David had earned certification to teach in the county schools, and Myrtle was teaching in a local seminary in nearby Powersville.[18] The following summer, in a hot, desperate, depression year, the Walkers again set out to farm their own land, joining that most spectacular of the Oklahoma territory openings—the run for the Cherokee strip in September 1893.

The *Lucerne Standard*, in an article in David's style, bade them farewell:

> Mr. and Mrs. D.W. Walker started last Monday on their trip to the Cherokee strip. Mr. and Mrs. Walker have left behind them a record of their work which cannot soon be forgotten. Honest, sincere, self-denying and tireless workers, they could not help but win the hearts of the people with whom their lot was cast and wherever they may tarry in the future they may always be assured that they are still remembered and that their influence is still felt by the people of Putnam county, that their brightest dream may be fully realized in their new situation is the most earnest wish of the Standard.[19]

Loading the covered wagon, they set out for western Kansas. One of four-year-old Mabel's earliest memories was of crying for a flower she spied in the dusty prairie, until her father stopped the team to walk back and pick it to please and distract her. With Myrtle and Mabel safely in Kingman, Kansas, with his relatives, David set out for the opening of the strip. More than six million acres were available for about 40,000 claims. There were 100,000 prospective homesteaders.[20]

David started from near Honeywell, Kansas, wisely accompanied by a hunter familiar with northern Oklahoma. At a signal the crowd surged forward, David charging with the leaders toward land at the Bitter Creek bottoms. But "sooners" were already encamped and all the land was flagged. Still hopeful, they raced for the Salt Fork bottoms; again, sooners had already staked their claims. Giving up the chase for the day, they pitched camp. In the morning David saw across the prairie "a seething mass of land hungry pioneers" and decided to return to the family in Kansas. En route, he arrived at a frame shack labeled "A.J. Blackwell, President of the Blackwell Townsite Co." He joined the line for townsite lots and this time was successful.[21]

Myrtle and Mabel were brought to their new Blackwell home, a nine-by-twelve-foot tent. The office of the new Walker-edited *Blackwell Times* was another tent eight-by-ten feet. The origin of the *Times* aptly fitted the description of the pioneer newspaper that pushed ahead of post office, school, and "all other institutions of civilized life," and David Walker seemed the archetypal frontier printer, "gripped with optimism," who rode into a new town and "threw in his lot with it."[22] With a wife and child, a tent home, and winter ahead, David did not lack for courage and enterprise.

The first issue of the *Blackwell Times*, November 1, 1893, followed the custom of "giving a salutary." The Walkers announced their decision to make the venture in the new town because their own interests would be "furthered by the superior prospects of Blackwell" and also to join with other publications in building up the town and county and promoting Oklahoma statehood. The *Times* pledged to avoid local partisan politics, since candidates were known to their neighbors and the editors believed men should be judged before party. Primarily, the *Times* was dedicated to boosting Blackwell and making the paper "such a readable and attractive sheet that it will be sought for by every good citizen and that the wide-awake businessmen will feel the need of using its columns as an advertising medium."

A page in the first issue provided a lyrical description of the central location of Blackwell and the booming surroundings of the Cherokee strip. This "trackless waste" had been changed in a month and a half to a scene of "prosperous towns." "Thousands of farmers" were building claim houses and readying the sod for corn and spring crops.

Blackwell had more than a hundred buildings. Saloons, a livery stable, feed stores, restaurants, and lumberyards had opened; doctors, lawyers, real estate salesmen, and two rival newspapers had arrived. In a few months, the *Times* joined one of its rivals to form the *Blackwell Times-Record*.[23] It was a heady beginning in unpropitious times.

Neither Blackwell nor the Walkers lacked excitement. After one heavy storm, a flood rushed through the town imperiling the fledgling *Times*, the printing press, the tent home, and Mabel. Hastily turning over the kitchen table, Myrtle set Mabel, kitchen utensils, and press on this improvised raft and held on until the waters receded.[24] In spite of this flash flood, summer on the plains was dry and searing. The railroad, bypassing Blackwell, was routed a hundred miles to the north. The deepening national depression of 1893 compounded these disasters, and the Walkers decided to move once again.

Faced with another new start, they stopped to visit and consider options with David's oldest brother in Kingman, Kansas. Pointing out that their county faced a shortage of teachers, the elder Walker persuaded David and Myrtle to stay with his family and teach for a session while deciding their next move. The younger Walkers moved into one room of the five-room farmhouse. Myrtle taught in the "home school" a half mile away; David rode a horse six miles to his post; Mabel, with her young preschool cousins, was cared for by her aunt.

In the excitement of Christmas Eve preparations, Mabel had an opportunity to learn a lesson at home. A young couple, the wife ill with tuberculosis, traveling to Arizona with their five-year-old daughter, set up their camp among the big cottonwood trees near the Walker house. Myrtle and her sister-in-law hastily prepared a Christmas box for the hard-pressed family and called four-year-old Mabel "into consultation." Shown a new doll on the Christmas tree and asked if she would like to "share" her doll family with the little girl in the wagon, Mabel stood a few moments, then hugged and kissed the doll, and said "with a hint of tears," "Give the poor little girl this one—it is the newest one, and anyway, maybe I love my old ones just as much."[25]

With the spring thaw, the Walkers moved back to Putnam County, near Powersville, again close to Myrtle's relatives, and began to farm on their own eighty acres. The farm income was supplemented by teaching in the winter months. Mabel had little formal schooling. In one interview, she explained that the Walkers never farmed near a schoolhouse that was within walking distance and a horse could not be spared from farmwork. Yet she learned much at home from her teacher-parents. Her mother introduced her to the beauty and mystery of nature, putting her out in the limited prairie shade when she was still an infant to let her "feel the caress of the southwind . . . its breath sweet from nature," and "hear the crooning love song of the mother bird to her wee ones." She learned to "catch the glint of the wings of many hued butterflies, hear the crickets at sundown, listen to the whip-poor-will," to walk out into the night and watch the stars.[26] She loved and she needed the closeness of nature all her life.

From her father she learned practical farm chores—milking, raking, caring for the chickens. She cherished walking behind the plow with him as he talked crops, business, or politics "man to man."

Both parents devoted time and care to the training of Mabel's character. David Walker recalled a scene in the Lucerne post office when Mabel begged for a basket of discarded letters to "sort out." He gave them to her after extorting the agreement that she would pick up anything that she dropped on the floor. Soon tired of playing, she walked away from the littered floor only to be reminded of the agreement. She paused a moment and announced firmly, "I have changed my mind, Papa." Her father recounted, "It required discipline and hours of patient endeavor for her to realize that a promise is sacred and once made must be kept."[27]

When she bit a pet cat's ear, David Walker bit hers. But Mabel appreciated a sterner lesson:

> As a child on a farm with a beloved cat and seven kittens, I faced their loss. Although food was plentiful, the mother cat had reverted to her predatory ancestry and was found not only killing chickens but teaching her half-grown offspring to do likewise. As a barefoot, seven-year-old child I hysterically begged for their lives, lashing myself into a tempest of appeal. It was a dramatic scene. . . . But my father, looking me over in his calm way, wisely thinking below the surface of sorrow to the opportunity for mastery the situation offered, said with his blue eyes flashing and with Jehovan sternness
>
> "Stop it! You're acting like a child. Go to your room until you can control yourself!"
>
> And bitterly sobbing on my bed—for having no brothers and sisters, these eight cats were my playmates and much beloved—into sorrow stole a healing thought. "You're acting like a child"—why then he must think of me as bigger, older, and with larger capacities than a child! To what seven-year-old is that no inspiration and challenge! Immediately, it was some-

> thing to live up to. Then, with what consideration and respect
> that wise father and mother treated me when, swollen-faced but
> master of myself, I re-entered the family circle.[28]

Formal religious training came through the services and Bible study
of the Christian church or the nearest church available. Mabel learned
more perhaps from her mother, who made her "first impression of
God not creed, but an all-enveloping love and an infinite strength for
times of need."

Her mother taught her to read, and her father let her help to set type
in their newspaper days. She was always fascinated with words and
read her way through the many books and magazines around the
house. The Walkers tried to help her with the meaning of each new
word. In the evenings, Mabel read aloud and tested ideas in lively
discussions with her father. When neighboring farmers stopped in,
there was talk of crops, mortgages, and politics.[29]

Connection with the larger world was limited. The arrival of a mail
order always proved exciting. Mabel recalled the delivery one time of
new dishes. While her parents puzzled over what the tiny round plates
included in the set might be, Mabel silently hoped that they were doll's
dishes sent by mistake. It was decided that they must be some new city
dish to set the teacup on while drinking out of the saucer, but they
wisely waited to see what a visiting city stranger from Chicago would
do. When the stranger put butter on the little plate, the enlightened
Walkers all followed suit.[30]

The visitor was probably the representative of the Chicago Orphan
Asylum, for in July 1901, the Walkers took Minnie Hickstein into their
home as a foster daughter, a companion to Mabel, and a help on the
farm. She was fifteen and was to stay with the family at least until she
reached sixteen. If she decided to remain two additional years, the
Walkers agreed to give her $100, a suit of clothes, and a Bible.[31]
Primarily, the Walkers were anxious for Mabel to have a companion as
she finally began her formal education.

It was the Walker credo that a girl should be brought up as indepen-
dently as a boy and fitted to earn her own living. Mabel had many
practical skills, a strong will, and a lively imagination. It was time for
her quick mind to have sustained schooling. In the autumn of 1902, the
family moved to Kansas City, Missouri, leaving friends, family, and
the farm they had so painstakingly developed. Mabel was to have an
opportunity to grow. The Walkers had no jobs, but as usual they were
armed with a testimonial to their good character, success in teaching,

and standing in the community.[32] Mrs. Walker completed a correspondence course in fitting glasses and went into the countryside selling and fitting spectacles; Mr. Walker first sold newspapers on the street and eventually became a carrier for the *Kansas City Star*.[33]

For Mabel, already uprooted four times, this was the hardest wrench. Powersville with a population of less than 50 was replaced by bustling Kansas City with a population of 320,000. The Walkers' first home was downtown on Cherry Street, only blocks from congested Main Street, which was clogged with electric streetcars, carriages, and huge drays. The Walkers' relocation again coincided with a natural disaster: a great flood swept down the Missouri River soon after their arrival. Sick in bed with whooping cough, Mabel chafed because she could not run to the bluff and "see the houses and things floating down the river."[34]

With Minnie as her companion, thirteen-year-old Mabel started school in the sixth grade. Although they were "like sisters," gentle, quiet Minnie did not have the drive, enthusiasm, and quicksilver mind to keep up with Mabel, who quickly moved to the head of the class. But Mabel did discover a new boon companion who could keep up. One afternoon she brought little Maud Hubbard home from school and asked that she become part of the Walker family. To hard-pressed David Walker, Maud appeared "dirty, ragged and indifferent," but Mabel was charmed by her intelligence, wit, and what seemed a sturdy independence.[35] Mabel's persistence and will and the Walkers' innate sympathy and concern over Maud's difficult home conditions won the day. Maud became the third teenaged girl of the Walker household.

In the next three and a half years, Mabel completed grammar school and some course work at Manual Training High School. The Walkers' choice of Manual for Mabel and Maud reinforced their early emphasis on practical learning and character training. Manual's mission was "to send the whole pupil to school." The curriculum combined hand and head work to surround students "not only in thought but in things, and to fit them for their environment." The faculty believed that an hour in the shop or cooking laboratory left a student eager and better fit for recitation in literature. More than 1,700 students and a faculty of 72 were involved in a demanding six-track program. Manual, as its bulletin warned, "was not a place for triflers."[36] Mabel elected the college preparatory program and excelled, even though she and Maud worked after school in a local doctor's office to help stretch a severely strained budget. By pooling the family resources, the Walkers were able to reward this diligence by sending Mabel with other Manual students and the school exhibit to the 1904 St. Louis exposition. Though her work seemed to preclude after-school activities with the glee club or basketball team, by 1905 Mabel was pictured in the Manual quarterly with the class leaders.[37]

While struggling with algebra, ancient history, zoology, botany, American literature, freehand drawing, sewing, and physiography, Mabel also continued to study on her own. A surreptitious reading of the *Rubaiyat* was paired with a public reading of the Bible. When she had first come to Kansas City, lonely and sick, she had crept out to sleep on the porch roof to watch the stars as she had on the prairie. They seemed the "only thing" in her isolation that had any "friendly interest in my intense longing to pierce the veil between our puny lives and God's power swinging them all in their places."[38] Particularly, she was strengthened by the New Testament declaration "Ask and ye shall receive" and the sense of partnership and responsibility it brought.

Whether it was a commitment to religious values, the attraction of the unusual self-help program, or the sure route to college, in January 1906, Mabel and Maud both applied for admission to Park Academy in nearby Parkville. On her application, Mabel listed the course work at Manual and indicated that she and her parents could meet the annual tuition of seventy-five dollars. She described herself as five feet, six inches tall, weighing 125 pounds.[39] It was a thin description for the young woman with the clear, blue eyes, wide forehead, infectious enthusiasm, zest, and determination.

Park College and Academy, like Manual, was not for triflers. Founded in 1875 to provide "cultural leadership for the expanding frontier," its motto was *Fides et Labor*. Its cofounder and first president, John A. McAfee, a Presbyterian minister, established the self-help program of the Park community. Students and faculty studied, worked, and prayed together; students cut the stone, erected the building, tended the cows, served the food.

Another school motto was "religion over all." At 5:00 A.M. a bell roused all students. By 5:30 they were assembled and President L.M. McAfee led the community in a Bible study period. Breakfast was served at 6:00, and Mabel and Maud waited on tables. Classes or work filled the morning. The noon meal was followed by chapel at 1:00, more classes, supper at 6:00 P.M., and then a half-hour religious service. Students knew that 'disloyalty to the common good, reckless selfishness to the detriment of the common welfare, greedy zeal for personal benefit and deliberate sacrifice of the community's well-being" were monstrous.[40]

Mabel and Maud joined the second-year class in the academy in September 1906. With their sixty-seven classmates they chose the class motto "Make use of the present day" and tried to become good members of the Park community. For Mabel this soon proved impossible. Study was a pleasure; Greek, physics, chemistry, mathematics, or modern language could be elected. Yet for the first time, Mabel was away from home and the staunch support of her parents. Schooled in the open schedule of home and prairie, and disliking rules and regulations, Mabel was bound to balk at the tight regimen of Park.[41]

The blow-up came in March 1907, probably at one of the Wednesday evening prayer sessions. Mabel, whose God was a partner, whose church was his world, challenged President McAfee on the doctrine of the virgin birth. Stern, meticulous, conservative McAfee brooked no question of doctrine and Mabel, arguing her first case against judge-jury-prosecutor McAfee, lost. The contest was never in doubt and she was "fired" from Park. While the dismissal was dramatic, the academic consequences were further complicated because Park refused to release the academic records of students who violated the pledge made at admission to complete the program.[42]

Though forced out of Park, Mabel did admire its broad purpose and philosophy. Sixteen years later, addressing the Conference of College and University Students, she quoted Emerson: "Character is higher than intellect; a great soul will be strong to live, as well as to think." Echoing Park's ideals, she argued that college should develop two habits, "love of work and spiritual development." She urged the students to develop a religious life based on conscience and the vision that "God is struggling to work" through them. Those "equipped with spiritual vision and love of work will transform any locality in which they move." The McAfees would have applauded.[43]

Meanwhile, Maud Hubbard was also forced to leave Park for treatment of a thyroid condition. Mabel helped her mother care for her and later contributed to the tuition that enabled Maud to return and finally graduate from the college in 1913. (She also managed to wriggle through the transom of the registrar's office to obtain Mabel's academic record.)[44]

Distressed but unrepentant Mabel traveled north with her parents to

Buckley, Michigan, for a fresh start and to allow David Walker to care for his ailing mother. A small lumber town near Traverse City, Buckley was "a wicked little place with four saloons on its four corners and lumberjacks reeling through the snow."[45] Ever the optimist, David Walker founded the Buckley Bank. True to the Walker tradition of bad timing, he opened for business in the "most stringent period" of the panic of 1907. Still, an advertisement in the *Buckley Enterprise* trumpeted the bank's opening and its motto, "A Square Deal to All." The same issue noted that a new cash grocery, meat market, and sawmill had opened. Buckley seemed to be booming.[46]

Though ousted from Park, Mabel had completed enough course work there and at Manual to pass the teachers' examination. Her first assignment was in a small country school a mile and a half from Buckley. She was in charge of five grades, but her adventures en route to school each day were perhaps more dramatic than the challenges of the classroom. Once she was lost in a blinding blizzard; another time she was trapped in a raging forest fire. After one year, she moved to the Buckley grammar school, beginning in the fourth and fifth grades and finally teaching two classes in the high school. During the summers of 1908 and 1909, she studied at Ferris Institute in nearby Big Rapids, Michigan. She was cited by the clerk of the school board (who was also her father) in a later recommendation as the best teacher Buckley ever had.[47] She seemed to have little trouble with discipline though her pupils were "as tough as sun-dried shark skin," so tough that when she was once forced to threaten one of the larger boys with a rod, he retaliated with a knife. Undaunted, Mabel captured the knife and then applied the rod in "an enthusiastic licking." Her father recorded this as a rare occurrence and reported that "she commanded the utmost respect from her pupils, not by fear that she would deal harshly with them, but by a winning personality that touched and called forth the good in the child nature." Though not identified with any religious denomination, she did meet twice a week with her students in a tiny house owned by the Walkers behind the bank, "reading to them and inspiring them with a love of higher spiritual truths."[48]

For all of the roughness of saloons and lumberjacks, life in Buckley was comfortable for the Walkers. Their own generous clapboard house was a gathering place for Mabel's friends. She found time to join a women's basketball team and enjoy lazy picnics at nearby Duck Lane in the summers. Leading the circumspect social life required of a young woman teacher, she was increasingly in the company of the

The Walker bank in Buckley, Michigan, 1909.

A gathering of the local Buckley basketball team, April 1909, with Willebrandt (center rear), gazing steadily off camera. *Below,* Mabel Walker at age twenty, just before her marriage to Arthur F. Willebrandt.

handsome, twenty-one-year-old principal, Arthur F. Willebrandt. In the winter of 1909 he survived a bout of pneumonia but was threatened with tuberculosis and decided to move to Arizona to regain his health. Ailing and appealing, he asked Mabel to go with him as his bride. Her Christian, romantic mother encouraged the match. Mabel later recounted that she saw herself as Joan of Arc. En route to Phoenix, they were married in Grand Rapids, Michigan, on February 7, 1910. One account dramatically described Arthur on a stretcher making the trip in a baggage car.[49]

She left behind the sure anchor that had supported her throughout the rapid changes in geography and family fortunes. The unity and harmony of family had been a safe haven. As she later wrote her parents, "But *you* who have loved me so hard" have "furnished my heart a sanctuary and a resting place" and "the certainty that the love of God makes me invincible."[50] Full of responsibility, hungry for new experience, buoyed by her mother's spirit of idealism and her father's unquenchable optimism, she was on her own, heading west.

The separation from father and mother, the threat of the deadly contagion of tuberculosis, the challenge of being wife-nurse were further heightened by the impact of the "wrinkled dryness" of territorial Arizona. It was a forbidding frontier of dust storms, searing heat, and flash floods. Yet its awesome physical presence could be a source of strength, and Mabel loved the dusty, rough, "challenging and irregular" West.[51]

For the tubercular patient, Arizona and the great Southwest were hailed as "The Consumptive's Holy Grail." The climatic conditions of clean air, almost constant sunshine, and dryness threatened to turn the area into one vast sanatorium.[52] Arthur and Mabel settled into a sanatorium close to Phoenix. Possibly they were helped in their choice by one of Mabel's English professors at Ferris Institute who now taught at the normal school at nearby Tempe. Pictures of the new home sent to her parents at Buckley showed a one-room wooden frame structure hung with canvas for easy opening to the health-giving sun and air. To the north and west were other cabins and the low central building of the superintendent, probably housing bath and kitchen and a gathering place for the convalescents. To the east was nothing but scrub pine and mountains. It was as spartan and simple as the old Kansas sod house, but Arthur could concentrate on bed rest and wholesome food; Mabel could nurse, cook, work, and explore their new environment.[53]

The first home of Mabel and Arthur Willebrandt, at a sanatorium near Phoenix, Arizona, February 12, 1910. *Below,* the view to the southwest from the sanatorium home.

Lazy days in Arizona, when Arthur Willebrandt was obviously on the mend,
May 1910.

Phoenix was an interesting city to explore in 1910. Built in the Salt River Valley, its founders and those of neighboring Tempe had traced the old canals of the vanished Hohokam tribes and used them to develop irrigation for the fertile countryside. Three to five alfalfa crops were harvested annually, 35,000 head of range cattle fattened, orange groves flourished, and honey was produced. Clearly, as one booster lyricized, "No oasis was ever such a paradise as sung by the poets of Araby." As the territorial capital and county seat of Maricopa County, it boasted a population of more than 11,000; the almost completed Roosevelt Dam promised further expansion and prosperity. A constitutional convention was about to convene in the city to complete the territory's long drive for statehood.[54]

In the summer, David Walker arrived from Michigan to visit and to tour Granite Dells, the old capital of Prescott, and camp with the young Willebrandts in the rugged mountains.[55] Arthur was regaining his health, and Mabel was ready to reduce her nursing role and to go back to school at Tempe Normal School. If she had to be the breadwinner, she was going to be fully certified as a teacher.

Like Phoenix, the normal school was booming in 1910. Starting in 1885 with a twenty-acre plot of pasture land and a $5,000 legislative appropriation, it had opened in February 1886 with one teacher and thirty-three students. Its purpose was to train teachers for the Arizona schools. The first president and sole teacher, Bradford Farmer, set the early curriculum. The school emphasized retraining in the subjects taught in the elementary schools and added courses in Latin, algebra, natural philosophy, literature, debate, political economy, history, and the history and philosophy of education. A practice school was established for the young student teachers. Students gazing out the windows from one of the square brick buildings could look directly into the eyes of cattle who came for shade under the roof of the wide porch ringing the structure. Tempe was small, friendly, open, and spirited, but Farmer "assumed that everyone in the school came to work, and considered attendance a privilege." Character, work, and experience were stressed: graduates who earned a diploma at the school were immediately granted a territorial teaching certificate.[56]

Building on the Farmer foundation, Arthur John Matthews became president in 1900 and guided the school for the next thirty-three years. Though there were still only 5 faculty members and 200 students, he planned for expansion, winning money from the legislature for the first dormitory, a new science laboratory, and improvement in the

A study of Mabel Walker Willebrandt's men: Arthur Willebrandt and
David Walker, 1910.

A snapshot for a postcard sent home to Willebrandt's parents with a notation of a 250-foot drop below "Queen Superior" surveying the world.

practice school. By 1910, when Mabel Willebrandt arrived, the campus boasted ten buildings, ambitious landscaping, a dedicated, stable faculty, and 246 students. The curricula included normal; Latin, for students continuing for professional or university degrees; and "subnormal" for students with no high school in their area.

Matthews was alert to building the reputation of the small school outside the boundaries of Arizona. In 1902, he visited the California state superintendent and so impressed him with the quality of Tempe's staff and program that a Tempe diploma was accepted as "of equal rank with the state normal schools of California." Holders of the degree would be granted a grammar school certificate for California districts without examination.[57]

Tempe undergraduates shared a rich community life. President Matthews, Cap Irish, the science professor-football coach, and other faculty members often led students on desert camping trips and picnics. The Walking Club and Hiking Club were two of the most popular organizations. All students belonged to one of the three literary clubs. In 1911 the first yearbook, "El Pecadillo," was edited by a busy Mabel Walker Willebrandt. The outstanding event of the spring semester was the arrival of former president Theodore Roosevelt to dedicate the first of his reclamation projects, the massive Roosevelt Dam. He exhorted the Tempe students: "You have that great material choice ahead of you. You can throw it away if you have not the right kind of men and women. Do not flinch; do not fail; and hit the line hard."[58] It was a speech Mabel Walker Willebrandt could have given.

Tempe completed its own sending forth at the annual precommencement lantern walk up Tempe Butte. Seniors carrying lighted Japanese lanterns handed them on to the juniors with song and ceremony on the rim of the butte and, having symbolically passed on the torch, walked down into the darkness and leadership in a wider world.[59]

Mabel Willebrandt participated in all of these activities, but she was far from the typical undergraduate. She brought three years of teaching experience to the practice school of Tempe. Here she added another nine months in the classroom, honing skills under supervision. But most unusual was the fact that she was married; it said much about her determination, Arthur's acquiescence, and their future estimate of her need to earn their living. In the midst of her studies, teaching, and caring for Arthur, Mabel became pregnant. It was a tubal pregnancy which could only end in pain, the physical and psychological devastation of a miscarriage, and, in Mabel's case, surgery that ended further childbearing. Facing not only the loss of this child but a childless future, she tersely described the tragedy as the "grave of my most cherished hope" and felt "engulfed in utter despair."[60]

She was tempered but not stopped by tragedy. Years of developing her inner resources in the changes of frontier homes, the comforting strength of parents, and her own questing spirit sustained and quickened her determination. In June, with a Tempe diploma and her teaching credentials, and anxious to put Arizona behind them, she and Arthur set out not for the security and haven of Michigan and family but to the west and California.

CHAPTER TWO

California: Professional and Progressive

Those women who are quietly, unostentatiously, and success-fully combining marriage and career are real pioneers. It is cruel that the world should exact of the girl who tries to climb up in business or profession the sacrifice of home and children.

MABEL WALKER WILLEBRANDT
"Give Women a Fighting Chance!"

The analyst of California is like a navigator who is trying to chart a course in a storm; the instruments will not work; the landmarks are lost, and the maps make little sense.

CAREY MCWILLIAMS
California: the Great Exception

W HILE Arizona was thriving in its last year as a territory and bustling with the new excitement of state-hood and expansion, California in 1911 was in the midst of an economic boom and the social and political ferment of progressivism. In the north it was dominated by cosmopolitan, open, labor-strong, Catholic San Francisco; in the south by morally upright, midwestern, Protestant Los Angeles. It was a land of Oz with two Emerald cities. Both struggled with their own demons. San Francisco reformers, editors, and businessmen battled the labor machine of Boss Ruef in a series of sensational graft trials from 1906 through 1908. In Los Angeles, dubbed "the chemically pure," reformers launched a purity crusade against gambling dens, saloons, and prostitution. They gloried in the knowledge that "many flaunting indecencies had been swept away."[1] Editors, lawyers, and business leaders attacked the city machine and its partner, the Southern Pacific Railroad. By 1909, the nonpartisan Good Government League hounded the machine mayor of Los Angeles into retirement with charges of conspiring with the police chief to monopolize the prostitution trade and with threats of a

27

recall movement. Charter amendments followed, establishing direct primaries and nonpartisan elections. Though a public backlash at the dynamiting of the *Los Angeles Times* building by radicals slowed the reform impetus temporarily, the Good Government forces kept pressing for efficiency, economy, and morality in the city administration.[2]

With these successes in north and south, the urban reformers joined in an uneasy alliance to redeem the state from the hands of the Southern Pacific organization. Their campaign finally triumphed in the election of Hiram Johnson as governor in 1910. For the next decade, he led the reform forces, beating back the "Associated Villainies" of the old Southern Pacific machine, and bringing California progressivism into the national arena—first in support of the candidacy of Theodore Roosevelt in 1912 and finally in the cause of his own presidential aspirations. Anyone entering California life and politics from 1910 to 1920 would need a compass and sensitive antennae.[3]

Mabel and Arthur Willebrandt first settled in the distant Los Angeles suburb of Buena Park, where Mabel, armed with four years of teaching experience and her new Tempe diploma, was appointed principal and teacher of the upper grades. Though she was successful, the couple decided after one year to move closer to the city. Mabel applied for a position with the South Pasadena schools.

Her application form and accompanying dossier provide a rich inventory of her talents and accomplishments. She listed a remarkable breadth of teaching specialties and subjects: English language, grammar, American history, modern history, civics, geography, arithmetic, and nature study. She cited competence in teaching algebra, geometry, botany, zoology, biology, physiology, physiography, Latin, English literature, English composition, elocution, English and ancient history, pedagogy, penmanship, public school music, and baseball. Additionally, she noted her courses in trigonometry, physics, chemistry, Greek, rhetoric, elocution, public speaking, European history, ethics, sociology, political science, physical culture, commercial law, commercial geography, freehand drawing, domestic science, household economy, clay modeling, and gymnastics. Beyond this prodigious academic preparation, she noted that her health was "*Excellent. I am never ill in any way.*"[4]

Academic recommendations were impressive. The head of the Tempe Education Department reported her "signal success" in the training school, adding: "Teaching is an instinct with her. She knows things to begin with and she has a rare power for clear presentation."

She disciplined "by sheer force of an attractive personality." She was "distinctly human," "the kind of person that young people take to." When she went into her room the work began and there was "nothing else done, but work." He concluded that "the community that takes her as a teacher is going to bless the day when she comes."[5]

Her English professor at Ferris Institute and then at Tempe, J.L. Felton, reported her "excellent" success as a teacher in Michigan. President Matthews of Tempe noted that her "testaments" on teaching were "very satisfactory" and added that she was considered one "of our strongest students. A woman of maturity and successful experience in teaching."[6]

Most effusive in his recommendations was D.W. Walker, clerk of the school board in Buckley, Michigan. Though he did not identify himself as her father, he wrote with pride: "She taught 3 years here, 5th and 6th, 7th and 8th grades. She was the best teacher we ever had, having the rare gift to inspire her pupils to see the higher things, mentally, morally, and physically."[7]

All agreed that morally she was above reproach. Felton affirmed that she made "a quiet profession of religion—reverent and not effusive." President W.N. Ferris of Ferris Institute cited her moral and religious character as "first rate." The chairman of the Tempe Education Department reported that she was an active member in the sunday school of the Congregational church and added, "I don't know that she is a member. She is just the person to do things both in church and in everyday affairs." Mabel filled in the blank on the personnel form next to "church attended" by simply writing, "the closest."[8]

She stated her age on the May 1912 application as twenty-five, a slight exaggeration, since she was still three weeks shy of her twenty-fourth birthday, but consistent with her Buena Park application, which had added one year for the maturity expected in a principal. Physically, she was described as "a good looking young woman—always neatly and tastefully dressed." She was "not handsome and yet she is what is called good looking. Her open countenance inspires confidence and trust and she keeps people her friends by doing things for them that are good." D.W. Walker described her proudly as "really a handsome woman." Only the clerk of the Buena Park School Board declined to recommend her "for we are so well pleased with her work here, that we want to keep her for another year."[9]

Such encomiums persuaded South Pasadena to engage her as the principal of Lincoln Park Elementary School at a salary of $100 a month. Lincoln Park was a large two-story red brick building with white columns framing the main doorway. It was a much more imposing structure than the frame schoolhouse at Buena Park. Mabel not only served as principal but taught the eighth grade and organized the parent-teacher organization, soon becoming a "leading personality of the community."[10]

She and Arthur moved into a small cottage on El Centro, two blocks from the school. When they were settled Arthur's mother, Rose Willebrandt, joined the household. Mabel now did most of the cooking, cleaning, sewing, and earning for three. She and Arthur also determined that they would study at the College of Law at the University of Southern California. For the first year, they agreed, Mabel would work full time and follow a part-time course schedule. The following year, Arthur would work full time to send Mabel full time. This never happened. For the next three years Mabel continued as principal and teacher at Lincoln Park, commuting to her evening law classes on the Pacific Electric streetcar that conveniently went past the school to downtown Los Angeles. Wearily returning home to South Pasadena at 9:45, she found little time to prepare classes for the morning and the next evening.[11]

Several different versions of what attracted her to the study of law seem partially true. According to one account, her father, when a banker in Buckley, yearned for a lawyer in the family and Mabel obliged. She gave two reasons in later interviews. She had really wanted to study medicine (her mother had been horrified to find her dissecting a cat on the farm at Powersville), but since there were no night classes, she settled for the law. The other reason was connected to her teaching. She was overwhelmed by the dullness of the civics textbooks.[12] Her own schooling had come from the lively discussions of farmers in Powersville and with her father on long buggy rides in the Michigan countryside. He posed hypothetical questions: would it be "right for an honest man to seek public office by allowing a corrupt political machine to conduct his campaign for election?"[13] In the classroom, Mabel challenged students with questions, games, and simulations to "help them realize the true meaning of the science of citizenship." She searched for books and resources to develop her ideas and finally decided to write a textbook herself. Then, "the absurdity of her presumption dawned on her"; she did not know the law.[14]

The College of Law of the University of Southern California provided a rigorous education in theory and practice. Located at First

Willebrandt (top, rear, seated) with her students at Lincoln Park Elementary School, South Pasadena, California, 1913.

Street and Broadway, it was within walking distance of the Los Angeles County Law Library, the sessions of the California Supreme Court, U.S. District Court, Appellate Court for the Southern District, and Superior Court of Los Angeles County. Five city police courts and four township justice's courts allowed advanced students to gain some actual practice even before their admission to the bar. When Mabel Willebrandt arrived in 1912, the College of Law, one of the few to admit women, had just formed a women's department. Women lawyers conducted four classes for the thirty-eight women students enrolled in 1912: criminal law, criminal procedure, torts, and domestic relations.[15] In addition, a women's room was provided, where women could gather, study, and generally encourage one another. The year before her arrival, a group of five women had founded the first chapter of Phi Delta Delta legal fraternity, which gave further support to the law students at Southern California and gradually built a nationwide network.[16]

The course of study was demanding but, with the exception of some emphasis on water rights and irrigation law, standard for the period. The first-year program included courses in contracts, criminal law, elementary law and Blackstone, torts, bailments, debating, personal property, agency, domestic relations, practice court, and use of books. The second-year courses included wills, private corporations, real property, equity jurisprudence, constitutional law, partnership, water rights and irrigation law, and again, practice court. In the third year, the courses were code pleading, bankruptcy, legal ethics insurance law, equity pleading, and federal procedure and practice court. The same faculty taught both day and evening classes, but the evening program stretched to four years. The typical program, which Mabel followed, included two years of night sessions, two summer sessions, and a third year with the regular senior class.

Mabel met the tuition costs for both Willebrandts out of her $100 a month salary: $45 a semester for the day and $35 a semester for night sessions. Fees added another not inconsiderable $22 for each.[17]

In 1915, Arthur Willebrandt successfully completed his program of study and briefly clerked in the office of one of their law professors, Kemper Campbell. Mabel, now committed to the law, left her position at Lincoln Park to teach at the Utah Street School, downtown in the Mexican section. She could meet an 8:00 A.M. course, teach, and then return for two evening classes, ending the day by doing the household chores. The pace of this schedule aggravated an already strained marriage. The disappointment of the failed commitment by Arthur to share equally in their progress toward degrees in law, the added burden of caring for Mrs. Willebrandt, and the exhausting schedule of studying, commuting, and teaching took a toll. In January 1916, Mabel Willebrandt left the home in South Pasadena and moved in with a young woman classmate. Friends sighed that "Art just couldn't keep up."[18]

The story was, of course, much more complicated. Mabel tried to share with her parents the sense of what had caused this second devastating loss:

> I think more unhappy marriages come from failure to share the inner religious and thought life with each other and for letting the whole relationship just drop to a dead level of bodily contact. Most people give a gift—or sometimes a caress to express love—when a far greater proof of it is to say an intimate and confidential thing. But to learn to share one's inner life— even with a person one may love takes patient effort because most of us do not talk on such subjects easily—and habits and sensitiveness and putting off the thing we may have an impulse to say till come another time—just wall us in and walls real happiness out—often I've wanted you to know how the most precious thing about our home life, which endears it to me more than anything is the way we talk about the things we think about.[19]

Clearly there was little time for talk or quiet sharing, but the overloaded schedule might also have been an indication of Mabel Willebrandt's acceptance that time would not bring the warm intimacy she so cherished in the Walker home.

Beyond the lack of emotional sharing, there was no partnership. She later wrote a magazine article on the "necessary adjustments" in marriage, "the preservation of *her* freedom, her self-respect, her intellectual and executive attainments, her economic independence and sense of civic usefulness and importance as well as his." The wife should work at "finding the best outlet for her energies, finding the best protection for her spirit, and establishing a basis of mutual understanding with her husband in order to have both a 'child' and a 'job' if she wants both." This was more important to the actual "preservation of their home than that he should cling to the outgrown 'manly theory' my wife can't work for a living!"[20]

But the failure of her marriage haunted her. She confessed to her classmate Myra Dell Collins that no matter what she accomplished later, she would always feel a failure because she could not sustain her own marriage. She considered marrying again but always balked. When, after years of separation, the divorce became final in 1924, she wrote to her father:

> Certainly all these years when I felt crucified *inside*, *lying* to the outside, *did* something to me and I know what it was—They just built up a fear complex at the marriage status. It is so cruel to a woman if she'd any pride. It will only be after a terrific mental struggle that I could bring myself to trust—not the man, that would be easy—but the social status of marriage—seems like I feel about it as an escaped convict must when he looks at a prison wall. Isn't it too bad the years didn't rob me of the power to love and want to be loved, since they robbed me of confidence in accepting these things at the price of matrimony.[21]

The divorce was handled quietly by friends with "no trouble and no publicity." She wrote of her relief to her father:

> I'm so deeply grateful for that. You have no idea what a relief it is to have that *over*. Tho of course it isn't over. It'll rise up to haunt me in questions as long as I live but at least *underneath* I'm free. I didn't realize myself what an almost exhausted feeling of relief it would create in me.[22]

Typically, she met her pain by redoubling her efforts in her work, but she had a new sensitivity and a sympathy for women and women's issues.

In February 1916, one month after she left the Willebrandts, her friend and former associate at the University of Southern California, James H. Pope asked her to serve as his assistant in the office of the police court defender handling women's cases. She accepted with alacrity. Pope, who had worked his way through law school as a reporter, had been admitted to the bar in the summer of 1915; he had lobbied for and had been the first appointee to the new position. Willebrandt, who had had ample time to see the treatment the law meted out to the Mexican neighbors of the Utah Street School, had also worked for the new defender's office. She was appointed while still in her last semester of study at the law school and still teaching a full schedule.[23]

Like many other programs in the progressive era, the office of the police court defender was launched in a burst of reforming zeal, financed on a shoestring, and dependent on the generous service of middle-class citizens. Each morning before the courts opened, police

Fred Horowitz (left), Willebrandt, and John Shepherd at graduation from the College of Law, University of Southern California, June 1916.

reported to the city prosecutor the arrests made and the evidence. The court defender and his assistant then consulted with those prisoners who wanted their advice or aid in court.[24] Mabel Willebrandt's day began with these morning meetings, which were followed by three hours of teaching, a lunchtime spent in tracking down witnesses, more teaching, a session in court, and finally evening law classes. The volume of cases was staggering. In his first annual report, Pope declared that his office had handled 1,650 cases before the police court or occasionally the higher court or the lunacy commission. His assistant averaged fifty or more cases a month.[25]

The major work of the office involved vagrancy, drinking, and prostitution charges. Los Angeles was a wide-open town. One *Los Angeles Times* reporter remembered: "Immoral houses were so common that very little was said about it. At Broadway and Sunset there was a long row of cribs extending northerly in which the women sat in chairs in large windows. . . . Men walked up and down the street in groups and made their selections like they select clothes." The reform administration brought in by the Good Government League made inroads but obviously did not eliminate the trade. The city council in its zeal formed a metropolitan squad to attack gambling and prostitution; a series of raids and patrols was carried out in 1916 and 1917.[26]

To meet the increased case load in the police courts and in response to the reformers' current emphasis on the prostitute as victim, Los Angeles experimented with a special women's court "away from the evil influences of police court surroundings" where women could "bare their hearts—not to a courtroom full of curious, leering men—but to a few women who understood." Judge Thomas White presided in this pioneer effort; he was frequently joined on the bench and assisted by the prominent woman attorney Georgia Bullock. A panel of volunteer clubwomen took turns attending court sessions and stood ready should a prisoner be released to accept custody and try to lift her "from the depths into which she had fallen."[27]

Willebrandt's contribution to the reform effort was procedural. Disgusted that little or no effort was made to apprehend the male partner, she began to take advantage of a court procedure that allowed the defendant to request a jury trial in which the appearance of the "john" involved could be required. Court costs escalated and the police court judges gradually changed their procedures. Both female and male offenders were brought to answer charges in Los Angeles prostitution cases.[28]

Willebrandt worked to understand her new clients. Their sullen indifference frequently "baffled her," but she did perceive: "These women are the same as I. Each has a story. I must make them feel that they want to tell it to me."[29] She not only won their trust but retained their gratitude. One appreciative client, still "making good," later wrote, "Never will I forget the day I stood before Judge Frederickson and you said to be lenient with me as I came from a good family in the East."[30] In another instance, Willebrandt's practicality showed through. A madam she had once helped came for advice on "going straight." She wanted to buy a home to raise her sons in a respectable environment. Carefully checking her client's resources and knowing the home she wanted to buy, Willebrandt ascertained how much longer the woman would have to work at her profession to earn the necessary funds. Her advice was to continue another six months; she also loaned her some money for this new beginning.[31]

Pope respected this practical, businesslike assistant. She "was not a softie, nor did she address women as 'dear' nor run her hands or fingers through their hair nor make a lot of talk about 'you poor girl' or 'that man certainly took advantage of you.'" There was no false emotion, he explained, "no petting or purring," but a simple discussion of the facts followed by prudent plans.[32]

In that same practical vein, Willebrandt was one of Pope's staunch supporters when he and others began a prison farm near Griffith Park. It supplied work for some inmates and improved the diet of all. Willebrandt, who had bought a small farm outside of Los Angeles, was a leading goat breeder. She contributed a small herd of Toggenburgs to the farm to aid the cause, and, Pope observed, to perhaps reduce the complaints of her neighbors at the burgeoning and noisy livestock on the Willebrandt land.[33]

In her work as assistant court defender, Willebrandt always had a special sympathy for the youthful offenders. The "Rosebud Baby Case" particularly moved Willebrandt to action. The Hearst paper, the *Los Angeles Herald*, followed her efforts to get a special police detail "to prevent owners of nickelodeons from taking little girls who came to the Saturday morning movies behind the silver screen and getting them with babies, rosebud or otherwise."[34]

The Los Angeles City Council finally passed a special resolution responding to the many complaints about "a number of low dives operating on Main Street under the guise of theaters where it is alleged lewdness and lasciviousness runs riot." The council urged immediate steps by the city attorney to eliminate these immoral places and to compel these movie houses to maintain "respectable exhibitions." The police mobilized so that such places might "no longer offend the sense of moral decency of the city of Los Angeles."[35]

In the summer of 1916, Willebrandt added to her heavy case load in the city courts by launching her private practice. Receiving her LL.B. and admitted to the bar in June, she opened offices with two close friends from the College of Law, Fred Horowitz and John Shepherd. The three had organized a highly successful study group in their last year at law school and decided that rather than eke out an existence clerking for someone else, they might as well starve together. Aided by Shepherd's lawyer father, who supplied a library and furniture, they opened "three beautiful offices" in the Douglas Building on Spring Street, lawyers' row, in downtown Los Angeles. Realizing the difficulties a woman faced in establishing a practice, Willebrandt joined by her two colleagues, returned to the College of Law to work for an LL.M. She continued helping in the police court defender's office and taught night classes to Mexican immigrants at the Macey School. It was a typical Willebrandt schedule. On the weekends, the three colleagues, all avid hikers, frequently joined the Sierra Club camping trips in the mountains.[36]

Willebrandt had definite ideas about the practice she wanted. Her experience with more than 2,000 cases in police courts made her decide to avoid criminal law. She also rejected divorce cases. Above all, she was determined to be an honest lawyer. She liked to quote Lincoln: "Resolve to be honest at all events; and if in your own judgment you can not be an honest lawyer, resolve to be honest without being a lawyer."[37] Cotton Mather was another favorite. His admonition hung behind her desk: "There has been an old complaint that a good lawyer seldom is a good neighbor. You know how to confute it, gentlemen, by making your skill in law a blessing to your neighborhood."[38] Diligence and character, Willebrandt believed, would win success.

Though James Pope used his old newspaper contacts to win her some publicity, Willebrandt's first case came from a contact at the Lincoln Park school. She had tutored one of her students in English after school, a considerable sacrifice of time in a heavily burdened schedule. The student's grateful brother brought her a case, seeking the dissolution of his dairy business and an $18,000 settlement from his partner. The presiding judge was well-known as tough but gregarious. He "liked to talk shop and discuss the details of upcoming cases" over lunch with attorneys. When Willebrandt began to present her case, the judge listened in a "bored manner" and then raised details he could have obtained only from the opposition attorneys. Realizing his luncheon habits, she challenged: "Your honor, you have talked with someone from the other side of the case. I am compelled to ask for a change of venue." It was a remarkable charge in her first civil case. After a long, uncomfortable silence, the judge agreed to disqualify himself. Her victory against six other attorneys was almost overlooked in the courthouse chuckling and appreciation of the audacity of this plucky young woman. More immediately, Willebrandt's bravery led to a quick dash to the rest room where she "got so sick . . . and vomited and cried and almost had hysterics." A year's effort in the case netted her a fee of $600. She was "so grateful," she explained, in having the case that she was "actually frightened" to send a larger bill.[39]

Another successful early case involved an elderly woman injured by a city streetcar. The company offered to settle all claims for $500, but since the injury involved the inner ear and the symptoms and disability were intermittent, Willebrandt advised her client to refuse settlement. She fully studied the medical aspects of the case (knowledge that would be helpful when her own ear problems developed) and five months later with her medical-legal argument won a $10,000 judgment for her client.[40]

Her practice grew steadily. A bank retained her as counsel. Land-title cases, mortgage foreclosures, damage suits, and guardianship cases expanded her work schedule to an eighteen-hour day. Between court sessions, she found time to lunch with juvenile court judge Orfa Jean Shontz and a young innovating penologist, Miriam Van Waters, for lively discussions on helping youthful offenders. She still found time for the underdog.

In 1917, when America entered the war, Los Angeles was selected for the site of an army camp. An apprehensive city council, girding to face the new conditions the soldiers would present to the city, resolved that "these elements which are ever prone to congregate near a large body of men will not be tolerated for a moment." In the first months of the war, the Los Angeles Police war squads' sweeps for vagrancy and vice netted 220 arrests. Clinical tests were administered to those apprehended. Women found to have venereal disease were sent to Los Feliz Hospital to remain until cured; men were sent to the East Side jail.[41] Willebrandt helped out the beleaguered police court defender's office. In the evenings she drove to Los Feliz to interview the women detained to see if they needed legal advice or help in contacting family or friends.

As cases from the sedition law, a war measure forbidding "disloyal, profane, scurrilous, or abusive language" about the Constitution, flag, or military uniform, began to clog the Los Angeles courts, Willebrandt again sided with the underdog. She defended an elderly German-American woman who was arrested for saying "not much more than La Follette had said." The real reason for her arrest seemed to be a neighbor's annoyance that she kept chickens in her yard. Willebrandt asked for and was granted a jury trial and won the case. It was a rare wartime victory in a sedition case in Los Angeles and she was congratulated by the jurors. In a letter to her father, Willebrandt reflected: "The real loyal American with German ancestry where that ancestry is known is placed in a hard position and all he can do is to bear all the things people say in silence feeling that it is a part of his burden in the war. . . . Anything he might be driven to say in a defense of his ancestry is misjudged. Bad as their plight is, however, it is undoubtedly preferable to that of an American's in Germany and in that most of them agree with me. It is the only consolation I can give them."[42]

The war brought another responsibility. In 1918 she was appointed chairman of the legal advisory board for District No. 11, the second largest selective service district in the city. She directed thirty attorneys in checking conscientious objector status and examining other pleas for exemption. Her most troubling case was Arthur Willebrandt's. When his draft number was drawn, he approached Mabel and asked her help in winning a deferment. Appalled at this new failure in responsibility, she stated that if he passed his physical he would have to report for duty and removed herself from his appeal procedure. Pronounced fit, Arthur Willebrandt was drafted and sent with the Ninety-first, the "wild west" division, to the front in France. He came home safely, but tragically, her colleague John Shepherd, perhaps "the only man Mabel ever loved," a lieutenant with the Ninety-first, was killed in battle in February 1918.[43]

Willebrandt and Fred Horowitz continued their law practice on Spring Street. Increasingly, her office became a center for young women lawyers struggling to establish a practice. Invited to join the fledgling legal fraternity Phi Delta Delta while at the College of Law, she actively supported its expansion. At one of the gatherings in her office in September 1918, Willebrandt was the driving force in launching the Women Lawyers' Club of Los Angeles County. Elected secretary, she began a lively correspondence with leading women lawyers like Florence Allen of Cleveland, asking them to share their experiences, which "would be inspirational and helpful to us in the west." Two years later she was elected president. Charter members included fellow Phi Deltas Elizabeth Kenny, Florence Woodhead, May Lahey, Orfa Jean Shontz, and Litta Belle Campbell. Caroline Kellogg was named the first president; Clara Shortridge Foltz, the first woman admitted to the bar in California, was given honorary life membership. Of the thirty-nine charter members, three would become judges; two, deputy district attorneys; and one, a United States assistant attorney general. A legislative committee of the club reviewed developments at Sacramento, and a delegate was dispatched to the State Bar Conference.[44] Primarily, the club provided a network to augment Phi Delta Delta and to cope with the "old boy" system of the Los Angeles courts.

Illustrating the gradual and grudging respect women were earning, Willebrandt reported the conversion of a particularly recalcitrant judge. She relished trying cases in his court because his "violent expressions—printed and verbal" on suffrage and women jurors "amused her." His harassment and paper rattling during a presentation and shouts of "Get to the point!" made his court a test of self-discipline and a "pretty maddening" experience. Finally won over, the judge called Willebrandt to concede: "I just wanted to tell you I think I've been all wrong about you women. . . . You're much better on juries and in court than I thought you would be." He added: "You women lawyers have some sort of a society, haven't you? Well, I will come to your next meeting. Yes, I should like to meet 'em all and tell them what I have just told you."[45]

On a broader scale, Willebrandt insisted that the woman attorney had a special responsibility to participate in the civic life and the politics of the community, at least "to the extent of studying and instructing groups of women on issues involved when she is requested to do so."[46] This participation, she pointed out, was also helpful professionally. She was a model of her own advice, joining the Professional Women's Club, the Women's University Club, and the socially prestigious Friday Morning Club.[47] When she joined anything, she was active. Secretary and then president of the Professional Women's Club, she also chaired not only its legislative committee but those of the

Friday Morning Club and the Los Angeles County Federation of women's Clubs. In 1919, she was one of three representatives dispatched by the Women's Legislative Council, a coalition of women's organizations, to argue at Sacramento for the married women's property bill. The measure passed only to be brought to referendum. The *Los Angeles Herald* reported Willebrandt as "prepared to go to bat" in May 1920 by donating a week's income to the cause and acting as co-chairman of the campaign committee gathering contributions to win the referendum.[48]

An already hard-pressed Willebrandt made arrangements to bring her parents to California in 1919. The Buckley Bank had failed in the wake of labor troubles in the logging industry. Her parents, though used to new starts and moving on, experienced a "horrible nightmare." David Walker worked in a Detroit factory trying to earn enough money to support the family and to pay off some debts. Distressed, Willebrandt wrote to him:

> I just can't think of you in factory work and it hurts that I who have received so much at your hands can't at this time, which I was so thoughtless to realize might come, step in and make good to prevent it being necessary for you to work like that. But I appreciate the truth of your statements that false construction might be placed upon your leaving the state at once and the fact that you are doing what you are will give the lie to their false whisperings as nothing else can do. Only do not prolong it any longer than you feel is absolutely necessary. We do need each other.

She added, "It's hard for a woman to judge in business life the many things that come up, for the problems are doubled for her when she thus steps out of the beaten paths of feminine endeavor. . . . I could never tell you how often I want your advice and actual aid in the work as it comes up."[49]

Meanwhile, Myrtle Walker, remaining in Buckley to reassure the creditors, faced the recriminations of friends and neighbors who had lost their savings in the bank crash. She later wrote of her anguish:

> To have those who have pretended to be your friends accuse you of making money out of their loss cuts you and freezes you inside. Many of these that Dave had favored in the past came to me after he had gone and called him everything but an honest man. All the time I knew their loss meant everything to them and that we were powerless to make good. The thought is *Hell* and it burns with an unending fire.[50]

Willebrandt bought a small piece of land in Temple City, California, for a chicken ranch for the Walkers. On January 1, 1920, she moved them to it. Home at first was a tent, as it had been in Blackwell, Oklahoma.[51] Fred Horowitz and Willebrandt's women lawyer friends were rallied to help pluck chickens and to buoy up the Walkers' spirits. This new start was further complicated by David Walker's serious bout with influenza, but with typical optimism and resilience he saw the possibilities in the growth of that "neglected mulberry grove" of Temple City. It might become a second Glendale. He began working with the chamber of commerce and developed a water company to add to the chicken business. Willebrandt spent as much time as she could with them, but her schedule had grown to the enormous proportions that always characterized her professional life. She liked to quote Lincoln: "Work. Work. Work is the only thing." More tellingly, she observed: "Love of work can only come by necessity—the inward compulsion of *having* to make good because of hope of parents or financial necessity." Her law practice was "dignified and growing;" her civic participation continued to expand.[52]

Willebrandt's sense of a lawyer's responsibility and her commitment to political issues and action did not extend to an interest in political office. She warned women attorneys that political office, "though most alluring," should be avoided: "If there is one sure 'bugaboo' that is liable to assail the inexperienced attorney it is that 'The politicians'll get you if you don't watch out.'"[53] Yet the bitter divisions and disputes that rocked California politics demanded that participants stand and be counted.

A progressive Republican, Willebrandt had brought her father's "true blue Republicanism" from the Midwest to California and then developed her own progressive philosophy. Her work as assistant police court defender identified her with the reform element; her work with professional and women's clubs and the bar association committees linked her further with the issues of social feminism that affected home and community. In her graduate thesis at the College of Law in 1917, she examined "Popular Government and Public Commissions" and concluded that "popular government" was "absolutely inconsistent" with the emergence and proliferation of appointed and unresponsive state commissions. The frustration of citizens led to drives for constitutional amendments. Like Theodore Roosevelt, she urged that federal commissions be instituted to deal with industries in interstate commerce. The government and the economic development

Myrtle and David Walker at the Temple City ranch in the early 1920s.

within the state should be left to the legislature and the people, not commissions.[54] It was a classic statement of frontier, populist, progressive faith in the power of the people, tempered by a lawyer's respect for the law and the Constitution and by Rooseveltian practicality.

Willebrandt's party in California and nationally had been riven by the bolt of Theodore Roosevelt and his vice-presidential running mate, Hiram Johnson, to the Progressive party in 1912. Defeated in that race, Johnson remained governor and then was reelected on a Progressive ticket in 1914. Two years later, the rift between Progressives and Republicans was thinly patched in a United Republican campaign that was strong enough to send Johnson to the United States Senate. Concerned with ensuring progressive control of the state party machinery, he lingered as both acting governor and senator until forced to leave for Washington and the special session called by President Wilson to consider a declaration of war.[55]

While the war blunted progressive reform efforts in Washington, in California the war years were labeled the downhill years. Johnson's appointed successor, William Stephens, found it difficult to control the legislature in the face of the criticism of Johnson loyalists, the reemergence of the powerful Southern Pacific combine, and traditional north-south divisions. Postwar issues further complicated the situation: Versailles, the League of Nations, and internationalism. Johnson, a leader of the "bitter-enders," those irreconcilably opposed to American participation in the League of Nations, worked to have the California Republican party stand with him. In the 1920 senatorial race, he backed Samuel Shortridge, "a conservative's conservative," over two progressive candidates who were not with him on the league or had not been, in his estimate, fully loyal to Hiram Johnson. Shortridge was the easy victor. The presidential primary fight between Johnson and Californian Herbert Hoover, who campaigned to strike a blow for the league, added to the divisions. For a progressive Republican like Mabel Walker Willebrandt, working in California politics in these downhill years was like walking in a mine field.[56]

In 1920, Willebrandt was in the middle of a Johnson-Shortridge, progressive-conservative Republican tussle. At issue was patronage; in this case the rich plum of a United States assistant attorney generalship. President Wilson had appointed the first woman to such a post, northern Californian Annette Abbott Adams, in the last year of his administration. California Republicans now wanted to claim that position for their own; it was logical that they too should woo the victorious suffragists by naming a woman.[57]

Senators Johnson and Shortridge, in uneasy tandem, had to work out an agreement on the California share of the federal patronage in the new Harding administration. In Southern California, Johnson's key lieutenant and adviser was law professor Frank Doherty. To Willebrandt, he was teacher, friend, and able mentor in the tangled political thicket. Doherty's suggestions all had the key qualification of loyalty to Johnson. He early recommended Mabel Walker Willebrandt as assistant attorney general.[58]

By June 1921, there were two leading women candidates for the post: Willebrandt and Clara Shortridge Foltz. The first woman admitted to the practice of law in California, Foltz was a strong suffrage leader, active in the Women's Republican Club, and, most important, the sister of Senator Sam Shortridge. A disturbed Johnson wrote to Doherty in late June about a *Washington Times* article citing Foltz as a likely choice: "Such appointments would be unfortunate and embarrassing. If you are interested in Willebrandt suggest you forward endorsements of Attorney General, or judges, men like Flint and of Republican organizations and women's clubs."[59] Shortridge had already claimed the United States attorney slot in San Francisco for his protege. Johnson wanted his share.

Doherty and Willebrandt moved into action. He won immediate endorsements from state senator Flint and judges; Willebrandt garnered the support of key clubwomen and reformers like Katherine Philips Edson, one of the eight women on the Republican national executive committee.[60] Supporters sent wires to Harding's attorney general, Harry Daugherty. James Pope wrote at some length to Daugherty, reviewing Willebrandt's work in his office and reporting: "She is one of the most unselfish and hard working attorneys I have ever met and if you make her a member of your staff you will have a live wire who will stay awake nights trying to think up new ways of giving more credit for the office." Her "loyalty is of that rare type which spends itself in seeing that the head of the office gets his just dues. If she gets into your office you will discover that your reputation is getting the boost of its life."[61] Daugherty, surveying this boomlet for Willebrandt, was also watching the counter groundswell for Foltz. Willebrandt feared he might end the impasse by deciding against both of them.[62]

By August 4, Johnson reported that he had done everything in his power for Willebrandt and would keep up the fight. He refused to budge on Shortridge's pleadings for Foltz and gradually forced him to yield on Willebrandt, stressing the strength of her Southern California supporters. In mid-August, Shortridge reluctantly admitted defeat. Daugherty, faced with a single nomination, quickly wired Willebrandt to come to Washington for a conference. She left California quietly on August 17; her office told hovering reporters that she was away on a vacation.[63]

The interview with Daugherty went well; it was followed by a successful meeting with Harding. Looking over this attractive, dynamic candidate, he observed that she had only one shortcoming, her youth. She laughingly assured him that she would soon outgrow it. On August 27, 1921, Attorney General Daugherty forwarded two recess commissions to Harding: Shortridge's candidate, J. T. Williams, as United States attorney for San Francisco, and Mabel Walker Willebrandt as assistant attorney general.[64]

Hiram Johnson immediately wrote of his delight to Frank Doherty: "She owes this appointment to you. Because of you I contributed what little I could to it." Her reputation and record had not only won her key endorsements, it had earned the enmity of conservatives. He reported: "Singularly enough, the most prominent women in your city wired protesting against Mrs. Willebrandt," alleging everything against her "from lack of experience and legal attainment to anti-vaccination."[65]

Willebrandt had her own reservations. Three years earlier she had considered and decided against taking the civil service examination for a post as deputy district attorney. "It would," she explained, "always be prosecuting and I prefer being on the other side." It would also mean dealing only with criminal law, and she intended ultimately to have a practice only in civil law. In addition, the salary would be $110 a month, only $10 more than she had earned as principal of the Lincoln Park school, and she would have to abandon her private practice. At the same time, she also considered running for police court judge. The odds, she decided, were too great "to warrant the expenditure of money it would mean, and losing, I might get branded a 'political seeker' in skirts and that I couldn't stand."[66]

Willebrandt accepted the appointment as assistant attorney general in August 1929 with additional apprehensions. She "fairly shuddered" at the possibility that she would be "relegated to an inconsequential groove" in a dull, colorless government post, a token woman, patronized and powerless. She worried about her parents, just relocated to California. They needed her, as she always needed their emotional and moral support. Her resources were so stretched that she had to borrow train fare to Washington and a blouse so that she could change on the trip. Finally, she was well aware of the truth in Harding's observation. She was a young lawyer. At thirty-two, she had just over five years of legal experience. She later reflected, "I was a young lawyer, much *too* young when appointed, for the responsibilities heaped on me."[67] But she had worked hard for the opportunity and had always thrived on challenge. As she began the long journey to Washington, she was excited and confident. She opened her Bible to the passage in Timothy (2 Tim. 1:7) that always sustained her: "For God hath not given us the spirit of fear; but of power, and of love, and of a sound mind."[68]

CHAPTER THREE

The Justice Department: Prohibition

*While attending law school, I used to wait late at night when
the law library closed on the corner of First and Main Streets in
Los Angeles for the interurban car to my suburban home. Indeli-
bly impressed upon my mind is the fact that scarcely a night—
never a week—went by without several drunken men reeling
past me from the five saloons near that corner.
No one noticed then—now one such incident would be news!*

MABEL WALKER WILLEBRANDT
The Inside of Prohibition

*National prohibition by constitutional amendment had begun
as the golden dream of thousands of devoted men and women. At
the end of the decade it had precipitated a struggle which was to
test the political wisdom of the American Republic.*

CHARLES MERZ
The Dry Decade

*M*ABEL WALKER WILLE-
BRANDT joined a Justice Department badly bruised by two of its
most controversial administrators. In the last years of the Wilson administration, Attorney General A. Mitchell Palmer, the fighting
Quaker, had expended his energies in zealous pursuit of suspected
foreign agents and radicals. His 1919 and 1920 "ship or shoot" policy
fed a Red Scare that seriously eroded civil liberties. Launching his
presidential ambitions from these Bolshevik hunts, he allowed the
leadership of the Department of Justice to drift. Charges of corruption were raised; prohibition and wartime cases crammed the federal
dockets.

Harding's appointment of his campaign manager, Harry A.
Daugherty, as attorney general did not augur well for a return of either
the department's reputation or efficiency. More lobbyist and politician

than lawyer, Daugherty saw himself as the power behind Harding and as the dispenser of patronage. Like his chief, he promised to build a staff of top professionals, but also like Harding he richly rewarded personal and political friends. Ill for much of his tenure, anxious at the serious illness of his wife and alcoholic son, rocked by the scandals of his aide Jesse Smith, he left the day-to-day operations of the department to his six assistants.[1]

Willebrandt was regarded as one of Daugherty's nonpolitical appointments, since she was so strongly recommended by bench and bar in California. Assigned a new division, she had jurisdiction over prohibition cases, federal income and estate taxes, prisons, war risk insurance, and minor acts to regulate commerce. In 1921 she had a staff of three assistants. Eight years later, with more than a hundred staff members and aided by several hundred more in the field, she led the largest, most active, and one of the best administered divisions.[2]

In "pestiferous appeals," publicity, and politics, prohibition was her greatest responsibility. Willebrandt had not been involved in the fight for a dry law in California, nor had she joined the Women's Christian Temperence Union (WCTU) or the powerful Anti-Saloon League. She was not a prohibitionist or even a teetaler before the National Prohibition Act, but once given the responsibility, she worked tirelessly to enforce the law.[3]

The task was staggering. The effort destroyed her major ambition to be appointed a federal judge and made her the storm center of the 1928 presidential campaign. The problem was to dry up America; in 1921 it was leaking substantially.

The United States had 18,000 miles of coastline and border to patrol. Ships and occasionally planes from Canada, fast rumrunners from Bimini, Cuba, and Barbados, and British and Scottish ships plying beyond the three-mile limit busily supplied the "real McCoy." New York garbage scows returned from their Atlantic dumps with small shipments of spirits; motorboats slid into the rivers and creeks near Savannah or into wide, inviting Biscayne Bay. One intrepid smuggler used torpedoes to land his wet cargo on Long Island.[4] It was even simpler to steal a car, pay $500 for Scotch in Ontario, and sell it for $1,500 in Detroit.

The thirsty did not have to import their drink. America was rich in alcohol. In January 1920, when the Eighteenth Amendment became law, more than five hundred distillers produced an annual output of 286 million gallons; more than twelve hundred breweries made hundreds of millions of gallons of beer. Five hundred warehouses bulged with 200 million gallons of liquor.[5] Not only were there millions of gallons available for illegal diversion, but distilleries were still able, with permits, to produce alcohol for industrial or medicinal uses. Breweries could make near beer that could be needled into real beer. Permits, medical prescriptions, and warehouse receipts could be forged. The director of the prohibition unit, Lincoln Andrews, conservatively estimated that 15 million gallons were annually diverted into bootleg channels.[6]

The moonshine trade was thriving and adventurous. Willebrandt lamented the ease of supply to Washington. One southern Maryland highway was renamed "Bootleg Boulevard." Fords emerged from the dirt roads of tobacco country to rendezvous with the speedy Lincolns that supplied the restaurants, speakeasies, and private citizens of the capital and Baltimore. Home brewers could avoid the bootlegger altogether; a one-gallon still cost only seven dollars, and recipes were available in the local library. The small entrepreneur, however, was increasingly elbowed out of the trade, given the magnitude of the supply and demand. Bootlegging became big business, with the organization and nationwide network that characterized other industries of the 1920s.[7]

Public support was essential in plugging up the leaks. At the beginning, success seemed assured. Prohibition had been won through the combined efforts of a broad coalition. Middle-class progressives fought the political corruption centered in the machine and saloon; social workers anguished over lost family paychecks; businessmen sought the efficiency and safety of the sober worker in the new "scientific management"; traditional temperance groups and fundamentalists pressed politicians and church leaders in a combined campaign for purity and progressivism. The nonpartisan Anti-Saloon League massed "an army of the Lord to wipe out the curse of drink" and joined forces with the Women's Christian Temperance Union to form the major lobby for local, state, and national campaigns. Their success was reflected in state triumphs well before the wartime Lever Act and final passage of the Eighteenth Amendment. Forty-six of forty-eight states voted ratification. No constitutional amendment had ever been repealed, and prohibition seemed the enduring law of the land. Texas senator Morris Sheppard concluded: "There is as much chance of repealing the Eighteenth Amendment as there is for a hummingbird to fly to the planet Mars with the Washington Monument tied to its tail."[8]

Willebrandt on the job at the Department of Justice. Photograph by Underwood and Underwood. *Below*, Willebrandt kept a cartoon collection. The frustration in prohibition enforcement was depicted by T. E. Powers in the *Washington Herald*, July 1928.

Give the Little Girl a Hand

Essentially the coalition marshaled dry, rural, old-stock, Protestant citizens and built on their traditional values of self-control and responsibility and their growing anxiety over the emergence of a problem-ridden urban America peopled by wet, Catholic immigrants. The fight sharply divided the nation on class, ethnic, geographic, and religious lines.

Willebrandt believed that "no political, economic or moral issue has so engrossed and divided all the people of America as the prohibition problem, except the issue of slavery."[9] The country, she perceived, would not be "Couéd" into acceptance. Communities and their leaders had to unite and demand respect for the new law. Like the suffragists after their constitutional victory, however, the drys faced new organizational problems and the need to develop new directions. They reduced their local and state activities and, as Willebrandt lamented, relied on the federal government as the "big boy" to end the illegal traffic.[10]

Federal enforcement proved to be an organizational nightmare. Responsibility for enforcing the ban on the manufacture, sale, transportation, importation, or exportation of alcoholic beverages was logically placed in the Treasury Department, which had long experience in taxing, licensing, and setting standards for the alcohol and drug industries. A new prohibition unit was created under the Bureau of Internal Revenue and charged with suppressing the illegal traffic in liquor and licensing and controlling its legal manufacture and trade. Major Roy Haynes, an Ohio editor and antisaloon supporter, was appointed by President Harding to serve as his prohibition commissioner. Described by Willebrandt as "a politician in sheep's clothing," he presided over a force of state directors and 2,500 agents that was explicitly exempt from the federal civil service. The unit was a giant plum tree. Field administrators advised applicants to secure endorsements from congressmen or the Anti-Saloon League. Agents, paid at a lower rate than colleagues in the other Treasury Department services, had little background and were given little training. Willebrandt characterized the unit as a "regime of preachers." Too many agents, "like ordinary policemen," adept at bringing in the retail bootlegger and logging an impressive number of arrests, were unable to carry out the sophisticated undercover work needed to dry up the source of supply or the protection money.[11] Most were "of the ward heeler class," "of uncertain character, limited intelligence." The U.S. attorneys bitterly complained of agents too inept to secure reliable evidence, too lazy to lie along a dark pier all night, or too afraid of the graft organization to do the needed job.[12]

By 1925, complaints were so widespread that the prohibition unit was reorganized under the assistant secretary of the treasury, General Lincoln Andrews. He promised to set up a "new clean business organization" and insisted that appointments would be made on merit. Andrews would be the "generalissimo." Willebrandt described the shift from Haynes to Andrews as one from "zealots to military organization." Instead of preachers, military cronies moved into prohibition posts. She particularly objected to one appointment in New York, where the candidate had already been dismissed by the Internal Revenue Service when the evidence gathered in four cases was worthless. Andrews made the appointment with the notation that he was "a good sojur, 'nuff said." Willebrandt fumed, "It will take many a day . . . for law enforcement to recover from the setback it suffered from General Lincoln Andrews."[13]

Cooperating in the prohibition effort were the Coast Guard, the Customs Service, and, in cases where the prohibition unit was unable or unwilling to collect evidence, the agents of the intelligence unit of the Internal Revenue Service. Coordination was the responsibility but never the achievement of Secretary of the Treasury Andrew W. Mellon. The Anti-Saloon League leader Wayne Wheeler had fought against Mellon's appointment because of his indirect interest in distilleries. Willebrandt concluded that "Secretary Mellon was *not* interested in doing a good job with his prohibition unit and paid no attention to the appointments or supervision." Attorney General Harlan Fiske Stone agreed that "law enforcement agents shouldn't be under *that man*."[14]

The organizational problems in the Justice Department were only slightly less severe. Politics was rife in the selection of U.S. attorneys and their assistants. Willebrandt lamented about the time lost in prosecuting the prosecutors. She marshaled a "flying squadron" of special assistants to the attorney general to try cases where the local U.S. attorney proved inept or untrustworthy. Federal commissioners, responsible for preliminary hearings of the evidence, were also political appointees. Serving on a daily fee basis some refused to hold more than one hearing a day. U.S. marshals were not always scrupulous in guarding juries or in keeping a secure lock on potable evidence. Many of them, Willebrandt complained, were "broken-down politicians fond of drink and low company."[15] Judges and juries tended to take on the coloration of their communities, wet or dry.

Willebrandt's problems in directing the efforts of her division were further exacerbated by the turnover in the post of attorney general. Harry Daugherty was harried by the Brookhart Committee's investigation of his administration of the Justice Department and the alleged influence peddling of his aide Jesse Smith. Pressure for his ouster was so strong by the spring of 1924 that Coolidge, facing an election, finally yielded and got Daugherty's reluctant resignation. His successor, the distinguished law professor Harlan Fiske Stone, energetically cleaned out inefficient political hacks until he was "bumped upstairs" to the Supreme Court in 1925.[16] A conservative Vermonter, John G. Sargent, was the next appointee and served until Hoover's inauguration in 1929. All of the attorney generals gave Willebrandt support, but the shifts in administrative style and personnel did not foster consistency or efficiency in the department.

The magnitude of enforcing prohibition was aptly illustrated in a 1928 cartoon showing Willebrandt with a mop trying to stem the waves on an Atlantic seashore. Her division handled more than 40,000 cases a year; 50 percent of the federal case load concerned prohibition.[17] She had never run from a fight and did not intend to drown now, but the effort to enforce the law made "Mrs. Willebrandt" a familiar headline and one of America's best-known and most controversial women.

She tried to share her routine and the significance and excitement of the work with her parents:

> Tomorrow just as a sample of an ordinary day, I have to appear before the Investigating Committee on Prohibition Enforcement . . . at the Capital at 11:30. Before that dictation at 8 A.M. and a conference with 2 detectives making a big case at 9:30. Noon Supreme Court for an hour and a half.
>
> Afternoon a conference with officials of Treas. Dept. on undercover operations to go into making certain smuggling cases on New Jersey coast.
>
> A conference with the new A.G. on some cases. See 3 attys applying for positions my dept. Meeting attys my division and probably 4 or 5 out of town officials who'll "drop in" then to be chinked in between—besides *mail* and office routine! Then at night I go to Louisville Ky. where Congressman Langley whom I indicted is to be on trial—US atty says political pressure so great—please to come! I'm going![18]

Knowing that community support was essential in enforcing prohibition Willebrandt spoke and wrote tirelessly on citizen responsibility. Typical was an exhortation to the Boston Chamber of Commerce:

> We are menaced by a "No Man's Land" in America . . . the upper crust which feels itself above and superior to the law and the "dregs" who strike beneath the foundations of American liberties. These two classes exist everywhere, especially in Boston where the oldest families on whom the nation looks as representative of the finest in American life violate the law, and in New England, because of the large foreign population.[19]

Speaking at an annual meeting of Republican women in Philadelphia, she argued that it was "idle for us to spend our time talking about affairs in Europe. No women's club or group can excuse itself by talking of foreign or national affairs unless vital local matters are first studied."[20]

At the Anti-Saloon League's national convention, local and national conventions of the WCTU, the League of Women Voters, and the National Woman's party, her message was repeated: it was up to the citizen to uphold the law. In May 1923, she wrote to her parents of a speech at Hartford, Connecticut, before "a big wet audience," noting: "I'm growing very bold in the assertion of my convictions (Perhaps you wonder when I was otherwise!). . . . I am enjoying giving a message I so much believe in as law enforcement but it breaks into my work which is terribly heavy to such an extent that I can't do much more of it and I'm turning down invitations right and left."[21]

In October 1923, she accepted a major invitation to address the Citizenship Conference in Washington. Other speakers included William Jennings Bryan, Gifford Pinchot, William Borah, and Rabbi Stephen Wise. In the midst of this pantheon of drys, Willebrandt's address on "Some Problems of Enforcement" was a rousing attack on local "sleeping sickness" in enforcing the law combined with a criticism of the Volstead Act as "puerile," "a puny, little toothless sort of thing!" Since all the "big violators" of the Eighteenth Amendment were "taxdodgers," she urged a double dose of prohibition and tax enforcement for the bootleggers.[22]

The same message of citizen responsibility was issued in her major interviews and articles. A long article in *Good Housekeeping* in April 1924 reiterated her question and plea, "Will You Help Keep the Law?" Pungently she used a war analogy: "If a regular warfare against the government were on, what a patriotic fever would burn in our veins, but since it is only an army of rodents scuttling the ship of state, how serenely do we sit on the deck and bask in the sun!" She warned that justifying the evasion of any law was "sowing dragons' teeth . . . from which spring those who, with different views of 'cherished liberty,' will justify evasion of other laws safeguarding property or business development."[23] In "Smart Washington after Six O'clock" in the *Ladies' Home Journal*, she reported that it was no longer fashionable to serve a cocktail. Knowledgeable citizens realized that they were supporting murder and bribery through their drinking. She stressed: "It may have been clever and smart to serve a thing forbidden and costly if the dregs in the glass were not so repulsive and disillusioning."[24] In "Half or Whole-Hearted Prohibition," in *The Woman Citizen*, she summed up her plea: "Let us then pull together—you catch the little fellow, punish him quickly and drastically, and then hold us in the Federal Government responsible if we do not mobilize every agency at the command of the Government to dam up the sources of illicit wholesale supply."[25]

As she took over the operation of the division, Willebrandt worked with the Treasury Department to dam up leaks from rum row and bootleg diversion of domestic alcohol. Her biggest case, breaking the Savannah Four, was generated out of this primary attack on smuggling; it also demonstrated all the difficulties of enforcement and coordination.

The leader of the four-family ring (Haar, Goldberg, Bailey, Baughn) was Willie Haar, the "King of the Bootleggers." He owned four schooners and a fast fleet of small boats that landed their cargoes from the Bahamas or Scottish supply ships in cement caves by the swamps and rivers until the liquor, crated as fruit or potatoes, could be shipped by truck or box car to New York, Chicago, or New Orleans. County sheriffs were paid "not to see things." An army of detectives and employees ensured the efficiency of the business. The operation seemed so protected and secure that Haar's men openly named their local baseball nine the Bootlegger Team.[26]

To crack the Savannah rings in such hostile territory would take a skilled, cooperative effort of the agents and lawyers of the Treasury and Justice departments. The task was complicated because the U.S. attorney's office was, according to Willebrandt, "worse than useless"; the local prohibition director was "absolutely crooked"; and the sheriff was in collusion with the bootleggers. In office less than six months, Willebrandt took on the challenge. In April 1922, she requested that the director of the Bureau of Investigation, William Burns, detail "two thoroughly reliable high class investigators" to Savannah to apprehend some of the Big Four.[27] The investigation was directed from her office and under her personal supervision in cooperation with Assistant Attorney General John W.H. Crim of the Criminal Division. By June, undercover agents had obtained evidence of a conspiracy and, as Willebrandt reported to the attorney general, "had a wonderful case worked up" until the local prohibition agents rushed in to raid one of Haar's places without a proper warrant. They queered the Justice Department's cover and ruined two months' effort. Outraged, Willebrandt discussed the costly clumsiness with Commissioner David Blair of the Internal Revenue Service and indicated that it was up to the Treasury Department to make amends by working up a case that could stand. To the attorney general, she argued that such big interstate investigations should be "generaled" by the Department of Justice. In an attempt to get more agents and support, she added that the beleaguered Harding administration, bombarded by allegations of scandal, could strike back with a success in one of these cases. She got both agents and backing.[28]

The strategy was to pursue the Haars and their colleagues for income tax evasion first and then build evidence of the liquor conspiracy that had produced the unreported income. Treasury agents searched bank accounts in New York, Philadelphia, Baltimore, Miami, Seattle, and Portland and estimated that the Haar brothers owed $1,900,000 in income taxes. An attorney was detailed from the staff of the solicitor of internal revenue to help the assistant U.S. attorney draw up the indictments; Willebrandt sent one of her assistants to help, stressing that it was extremely important that records be kept.[29]

A special assistant to the attorney general would be named to present the evidence to the grand jury in August and later to try the cases. Aware that the department dared not send a northerner to appear before "the patriotic citizens of Savannah," Willebrandt searched for a border state southerner. A quintessential southern gentleman and highly respected Chattanooga lawyer, White B. Miller, was appointed and dispatched to Savannah.[30]

While the Treasury Department investigators developed the income tax cases, the Bureau of Investigation men worked "to insinuate" themselves into the liquor organization. Willebrandt wrote to Commissioner Blair of the need for cooperation and of her anxiety over interdepartmental jealousies, for the cases were "too important

"AT THE BOTTOM OF THE LADDER"   By KESSLER

MRS. MABEL WALKER WILLEBRANDT, ASSISTANT UNITED STATES ATTORNEY GENERAL, BEFORE SHE WENT TO SCHOOL LEARNED TO SET TYPE IN HER FATHER'S PRINTING OFFICE IN BLACKWELL OKLAHOMA.

Kessler's cartoon in the *Newark Ledger,* October 1, 1924, illustrates not only Willebrandt's identification with prohibition enforcement, but a steady public interest in her background and private life.

Willebrandt in her typical office or court attire—a tailored suit and soft blouse. The hair style was carefully prepared to hide her hearing aid.

to let any departmental rivalry or boundaries of official duty spoil them." Miller coordinated the agents locally and reported to her. She wrote to her parents, "I'm just beginning to plumb the power I have in the gov't game."[31]

From Washington, she encouraged the investigators and urged them to take particular care in drawing up complaints. A former sheriff, miffed at the local machine, joined the undercover agents, helping to gather evidence and checking on jurors. Sixty intelligence men and three attorneys were on the scene to organize the case against seventy-two bootleggers. Willebrandt arrived in early August to join in drawing up the indictments.[32]

She discovered that Miller though a good lawyer was a "punk executive," and pitched in to clean up the details. She worked everybody so hard that Miller buckled. She reported in some disgust to her parents: "The 2nd day he got sick! Couldn't keep the pace. When he left for the Drs. he kissed my hand—like a true Southern cavalier. To poor old White Miller, I'm a whirlwind. He's a fine lawyer, but slow. Oh!" But she added, "He's really fine. I use him as a symbol. He's the best of the brand!" Somewhat guilty that perhaps she had brought on his optic neuralgia, she worked to spare him for the grand jury.[33]

The first of the indictments was made on August 11. The government succeeded so effectively that Willebrandt was exuberant. "The Savannah case has broken wonderfully. It's the biggest of its kind anywhere in the country." She sent off a barrage of congratulatory letters to White Miller, Commissioner Blair, and key Treasury intelligence men.[34] She encouraged the leader of the agents from the Bureau of Investigation to keep up his splendid work but also pointed out that the case against Willie Haar was not as good as it ought to be. Preparing for the trial, agents should use the evidence gathered in the grand jury proceedings to work for "squealing" by some of the "little fellows." While recognizing that it was useless for her to make too many suggestions to agents in the field, she did caution against drinking and warned again that jealousy between Justice and Treasury men should be avoided. Specifically, Willebrandt directed that at no time should intelligence bureau agents confer with any prohibition agents, the U.S. or assistant U.S. attorney, or confer with the U.S. marshal or his deputies, concluding, "I'm not for taking any chances."[35]

In Washington, faced with a full case load before the Supreme Court, she worried about efforts to delay the trial. She wrote to Commissioner Blair that her heart was set on letting nothing prevent it and she spoke of the boasts of the defendants that they would never be tried. Some modest but unsuccessful intervention was attempted through Coolidge's assistant Bascom Slemp, but in September, Willebrandt reported to her father that the case had "come to a head nicely." She dispatched fifty-eight agents to keep watch on witnesses and jurors.[36]

The preparation bore fruit. On November 24 a wire arrived affirming that all of the Haars were found guilty. Willebrandt cheered, "Oh, Gorgeous—Thank the Lord." She wired Miller: "Wonderful news making a real Government Thanksgiving"[37] and suggested to Attorney General Daugherty that he might want to issue a press release. She drafted one for him just in case.

The Daugherty-Willebrandt press statement was issued December 11. It cited the series of Savannah trials as "probably the most noteworthy since the passage of the Eighteenth Amendment." Sentences totaled twenty-nine years and four months and $153,000 in fines. The release noted: "The cases were prepared, instigated and developed under the personal direction of my assistant, Mrs. Mabel Walker Willebrandt." Willebrandt saved the adjectives for Miller's "Herculean task" and concluded that this case proved the contention that the law could be enforced when the federal government pulled together.[38]

In the aftermath of these major indictments, "the little fish fell in line" in Savannah. Willebrandt noted the "supplemental killing" the agents made and wrote to Rush Holland, assistant to the attorney general: "I hope you can raise their salaries. They honestly *deserve* it!" The litigation and negotiation with the big fish over the income tax owed would not end until 1929.[39]

At the same time that Willebrandt was planning her strategy in Savannah, she marshaled her forces for a massive sweep of the bootleggers in Mobile, Alabama. In June 1923, more than fifty agents, including the celebrated master of disguises Izzy Einstein, were dispatched to gather evidence. A series of raids in November netted $100,000 worth of liquor. Eighty-five warrants were served. Einstein reviewed the haul: "I have never seen such a variety of booze in all my experience. I have tried every thing from the rarest vintages that are worth three figures a pint to the vilest shinny that would kill an elephant. The poison that is sold here as booze is the most criminal thing I have ever witnessed."[40]

To head the prosecution, Willebrandt recruited the young crusading Birmingham attorney Hugo Black. A convinced dry and a prominent

Democrat, Black tried the case "with characteristic vigor." More than 150 witnesses were called in the bitterly fought twenty-five day trial. The chief of police, a city attorney, a legislator, five deputy sheriffs, county officials, and more than one hundred others in Mobile were charged in a conspiracy headed by the Mobile "Big Six." Again, Willebrandt concentrated on the "big fish." Thirty-three of those indicted were found not guilty, but five of the Big Six were sentenced.[41]

The cases against the Savannah Four and the Mobile Big Six were highly publicized, but the federal campaign to end smuggling along the shores of Florida was a more difficult undertaking. Willebrandt fought hard for more power to conduct investigations. With Attorney General Stone's backing, she was able to report some success in 1924, even with her continuing nemesis:

> The unexpected has happened. Today at Cabinet meeting Mellon gave a letter to AG Stone authorizing our dept. to conduct investigations in Pro. smuggling etc. according to *my* (!) plans outlined at the conference with the Director of the Budget the week before I left!!?! Mellon promised to transfer $150,000 to $200,000 to be expended under my direction, and furthermore to furnish a fast boat to us, and full cooperation of his units!

Her admiralty assistant and investigators exulted and she concluded, "Think! I'll maybe rope a US Senator in this."[42]

Florida was so hostile to prohibition enforcement that when the Coast Guard opened an operating base, local shipyards in Miami refused to repair their vessels or make a wharf available. After the base was shifted to safer Fort Lauderdale, a conspiracy to assassinate an officer was discovered. A Coast Guard undercover agent asserted that the federal judge was either incompetent or crooked, and the U.S. attorney had a partner in his private practice who was the "most notorious bootleg attorney." Information given to the U.S. attorney's office was immediately leaked. The bailiff of the U.S. District Court at Miami was under federal indictment in Georgia. The people of Florida were so intimidated they were afraid to complain.[43]

Willebrandt launched a four-year effort to reorganize the U.S. attorney's office in Florida. In 1927, a flotilla was sent to rout the traffic from Cuba and the Bahamas. The Treasury and Justice departments and the navy cooperated in dispatching a fleet of eleven destroyers, nine large patrol boats, and thirty smaller craft and two amphibious planes to interdict the illicit trade.

The chief intelligence officer of the Coast Guard reflected on the years of the Florida effort and concluded:

> Mabel Walker Willebrandt has been a tower of strength to the Coast Guard. She has helped us in every way possible, both in prosecuting criminals and in defending our men against unjust persecution and prosecution and has many times stretched her authority to the elastic limit in her efforts to produce results and to maintain the morale of our personnel. Her courage, tenacity and knowledge are remarkable.[44]

The rum row campaign was paralleled by the effort to stop the domestic leaks and diversions from distilleries, breweries, and warehouses. The sensational George Remus case indicated the possibilities of using the loopholes in the Volstead Act, which provided for the manufacture and distribution of alcohol for medicinal and industrial purposes. Remus, a successful Chicago lawyer, purchased licensed distilleries with supplies of bonded liquor in their warehouses, acquired drugstores for distribution points, and cultivated federal prohibition agents for the permits necessary to get the liquor "legally" from distillery to drugstore to consumer. Remus moved to Cincinnati for ease of access to his distilleries and began his operation. In thirteen months, he amassed $3 million.

By the summer of 1921, U.S. Attorney James Clark, alarmed at the size of the Remus trade, wrote urgently for help to Daugherty. One of Remus's distilleries had shipped out 3,200 barrels and 18,000 cases of liquor between June and August 1921. Forged permits sent the cargoes to nonexistent consignees. Actually the merchandise was convoyed to Remus's Death Valley farm near Cincinnati for distribution. Enough liquor was also dispatched to Remus drugstores to "meet the prescriptions of physicians of the whole United States."[45]

Willebrandt charged Remus with five counts: two under the old Internal Revenue statutes and three under the conspiracy and Volstead statutes. Remus's fortune had reached an estimated $6 million. He controlled nine distilleries and employed three thousand people; his business volume was $50 million annually.[46] Remus was certainly not cowed by the indictment. Free on bail, he gave a New Year's Eve party in his new mansion. The real stuff flowed liberally. At the end of the evening, each man received a diamond favor; each woman found a new Ford car waiting for her ready to join a parade of one hundred new autos to greet the New Year of 1922.[47]

Remus's trial in May ended in guilty verdicts for him and thirteen confederates. Remus drew two years in Atlanta federal prison and a fine of $10,000 on conspiracy charges, and a one-year sentence to be served in the county jail for running a nuisance at the Death Valley farm. His lawyer immediately appealed. Willebrandt sent the U.S. attorney her congratulations and the "intense satisfaction" of the department. She also filed an appeal on the judge's ruling that the Volstead statutes applied in the Remus case and superseded the stiffer Internal Revenue statutes. Always chafing at the weak punishment allowed under the prohibition law, Willebrandt did not want to lose the heavier penalties for evading the tax on liquor sold for beverage purposes.[48] She won her point in an opinion delivered by Justice Holmes in the October 1922 Supreme Court session. Especially pleased at Holmes, "whom I love dearly—from afar," she reported to her parents that "since everyone was convinced I couldn't win on that point, it is regarded as a great victory and congratulations have just been pouring in."[49]

Unsuccessful in his appeals on a search warrant technicality and double jeopardy, Remus went off to Atlanta in a show of bravado with his colleagues in his own private railroad car. In March 1924, Attorney General Daugherty wired the warden of a report that Remus was receiving special privileges. Willebrandt wrote a follow-up letter observing that when agents investigating the Jack Daniels Distillery case arrived in Atlanta to interview conspirators they found that the witnesses had been instructed by Remus not to provide any information. The agents and Willebrandt were puzzled at Remus's advance knowledge. Though suspicious, she accepted the warden's assurances that "this wealthy and notorious bootlegger" was enjoying no special privileges.[50]

Remus remained busy in the spring of 1924. He was called to testify by the Brookhart Committee on his allegation that he had paid Daugherty's aide Jesse Smith $250,000 in protection money. In May, he wrote Willebrandt requesting that he be allowed to complete his entire sentence at Atlanta. It would be better for his health, save the government the expense of moving him, and allow him to finish the socially beneficial work he had undertaken there. In August, he wrote again seeking a writ of habeus corpus on the grounds that the sentencing judge had not made it clear when, specifically, his incarceration would begin in each prison. Willebrandt was angry and adamant, writing to the solicitor general: "Remus was the most notorious and defiant bootlegger the Government has had to prosecute and he should be compelled to serve his full sentence, if possible. He was the ring-leader of this gigantic conspiracy and has given the Government no end of trouble."[51]

In trying to dry up the leaks from permits issued for distilleries and breweries, Willebrandt urged prohibition agents to be more stringent and discriminating in issuing permits. Each applicant should be fully investigated. She pointed to the permit issued to a small-town Texas drugstore releasing two hundred barrels of 90-proof Jamaica ginger. This "would take care of quite a sizable quantity of old-fashioned tummy-aches—many more, in fact, than would be likely to occur in a sparsely populated Texas community."[52]

The drive to shut down illegal production was matched by a deter-mined attack on distribution in speakeasies, restaurants, and shops. Sections 21, 22, and 23 of the National Prohibition Act authorized issuing an injunction against places that manufactured, sold, or pro-cessed liquor as a "common nuisance" and provided for their abate-ment and closing. In 1923, the U.S. attorney in New York City wrote Willebrandt that he was developing a card index file on places selling liquor in New York. Far from complete, it already included 1,100 saloons and 300 to 400 restaurants. He submitted an expense request for padlocks. In March 1924, his successor announced that he was grinding out padlock cases with a pretty good record. In one month, he had sought injunctions in 116 cases.[53] Willebrandt wrote her en-couragement: "This is splendid work and I hope it will continue."[54] Three years later another active padlock effort was under way in New York; 113 complaints were issued in August 1927.

The tactics were familiar, then, when federal marshals and prohibi-tion agents swept down on speakeasies in a series of spectacular raids in July 1928. The timing of the raids, however, coincided with Governor Al Smith's nomination for president by the Democratic convention. The New York Democratic press immediately charged foul play. The sweeps had been well planned. Prohibition agents were brought in from Denver, Fort Worth, and Kansas City. Their wardrobes were chosen with care, since New Yorkers knew that "the man who looked the most like a bum in any night club would be the agent." For further cover, women accompanied the agents to collect the evidence.[55] Pad-lock proceedings were started against thirty-six Broadway restau-rants. The list of prominent New Yorkers present during the raids and the notoriety of the clubs attacked, including Texas Guinan's and Helen Morgan's, ensured major headlines.

A concerned Willebrandt wrote to vacationing Attorney General

Sargent that the spectacular stories were bound to discredit the cases and urged him to impress on Charles Tuttle, the U.S. attorney in New York, that he should make no statement to the press. A major breakdown in communications ensued. Tuttle moved to indict the waiters and entertainers apprehended in the raids. Willebrandt, wanting as always to use the federal power to stop the suppliers and the protection apparatus and perhaps stung by press allegations that only the "little fellow" would suffer, instructed Tuttle to arrange for an attorney from her office to present additional evidence from documents obtained in the raids. More than a hundred subpoenas were issued to prominent citizens who were caught and to New York police inspectors who seemed implicated. The scene at the Federal Building was described as a Roman holiday as witnesses assembled.[56]

Tuttle, returning to New York after a brief absence, issued a statement objecting to such wholesale subjection of citizens of New York to publicity. Describing the exercise as a fishing expedition, he also claimed he knew nothing about the Justice Department plans.[57] Furious, Willebrandt wired Sargent that Tuttle's alleged ignorance was "positively untrue." She had personally informed him of the planned procedure and raged at his "indefensible" and "cheap newspaper grandstand play." She asked Sargent to wire Tuttle to say nothing, adding that she believed the cases would "come out all right if Tuttle would keep matter out of controversial zone." Later, she wired the Justice Department attorney presenting the witnesses to the grand jury to try to keep "Washington/myself or H[oover] out of it if you possibly can."[58]

Finally, she sent a blistering telegram to Tuttle that she was "constrained personally" to tell him that the "unfortunate publicity" in the face of the department's request to say nothing regardless of pressure "has done untold damage" to the government's chance to enlarge the cases. Witnesses had cooperated before his outburst, but "willingness to talk has declined." Though the acquittal of Helen Morgan and Texas Guinan on charges of running a nuisance garnered the major headlines, the final results of the raids were not as disappointing as Willebrandt anticipated. Eighty trapped in the raids pleaded guilty; of the eighteen who stood trial, fifteen were convicted. In her 1928 annual report, Willebrandt cited the padlock or injunction proceedings as "one of the most notable gains" in prohibition enforcement, and, to put the New York raids in the context of business as usual, noted there were 7,000 petitions for injunctions.[59]

Interrupting rum row operations, shutting down the Remus ring, and closing New York speakeasies did not strike at the root of the problem of law enforcement. Willebrandt defined that in one word—politics. This was the source "of all the present evil."[60] When major political figures were involved in a case, she was usually present to help the U.S. attorney argue for the government. Her presence emphasized the commitment of the Justice Department. Because she was a woman, and sometimes the first to practice in a federal district, she always drew additional attention to the case.

The trial of Congressman John W. Langley of Kentucky is an example. Receiving permits from a friendly federal official to withdraw 4,000 cases of whiskey from a local distillery, Langley sold the whiskey for $196,000. Withdrawn for alleged medicinal use, the liquor was diverted into bootleg operations and Langley and his partners were indicted for conspiracy. The veteran representative was also accused of trying to corrupt the prohibition director of Kentucky.[61] Willebrandt, who cross-examined witnesses and addressed the jury in the government's summation, described the crowded courtroom scene in Covington to her parents:

> The jury was made up of farmers. Langley, the principal defendant is a Congressman from Ky. who joined purpose with a lot of New York bootleggers and tried to corrupt the Prohibition director of Kentucky. Three Philadelphia lawyers, two prominent members of the Washington bar, one local man and two from Cincinnati were on the side of the defense. That's why the Dist. Atty called for me. It has been a battle royal all week. Our side of the case stood up splendidly and unless the jury is overawed by the character witnesses who appeared, Gov. Morrow, former Republican Gov. of Ky. and Gov. Price, present Democratic Gov., I feel they *must convict*. I do hope so. They all are clearly guilty and if a Congressman is sent to the penitentiary it will do more to clean up prohibition enforcement in this country than anything else.[62]

Langley was found guilty; to register sympathy and support, however, the governor named his wife to complete his term.

In 1925, Willebrandt prepared for a conspiracy case "seething in the political pot of Ohio." It would demand, she knew, "the wisdom of Solomon and the guile of a serpent, the intuition of H.G. Wells and the self control of Lincoln." The case again involved withdrawal receipts and the alleged connivance of the state prohibition director and his assistant. Ten carloads of whiskey were seized. All of the conspirators except the two federal officers pleaded guilty. A Cleveland bond broker, who had handled some of Harding's stock transactions, turned state's evidence in return for leniency. Allegedly some of the proceeds from the conspiracy had been added to the Harding campaign fund. Daugherty's aide, Jesse Smith, appealed to Willebrandt to dismiss the case, but Coolidge in spite of calls to the White House "didn't call her off." Mellon, she complained, had "allowed it all to happen." Finally, she exploded: "God, how the government does *need* officials who have honor."[63]

The two-week trial was argued in 90-degree heat. The defense mounted a distinguished team led by Luther Day, son of a former Supreme Court justice. The drama centered on allegations that one defendant paid $50,000 to Jesse Smith to kill the case and on inferences of Harding's involvement because of his appointment of the prohibition director and friendship with one of the accused. Willebrandt examined witnesses for seven hours. She had confidence in the U.S. attorney, but felt keenly that the case was her responsibility. The press did not cover her well, she believed, because she did not "yell and shout or make flamboyant statements," though she did colorfully accuse the defense of "parading the shroud of a dead president." The judge, citing the "ferocity" of the case, praised her argument as "most logical, convincing, and in two places, startingly 'clever.'"[64] Luther Day acknowledged that not only was Willebrandt one of the ablest lawyers he had faced but that if she had not been on the case he would have won. Cheered at the verdict and the praise, she wrote her parents, "It was a gorgeous victory, and one of which I am prouder than of anything I've done so far!"[65]

Dry groups presented other political hazards to prohibition enforcement. The Methodist ministers at Fort Scott, Kansas, proved particularly troublesome. They were aroused by an incident in which the U.S. commissioner was stopped by the sheriff, apparently in the act of removing from the courtroom potable evidence seized in a previous case. The commissioner quickly flashed a "release order" from the judge and announced the liquor was en route to St. Francis Hospital in Kansas City. When it transpired that there was no release order nor a St. Francis Hospital and that the U.S. marshal had destroyed the rest of the stored evidence without making a proper inventory, Kansan and federal suspicions were aroused. The commissioner asserted he was just playing a joke on the sheriff; the sheriff admitted he had only seen a piece of paper and could not testify that it was a release of any kind. Kansas senators Charles Curtis and Arthur Capper pressed Attorney General Stone for a thorough investigation. He agreed that "this whole story is so fishy that I am unwilling to let any public official rest under the impression that I would swallow it without a thorough investigation."[66] The U.S. attorney investigated. A year after the incident, in February 1926, no indictment had yet been filed. The U.S. attorney could find no evidence, and he advised abandonment of the case. The local leaders still fumed that nothing was being done.

At this impasse, Senator Curtis asked if Willebrandt, in Kansas City on business, could meet with the Kansas attorney general and journey to Fort Scott to pacify the Methodists. Wiring the attorney general that she did not see what good could be accomplished, she added reluctantly: "Perfectly willing as good soldier to see groups of objectors and mollify them but regard it as undignified."[67] She used her meeting with the Kansas attorney general to emphasize to him and to the press that two investigations had been held and that there was no evidence to justify a prosecution. Acknowledging the "mess at Fort Scott," she added a personal note: "It has hurt to have the imputation that I have attempted to cover up something in Kansas, of all states—my native state, the prohibition state. I was born at Woodsdale, in the Southwest corner of the State and in the department I am known as very dry."[68]

Her reception at a Fort Scott meeting of Methodist ministers was mixed. One minister commented that she was "a brilliant little woman in a bad hole." Willebrandt wrote a terse memo to the attorney general enclosing pro and con clippings of her mission and reporting: "That Fort Scott errand was a difficult one and put to the test all the self restraint I possess. I pity anyone who comes up frequently against Methodist ministers of that type who know no law and seem utterly unable to see beyond their own prejudices."[69]

By far her most difficult and personally troubling case involved the Nations trial in St. Louis. It was a confrontation with the Anti-Saloon League. She wrote to White B. Miller, still involved in the tax disputes of the Haar case:

> I have just been out in St. Louis trying a case against a grafting brother of a loud mouthed K.K.K. Anti Saloon League Prohibition Director. We got one Klansman on the jury and he held them out for twenty-four hours but we got a verdict of guilty. It was a great victory, because the organizations to which this

defendant, Heber Nations had appealed had flooded the city with dodgers proclaiming his innocence and appealing for an arrest of the trial, raising a most unusual situation.[70]

More than 200,000 broadsides distributed in St. Louis and throughout Missouri and a flood of letters to the White House laid out the defense. Heber Nations, editor of a Republican Jefferson City newspaper, had been a fearless dry champion. His brother Gus O. Nations, an agent of the prohibition unit, had discovered that the Griesedieck Brewery was making real beer and led the raid. In revenge, the wet interests had framed Heber and charged him with giving protection to the brewery. The case was to be tried in wet St. Louis. A typical editorial in the *Christian Evangelist*, May 21, 1925, asserted that Gus caught forty-four men red-handed. One of the bootleggers had testified that he had paid for protection. "For this 'evidence' all of the 44 culprits at a brewery plant which was an old offender were set free." Enemies were trying to railroad "two fine young Christian men."[71]

It was a case of word against word. The government used the testimony of Griesedieck that he had paid $15,000 for protection while manufacturing real beer. He gave the money to the former state food and drug administrator Charles Prather; Prather charged he gave Heber Nations $1 for each case of beer sold to use his influence to deceive the public and enforcement officials. All in the conspiracy pleaded guilty except Heber Nations.

Willebrandt dispatched six special undercover men to check on the defendants' activities and to guard against jury tampering. When she arrived to join U.S. Attorney John Dyott she wrote her parents that she expected "the hardest three days" she had experienced since the Cleveland case. St. Louis was embroiled in a wet-dry war. The broadsides and dodgers spurred a massive outcry from Methodist unions and the WCTU. The Boy Scouts had thrown dodgers on everyone's porch in St. Louis with the appeal to "stop" the trial. She concluded: "It presents a nasty situation—only a moron will be eligible for jury duty for everyone else will have opinions."[72]

As in Cleveland and in the Langley trial, Willebrandt examined the key witnesses and participated in the government's summation to the jury. The *St. Louis Globe-Democrat* noted her simple gestures and unspectacular manner of arguing. The "quiet earnest voice of a woman—hardly carrying to the far reaches of the courtroom, filled with an attentive audience, argued and summed up the points of what

she called 'a splendid, going, grafting concern.'" Mainly, she worried
that there would be a hung jury due to "K.K. propaganda" and their
"terribly sinister influence."[73] Once more she had to leave for Washington before the verdict of guilty was in. Heber Nations was sentenced to serve eighteen months in Leavenworth and pay a fine of
$3,333. His attorney immediately appealed on a charge of prejudice by
the presiding judge. Nations won his appeal and was retried and found
guilty; he again appealed and won. In October, 1933, when the government considered retrying the case, it concluded that the repeal of
prohibition would be enacted before the case was completed.[74]

In the interim, Willebrandt had written *The Inside of Prohibition*,
which was syndicated in twenty-one major urban dailies. Gus O.
Nations sued her for libel in those jurisdictions where the series was
carried, since she identified him as a "crooked and popular agent"
whose removal was opposed by the Anti-Saloon League. She was
convinced that Gus had cooperated with Heber in the protection, but
the government had no evidence to make a charge. Willebrandt successfully defeated Nations in each libel case, but the drawn-out nature
of the proceedings after she left office was intensely painful.[75]

Willebrandt was also present in the courtroom, but as a nonpar-
ticipant, in the prosecution of San Francisco prohibition administrator
Colonel Ned M. Green. Green freely admitted removing some liquor
from the federal vault. He knew some of the "good stuff" should have
been destroyed but reasoned, "Now there are a couple of bottles of
especially good liquor and I will take them along with me." If he found
someone in a hospital who could be helped, he delivered the liquor. He
had also ordered his men to hold back from a raid in one San Francisco
restaurant because it was "a good place." His attitude was that there
was too much to accomplish; the San Francisco police ought to carry
out the major enforcement. Though the government believed it had a
strong case, Green was acquitted. Willebrandt observed that the
judge's instructions to the jury had been fair and his comment indicated that he believed absolutely in Green's guilt. However, she concluded, "it is too much to expect a wet county to convict a man
generous with liquors whether they were his or the government's."[76]

While preparing and arguing cases in the federal district courts and
trying to stem the bootleg rackets and political influence, Willebrandt
also worked to better marshal the forces of the Justice Department. At
the request of Attorney General Stone in the spring of 1924, she drew
up an analysis of the status of cases and personnel in each federal
district. She suggested that when the dockets were clogged, a confer-

ence between the presiding judges of the circuit court of appeals and the attorney general might result in reassigning judges to those areas with heavy case loads in New Jersey, New York, Boston, San Francisco, and Colorado. She also completed a special statistical analysis for Stone of the U.S. attorneys' offices, particularly detailing the situation in Boston, New Jersey, and Pennsylvania. Stone, impressed, dispatched a copy of her report to all of the U.S. attorneys. Willebrandt commented, "THEREAFTER THE FUN BEGAN!" U.S. attorneys who were criticized retaliated with indignant news releases. The attorney general, who had no power to force removals, began his own investigations. Stone's approach was to interview each of the controversial attorneys, try to make a decision on his honesty, and then give him time to clear up his cases—otherwise he tried to obtain a promise of resignation.[77]

The U.S. attorney in San Francisco, John T. Williams, protege of Senator Shortridge, was pressed for his resignation. Serving in a notoriously wet city, he had won some significant convictions, but there were also complaints that he drank on duty and consorted with known underworld figures. One complainer was Senator Hiram Johnson, who charged that Williams "was a disgrace to law enforcement." In Willebrandt's presence, Stone arranged for an interim appointment, phoned Williams to ask for his resignation, read him a bill of particulars, and offered him an opportunity to leave gracefully. Williams complied, and Willebrandt was dispatched to urge Hiram Johnson not to agree with Senator Shortridge on a replacement, but to enable an interim appointee time to clean up the city. Johnson was able to delay the agreement for a year and a half. Shortridge never forgave Willebrandt for her part in the maneuver and steadfastly opposed her most cherished hope for appointment to the federal bench.[78]

In Boston, U.S. Attorney Robert Harris was an outspoken opponent of prohibition. Described by Willebrandt as "*not* a bad sort," except regarding violations of the Eighteenth Amendment, Harris took no graft money. He just did not vigorously enforce the law. After Willebrandt marshaled the accumulated charges of inaction, Harris was called to Washington for an interview with Stone in which Willebrandt was instructed to do most of the talking. Returning to Boston, Harris reported that he was being attacked by Mrs. Willebrandt. One newspaper headlined: "Meddling Mabel Defied by Mayflower Club." Harris refused to resign and Coolidge finally signed an order removing him.[79]

The most difficult situation involving a U.S. attorney's office was in New Jersey. Willebrandt so distrusted Assistant U.S. Attorney Walter Van Riper, the former campaign manager of the popular Senator Walter Edge, that she worked out an agreement with his "well-meaning" superior that Van Riper would handle no prohibition cases.[80] When the Hudson County prosecutor broke a major smuggling case in 1924 involving New Jersey "political big wigs," Van Riper moved into action and requested a federal grand jury investigation. To forestall this obviously pre-emptive move, Willebrandt immediately wired that the state litigation should be completed before any federal initiative was taken. In response. Van Riper announced that Mrs. Willebrandt was trying to call off his investigation and interfere with his clean-up of New Jersey. With Stone's backing, Willebrandt wired Van Riper that he should have nothing to do with the case and released the wire to the press. Privately she noted, "Van Riper *is* Edge and we all know it."[81]

Stormy conferences between Edge and Stone followed. Willebrandt wrote: "The papers boil. I don't read them much. The newspaper men swarm. Edge is leading a fight on me in the Senate. Everybody buzzes at me. Meantime I *have* the evidence on Van Riper and he must be fired. I'm confident the AG will so act. That will stab Edge. He deserves it. He will take his pestilential influence out of appointment of law enforcement men or I'll get evidence on *him* and have him indicted and headed toward the Atlanta Penitentiary before his term of office expires. If I dethrone Edge in New Jersey, I shall not have lived in vain."[82]

Willebrandt became further involved in housecleaning when her letter to the Law Enforcement League at Philadelphia was released during the election campaign of 1924. She had written a confidential statement on the situation in the U.S. attorney's office. She contended that most were hard-working faithful officials but added, "There are maybe nine or ten of them, whom, if I had the power, I would summarily remove, because of their inactivity or political evasiveness in enforcing Prohibition statutes."[83] Coolidge's political enemies, particularly a New York lawyer backing Robert La Follette for president, charged that the president's refusal to act in these known instances contributed to Willebrandt's published charge that "political stagnation runs all the way down the line in Pennsylvania."[84] Keenly conscious of the embarrassment to Stone and Coolidge at the publication of her letter, Willebrandt was encouraged by the backing of the attorney general, who advised her to keep "plugging at 'em" and assured her that he never put anyone under a ban of silence.[85] Coolidge announced that he was reviewing the cases and that ten resignations or removals were in process.[86]

There was further newspaper publicity in the summer of 1925 when the *New York Post* and the Associated Press carried a story that Willebrandt had sent a questionnaire to all U.S. Attorneys asking them to assess the problem of enforcement in their district, to list the reasons why they were obliged to dismiss so many cases, and to give suggestions for better tactics in gathering evidence. The letters had again been sent confidentially to elicit a reply that might be helpful to General Lincoln Andrews as he began his reorganization. Again, the survey made page one.[87]

Beyond working with the Treasury Department to stem the liquor traffic and organizing her division in the Justice Department for efficiency in enforcing the law, Willebrandt had the major responsibility for briefing and presenting prohibition cases to the Supreme Court. By 1929, she had submitted 278 cases *a certiorari*. In the total number of cases argued before that body Willebrandt stood fourth among the members of the bar.[88] An *American Mercury* article, "Portia in Wonderland," reported that "her graceful tailored figure has become a regular adornment" before the court.[89]

She loved the challenge of arguing before the Court and against the best. In March 1926, she faced John W. Davis, the 1924 Democratic candidate for president and to Willebrandt "the foremost lawyer of the U.S. in learning, polish, beauty of diction, cleverness and scholarly presence." Davis always drew a crowd; in this instance it included the British ambassador. Willebrandt wrote to her parents that pitting her against Davis was "like matching a Ford car with a Pierce Arrow. But I did the best I could. I sincerely prayed to do my best. I think I did well. The court was respectful and the spectators showed admiration."[90]

The volume of prohibition cases was unrelenting. Willebrandt's annual reports cite 49,021 criminal prosecutions and 4,109 civil cases in 1922–23; in 1924–25, 51,688 cases were filed; in 1927–28 there were 55,729 criminal prosecutions.[91] In August 1923, she wrote: "Just been assigned five cases in Supreme Court to argue; working day and night on them." In February 1927, she argued four cases and then commented: "Much to my surprise the Supreme Court moved up a couple of other cases that I had not anticipated reaching before late spring. There was nothing else to do but plunge in, and the men here in the division stood loyally by. One night we worked all night. I went back to the house at 7 o'clock for breakfast and then came back down for a day's work."[92] In spite of the pressure and the occasional unpreparedness, she had a high winning average. In 1924, she won 37 of 39 cases on appeal to the Supreme Court.[93]

Faced with a new law, Willebrandt was anxious to establish its meaning and limits in the courts. In October 1922, she wrote an opinion for Attorney General Daugherty on liquor coming to American shores in foreign or domestic liners or merchant ships. Daugherty issued her opinion virtually unchanged. Domestic merchant ships were cited as part of the territory of the United States when on the high seas and therefore covered by the Eighteenth Amendment. Since Congress had acted to withdraw liquor as legitimate ships' stores, American merchant vessels were forbidden to carry liquor. Concerning foreign vessels, the Willebrandt opinion held that it was unlawful to carry liquor into American territorial waters. Coolidge issued new orders for ships using American ports following the attorney general's ruling. The Cunard Line promptly challenged the new regulations in the courts.[94]

Willebrandt hoped to argue these cases. She confessed to her parents, "All week I've been blue fighting it, but feeling badly because I probably won't get to argue the Shipping Board cases." The solicitor general could argue any case he chose, and he chose these. Willebrandt fumed, "because they're *big* cases and will surely be won—Makes me sick. 'They're my baby!' I wrote the opinion and fought everyone for it. But I'll stop crying. One can't have everything. I'm still hoping that maybe I'll get to argue part of the points at issue."[95] She was ready when Solicitor General Beck relented and she did participate in the argument. The decision affirmed the government in only the foreign aspect of its case. Domestic ships were judged part of American territory only "in a metaphorical sense" and hence exempt from the strictures of the Eighteenth Amendment on the seas.[96]

Another aspect of the law that Willebrandt was eager to test in the courts was the responsibility of the bootlegger-tax dodger. In colorful language she excoriated one of the "chief vices of the bootlegger—a worse one in my opinion than his moral effect on the community—his dastardly evasion of the payment of income taxes."[97] The case that settled the matter was *United States* v. *Manly S. Sullivan*, decided by the Supreme Court in May 1927. Sullivan, a Charleston attorney and bootlegger, argued in the lower courts that to reveal how he had earned his income on his tax form would force him to give evidence against himself. If he did not report the income, he would be liable for prosecution for deliberate nonpayment; if he reported it from another source, he would be liable for perjury. While Willebrandt argued the case, her concentration was broken as one of the justices reading the transcript of Sullivan's histrionics in the lower court chuckled delightedly. Still, she won. A *Washington News* editorial reported the victory; the bootlegger had to share his profits with the community just as did the saloonkeeper of old. It explained: "When a bootlegger's car has been shot out from under him, heretofore he has said, 'Well, there goes that,' and thought no more about it. Now he'll make a note of the matter and figure it into his next tax schedule as so much loss of rolling stock."[98]

A crucial decision, useful in the New York padlock raids and elsewhere, was the Supreme Court's ruling in *Marron* v. *United States* in October 1927. Prohibition agents acting on a warrant issued to search for liquor on the premises could also seize account books and documents not described in the warrant but used in carrying out the illegal enterprise.[99] Willebrandt argued and won another significant search case, *United States* v. *Carroll*, in which the Court ruled that a car could be stopped without a search warrant if the agent had observed the car enough to be reasonably certain of its violation of the law.[100]

Though anxious to affirm the government's powers of investigation in prohibition offenses, Willebrandt asked to be excused from the "whispering wires" case. Agents had cracked a major Seattle-Vancouver ring and brought ninety-one indictments. The Olmstead ring was a sophisticated smuggling operation; Mrs. Olmstead apparently used the family radio station to broadcast coded information to incoming ships while she ostensibly presented bedtime stories. The major part of the government's case, however, was built on evidence secured from phone taps. Willebrandt, always valuing her own privacy, believed that to invade individual privacy in the home was a dangerous and unwarranted practice to follow in enforcing the law. But the Supreme Court decided that the protection of the home in the Fourth and Fifth amendments did not pertain to telephone wires.[101]

Other cases affirmed the use of the injunction to padlock a nuisance, the prohibition of physicians' prescribing intoxicating malt liquors, and the liability of prohibition agents for failure to report violations of the law. In 1922, Willebrandt reassured a WCTU correspondent: "In my opinion, the Supreme Court has always displayed a remarkably helpful attitude in interpreting close questions of law that arise under the prohibition statutes, to the end of always carrying out the purpose of these statutes." Five years later she again registered the "great gratification to all" that "the Supreme Court is issuing so steadily opinions so helpful in the orderly and vigorous administration of the prohibition law."[102]

Willebrandt was also active in appearing and testifying before Congress. In 1924, 1925, and 1926 she was a witness before congressional committees investigating prohibition enforcement and seeking ways to reduce congestion in the federal dockets and minimize inequities in sentences meted out by the courts. She worked successfully for the passage of the Jones "Five and Ten" law allowing a maximum of five years and $10,000 fine or both for prohibition violations.[103]

In 1929, reflecting on eight bone-wearying years in government, Willebrandt determined to set the record straight on the prohibition fight. In her syndicated column, "The Inside of Prohibition," she repeated the question, "Why not be honest and admit enforcement is impossible?" She was not ready for that admission. The essential way to enforce any law, she argued, was to establish personal responsibility for it. This was never done for the Eighteenth Amendment or the Volstead Act. What did emerge was "The Buckpassers League" and the "not me" position of courts, grand juries, sheriffs, prohibition agents, U.S. attorneys and others.[104]

The responsibility began with the president. He could ensure sound appointments in the Justice and Treasury departments and establish an accountable chain of command. He could end divided responsibility and coordinate the "evidence-collecting branches of the Treasury Department with the prosecuting-evidence collecting agencies under the Department of Justice." He could appoint *"one head to determine policies."*[105] With that authority assigned, specific steps could be taken to cut off the alcohol supply through restricting permits; strengthening regulations on the production of industrial alcohol; coordinating border units in the customs, immigration, and prohibition offices; and developing better cooperation with Canada. Professionalism should be emphasized in all of the law enforcement agencies. Although the prohibition agents were placed under civil service examination in 1927, one-third of the force were still political appointeees. U.S. attorneys' offices and U.S. commissioners and marshals should be depoliticized.[106]

In the end, she concluded, prohibition was a shared responsibility.

She reflected on the "No Man's Land" near her birthplace, a haven for criminals and the scene of her uncle's death at the hands of a "lawless mob." Throughout the land, she asserted, there had developed a "psychological no man's land which was a refuge for the worst in America—bootleggers, grafters, murderers." Citizens could organize. "The bootleggers and their allies still and will be routed. This is not blind optimism; it is common sense based on a knowledge of the character and strength of the American people, who will not surrender to confused thinking and the defeat psychology current on this subject."[107]

Hindsight and evidence indicate that she accurately analyzed the problem. Certainly, prohibition had "worked" in the early years. Statistics register a downward trend in arrests for drunknness and hospitalization for alcohol related diseases. Indeed, as one historian argued, until 1922 or 1923, "prohibition was generally a success. Certainly there is no basis for the conclusion that prohibition was inherently doomed to failure."[108]

A shift in public perception, however, took place in the mid-twenties. Willebrandt expressed her frustration in the autumn of 1924, writing, "Got so blue over the blooming hypocrisy in law enforcement on every hand that I had to leave the office for an hour or two and walk in the P.M.—*fast*."[109] By 1924, the crime wave of "Alcohol and Al Capone" had developed. Reading headlines and observing their own friends and families, many in the middle class concluded that drinking had increased, whereas it had actually decreased particularly among the working class. Interest groups emerged to lobby strenuously for repeal. The Association Against the Prohibition Amendment and the Women's Organization for Prohibition Reform provided an avenue for protest by business leaders chafing under tax burdens and eager for the revenues generated by brewers and distillers, by conservatives concerned at the invasion of personal liberty, by wet industries seeking a return to production, and by urban politicians representing thirsty constituents. They utilized the Anti-Saloon League and WCTU tactics gradually to win over public opinion in the counties, states, and nation. Persistent, well-organized, well-funded lobbying, the onset of the Great Depression, the frustration over enforcement, and the search for revenues finally ended the noble experiment.[110]

Willebrandt insisted that prohibition could have been enforced if the legislation had been properly drawn. The responsibility of the federal government should have been only to control the traffic in alcohol. Instead, the law "tried to do too much all at once, and states and counties that had hitherto accomplished" much, just relaxed. Good leaders, good citizens, and a careful delegation of responsibilities might have brought at least a chance for success.[111] She never flagged in effort or energy to meet her responsibility. In her last year in the Department of Justice her division carried out 59,786 criminal prosecutions, winning thirty-two convictions for every acquittal. She wrung funds from Congress to employ more special assistants to help with the most difficult cases. Perceived as a dry zealot, she was primarily zealous for law enforcement and meeting her responsibility. She shared her own perception of her prohibition effort with her parents on Easter Sunday 1929: "One hard thing about my service has been that so much of it is like the little boy who stood for hours with his arm in the hole in the dike. I've *prevented* floods of wrong things, but it's a wearing way to be a 'hero'!"[112]

CHAPTER FOUR

The Justice Department: Prison, Taxes, the Judgeship

We are doing so much in the prisons work that that keeps me consoled for the little that is being accomplished right at the present time in prohibition enforcement. . . .

MABEL WALKER WILLEBRANDT
November 9, 1925

*W*HILE her prohibition efforts were increasingly frustrated, Willebrandt's other Justice Department responsibilities in prisons and taxes brought hard-won accomplishment. In an administration renowned for caution and tight money, she spearheaded the successful drive to establish both the first federal prison for women and the first federal reformatory for young male offenders. The energy concentrated on expansion and reform of the prison system was matched by the intensity dedicated to the complex tax litigation flooding the federal courts. The internal administration of her division, the fastest growing in the department, and the adaptation to the changes in leadership and policies of four attorney generals, posed another challenge. In each area she achieved major successes, only to be thwarted in her own personal ambition—to be appointed a federal judge.

In 1921 when Willebrandt joined the Justice Department the federal prison system faced a crisis in numbers and direction. The Harrison Act of 1914 and the Volstead Act were flooding the federal dockets with drug and alcohol cases. Only three penitentiaries, Leavenworth, Atlanta, and McNeil Island were available to house a burgeoning population. Short-term federal prisoners were boarded in local, county, and state prisons. The small system was administered by a superintendent of prisons who reported to Assistant Attorney General Willebrandt. Harding's appointee was gentle Heber Votaw, a former missionary. Inexperienced in prison management, he had the more significant credential that he was the president's brother-in-law. Prison proposals could win the ear of the president, but prison management languished.[1] To complicate federal prison administration further, public and professional attitudes toward crime and punishment were changing. Public reaction to the crime waves of the 1920s was to press for a "get tough" policy in courts and prisons. The progressive penologists' emphasis on prevention and rehabilitation, an emphasis shared by Willebrandt, was replaced by the drive to protect society from the violence and contamination of criminals and misfits.[2]

Faced with an emergency in numbers and the pressure of shifting attitudes, Willebrandt and Votaw set an agenda with three major priorities: the establishment of a federal prison for women, the institution of a federal reformatory for young male first offenders, and, providing a program of work for federal prisoners.[3] All three were accomplished within the next seven years. Willebrandt's drive to achieve the first provides a model of the political and organizational skills needed to win reform. Her work with women, for women, created the most lasting accomplishment of her administration.

Public attitudes toward "fallen women" had veered from the nineteenth-century assessment of them as pathetic moral degenerates to the early twentieth-century analysis of women as victims of poor home environment, economic deprivation, or exploitation by organized crime. As assistant police court defender, Willebrandt had shared the convictions of reformers like Miriam Van Waters on the healing power of environment, work, and discipline. Sensitive to her clients' background and needs, she developed "a very real aversion to putting people in jail" while it was a breeding place of crime rather than a source of "reformation and redemption."[4] During World War I, as other reform efforts yielded to mobilization, advances in the prevention of female crime and the rehabilitation of female criminals halted also. Woman as victim was replaced by woman as threat and pariah. The round-ups of prostitutes that filled Los Feliz in Los Angeles were part of a nationwide effort by the federal Committee on Training Camp Activities to safeguard soldiers from that "greatest destroyer of man power." The determination to lock up society's misfits, combined with increased alcohol and drug violations, brought a crisis in numbers and a call for action. As former prison warden Mary Belle Harris wryly observed: "Appeals for help gain potency if there is a flagrant emergency."[5]

To Willebrandt and Superintendent Votaw, the plight of federal women prisoners constituted that obvious emergency. Two hundred and fifty women, most convicted on drug and liquor charges, were boarded in state and county jails. Supervision, food, and medical treatment varied from good to intolerable. The federal government had no control and only one federal inspector to monitor conditions. By 1923, the per capita cost of the best local facilities exceeded the payment allowed by the federal government. Overcrowded state and county institutions were not inclined to accept either the low payment or the federal guidelines for prisoners. Only California and New Jersey institutions were still admitting federal women prisoners, and their prisons would soon be filled. The warden of the West Virginia state prison asserted he would have to turn out twenty federal women prisoners he was boarding. Votaw summed up the situation: "Practical necessity, unmixed with sentimentality, demands immediate action."[6]

Aware that within two months there would literally be no available place to incarcerate federal women prisoners, Willebrandt and Votaw journeyed on a gray, rainy day in January 1923 to the Blue Ridge Mountains to inspect the facilities of a Department of Agriculture weather station on Mount Weather. The cost was low, the climate healthy, the water supply adequate. It was immediately available. Willebrandt's division drafted the enabling legislation to secure the Mount Weather land and buildings. Congressman Wells Goodykoontz (Rep., W.Va.) and Senator Charles Curtis (Rep., Kansas) agreed to introduce bills simultaneously. Though temporarily slowed by the grippe in the first two weeks in February, Willebrandt lobbied hard and testified before the Senate subcommittee on February 23. She energetically rallied representatives of women's organizations through the Women's Joint Congressional Committee (WJCC), which forged a coalition of the League of Women Voters, the Women's Christian Temperance Union, the General Federation of Women's Clubs (GFWC), the National Federation of Business and Professional Women, the National Consumers' League, the National Women's Trade Union League, the National Congress of Mothers and Parent-Teacher Associations, the American Home Economics Association, and others. It was a powerful lobbying force marshaled to work for legislation of interest to women. Led by Maud Wood Park, president of the League of Women Voters, the WJCC closely monitored the progress of the bills for a federal institution for women.[7]

The General Federation of Women's Clubs proved a strong ally. Willebrandt worked closely with the GFWC executive director, Lida Hafford, to distribute copies of Congressman Goodykoontz's remarks on the Mount Weather facility in the *Congressional Record* to club members. In April, she alertly sent information to Mrs. Edward White of the GFWC legislative department urging her to "personally take a hand" to win support at the Legislative Council meeting in Atlanta. Armed with the dates of other national women's conventions, Willebrandt galvanized her staff, writing: "This is fine—go at it systematically and send literature and ask for endorsements and check them off when they come in."[8] Meanwhile, her friend Mrs. Harriet Taylor Upton, a Republican party leader, interceded with Harding. She pointed out the dismal party showing in 1922 and the need for female support in 1924. Mrs. Harding also pressed her brother's prison project.[9]

The intense lobbying of the women and modest presidential persuasion failed to win Congress for the Mount Weather legislation. The ostensible reason was a minority report critical of water conditions and sewage and transportation difficulties. The real obstruction came from the objections of the Virginia congressman R. Walton Moore and his colleague Senator Swanson in response to the complaints of their constituents who did not welcome a federal prison as a neighbor.[10] Angered but educated, Willebrandt and the women's organizations regrouped.

Working with Julia Jaffray, head of the GFWC's Committee on Institutional Relations, Willebrandt pressed for a special conference to organize support and plan strategy. On September 21, leaders of twenty-one national groups answered Jaffray's call to gather at the GFWC's new headquarters building in Washington. The women were there in force. Representatives from the American Association of University Women, WCTU, the Daughters of the American Revolution, National Council of Women, National Congress of Mothers and Parent-Teacher Associations, and National Federation of Business and Professional Women's Clubs joined leaders from the American Prison Association, the Democratic and Republican national committees, the National Committee on Prisons and Prison Labor, the National Committee on Mental Hygiene, the American Home Economics Association, and others.[11]

Willebrandt opened the conference with a strong statement on the three priorities of the federal prison system: an institution for federal women prisoners, an industrial reformatory for young men, and employment for prisoners in the three federal penitentiaries. Heber Votaw followed with supporting statistics. A distinguished panel of state prison administrators, Katherine B. Davis, Jessie Hodder, Florence Monahan, and H. Crittenden Hawes, underscored the urgent need for a women's prison. By the end of this high-powered session, the conference agreed that a separate institution for women prisoners should be established. A special committee, headed by Willebrandt, was charged with drafting a detailed proposal to submit to the afternoon conference session. The blueprint emerged with a speed and dispatch that suggested that specifics had been thrashed out well before the conference deliberations. Recommendations included establishment of a federal institution for federal women prisoners; appointment of a woman superintendent; capacity for a minimum of seven hundred prisoners; land of 500 acres; site selection by the Department of Justice; structure based on the cottage plan. The proposal was unanimously adopted with the added pledge that the legislative representatives of the organizations would gather the support of their members.[12]

By Thanksgiving, the bill was drafted and a campaign mapped out. When Congress convened in December, Willebrandt wrote Senator Curtis that she was "so glad" he again agreed to sponsor the legislation, adding, "Anything you can do to speed up consideration of the bill will therefore be greatly appreciated by the Department of Justice and by me personally." Congressman George Graham (Rep., Pa.) was assured that his name on the House measure "insured its success." Taking no chances, the women backers aggressively lobbied. Willebrandt expressed her regret to Graham that she had not been able to join Mrs. Park and Mrs. Hafford when they visited his office.[13] Clearly, the heavy female artillery was deployed. Representatives of women's organizations were highly visible at the congressional hearings when Willebrandt testified to the urgent need for the prison and stressed that in this bill the site selection was left to the attorney general, the secretary of the interior, and the secretary of war. There would be no obstructionist local opposition this time.[14]

She rallied broader support in two trips to New York. In November she visited Adolph Lewisohn's home on the Hudson River to urge the energetic support from his National Committee on Prisons. She addressed the New York Bar Association, using a memo from Votaw that emphasized the urgent need for both a women's prison and a men's reformatory.[15]

The women remained the essential shock troops. In January, Willebrandt gathered resolutions from the executive boards of the WCTU, GFWC, League of Women Voters, American Home Economics Association, Service Star Legion, Girls Friendly Society, the National Council of Jewish Women, and National Council of Women, and forwarded them to Congress. When the secretary of the National Council of Churches wrote asking if his organization could help, she scrawled her response: "Tell them Yes—Graham." In California, her Phi Delta Delta colleague Georgia Bullock rallied the members of the Women Lawyers' Association. A grateful Willebrandt thanked her for the good work but worried that Congress was in "such a hub-bub of investigations I despair of any legislation getting through."[16] By the end of May, prospects were brighter. To Lida Hafford's query if any action at the annual GFWC convention would be helpful, Willebrandt answered that it looked as if the measure would finally pass. The Democrats were working hard "*if not* harder" than the Republicans. Meanwhile, the GFWC might keep the pressure on by wiring House Speaker Gillett and others. She turned down an invitation to address the convention so that she could stay on the scene in Washington to press for passage.[17]

She kept Congressman Graham apprised of the urgency of the situation, reporting that almost six hundred women were housed in jails "absolutely inadequate to care for their health and comfort." One federal judge had refused to sentence any more women until the Justice Department could assure adequate quarters. She also reminded Speaker Gillett that the prison bill would be more valuable than any other to the Republicans in future elections. On June 5, she triumphantly wired Julia Jaffray: "Women's Prison Bill Passed."[18]

The choice of the site was the next hurdle. Well before the measure was approved, localities began lobbying for their selection. West Virginia was the most effectively organized. The governor appointed a special West Virginia Industrial Farm Commission to press the case for the state. Within four days of passage of the bill, the secretary of the commission wrote to Attorney General Stone recommending a site near Alderson. West Virginia congressman Guy Goff, formerly Daugherty's assistant, wrote to Superintendent Votaw and Interior Secretary Hubert Work. E.E. Dudding of the Prisoner's Relief Society joined in urging the attractive Alderson site, as did K.T. Crawley, manager of the Agricultural and Industrial Department of the C & O Railroad, which serviced the area.[19]

In August, Willebrandt and her friend Fannie French Morse, superintendent of the New York Women's Reformatory, set out on an inspection tour through the West, canvassing for possible sites. Votaw traveled to Indiana. Concerned West Virginians urged that Alderson be included on the itineraries. Crawley wrote to Coolidge's secretary, C. Bascom Slemp, that a quick decision for Alderson would help to carry the Republican ticket in West Virginia. Willebrandt's friend Mrs. Lenna Yost, a WCTU leader, loyal West Virginian, and prominent Republican, wrote offering to "show her the place" at Alderson and inviting her to speak there to Republican women, adding, "Please do come we need you."[20]

Instead, Willebrandt dispatched her Phi Delta Delta colleague Judge Mary O'Toole with a delegation to visit Alderson. A West Virginian, Judge O'Toole reported that the Rose Farm, contributed as an inducement by Alderson citizens, would be suitable. The 1,600-foot altitude provided a healthful atmosphere; the nearby Greenbrier River supplied ample pure water; the land had fine farm and woodland resources; and, finally, the neighboring population was composed of Anglo-Saxon stock, "apparently wholly free from the use of ales or liquor." With this endorsement and yielding to the continuous West Virginia invitations, Willebrandt visited Alderson in October. After thoroughly inspecting the site, she was convinced that it met the requirements. She urged the local chamber of commerce to draw up an estimate of costs. When that was not forthcoming two days later, she wrote Crawley for action. He pressed the chamber, commenting, "I think you will agree with me that Mrs. Willebrandt is going to be the one that really will name the site to be selected."[21]

Willebrandt now wrote to the three cabinet members, stressing the low cost of Alderson. To Secretary Work, she noted the "distinct moral and religious tone" of the community and its isolation, which would forestall both narcotics smuggling and escapes. When the final cost estimate of $45,000 arrived, she immediately forwarded it to Stone, Work, and Secretary of Labor Davis. The cost might seem high, but she pointed out that it was well under any other offer and included three houses, twenty-one large silos, barns, and equipment. Still without the needed approval a month later, she again wrote to Stone rehearsing all the reasons for Alderson: economy, location, the cooperative spirit and religious nature of the community, and its isolation. Only one objection had been raised, by a West Virginia federal judge, at the stigma that would come to the state in housing a women's prison; his objection may have been prompted by the prison's location only ten miles from his brother's property.[22]

Attorney General Stone finally responded on January 17. Instead of approval, he raised a series of questions. What of the service road, sewage disposal facilities, and the water supply? Willebrandt immediately forwarded his letter to the Alderson Chamber of Commerce. In four days the chamber replied with a promise to build a road, guarantee the right of way for a water line, and an explanation of the delay in the sewage work. After the cabinet members journeyed to Alderson and its only remaining rival site, Delphi, Indiana, Willebrandt pressed for action. The last day to forward an appropriation request to Congress was February 1. To miss that deadline would delay the project another year.[23]

Finally, on January 29, Willebrandt could relate the last hectic moments ensuring the Alderson success:

> Today I just got the location of the women's national prison thru. It will be a great monument to my work here. I despaired of getting anything done before Stone left, for Secys Davis & Work listened to a political appeal from Senator Watson [Rep., Ind.] who wanted to locate it in Indiana and tried to hold this up for political purposes. I was discouraged for there is but a *week* more to get the appropriation thru the budget committee. So when Sec. Davis today at 3:45 finally said he'd agree but was leaving on a 4:30 train and would sign the report to Congress when he returned I said No I'd meet him at the train to sign. Which was done! Now a big weeks work getting the budget thru and in 8 months the institution will be on the way to conclusion.[24]

The appropriation bill was carried on March 4, and Coolidge approved the $909,100 to start construction. Within three weeks Willebrandt completed the search for a woman superintendent. Her first choice had been Katherine Davis of New York, but neither she nor Fannie French Morse or others with major state appointments would be willing to leave their positions for the federal annual salary of $3,000 to $5,000. The final choice was Dr. Mary Belle Harris, whom Willebrandt met as superintendent of the New Jersey State Home for Girls. She knew her as a "woman of great refinement, executive ability, and intellectual attainments." A leader in the prison self-government movement needed in the cottage plan at Alderson, Harris had experience ranging from the New York City workhouse to New Jersey's model prison farm at Clinton. Her war experience had been similar to Willebrandt's at Los Feliz. She had just accepted the post of executive secretary of the International Policewoman's Association. Willebrandt confidently left the major decisions to Harris. The new superintendent accepted the challenge, knowing Willebrandt "well enough to feel confident that I should enjoy working with her."[25]

As the first buildings took shape, Willebrandt had to win a second appropriation from Congress. Again, she was backed by the women's organizations. Their lobbying was so effective that members of the House Appropriations Committee complained that she was using the GFWC and others for propaganda. Julia K. Jaffray, newly named a member of the Board of Advisers of Alderson, issued a stinging denial. Willebrandt had canceled her address before the GFWC Atlantic City gathering, since the appropriations were pending and her remarks might be "premature." Jaffray insisted that Willebrandt had gone out of her way to avoid controversy. The GFWC president, Mrs. John D. Sherman, added: "Of course we are trying to get the appropriations for this institution. We initiated the project and it is one of the main objects of our public welfare program."[26] The appropriation bill soon passed.

The first inmates were admitted to Alderson in April 1927. That this institution was to be different was obvious the first night. Prisoners entering the dining room were bewildered that the tablecloths and napkins were meant for them. Some wept. There were no walls, no guards with guns in turrets. From the outside, Alderson could be mistaken for an attractive college campus. Two quadrangles of brick cottages were anchored by administration and educational buildings. Harris immediately established a scientific classification system to set the right work and training for each inmate to prepare her to return to society. Each cottage developed an organization for self-government. The entire cost of this handsome red brick plant, Harris pointed out, was less than $2,500,000, little if any more than required to build conventional cell blocks.[27]

The formal opening ceremony was November 24, 1928. Attorney General Sargent handed Harris a symbolic key to the institution. He warmly praised the work of Willebrandt, who "cared for and fought for" Alderson as a "mother for her child."[28] Willebrandt gave the keynote address, "The New Note in Penology." Dr. Harris described the event:

> Mrs. Willebrandt's speech will never be forgotten by the thousand who heard her as she sounded the "New Note in Penology" with a clarion ring that will reverberate in the lives of every woman who enters our doors. All were stirred by her plea for individualization in the treatment of the personalities caught in

the toils of their own weakness and imperfections and by her challenge to us to use the facilities of the government for the permanent redemption of those who come under our care. . . . [The two hundred women] had an enlightening glimpse of the unselfish devotion to an impersonal cause that was embodied in the woman who had struggled and sacrificed to make their government mean justice to them.[29]

Without Willebrandt, Harris reflected, the outcome would have been quite different, "for it needed someone on the spot to hurry things along, to win over the hostile and inspire the indifferent. She was the cutting edge that hewed out the needed legislation and appropriations."[30] Fittingly, Harris named the school and assembly building, which also housed a law library and small chapel, Willebrandt Hall.

The first priority in prison reform was accomplished. The second, to establish a federal reformatory for young male first offenders, closely paralleled the struggle for Alderson. In December 1922, the overcrowded federal prisons were further threatened by 18,000 prohibition cases awaiting trial. Reviewing the urgent need for additional facilities, Willebrandt urged that instead of establishing another prison like Leavenworth, a reformatory for first offenders be built. Camp Grant, near Rockford, Illinois, like Mount Weather in Virginia, was immediately available and could house 200 to 300 prisoners. The Camp Grant legislation, however, met the opposition of Illinois neighbors and suffered the same fate as the Mount Weather bill.[31]

Again, the supporters regrouped. A conference in September 1923 at the GFWC headquarters had called for the National Committee on Prisons and Prison Labor to organize another conference devoted to the reformatory question. Within two months this conference met at the GFWC headquarters. Votaw presented the major proposals for both the first offenders' institution and prison labor. Representatives of the American Bar Association, American Council on Education, the Chamber of Commerce, Kiwanis Club International, Federal Council of the Churches of Christ in America, Knights of Columbus, Young Men's Christian Association (YMCA), and others agreed to be present at the congressional hearings and to rally their members. Women's groups also passed resolutions of support.[32]

Testifying for a new measure introduced in the sixty-eighth Congress, the Foster Bill, Willebrandt reviewed the "growing perplexity" of handling young male prisoners and public criticism of the light sentences that judges meted out. The accused man was invariably described as of good character; if he were sentenced to a federal penitentiary, he might be corrupted rather than reformed. The solution, she argued, was not to excuse the offender but to provide a place where "his criminal tendencies will not be increased but he will be reformed out of them."[33] The choice of location for the reformatory would be left to the secretaries of justice, interior, and labor. The measure passed on January 7, 1925, three weeks before the approval of the Alderson site.

Willebrandt asked the War Department to provide a list of all its properties of more than a thousand acres suitable for the reformatory. Six were suggested. Camp Grant was ruled out immediately; four others were rejected because of climate. Camp Sherman, at Chillicothe, Ohio, became the prime candidate. As at Alderson the local chamber of commerce was eager for the facility. The site could accommodate 1,400 men; sewage facilities and roads were adequate; railroad connections were good; diversified farming, pasture, and wooded land was available. Moreover, it could be put into use almost immediately.[34]

Willebrandt wrote to Senator Walter George (Dem., Ga.) of the Senate Judiciary Committee that she hoped to acquire the Chillicothe site but was worried because the National Guard of Ohio had also requested it. A further complication was the insistence by the War Department that if authorized to sell surplus property for a reformatory, it would get an advance or immediate credit of $730,000 for its permanent housing program.[35] Willebrandt obligingly set up a conference with General William Lord, director of the Bureau of the Budget, the attorney general, and Secretary of War Davis and had the papers drawn up for transfer if Lord agreed to the War Department credit. Meanwhile, the Veterans Bureau, which had been leasing Camp Sherman for a hospital, raised an objection. General Hines, head of the Veterans Bureau, forwarded the concern of the hospital administrator at having a federal penitentiary housed next to his facility. Willebrandt, speaking on a Chautauqua tour, was kept apprised of a flurry of Veterans Bureau objections, and wrote trying to stir up the American Legion in Chillicothe to support the measure. Finally, in September 1925 the matter was agreeably settled; the War Department would get its funds and Veterans Bureau sensibilities were soothed. Willebrandt wrote exultantly to Attorney General Sargent: "Here it is at last—for over 1100 acres!"[36] Two of the three priorities in the federal prison establishment had been achieved.

In accomplishing the third priority, improving conditions in the three federal penitentiaries and providing work for the prisoners, Willebrandt faced the same problem she had with prohibition enforcement—the incompetence of political appointees and the need for dedicated professionals. The Atlanta prison proved the most troublesome.

On a trip to Atlanta to inspect the facility in April 1923, Willebrandt arrived just after the sensational escape of two prisoners. Police overtook the fugitives fifteen miles from prison and recaptured them in a running gun battle. One of the wounded escapees brought back to the prison hospital succeeded in bribing a nurse and escaping again. Four months later, Willebrandt made another Atlanta stop. Though she wired ahead to Warden A.E. Sartain, a Daugherty political appointee, to meet her, he "appeared half drunk, and talked most uncouthly." Outraged, she reported to Stone and urged an investigation.[37] Agent Franklin Dodge, fresh from his success with the Savannah Four, was dispatched to begin assembling the "facts of mismanagement." Further troubled at a report on narcotics in the prison, she recommended that the Bureau of Investigation be asked to trace the outside source and to send an inspector inside the walls. By October, two bureau agents were directed to "proceed with discretion and not arouse suspicion."[38] An "ugly story" of favoritism and bribery involving both Warden Sartain and the Catholic chaplain began to emerge. Alarmed, Stone asked Willebrandt whether peremptory instructions should be issued to end all favoritism, "or is it better to let matters rest until we can take drastic action."[39] She opted for drastic action. Stone brought in Assistant Attorney General William ("Wild Bill") Donovan, a Catholic, to work closely with Willebrandt and be the intermediary with the church hierarchy.

The story broke in November. Sartain was called to Washington and his resignation requested. Stone issued a statement that he was "satisfied that there was a negligent administration at Atlanta and that there was a great deal of favoritism." Sartain admitted that his resignation had been called for on the grounds that he was too soft on his bootlegger prisoners, but he insisted that he was ousted because he was a Daugherty appointee and "solely for the purpose of paying off old scores on the part of certain individuals."[40] He complained that in the past months his mail had been opened, his telephone tapped, his private bank account investigated, and his prisoners intimidated. A grand jury in Atlanta charged Sartain and his deputy with soliciting and accepting bribes from prisoners.[41] Willebrandt's Christmas letter to her parents outlined the case:

> Meantime Atlanta Penitentiary! . . . It is an ugly story. The Catholic Chaplain several days before the 4 Savannah millionaire bootleggers arrived, met Willie Haar, their chief and took him over the jail exhibiting the promised land.
>
> It was decided that "Willie's Boys" were to have pleasant jobs, and several of them were to bunk in a room back of the chapel and have their meals specially prepared & cooked and served there. Chicken, eggs and delicacies were in the contract. $10,000 was paid. The chaplain also received a fine new car. A number of wealthy bank robbers, and mail holdup men (with a million still hid away someplace, taken from a mail car in N.Y.) came in too. The Warden, Deputy Warden and Chaplain all prospered. *Friday a grand jury indicted them all!*[42]

Collecting the evidence on officials in charge of a prison with 2,700 men "all anxious to mutiny and escape" was "no small matter." She concluded, "Donovan and I have done it all, firing the men, hunting provisional wardens and choosing permanent appointees. Being much more familiar with it all I had it most to do."[43]

Willebrandt brought in a "corking fellow" as interim warden, a six-foot-four-inch tall former Texas ranger. For the permanent position, she chose John Snook, the warden of the Idaho State Penitentiary, writing, "It was a lot of work, but the only way to get the right man. And I didn't even inquire whether he was Republican or Democrat! But if the Federal penal system can be made a fine one it'll all be worth the work." Reviewing the year, she asserted: "Slowly I'm clearing out the politicians and getting real prison experts."[44] Yet, Warden Snook, who had the backing of William Randolph Hearst and the powerful Idaho Republican senator William Borah, proved to be a highly political warden indeed.

Snook began his duties energetically, cutting down privileges and vowing to stamp out narcotics in the Atlanta prison. Six months into the job in July 1925, he reported that he believed he had raised standards at the prison and had reduced drug traffic and usage. A year later, charges of Snook's mismanagement began to emerge. Former guards grumbled that Snook was replacing experienced Georgia guards with inefficient men from Idaho. Objections to Snook's behavior were also raised by the U.S. attorney in Atlanta.[45]

Cautious and supportive of her own appointee, Willebrandt moved slowly. In September, she asked the assistant superintendent of prisons to gather the charges and apprise Snook of them. The warden's aggressive response brought a bristling rejoinder from Willebrandt. To his suggestion that the critical letter, signed by her, might have been sent without her full consideration, she angrily asserted: "Very routine matters may occasionally pass under my signature without my knowledge, but generally speaking, if you have not yet learned I am sure before your tenure with the office is concluded you will learn I am not a 'rubber stamp' in the Department." Reviewing his actions, she noted, "I should not be obliged to take as much time on this matter as your attitude of self-justification and refusal to accept a correction from the Department makes it necessary for me to do." At the end of this chastising, she affirmed that she still had confidence in his capacity to run "an *excellent* institution," but she was "constrained to say in all fairness you should try to adopt a less czaristic and egotistical attitude in your dealings with the rest of the Government."[46]

Charges against Snook increased rather than diminished. A particularly sensational accusation was aired in a muckraking series in *Atlanta Life* that the leading lady of incarcerated nightclub figure Earl Carroll had been given special visiting privileges and had been entertained as the warden's guest. The Bureau of Investigation chief J. Edgar Hoover sent a copy of the July story on Carroll to Willebrandt. That same month the U.S. attorney at Atlanta complained of the "intolerable" and uncooperative attitude of the warden. The wife of one of the disgruntled guards wrote Coolidge charging Snook with "selling paroles." By October, Willebrandt had had enough. She wrote to Hoover, acknowledging that though these charges were not substantiated, there were enough to cause the attorney general to check the Atlanta prison. She asked of his progress in placing an agent inside as a prison guard (since he had abandoned the practice of using "inmate" agents). A cautious Hoover requested instructions on the civil service procedures for appointing a guard and then reminded Willebrandt that he had given up the inmate method with her sanction. Willebrandt observed that she preferred the use of an inmate agent, believing it brought better access to facts, "but if it can't be done, it can't."[47]

Finally, two investigative routes were followed. An agent, who had helped to develop the Sartain case, was dispatched to interview former guards and the editor of *Atlanta Life*. Another agent was planted as a prisoner inside the penitentiary to gather information. Beleaguered and anxious, Warden Snook wrote to his old friend, Senator Borah, in

September 1928 denouncing the "inopportune" investigation so close to the election. He insisted that he was efficient with both money and personnel despite severe problems in overcrowding. His health had been broken by working fourteen to sixteen hours a day. Since he was not a yes man, Willebrandt seemed determined to drive him from office. Though not *averse* to the investigation, which he believed would clear him, he found the methods employed "nauseating."[48] Willebrandt, meanwhile, conceded to her parents, "The Idaho warden I brought to Atlanta is proving much too small for the job and giving me a great deal of trouble."[49]

For the next six months, Snook fought for his job through Senator Borah, Senator Walter George, and the press. He charged that Willebrandt was driving him from the service and blackening his name without a trial. He discovered that prisoner 26206 was really agent William Larsen. When the press reported the story, Willebrandt accused Snook of giving out the information. He complained that she grilled him for more than three hours without giving him access to any of the charges made against him. She was prosecutor, judge, and jury, and had "stampeded" Attorney General Sargent.[50] He urged Borah to use his influence with Sargent.

Meanwhile, Willebrandt wrote to Snook on October 18 explaining the new system of using agents in prison that had been adopted "some months ago." The wardens had unfortunately not been informed at that time and a misunderstanding had arisen. She explained that the department believed it would be helpful to have an assessment of the prisons from the vantage point of the incarcerated. This could be used as a periodic check. It had no relationship to previous criticisms or investigations. "Its purpose is to put a thermometer into the morale of the prison body"; it also avoided the testimony of "stool pigeons."[51]

The Atlanta investigation continued. When a Bureau of Investigation agent complained that he had difficulty in gaining Snook's full cooperation, Willebrandt wired the warden:

> You are directed either to render full and uncomplaining cooperation to government inspectors or to forthwith absent yourself entirely from the institution leaving deputy warden in control. Department makes this alternative order out of consideration for possibility that although you report recovery your last summers illness may have left you too nervous to hold morale of the institution firm but investigation must proceed without interference or any recurrence of publicity from you.[52]

Snook turned again to Borah and George and his Idaho supporters. In February 1929, after the furor of the 1928 election had somewhat subsided, he promoted a visit to Willebrandt by a delegation of Idaho congressmen and Senator John Thomas. Willebrandt described the session to her parents: "They were all pro-Snook and pro 'Idaho-stick-together.' Senator Borah phoned. I said an earnest prayer before they came and while they were there. We talked. I was calm, reasonable, but definite and frank in stating the job was big and Snook very little."[53] Thomas, who had served on the Credentials Committee with her at the 1928 Republican convention, proved an ally, stating, "to save Idaho embarrassment," Snook should be told to resign. He and Borah supported her against the rest of the delegation and "sent Snook word to resign!!" They also "quieted" the Georgia senators who were alarmed at the Atlanta furor. She concluded: "Isn't that marvelous—I surely did work hard at the Reading Room over that—If I can eliminate Snook without a scene and a public fight how thankful I'll be."[54]

The warden was not finished. In March he discovered that still another agent had been committed as a prisoner in Atlanta by Willebrandt. The press again reported the "spy discovery" and then fully covered the decision by the new Attorney General William Mitchell to end the practice. On March 7, Willebrandt finally dispatched the letter requesting Snook's resignation. Mitchell informed him that she wrote at his direction and after he had conferred with Senator Borah.[55] Still fighting, Snook wrote to Borah that he hoped the senator would compel Mrs. Willebrandt "to sheathe her claws before she ruins the Republican party."[56] Willebrandt explained to reporters that Snook's resignation was requested due to his "utter lack of administrative ability." The *Birmingham Age Herald* speculated that Borah's opposition to the spy system might finally lead to Mrs. Willebrandt's undoing.[57] Atlanta had taken its toll.

Politics also collided with Willebrandt's drive for reform and professionalism at the penitentiary at Leavenworth. In the spring of 1926, she urged the dismissal of Warden Biddle. She wrote to her parents of her frustration: "I've had bad luck lately. I cannot understand the Atty Genl's refusal to fire a warden at Leavenworth who is crooked—and incompetent. That's hardly true. I do *understand*. He was willing to dismiss him when Congressman Anthony who runs from that District, went to the President and told a warped story of it and the President told the A.G. to go slow."[58] The investigation of malfeasance continued, by agents within and outside the prison, while the warden and Congressman David Anthony started "all sorts of annoying and disgusting backfires." The tense situation was compounded for Willebrandt because Anthony was a ranking member of the Appropriations Committee. She faced rough handling and was "humiliated" at the hearings for the Alderson appropriations.[59]

Biddle finally submitted his resignation in November 1926. After a tour of Leavenworth two years later, Willebrandt wrote with satisfaction: "the warden from Texas whom I brought in to manage Atlanta after the probe is now warden. He and his wife are fine and it was a great pleasure to see the faith I had in him in 1924 vindicated."[60]

One reform remained to be accomplished from the triad set by Willebrandt and Votaw in 1923—to develop employment for every prison inmate. In one of her first tours of Atlanta prison, struck by waste and idleness, she noted: "They sat and stood around the yard and in the halls in squads. The terrible idleness of the institution freezes my blood. Most of them got in prison because they had never learned the joy of honest sweat and a hard days work and for the government to continue to encourage such habits is no less than criminal."[61] With 2,600 men, there were ten or fifteen for each available job. There was a farm where 150, under "quite tolerable" conditions, worked to supply commodities for the prison and operated a planing mill. They lived "a very wholesome life." Inside the walls, a duck mill, authorized as a war measure to supply mail bags for the post office, employed another 700 men, but it had recently been cut back in the face of pressure from private contractors. Willebrandt complained, "It is the best thing there is in the whole Federal prison situation."[62] When a promising suggestion to establish a shoe factory met the objections of firms that had large contracts with the military, Willebrandt declared, "It sure is an indictment on the patriotism of these business concerns."[63]

As in the Alderson and Chillicothe campaigns, Willebrandt gathered support for the needed legislation. A start was made at the September 1923 conference at the headquarters of the General Federation of Women's Clubs, which had organized the Alderson drives. Willebrandt, Votaw, and Dr. E. Stagg Whitin, executive director of the National Committee on Prisons and Prison Labor, all spoke strongly for prison industries. Whitin argued that the time was particularly apt, since new standard specifications for all commodities used in government institutions were being established by the Department of Commerce. New industries could be developed to fit exact government needs and specifications. Willebrandt stressed the sound results of prison labor "from a disciplinary viewpoint" and the better prospects of a man with a trade and some savings for an effective reentry into society.[64] A spate of articles in 1923 in the *Atlantic Monthly* and *Century Magazine* by Adolph Lewisohn backed prison labor as an essential prison reform. Each prisoner should be classified for work and released when competent to take a useful place in society. His wages could be applied toward his keep or to help his family.[65]

With lobbying forces set in motion, Willebrandt worked with Votaw to gather information for the Senate hearings in September. Six months later, she noted with satisfaction that Congress had authorized the installation of a shoe factory at Leavenworth. The men would be paid a nominal sum for their work to support their families or for savings to reinstate them into society at their release. She repeated her conviction that teaching "habits of industry and the necessity and dignity of labor within prison walls is the best kind of prison reform."[66]

It was a constant struggle to maintain the appropriations to support prison enterprises. Superintendent Luther White, who replaced Votaw, was an effective advocate of prison labor, but with his death in 1926, Willebrandt had to attend more alertly to congressional appropriations hearings. In February 1928, she wrote wearily to her parents, "Today I had a hard task. While I was gone the appropriations for prisons went bad. Capt. Conner [A.J. Conner, another Borah appointee from Idaho] apparently laid down on the job. Took *no* for an answer—didn't fight—Consequently items were cut out which provided for new industries to put men to work and pay their wage." She ended, "and I went to the Budget Bureau and argued—at the end of which Genl Lord said send the items up. Then we made much talk over the prohibition—resulting in Genl Lord saying he would get the President's ok to appropriate to me $150,000 more for lawyers for prohibition."[67]

Willebrandt's prominence in the prohibition fight guaranteed headlines for her struggles for prison reform. In both areas she faced the influence of politics and public indifference; in both, her energy and perseverence finally gained organizational change and increased professionalism. Her highly publicized confrontation with Warden Snook resulted in a sweeping Justice Department study and report on the federal prisons for Congress. A new Bureau of Prisons was created and Willebrandt's final legacy to federal prison reform was in securing the appointment of penologist Sanford Bates as the first bureau chief.

She was consequently stunned by the allegations of a Hearst editorial in the spring of 1929 that Bates could do nothing unless prisons were separated from her department. She fired off a wire to Attorney General Mitchell (with a copy to Herbert Hoover's secretary Larry Richey) pleading for fairness:

> I think you owe it to me to make a statement of facts in reply that Bates was my friend appointed on my recommendation; that it is due solely to my labor and vision that the prison bureau is reclassified into a scientific major bureau. That for eight years I have made prison betterment along the best scientific lines a study and as a monument to my hard work a young man's first offenders reformatory has been established at Chillicothe, Ohio, where first offenders may be segregated from hardened criminals. A modern woman's institution established at Alderson, West Virginia, and industries started at Leavenworth putting hundreds of idle men to work, receiving wages to help their families. That I have also handled the legal end of prohibition. Has nothing to do with my competency in other lines. That in prison work I was awarded the international gold medal in 1924. The same as given to President Coolidge this year and I have had the approbation and support of such penologists as Hastings Hart, Sanford Bates, Burdette Lewis, Calvin Derrick, Dwight Morrow and that you as attorney general could do nothing worse for prisons than to remove from it my active support and interest. . . . I hate to ask you for self serving statements but I cannot longer endure the belittling of my part in every accomplishment resulting from years of devoted labor in other than prohibition lines. It is unjust to give you, a newcomer to the whole problem sole credit and picture me as a danger to prisons and I think your sense of fair play will make you willing to break silence. . . .[68]

She had fought too hard and accomplished too much to allow any distortion of what was her proudest record of achievement.

While meeting the heavy responsibilities in administering prisons and developing prohibition cases, Willebrandt supervised cases of income, estate, and corporate taxes. After the ratification of the Income Tax Amendment in 1913, federal tax legislation was prolific and complex. The Revenue Act of 1916 was followed by the war revenue measures and an excess profits tax. In the 1920s, the Mellon program of tax reductions produced the Revenue Act of 1921, the surtax in 1924, the estate tax in 1926, and finally the Revenue Act of 1928. In the first years of the decade, Willebrandt personally argued mainly those income tax cases that were related to prohibition. In other tax areas, while her division wrote the briefs, a special assistant to the attorney general, Alfred A. Wheat, presented the cases. By 1925, her Supreme Court appearances on tax matters increased, particularly, as in prohibition litigation, when a case promised to set a major new interpretation or extension of the law. In the Chile Copper case, she convinced the court that a $90 million holding corporation engaged in financing its subsidiaries was at least "a sentient form of corporate life," and was subject to a capital stock tax. In the next year, she persuaded the court in the Helmich case that when a corporation dissolves and distributes its assets these assets are profits not dividends. Tax must be paid.[69]

By 1926, she reported a "steady development of tax law." Though the law "was by no means settled," the decisions "were highly important, not only as an aid to the efficient administration of the law by the Treasury Department, but from the standpoint of the taxpayers whose rights and liabilities under the law have been made more certain." While only "time and experience" would bring "complete stability," there was considerable progress in establishing the implications and limits of federal taxing power.[70]

As in prohibition, the case load radically escalated. Tax cases demanded almost half the effort of her division. Willebrandt's annual reports are punctuated with statements of a "marked increase," "considerable increase," "substantial increase" of tax cases. In the spring of 1927, Attorney General Sargent ruled that all of the appeals from the United States Board of Tax Appeals should go through her division and be filed in the circuit courts of appeals in her name. Fifty cases were pending. She asked for but was denied additional assistants to face the fifteen to twenty cases each month. In only a few instances was Willebrandt able to review the briefs or argue the cases. In February 1928, a year in which her division prepared 226 tax appeal cases, she recorded a "solar plexus blow about a part of my own work in which I have taken a great deal of pride."[71] A judge of one of the circuit courts who had served as a U.S. attorney under Willebrandt wrote to her lamenting how poorly a tax brief had been prepared and the case handled. Willebrandt complained that it "would be possible for any *man* Ass. Atty. Genl. to have his name emblazoned on the outside of a brief and if that brief were poor, and the govt. lawyer sent out to argue presented it inadequately, no one would give the matter more than a shrug, but my name attracts notice and comment."[72]

Stung, she redoubled efforts to get the needed assistants and reorganize the work. In the meantime she set up a new system and determined to argue as many cases as she could and, when she couldn't, to send out her talented assistants. She set her agenda:

> I am going to set up a system whereby I will know at any moment just how many of these tax appeals cases I have pending in any one circuit in the U.S.—who is assigned to handle it and how many days we have on the briefs. All that I possibly can I intend to argue myself. At least I intend to try in circuits, if I can possibly make the rounds. Howard Jones [an assistant] is going down to argue one for me in the Fourth Circuit next month. It will be his first time, and I hope he does well. I have already appeared in the Fourth Circuit, and all the judges I regard as personal friends, so that I should enjoy making the trip down to Richmond were it not for the fact that it seems a propitious case and place for Jones to make his first effort.[73]

Willebrandt also worked, by encouragement and admonishment, to get maximum results from the U.S. attorneys managing tax cases at the district level. She wrote to the U.S. attorney in Omaha simply, "It is trusted you will win the case."[74] To the U.S. attorney in Chicago, she observed:

> I may add that there have been some fears expressed that you were not enthusiastic about this prosecution. Knowing you as I do, however, and your fine record in the prosecution of Government cases, the Department, of course, knows that these fears are without foundation. I am sure you will do everything possible to have the case tried on the 20th instant . . . and that you will strive for a conviction.[75]

Her growing expertise and responsibility for tax matters won her an appointment to the Taxation Committee of the American Bar Association. She was interested in the committee work but also described "a constantly accumulating irritation that I know so little about the subject and that I have so little time to study and become thoroughly familiar with it. One just has to live and breathe that tax work daily over a period of months, perhaps years, to become facile in thinking in its terms."[76]

In both tax and prohibition cases, Willebrandt fully appreciated the opportunity to develop and argue cases for the Justice Department. In late 1922, she wrote of hoping to "get away" to argue two railroad cases, adding, "It's hard for me to hold back, it's such *good* experience to go out in the field and handle these cases, but I really neglect the executive duties of my position when I do so."[77]

Meeting the administrative duties of the busiest division in the

Justice Department was a challenge that at times paralleled her efforts in prohibition, taxes, and prisons. While trying to reduce political influence in all the areas of her responsibility, Willebrandt ironically was laboring in the highly charged political environment of the Justice Department. It was certainly most politicized under Harry Daugherty's administration.[78]

In 1922, Daugherty met growing congressional criticism at the slowness of the department in prosecuting war-fraud cases. The attorney general reported that he had used a $500,000 appropriation to set the War Transactions Section to work but that it was difficult to make progress, since Congress had trimmed $3 million from the departmental budget.[79] In the fall his troubles mounted. Minnesota congressman Oscar E. Keller, responding to Daugherty's sweeping use of the injunction against striking railroad workers, charged him with malfeasance in office and began the machinery to institute impeachment proceedings. Keller introduced a grab-bag of fifty-three different charges, including failure to prosecute the war-fraud cases, failure to enforce railroad safety, failure to act vigorously in antitrust cases, and the appointment of controversial William J. Burns to head the Bureau of Intelligence. Ironically, Daugherty was also criticised for not requesting a large enough appropriation for the Justice Department. The most significant charge was that Daugherty had abridged freedom of speech in the railroad strike.[80]

The Judiciary Committee hearings dragged on until January 25, 1923. Willebrandt described the crisis from within the department to her parents: "Of course you've been reading about the Impeachment. I've been *living* it." The department received the specifications of charges on Friday, December 1, and worked through the weekend preparing a printed response. All of the divisions were involved, but Willebrandt explained, "These matters fell in my jurisdiction and I dug them up and answered."[81] Her major responsibility was meeting the railway safety charge and the claim that Daugherty should have filed for an injunction against the railroads to enjoin their workers from running the locomotives. Samuel Gompers testified. An unsympathetic Willebrandt described his appearance: "There was something pathetic about him. He is so old, and so wrong and so single tracked. He's such a short stubby little man with a head so bald and shiny as a billiard ball except for a few spots of tufts of thin long hair hanging over his collar which gives his head a weird appearance as of a cadaver whose hair has grown after death."[82] Her own role was not only to testify on railway safety but also to assist in cross-examining witnesses called to substantiate Keller's charges. Most of the witnesses from the Interstate Commerce Commission and the railroad brotherhoods, she believed, "really proved the energy and zeal" with which the problem had been handled by the department. Her own testimony traced the efforts to gather the evidence needed for an injunction and noted that the railroads, crippled by the strike, had difficulty repairing boilers. She charged that many boiler explosions had been caused by irresponsible agents who doctored the engines with nitrate of silver. Daugherty's attorney, Paul Howland, was particularly pleased with her testimony. She observed: "Funny little thing about him! . . . He's an old anti-suffragist of the ultra-positive variety. I do realize his tendencies at those first meetings to soft pedal *My* matters, but now he openly declares he wishes he could defend all counts by my testimony and in reliance upon the record my division made in handling the case."[83]

The hearings came to a bizarre climax when Congressman Keller, claiming a whitewash, refused to testify or even to respond to a subpoena. Willebrandt loyally asserted that contrary to a whitewash, the committee had listened to "trivial and irrelevant facts" until members began to protest "are we to go on listening to stuff that *is not* evidenciary but only accusatory in nature for months?"[84] The House finally voted 204 to 77 to sustain the committee report finding Daugherty innocent of the charges.

Shortly after Daugherty's exoneration and in the face of his growing physical and political frailty, Willebrandt began to ponder her own future. She wrote to her parents, "He is really in a much more critical condition that anyone realizes and should he remain nominally still the head of this Department, I would not feel in conscience or honor, I could resign and wish upon him the perplexity of choosing a woman substitute."[85] She asserted that her resignation would cause him more embarrassment than that of any of his other assistants, adding, "I do not say that alone on the quality of the work I am doing, although in justice to myself and in tribute to him, I know he regards it highly." It would be more complex to find a woman replacement and "with the Republican Party in the condition it is today, of course, it would have to be another woman."[86]

In the spring of 1923 she was content to wait. Another year of Supreme Court experience and the opportunity to become a "factor in the National Bar would be worthwhile." Daugherty continued to

express his appreciation of her work, citing her as "the *best* appointment he had made." Willebrandt wrote enthusiastically to her mother:
"Isn't he a peach. He sure appreciates loyal service—I don't always do
what I think he wants either! He sent a wire about delaying a prohibition case and I sent a wire to him that unless he *ordered* it I *wouldn't* for I
felt it would be a mistake and he told the attorneys—my judgment
went!"[87] Indeed in this time of weighing a return to California practice
and in the full confidence of Daugherty, Willebrandt felt invincible.
When Secretary Mellon phoned for a delay in a pending indictment at
Pittsburgh, she again said No and reported to her parents, "I'm having
the devil of a good time."[88]

In the summer of 1923, Daugherty's hour of crisis arrived. Against a
background of charges of corruption and influence peddling, his aide
Jesse Smith committed suicide. His son made headlines fleeing a
sanatorium where he was being treated for alcoholism, his wife was
seriously and painfully ill, and Daugherty himself became increasingly
weak. With rumors of his resignation, Daugherty and Willebrandt
met to discuss her future. The attorney general assured her that he
would not resign and that she had done "very wonderful work," far
exceeding his expectations of what a woman could do. He hoped she
would remain, at least until he regained his health or found someone
to replace her, adding poignantly, "nobody ever lost by sticking by me
yet and you just stay by the ship." Two months later President Harding died, struck down as a flood of scandals began to drown his
administration.[89]

In the wake of the Teapot Dome oil revelations and in a housekeeping mood before the upcoming 1924 election, the Senate adopted a
resolution by progressive senator Smith W. Brookhart of Iowa calling
for another investigation of Harry Daugherty and his bedraggled
department. When Daugherty declined to forward Justice Department papers to the Senate committee, Coolidge forced his resignation.
A worried Mrs. Walker wrote to her daughter from California: "Now
my *own* sweetheart just *know this*. We are back of you. If you think best
to resign should A.G. be forced out we will know it is best." But she
added, "Still, dear heart, it may be the only way to break the corrupt
party rings to have some of those who have believed in strong conservative organization to be shown how cruelly those who have done
much will be disgraced when it serves personal interests as a reward for
faithful loyal work."[90]

The Brookhart Committee investigation extended from March 12 to June 19, 1924. The most energetic committee member was Senator Burton K. Wheeler of Montana, who had been indicted after a Daugherty-inspired investigation for conspiracy to defraud the government by practicing law as a senator before an agency of the government. Wheeler was an aggressive interrogator seeking evidence to prove that Daugherty had failed to prosecute antitrust cases properly and to arrest and prosecute those involved in the Teapot Dome scandal. Underscoring the political overtones of the hearings, the first witness called was Jesse Smith's embittered ex-wife Roxie Stinson; she was followed by Gaston Means, a former Bureau of Investigation agent who was under indictment in New York for accepting bribes.

The newly appointed attorney general, Harlan Fiske Stone, arrived to find the Justice Department in turmoil. He quickly moved to shore up and defend the operations of the divisions by urging the senators to provide department personnel the opportunity to testify when their area was under investigation. Willebrandt was called twice in the last three days of the hearings. In lengthy testimony on June 17 she was sharply questioned by Senator Wheeler and Senator Jones of Washington. She defended the Justice Department's record on prohibition, stressed again the responsibility and problems of enforcement and prosecution, supported Daugherty, excoriated political influence, and finally succeeded in reversing roles and questioning Wheeler.

The exchange began to be heated when Wheeler charged that the Department of Justice and the Treasury Department's prohibition unit simply kicked "this whiskey business around as a football," each shifting responsibility to the other. He asserted that Justice Department agents stood "idly by" while crimes were committed. After several "wait a minutes," Willebrandt interrupted: "Senator, the thing that is the matter with prohibition enforcement in this country today more than any one other thing, in my opinion, is not passing the buck back and forth; . . . it is the political control of the people who are put in to gather the evidence and enforce the law." She concluded, after another exchange, that "the stultifying . . . thing is the fact that some politician, some Congressman or Senator, or someone in charge of some activities in a locality comes in to demand a permit for someone who had no business to have a permit, or to demand the appointment of some man who has no training." When Senator Jones questioned her on her authority and freedom in carrying out prohibition matters she replied that her "hands have never been tied in any respect," and emphasized that Daugherty had stood behind her even when she "got awfully hard pressed again and again by politicians." Jones then raised the question of Jesse Smith's influence on Daugherty. Willebrandt described him as "a kind of glorified personal servant," which led to the following Wheeler-Willebrandt exchange:

> SENATOR WHEELER: You do not think it is customary for the Secretary of State to invite a personal valet of some Cabinet officer to attend any of his functions, do you?
>
> MRS. WILLEBRANDT: Probably that is why I used the word "glorified" before it.
>
> SENATOR WHEELER: You would hardly think that a glorified valet would be attending functions at the White House and riding down on the *Mayflower* and attending functions at the house of the Secretary of State, would you?
>
> MRS. WILLEBRANDT: I think we are quibbling now over what that word "glorified" means. I never said I knew he was a valet. I said he acted around the Department of Justice like he was a kind of half servant and half glorified valet. He did personal errands.
>
> SENATOR WHEELER: It is not customary for a valet or a glorified valet or a half servant to occupy——
>
> MRS. WILLEBRANDT: I know less about the custom of Washington than you. I will have to leave your statement for that, because I came from a long ways, clear from California. I do not know what is customary.
>
> SENATOR WHEELER: You do not think it is customary for a servant or a glorified valet to attend these various functions do you?
>
> MRS. WILLEBRANDT: Customary?
>
> SENATOR WHEELER: Yes.
>
> MRS. WILLEBRANDT: I have already answered that I do not know what is customary.
>
> SENATOR WHEELER: You do not know what is customary?
>
> MRS. WILLEBRANDT: No.
>
> SENATOR WHEELER: I am sure if you do not I do not.
>
> MRS. WILLEBRANDT: I can not even get by an ordinary tea and know that I have everybody properly in line.
>
> SENATOR WHEELER: Well, you do fairly well whenever I have seen you. That is all, Mrs. Willebrandt.[91]

During the investigation, Willebrandt wrote a little more candidly about Jesse Smith to her parents, describing him as a weak man whose only strength was his "abiding loyalty and love" for Daugherty. He was "flighty" and "never knew his facts." She had no doubt that people tried to use Smith's closeness to Daugherty and might have succeeded, for "no one could be more easily gulled." Her own treatment of Smith was to stand up when he came into her office so that he would not stay long or if he were depressed to try to laugh him out of it.[92]

When the Senate investigation ground down it was determined from 3,000 pages of testimony that Daugherty was an ineffective administrator but that he had not been implicated in the oil or veteran scandals. There would be other investigations and a trial for Daugherty. Throughout, Willebrandt remained consistent and loyal in her support and testimony. During the Senate investigation, Daugherty asked her to come to Ohio to speak for him in his struggle to win a seat on the delegation to the Republican National Convention. Willebrandt went, but with a heavy heart, knowing that her presence would help to make credible that he had "not been crooked" in his work. She wrote: "He hasn't—and it is my duty to say so—now when he needs it most but never was I called on to do a more unwelcome thing. I'm tired. I'm very disgusted." She also agreed to sign a letter with five other assistant attorney generals citing Daugherty's courage, industry, and integrity.[93] In February 1927, when Daugherty was tried for his involvement in the favoritism by the Alien Property Custodian in the American Metal Can Company case, Willebrandt again was called to testify. She observed: "I am sorry and yet I do not think any harm can come from telling the truth. I think it will do much for Daugherty to lend a tone of respectability to his case. Likely I'll be considerably panned by radical editorial writers, but I'll survive."[94] Privately, Willebrandt later wrote to the biographer of Harlan Fiske Stone: "There was no Daugherty administration. He was seldom in his office and he paid very little attention to what was going on. He was manifestly utterly unqualified as a Law Enforcement Executive. . . ."[95] But publicly and as long as he lived, Willebrandt remained loyal.

Willebrandt was certainly happiest during the one-year housecleaning administration of Attorney General Harlan Fiske Stone. When he was "bumped upstairs" and replaced by conservative John Sargent, she again faced adjustment and reassessment of her future. She considered both Washington and New York as possible places to set up practice; Daugherty had twice suggested a position with a New York tax firm with a guarantee of $50,000 in the first year. She was also attracted to an offer with a firm specializing in estate cases, "my favorite brand of Washington practice."[96]

When she met with Sargent, her first reaction was to be "much pleased with him" in spite of his record of opposition to women's suffrage and prohibition. He in turn was supportive and even complimentary but, she complained, so reactionary that nothing new could be undertaken.[97]

In spite of all the changes in administration, Willebrandt worked to keep her own division working efficiently. Her own drive drove her staff. Marathon sessions to midnight and beyond were loyally supported. She exulted, "the other asst. a.g.'s say they can't get any stenographic help at night, why, *My* girls come *any* time I ask!"[98] At a particularly gloomy period, returning to Washington from the West, she remarked: "I'm gritting my teeth and going to it but goodness this can be the vapidest place on earth. The only thing is work. I know now why I worked so hard last winter—to escape officialdom! But my office force truly care for me and there at least is a little oasis of real friendship."[99] Their appreciation and friendship obviously sprang from hers. In October 1924 she reported that eight Supreme Court briefs were written in two days:

> The latter of course I did not *write* couldn't that many— [Mahlon] Kiefer did practically all the work—but they must be gone *over* as its my responsibility—But Kiefer is so fine. He and his wife are so grateful to me. . . . I tried him out—and then put him in charge of appeal work in my division and he has certainly made good. He says being with me has meant everything in that I make my assistants feel their own powers, and am so generous about giving credit—Jones is the same way—I *know* I've *made* him and he's so generous about feeling it. He's in charge of administrative meetings. Then Henderson, working on rum ships is so clean and fine and manly and earnest—and able. They're a loyal group, and I shall always know their friendship is *real*.[100]

She fought vigorously not only for the advancement of her staff, but also for their salaries. In February 1928 she raged at the attorney general's diversion of prohibition funds she had won from Congress to the department's work on alien property cases. The decision was made in her absence and she fought Sargent with "blood in my eye." His evasion made her "just manufacture hate" and admit, "I can produce venom faster than a rattlesnake when I get mad and I haven't nature's means given to the lovely reptile of hollow fangs to get rid of it. As a consequence, it makes me sick." Her explosion won back two of the three contested increases. Through controversy and change she

managed to run one of the most effective divisions in the department.[101]

The years of work, investigations, testimony, administration, and
fighting took their toll. Throughout the decade her work for the
Department of Justice was paralleled by a growing longing to leave
those responsibilities and be appointed to a federal judgeship in
California. She had labored loyally for the party; her record before the
Supreme Court and the federal circuit and district courts was impressive. She consistently had the support of each attorney general. Three
major obstacles remained. Her prohibition work won her the support
of the drys, but it made her appointment abhorrent to the wets. The
two California senators remained bitterly divided. Shortridge was
conservative and sympathetic to the wets; Johnson was progressive
and dry. They had tangled over Willebrandt's appointment as assistant
attorney general; they continued to battle over patronage, generally
forcing Harding and Coolidge to side with one or the other. Increasingly, Coolidge supported Shortridge's nominations. Finally, there
was the matter of sex. No woman had ever been appointed to a federal
judgeship.

Yet in 1923 there seemed good reason for Willebrandt to hope. Early
in the decade, the women's vote was still an imponderable factor for
both parties and, after the congressional returns of 1922, the Republicans clearly needed to strengthen their forces for 1924. Party vice-
chairman Harriet Taylor Upton had a long discussion with Harding
before his fatal cross-country trip in the summer of 1923 on the need to
appoint more women to federal posts. Harding indicated that when he
returned to Washington he would make some appointments; Upton
believed that he would have named Willebrandt to the federal bench.
Harding's chief patronage adviser, Attorney General Daugherty, had
told California politicians that he would like to see his assistant Willebrandt appointed a federal judge. With the death of Harding, however, Willebrandt wrote her parents: "It is quite a different matter now.
It *may* be possible—thru God as things are. I wish it might be, but
perhaps it isn't best—who knows."[102]

She continued to hope through the autumn of 1923. In September,
she wrote her father: "How I should like to have such an appointment.
It would give me the opportunity to *study* and my type of legal mind (if
any) is judicial rather than an advocate's. I somehow cannot bring
myself to seek it, however, either through the attorney general or

Senator Johnson who have already honored me by conferring on me in spite of my youth a powerful national position."[103] Two months later, she wrote her mother: "Mama, dear, do help just as hard as you know about the judgeship. I want to come home with it so—but I'm afraid I won't get it because they'll want me here to campaign."[104] Harriet Taylor Upton did urge her to help in the campaign efforts but also promised to see Coolidge about the judicial appointment. Willebrandt confided her tensions: "For almost two weeks I couldn't get hold of myself—my spirits were just *flat*. I wasn't sick—I slept, but wasn't rested. I don't know what was the matter. It was just as tho I had a ball and chain in my soul." But she rebounded, declaring that she would not care whether the judgeship came her way or not. "I shall know that if it doesn't I shall be glad."[105]

In December, Coolidge still had made no appointment. Newspaper reporters "sprang the question about the Judgeship at her," and one Associated Press reporter wondered "if Coolidge can realize how well received your appointment would be over the entire country." Willebrandt responded that she "personally was doing nothing about the matter." She wrote home that the press had been wonderful because she was "frank and never double crossed them."[106] Her family always sent encouragement. From Shanghai, Maud Hubbard Brown wrote: "What happened about the Judgeship? Is it decided yet? I'd think the wets would buy you a governorship to get you out of your present job!"[107] Her faithful mother reassured her: "I still am so sure that you will be appointed. If I am mistaken I shall be very happy anyway for I know by that your influence is needed elsewhere. I only pray that God's will may be done in you. If this is your work *nothing* can keep you from being appointed and I surely feel *sure* that it is."[108]

Coolidge still had no consensus candidate from the two California senators. Hiram Johnson's loyal lieutenant Frank Doherty wired Willebrandt about her backing and her opinion of what Coolidge would do if Shortridge and Johnson remained deadlocked. Her return wire was hopeful but realistic:

> No question about recommendation from my boss. He has already talked to president but latters action, no human can tell. Sat beside President at dinner Monday after which he volunteered comment to host on my intellect and legal attainments and similar prior statements from other sources have come to me. His political secretary is disquieted I understand because I'm liable to know too much going on over prohibition and he fears

our sector will make capital of refusal to make outstanding woman appointment but they are counting delegates so closely that its like a game of checkers. Shortridge named Ferrigan north and McCormick south. Hoover for latter too. Do not let any consideration for me prevent your doing what will be best for interests of our California friends. A friend at Slemp's request preparing memorandum on my history etc. for Chief Justice January third. May mean nothing. Informed nothing doing before January.[109]

Doherty, reporting to Johnson that Shortridge's secretary was boasting that Shortridge would dominate California patronage, advised the senator to determine if Coolidge would really consider Willebrandt. If not, Paul McCormick would be a good compromise and a popular choice. It was imperative that Johnson make up his mind so that Shortridge could not claim sole credit for the McCormick appointment. A disappointed Willebrandt wrote her mother January 25, 1924, "McCormick will be the man." She added, "If it were anybody else except McCormick I wouldn't care so much, but I hate to see Hoover and Shortridge run the State. . . ."[110] Two weeks later, she was philosophical and shared Johnson's advice to her, writing:

> I cannot bring myself to feel very badly about it. . . . Anyway I couldn't get it without what I would consider political humiliation and I decided I didn't want it that badly. Did I tell you that a few weeks ago Senator Johnson called me up and asked why I didn't go personally to Senator Shortridge and get it. He hinted what I had been already led to believe that if I would put myself in the *personal debt* of the august Shortridge he would look with favor on urging it before the president. I said to Johnson, "Ten judgeships would not be worth it. I have to *respect* at least, anyone of whom I will ask a favor," and I have not been sorry since the decision.[111]

In November 1924, after the election of Coolidge, there was an opening on the federal bench in northern California. Doherty immediately wired his encouragement to Willebrandt. Her mother wrote in a light tone that "papa" had said "she could hardly swing as big a thing as that." Receiving a gloomy letter from Willebrandt, she responded:

> I still expect you to get the appointment and will until someone else is named. I am sorry you gave up as a metaphysical law was broken when you gave up. If you read your Bible you will realize that always in healing or in victory of any kind it was

performed after to a material sense the thing was impossible. However, I am sure if the Judgeship is your place *no one can keep you from it*.[112]

The *New York Times* reported speculation over Willebrandt's appointment and growing opposition from northern Californians, who wanted one of their own for the judgeship. Shortridge, who had just watched his protege, U.S. attorney John Williams, harried out of his post by Attorney General Stone and Willebrandt, was adamant in his opposition. He pressed the nomination of northerner A.F. St. Sure. Johnson bitterly opposed St. Sure, and claiming he was apprised by Willebrandt that she had Coolidge's word that if Johnson endorsed her she and not St. Sure would be named, he again supported her. Since Johnson was sympathetic to the northern Californians' position that the nominee should be from that area, however, his support this time was less than energetic. Indeed, the *New York Herald Tribune* reported that he was backing Judge J.H. Langdorfer for the post.[113]

At the end of January 1925 Willebrandt wearily wrote home that St. Sure had been appointed. She noted, "all the nasty attacks" had left her "almost sick." At a particularly low ebb, she added:

> Tho outwardly I showed no disappointment, and at first wouldn't confess [it] to myself, really at heart I care terribly— For I just feel it was a sign from God that my life's work and field of service lie in different ways than I hoped or desired. If this had come, the future was so beautiful—and all mapped out. Now in my heart I feel I may stay East and *possibly* never come back. I'm plunged into doubt again and a feeling that destiny is a thing one's desires cannot deflect nor toy with as perhaps I have tried to do unwisely.

Once again her mother wrote to try to assuage the disappointment, questioning: "Do you know I am wondering if with all the new association and prestige and honor that has come to you if you will be as happy to come back here (unless of course you should get a judgeship) as you will, to accept something that is sure to come to you some place in the East."[114]

Within two weeks it all started again. The *Los Angeles Times* reported that federal judge Benjamin Bledsoe would resign to run for mayor of Los Angeles. This time Willebrandt had Johnson's strong backing, which immediately ensured Shortridge's opposition.[115] Justice Stone, who spoke to Coolidge in her support, urged Willebrandt to be patient and "let the tree grow." Willebrandt tried to convince the

An uncharacteristically unbuttoned Calvin Coolidge and Willebrandt about to be joined for a picture on the White House lawn by delegates to the Phi Delta Delta national convention in 1924.

president through Stone and Attorney General Sargent that if he continued to name only Shortridge's choices he would easily ensure the senator's reelection in 1926, a victory she believed he did not want to encourage. Sargent, perhaps aware that she would not win this time, earnestly asked if she "really" wanted the judgeship. Wouldn't she rather stay on with him awhile?[116] She replied that she was willing to stay if needed, but she confided to her parents: "Personally I like him very much but the work is not going to be interesting with him as it was with Stone." She added philosophically: "Of course I hope against hope for the Judgeship but should it not materialize I fancy in later years I'll be glad—I've been getting out for a walk in the early morning. Spring is in the air, the cherry blossoms are puffs of loveliness and I've felt quite sure the future must be filled with promise—so we shan't worry, just pray—Won't we?"[117] In April she admitted that the cause was lost because of Shortridge's opposition.[118]

In the spring of 1926, Willebrandt saw another hope from a bill introduced in Congress to expand the judiciary; two new California judgeships would be created, one in the north and one in the south. On Decoration Day, Willebrandt wrote home cautiously:

> You must not think about the judgeship. Heaven knows I want it but I question the choice politically run as the government now is. It's rather a paradox that never have the people been so satisfied and never has the government been turned over to a greater degree to the predatory interests than now. "Lower taxes" "Economy" Everyone who knows laughs. Some taxes, yes, but made possible by the vast prosperity—not economy. The president is the fiscal agent of the money interests and I do not say that meanly. He is not hypocritical. He really believes that is best for the country.[119]

She later reported that she had no news on the judgeship, only a remark by cabinet officer Lyman Wilbur that she was a fine woman but that he was against a woman being a judge. It was, he believed, "against the law of nature and of God." Willebrandt caustically observed, "God had, I fear lots to answer for when he made some men's minds." More serious than Wilbur's scruple was Coolidge's statement, reported in the *Los Angeles Times*, that the "rapid advancement of women in politics" had not yet reached a point where "he would feel justified in appointing a woman to the federal bench."[120]

But Willebrandt was determined to make a major effort this time. In July 1926 she had a stormy session with Frank Doherty when she proposed endorsing Shortridge in his bid for reelection. Ray Benjamin, Shortridge's secretary, had promised that if she backed the senator, he would work to get the recommendation of Chief Justice Taft for her judicial appointment. Doherty stormed that if she supported Shortridge, Johnson would never forgive her. Several days later, he wrote more temperately that he knew that her "heart has been set" on the judgeship and loyally asserted that Johnson would not want her to act contrary to her judgment and against her advancement. He added his own distrust of Shortridge but accepted that he would certainly win election and increase his influence with Coolidge. He advised, "do as your judgment directs."[121] She gained the bitter enmity of Johnson without winning any tangible support from Shortridge.

She remained at her post with "the gambling chance" of winning the appointment. The gamble lasted into 1927, when Congress adjourned without acting on the judgeship measure. She realized that Ray Benjamin believed she would finally grow tired and resign, allowing Shortridge to put in a man who could be controlled as judge and at the same time appoint a woman to the assistant attorney general post. Benjamin acknowledged that as a judge she would not be "half cocked," but he also knew that she would not "yield a conscienceless opinion."[122] Willebrandt concluded with spirit: "I hate like fury to just let them *tire* me out. If I resign under such conditions I fear I'd always feel that had I staid [*sic*] I'd have fulfilled my destiny a little better than if I quit. . . . The great trouble with me is that I just don't seem able to neglect the days duties as they come in this job and use the time to finess and do political things. I know how, but I never get time!!"[123] In early February, she made an attempt to do the political thing, hosting a Washington party for a California friend, Hollywood producer Louis B. Mayer. Shortridge was an honored guest. From California a disgruntled Frank Doherty wrote to Hiram Johnson of the "great social event," noting the guest list would have been complete if Harry Daugherty and Ray Benjamin had been included.[124] It was all in vain as the judgeship bill went down to defeat.

In March another federal vacancy opened in northern California. Willebrandt's Easter letter home reported a friendly letter from Ray Benjamin, but she remained unsure whether Shortridge would "get up the courage" to name her. She added, "As you say, Mama, I know the appointment will come if it's right, I'm not afraid of either future as a judge—or as practicing."[125] In September, she took the opportunity of having her parents more directly involved. She arranged an introduction to Coolidge, writing: "I think . . . his meeting you may help me. He's *abstract* in his thought of women unattached to some man—and meeting you may humanize me to him a little bit, a thing I have regretted he has not felt in the past."[126] In January, she postponed a trip to California fearing it might start the local newspapers speculating about why she had come before "this judgeship matter is settled."[127] It was never settled in Mabel Walker Willebrandt's favor. In 1928, her loyal participation in the political campaign finally dashed this most cherished hope.

CHAPTER FIVE

Extending Family and Profession

*How are the materials of personality balanced, fired, or tipped
in the making years, to bring talent and genius or lawless tendencies to the surface?*

How significant are the years of infancy?

MABEL WALKER WILLEBRANDT
"First Impressions"

*When we sum up the columns that make "success" for the boy
on the one hand and the girl on the other, you find the girl has the
much longer column to add.*

MABEL WALKER WILLEBRANDT
"Give Women a Fighting Chance"

*F*AMILY was always the first source
of shelter and strength for Mabel Walker Willebrandt. An only child,
she was nurtured by the full attention and love of devoted parents.
They remained the dominant influence in her life. Faced with 3,000
miles of separation in her Washington years, she wrote and visited but
also created an extended family by adopting a two-and-a-half-year-
old girl. She considered and rejected marriage and maintained and
expanded a strong network of personal and professional friends. The
prodigious energy and responsibility generated by her work was almost matched by the care and support lavished on family and friends.

Daughter and parents kept close through a stream of transcontinental letters. Willebrandt used this correspondence as a substitute for the
journal she never found time to keep. Her letters are full of prohibition
and prison matters with a few glimpses into her social life and developing network of friends. The Walker letters, written mostly by her
mother, are compendiums of progress on the chicken farm, the
growth of Temple City, pride in Mabel, and reassurance.

Money and work were continuing themes. Typical was Mrs.

Walker's assertion: "Mabel we do not need *any* money, don't send even $100." In May 1923, she reported that Temple City was being graded and plotted. The business district would be built on the first street east of their house and the land in front of them would be divided into "high class" lots. She wrote enthusiastically, "We are sure headed to make a good thing out of this land." There were rumors of oil and a test well was being driven a half mile away. By the next summer, when the curbs rimmed the streets and the streetcar was extended from Los Angeles, her mother announced: "Everything seems to be coming along in Temple City."[1] When the opposition of bankers in San Gabriel blocked a national bank charter for Temple City, Mrs. Walker called in her daughter's influence, writing: "If you think it would help and are in line so it would be all right for you to do so, it might be well for you to point out to the bank commissioner that Temple is a growing and developing place and that those who are fighting the move are simply doing it through a narrow jealousy."[2] By the following spring, Temple City had its bank, and the Walkers were among the first shareholders.

Running the chicken ranch taxed the energy and resilience of the Walkers, now in their sixties. Winds blew tumbleweeds in piles against the small cabin and sent dust swirling through the windows "like falling snow." David Walker worked a sixteen-hour day, seven days a week, to care for their 1,100 chickens. Mrs. Walker, who accepted some household help paid for by Mabel, estimated that they could profitably put fourteen hands to work. Both mother and daughter tried to persuade David Walker to ease his schedule. Once when they were successful, he was dragged off to the movies, but he "got even" by taking his wife to the Kansas and Missouri state picnics.[3] In the summer of 1924, they decided to abandon the chicken business. With the help of Willebrandt's friend and law associate, Fred Horowitz, they rented part of their acreage and brooders and began building small rental cabins. Their own cabin was included in the rental scheme. Facing the prospect of camping out in a neighbor's garage while their new larger house was being built, Mrs. Walker reflected wearily, "I dread to tear up and be torn up for so long. . . . Sometimes I wish I had nothing then I would not have to bother just travel around and not bring any furniture or books. It just seems like I will always be torn up."[4]

When the new "clean and cozy" house was completed in January 1925, Mrs. Walker reported: "I like it after it is done but so hate to do it." Her pleasure came in planting the garden with roses, fuchsias, Australian broom plants, and shrubs. She despaired of persuading her husband, "no lover of trees," to give space to anything but a practical fruit tree. Finally settled and content, she wrote Mabel, "The fireplace is great and when we get the draperies the house will be *so dear*. I know you will like it."[5]

More secure from their rental income, the Walkers sold off the chickens for $2,400. David Walker, who had organized Walker's Poultry Cooperative, now began to sell insurance and to plan a waterworks company. Mrs. Walker earned extra money by writing local items for the Temple City newspaper. She reported suffering from "Autoitis" from exploring Temple City in the new car Mabel had bought.[6] Although her parents were more comfortably settled, Willebrandt's extended family was not.

Minnie Hickstein, viewed as family from the day she first joined the Walkers on the Powersville farm, had married Ira Wells and had raised two children, bright and energetic Helen, and Mabel, gentle like Minnie but hampered by a learning disability. Minnie's husband had a job at a radiator factory in New Mexico; he also had a history of uncertain health and intermittent employment. A concerned Mabel wrote to her mother in 1924: "I'm worried about Minnie. I have to get them out with us. She's such a liability and drain on you. I want to help Helen thru school, and mean to, but hate you to have to shoulder grandma-ing the whole family. Shall I send her some money do you think, or if you will—let me know, I'll add it to what I send next month."[7] Mrs. Walker advised her to send clothes but no money, for Ira should not get "in the habit of expecting help from you—money help." In a real crisis, she promised, the Walkers would take them in. Mabel did send Helen Wells $150 to begin normal school in 1923, reporting to her mother: "It'll probably cost about $500 per year but is worth it I think. She seems a nice girl and somebody should be salvaged from that family."[8]

Whereas Minnie Wells struggled with money and family illness, Maud Hubbard Brown's life and problems were more exotic. Mabel's affection for Maud remained strong. While meeting the costs for herself and Arthur Willebrandt at the University of California law school, she had also sent tuition money to help Maud complete her degree at Park College. Mabel and Arthur journeyed to Parkville in 1913 to see Maud graduate and then drove her to the Walkers in Michigan for a vacation before she married her Park classmate, handsome J.W. Brown. Five years later, Mabel and the Walkers saw "Muddie" and J.W. and their two sons off for China, where Brown had contracted to serve as an accountant with the Methodist Mission Board.[9]

In the autumn of 1924, restless and bored in China and expecting another child, Maud considered returning to stay with the Walkers while awaiting the birth of the new baby. Mrs. Walker wrote to reassure Mabel, already worried about her parents' burdens: "Dearie, you need not worry. Muddie will not leave China to come here. She would not put up with the heat and the dust and being in a rough shanty all crowded up. No, I know Muddie too well. She is like a cat. She likes comfort and luxury too well. . . . it is rough and dusty and hot in the middle of the day and cool at night and nothing very nice, me so busy outside that much of the time we eat in the kitchen on oil cloth. Don't worry she could not stand it. She would soon go some place else."[10] Mr. Walker warned Mabel that J.W. was "quite willing to shift" costs if he could and insisted that he must meet all expenses.[11]

Maud was not deterred. She returned to join the Walkers, but in the hot dusty summer of 1925 took the boys to visit friends in Kansas City and Michigan. Mrs. Walker reported that Maud had forgotten "how much work there was in America." Still, she offered to keep the boys during Maud's confinement and to provide one of the small cabins on the chicken acreage should she choose to remain. When Mabel considered bringing Maud and her sons to live with her in Washington, she quickly had to reassure her horrified parents that she "only *desired* to do it."[12] It was an impossibility.

She eagerly looked forward to Maud's new baby, writing in June 1925: "I *wish* I could have it. The regret that, now, in the height of my powers, I cannot have one makes me tender with everyone who does—particularly Muddie—I do love her very dearly. She holds a place in my heart no one else will ever fill."[13] Mabel managed to spend Christmas eve in California and to visit the Walkers and Maud's new baby. On the return trip to Washington she wrote, "The baby is adorable. *How* can you stay away from him Papa—oh, I wish he were mine—or that I could be close enough to watch his growth."[14]

The arrival of Maud's baby and the temporarily settled state of the Walkers may have finally spurred Mabel on to a course she had long considered. She first raised the question in a tentative letter in August 1923: "Mamma, would you *mind* if I adopted a baby girl if I could find one that was from good parentage—I'd board it out."[15] The next year her search began in earnest. She wrote in October 1924, "I've been going to orphanages. Tomorrow I go to a foundling home. A little baby—a wonderful one was found abandoned. The finder, a fireman, tho wants it. There are a great many abandoned babies here. It would be rather nice to take one like that wouldn't it, providing it were of good health. Life is all a gamble anyway. You and Papa drew a lemon. I can't do worse than you did with your own—No? Reaching—always—for stars—and grasping nettles!"[16] Within a week, she was back at the orphanage seeing "the loveliest 8 day old little boy—guaranteed by the Dr. as from unusual parents." But she was also drawn to "a bright little 2 months old girl." She wrote, "I'm seeing whether she may be for adoption. She's illegitimate and the mother is over thirty years of age. You see I'm in earnest about finding one." As always, her mother responded with encouragement and support, hoping that she would find just the baby she wanted.[17]

The network of Willebrandt's friends was alerted to help in the search. She wrote to Fannie French Morse in December 1924: "You haven't found that baby girl yet for me have you? I'm still looking." Later, the same month, frustrated and depressed that she could not seem to save enough money to adopt a child, she vowed to "step high and have a good time."[18] She had no anxiety about raising a child as a single parent; money, as always, was the major deterrent.

The Willebrandt-Walker letters are punctuated with money concerns. Guilty at not being with her parents and worried that they were exhausting themselves, Mabel tried to send them $100 or $200 each month. In January 1923, a difficult financial period, she wrote apologetically for being "such a rotter not to send more money at the times you need it."[19] In March she confided to her mother:

> I've been worrying financially. I might just as well express it. The combination of my insurance ($600) some left over Xmas bills pending and so forth, income tax and a new dress for speaking before the New York Bar Assoc. put me under. It costs so much to live, and I'm so hopeless about being able to save the way many can. I'm *not* extravagant in the sense of buying lots for myself but I just don't watch details as I should. Furthermore I've thought a great deal about returning home lately, oh, for the last two months—and I'm face up against the idea that that means cutting off what I'm sending you and having little or nothing coming in for several months. And I get to thinking how hard you work and I feel terrible.[20]

Trying to make money faster, she decided to invest in one of Fred Horowitz's real estate projects, a hotel he was building in Los Angeles. She wrote home: "I hope we *can* make some money. I'd sure like the feeling of it in the Walker family. But I'm a poor fish at it. I really can't keep my eye focused on the money end of anything I do—I fear I'll always be more or less of a parasite on my friends and wind up in an old ladies home, but I'll have a fine time on the way there!"[21]

Her mother wrote reassuringly: "Truly if we should need money I will send you an SOS call. I *truly will*." Unconvinced, Mabel sought her father's confirmation that they could manage on $100 a month instead of $200 from her. She was trying to save for a new start. By the spring of 1924 she had amassed $2,000 but still worried. Reflecting on her success in Washington and "feeling puny" in California, she explained: "At home it's making money—economic struggle, here it's dealing with *human* forces—and the direction of human endeavor and purposes. They, I *know* and can control." Economic forces made her feel "utterly inadequate."[22]

Money worries were intensified by her health concerns. Since her student days at the University of Southern California, she had been troubled with an increasing hearing loss. She compensated by fierce concentration and focusing closely on whomever was speaking. Early magazine interviews stressed her large eyes and level gaze. Her difficulty and frustration were particularly acute when arguing before the Supreme Court. Not only did some of the justices "speak . . . softly," but they could not all be easily encompassed with her eyes, particularly when her concentration was fixed on the complexities of the argument. At congressional hearings or committee deliberations in the Justice Department, she sometimes had to ask for repetitions or she would occasionally guess at the question raised. She used a hearing aid, painstakingly arranging her hair for an hour each morning to conceal the device. In the evenings, with a different hair style, she concealed the batteries for the hearing aid in her bosom, leading one perplexed dancing partner to exclaim, "My God, Mabel, are you wearing armor!"[23] If the batteries failed in court or in a congressional hearing, she desperately sent word to her secretary to bring an emergency supply as soon as possible. Her anxiety and frustration emerged in a letter to her parents at Christmas 1922:

> The dread shadow of deafness all but submerges me. For Mama and Papa, dear, when from every quarter and indirectly . . . I hear the most extravagant marvelings at my capacities over the way I handle myself before the court, and when presiding at trying conferences, that surge of bitterness rises even at their praise when I think, "Damn you, you think that's *good*, do you know what then could I do if I weren't struggling under the

most horrible handicap that you do not guess." In other words if I could use in intellectual energy that extra attention and nerve and will-power that I *always* exert to even *keep the drift of what's going on* what couldn't I do! It cuts so deeply to be thought stupid or appear so because you haven't heard.[24]

A troubled Mrs. Walker tried to help by sharing her new found faith in Christian Science and her confidence in its healing. She wrote Mabel, "You may be slow to cast out from your consciousness the *fear* of deafness but *you will* sometime realize enough of the Truth to rise above all fear and when you do you will hear *perfectly*." She urged her daughter to find a good Christian Science practitioner in Washington, since her schedule allowed her no time to "give the problem full justice. . . . I have read many testimonies of people who are cured of catarrhal deafness. Nearly all write that the *fear*—has been so *great* that the cure has been slow."[25]

Mabel did begin reading the Christian Science lessons, but as her mother predicted, found it a difficult task to accomplish each day. In October 1924, her mother admonished her for worrying that she would be unable to provide for the family when she was deaf: "Oh, ye of little faith. . . . If you say 'when I am deaf' you are forging in your body a deaf condition."[26]

Six months later, Mabel wrote of finding a Washington specialist who had developed an "osteopathic treatment restructuring the Euctacian [*sic*] tubes." After examining her, he believed that with treatment her hearing could be restored. She worried, however, about the possible impermanency of the cure and concluded that with her current expenses, she could not take the risk.[27] She balanced her hope for renewed hearing with her determination to have a child. She chose the child.

On August 2, 1925, an exuberant Mabel wrote her parents from Chicago: "I have Dorothy with me. . . . the dearest, wisest little two year old I ever saw," who "*honestly*, no joking *looks* like Papa—the same blue, blue eyes & with quite a similar expression and a mouth with large full lips like all us Walkers are cursed with! And her forehead is like Mama's! First thing you know I'll talk us into a scandal in the family." She urged the Walkers not to say anything about Dorothy, since she did not want the papers "mulling over it until everything was settled."[28] Her mother immediately answered: "You will be such a fine Mother. Any child you take will seem very, very near to me. I love children and will rejoice in them as a grandmother."[29]

Dorothy had come from a farm in Michigan. A woman who had

sought out and been rescued through Willebrandt's help in Los Angeles when she was assistant police court defender kept in grateful correspondence after she returned safely home to Michigan. In 1925, however, she faced another crisis. She was raising her young son and a little girl she had taken into her home with the meager earnings from a farm and a part-time photography business. Planning remarriage to a minister, assessing their slender resources, and knowing that Willebrandt was looking for a child of her own, she wrote suggesting the little girl as a perfect choice.[30]

En route to business in Chicago, Willebrandt arranged to meet Fred Horowitz in Michigan and journey to the farm to see Dorothy. Immediately entranced, she suggested that she take her for the weekend to see how they got on. At the end of two days, she sent a wire to Michigan that they were a match.[31] Dorothy had a new home.

It was a bewildering change. Dorothy's first day with her new mother was spent watching her dictate to her secretary and take care of Justice Department business in Chicago. Willebrandt had hoped to show Dorothy to Maud Brown, then visiting in Michigan, but her usual hectic schedule forced her to return instead to Washington to prepare for an arduous Chautauqua tour. Arrangements were made to leave Dorothy with a young Washington couple while she toured, but Mabel wrote to her parents of her determination to revise her life so that she could be with her new daughter, asserting: "She's precious and I want to watch her mind develop. I don't see how I can go on the Chautauqua and leave her so long!"[32]

Her happiness was deep that August. From New Hampshire she wrote exuberantly that if she had the money she would like to adopt another girl or boy too sometime but added that without a judgeship that was impossible.[33] Returning to Washington, she made Dorothy the center of her intense energy and attention. She needed "everything." A seamstress was commissioned to make dresses. Her measurements were dispatched to Mrs. Walker, for, as Mabel explained, "I'd love her to have anything you made most of all." "Only a beneficent destiny," she believed, "could have led us together." She considered changing Dorothy's name until she discovered that it meant "Gift of God." She was full of a new mother's details in writing to the Walkers. Dorothy could almost entirely undress herself and was angry if anyone tried to help her. She neatly hung up her clothes. Willebrandt confessed the obvious: "I'm just foolish about her and do hope I can

Willebrandt and Dorothy share the pleasure of opening a gift.

have her with me this winter so that we may have a romp in bed in the morning. That would be about the only time."[34]

She toyed with the idea of renting a house in Chevy Chase and inviting Maud to come to stay with her. Maud could "train her little mind marvelously," but she also feared that Dorothy, already well trained in table manners ("You should see her use a finger bowl!"), might acquire Justin Brown's bad habits at the table. Instead, she decided to make a home with her friends Annabel Matthews and Dr. Louise Stanley. Matthews, Mississippi born, had, like Willebrandt, taught school before choosing law. A lawyer with the Treasury Department, she would be appointed the first woman judge on the Federal Tax Board. Dr. Louise Stanley headed the Bureau of Home Economics of the Department of Agriculture. Rounding out the household, and to Dorothy the central person in her upbringing, was Rosa (Willebrandt always called her Rose) Gainor, a young black mother who had been helping Willebrandt to entertain and to keep house. The "aunts" Stanley and Matthews, Rosa Gainor, and eventually the Walkers, all shared some responsibility for Dorothy. For a little girl fresh from another mother and a Michigan farm, it was overwhelming.[35]

Though bolstered with this support, Willebrandt sought the best scientific advice in meeting her new responsibility. Before she left for the Chautauqua tour, she had five psychologists examine Dorothy. They rated her abilities at three to three-and-a-half years in everything but sentence making. All agreed that she was "an unusual *find*."[36] In a decade rife with interest and theories on proper child rearing, she did not lack constant advice. Behaviorist John Watson's *Psychological Care of Infant and Child* had recently been published. Seventy-five institutions were devoted to educating parents. The Laura Spelman Rockefeller Foundation expended $7 million between 1923 and 1927 on research and institutes on child rearing.[37] After study and some personal experience, Willebrandt contributed advice of her own in "First Impressions," an article in the May 1928 issue of *Good Housekeeping*.

Reflecting the current psychological wisdom, she emphasized the crucial necessity of building good habits from birth. She supported Dr. Herman Adler's "solemn warning": "It is characteristic of all spoiled children that they can not change the behavior pattern which they have developed as the result of being spoiled. It is their tragedy. Such a child never learns from experience. He takes an experience, twists, turns, distorts, reshapes it until it fits into his pre-determined scheme of things."[38] It *did* hurt to spare and spoil the child. She worried about too much attention to the "material aspects of housekeeping," explaining:

> Any one who has had the good fortune to come into close contact with the homes of the poor has seen innumerable instances where a smelly immigrant shack combines all the real elements of home, which are so often conspicuously absent from many a cleaner house faultlessly managed by a material-minded "Martha" mother. I should infinitely prefer my child to spend early years in the former. I should rather run the risk of his acquiring culture later, if down deep in the recesses of his babyhood impressions had been packed truth, helpfulness, self-reliance, and the real meaning of love. For it is in the substrata of behavior and feeling that genius and talent root.[39]

She knew that the mystery of human development did not yield to an exact science and accepted that the determination of parents and their hopes could sometimes overcome the predictions of psychologists and "hereditists." Central to the child's development was "love expressed in mutual respect and tolerance. . . . It is the soil in which child growth is rooted. It gives value to all else. A tiny infant responds to its atmosphere and develops properly in no other."[40] Love and obedience led to liberty and self-reliance.

Grateful that her own mother had "made my first impression of God not creed, but an all-enveloping love and an infinite strength for time of need," she related an incident that she had shared with four-year-old Dorothy. As the two of them sat along a riverbank, they watched a caterpillar inch along the limb of an elm tree until it reached "to the edge of the farthest leaf that drooped with the tiny weight." Then,

> Lifting with inquiring instinct half of its body, it groped into space beyond the leaf. Then its feet slipped, and it fell. I heard the swift intake of the child's breath beside me. But the worm had not disappeared into the stream below. Midway, swaying gently to and fro, it hung by a silken thread spun from itself to the place from which it fell. Slowly, tortuously, it made its way back to the green leaf and safety. The little girl, with shining eyes, turned to me and said:
> "Oh, mother, look! God pulled it back again!"[41]

A child raised to obedience, she concluded, "where reliance was placed in spiritual force and courage, *may* slip far over the edge of things, nevertheless before actually dropping into the abyss of lawlessness and moral waste, the silken threads of that home's first impressions will sustain him and pull him back to safety and a new start."[42]

Years later when Dorothy was expecting her own first child, Willebrandt sent her books on child rearing, checking and annotating passages and providing a blueprint on how she tried to raise her. In Leslie Hohman's *As the Twig Is Bent*, she checked the passage: "If we want to make absolutely sure that our children will not be included among the world's disappointed or utterly defeated persons, we must not leave their psychological education to luck. From the day we bend over their cradles we must follow a definite plan to build the automatic emotional attitudes and skills, the character and disposition that are essential for their complete self-realization."[43] She wrote in the margin, "I sure *tried* but I think he's a little over enthusiastic." Next to the admonition that "we must instill the fundamental qualities that promote happiness and usefulness," she wrote simply, "How?"[44]

Determined that Dorothy be physically strong, mentally challenged, obedient, civilized, honest, and resourceful, Willebrandt asserted that "Life has few petted darlings."[45] Dorothy would not be one of them. She had Dorothy join her in her cold bath in the morning. When she was a few years older, a little sleeping tent was extended from her bedroom out onto a second floor porch. She was to eat what was placed before her. Warned when she asked for a glass of buttermilk that she might not like it and would have to drink it all, Dorothy wryly recounted "it wouldn't be like mother to give me a little glass."[46] When Dorothy balked at eating her spinach at lunch in the Senate dining room, Willebrandt excused them both, took her off for a brief talk and spanking, and returned. When Dorothy remained recalcitrant, the scene was repeated and repeated again until the spinach was consumed. Willebrandt always recounted that adventure with particular relish, since spinach became Dorothy's favorite food. Should Dorothy prove reluctant to eat, she did not hesitate to cut off all food until she was hungry enough to eat without protest.[47]

At bedtime, she tried to help Dorothy adjust to her new surroundings by placing a little music box beside her in the crib. When Dorothy adventurously scaled the crib sides to toddle over to her mother's bed for company, Willebrandt cured the practice by the strategem of lowering the sides and removing the challenge.[48]

In trying to impose a routine for Dorothy when she was not at home, Willebrandt ran into the problem of the "aunts" and particularly the warmth of Aunt "Weezie" Stanley. She also faced the strong will of Dorothy, reporting that the three-year-old "has infinite capacity for naughtiness and *absorbs* punishment and it takes a good deal to shape habits." Sometimes she would try isolating her in her room, but this generally proved ineffective.[49] Continually frustrated by the problem of time, she wrote in the margin of *As the Twig Is Bent* next to advice on setting a routine: "A mother in a home over and over." Worried about the speed at which Dorothy's mind was developing, she searched for a nursery school to provide the education that she could not schedule at home. She rejected a Montessori school as "not satisfying," and finally settled on Miss Tuthill's school in 1927, beginning a career for Dorothy that would take her to the Friends School in Washington, the Sacred Heart nuns, brief stints in the California public schools, Principio in St. Louis, and finally the Madeira School in Virginia.[50]

She also concentrated on Dorothy's emotional development. Willebrandt wanted her to be both strong and loving. On one visit to Alderson prison, Dorothy was knocked down by a large dog and a "big chunk" gouged from her head. Terrified, she remembered standing screaming under a shower with blood coursing down her head while her mother spanked her because she was screaming.[51] Yet, Willebrandt could be warm as well as stern. She worried at Dorothy's quiet withdrawal, writing: "I'm loving Dorothy so. She's a real joy. I wish she talked a little more. She doesn't express her emotions much, except in response to her kitty."[52]

Planning her Chautauqua tour in 1926, Mabel urged her parents to join her so that they might enjoy getting to know Dorothy and vacationing in the green New York countryside. Failing that, she hoped for a rendezvous at the Bar Association convention at Estes Park, Colorado. Finally, she considered sending Dorothy out to visit them. Her letter revealed domestic life in the Willebrandt home in Washington, as she wrote of Dorothy:

> She is no trouble; but that means that discipline is never relaxed. She is a loving little thing, and as bright as she can be; but she needs an iron hand, and she shows the effect of spoiling quicker than any child I ever saw. I fear if I did send her back she would get "choosey" and think her wishes had to be consulted above everything else, and lose some of her self-reliance. As it is, she now not only takes her own bath, but she fixes my bed and wakes me up and brings me my glasses of water and gets my shoes out and helps me dress and feels a responsibility for keeping our clothes closet in order, all the shoes in a row, and a lot of

things like that, that I think are very good for her. She could easily be a little tyrant if she were spoiled. Dr. Stanley is inclined to stop and listen to her demands, and you ought to see the way Dorothy will order her around, if she can—and she usually can. She has quite a different attitude toward me. She loves me just as much—more, in fact, I think—but she doesn't try to tell me to get up when I am reading a book and go and get her a pencil, the way she demands her Aunt Louise to do. I have a sneaking suspicion that she would "bully" her grandmother in a good deal the same fashion she does her Aunt Louise; and if she did, you would get awfully tired of her.[53]

The Walkers opted for a later California visit and Mabel took Dorothy with her on the Chautauqua tour "to get acquainted." She was delighted with her progress:

She's just developing imagination. She insists a kitty cat goes with her everywhere and that it's white. This morning she came into breakfast looking backward and talking to it and insisting it followed. Then she said, "I can't smile at a kitty cat. I got look like Mudder does" at which she rolled her eyes and frowned the way I do at her when I punish. She then related the reasons she couldn't smile and loaded off on the imaginary kitty cat the whole list of things she had been punished for. She said: "It get in a chockalets; it touched rings on a table; it didn't keep its word to her, it didn't go to sleep and it broke the laws."[54]

To housemate Annabel Matthews, she related driving through a pelting New York rainstorm with Dorothy philosophizing and asking, "Do you like the sun or rain, Mudder?" Mabel reflected, "I thought the comparison was good. She is developing so rapidly. Maybe not so much as that before I never was with her continuously day after day. But I am constantly marveling at her vocabulary. . . . Everyone thinks she's marvelous."[55]

Their schedule on the road called for sleeping until eight o'clock. They spent the day together. By seven o'clock Dorothy had eaten and was put to bed, while Mabel dressed for the lecture. She generally was "dead asleep" before her mother left. One evening, when Dorothy had been sent upstairs to get ready for bed, her mother stayed in the dining room finishing her coffee. She noticed amused glances fixed on the stairs where a stark naked Dorothy announced that she could not find her pajamas. Unperturbed, Mabel reminded her where they were and finished her coffee.[56] On this trip, Mabel again thought about adopting another child, even considering one little boy she visited on the tour; again, she was deterred by money as well as an unsettled future.

At the end of the summer, Dorothy did have her visit with the Walkers. She reveled in the simplicity and the easier routine of Temple City and loved strolling with her grandfather in the afternoons and racing in terror from the "giant" trolley cars plunging down the street. He built her a swing for lazy summer afternoons. Mrs. Walker gave her an egg beater and a little iron to play with. Even better were a few remaining chickens. On the train home, Mabel reported that Dorothy was melodramatically describing the dismantling of the swing and the loneliness of her grandparents at her departure.[57]

After the crucial months when she was campaigning for the Republican ticket in 1928, Mabel again turned to her parents for help with Dorothy. She worried about her absence and the warm but yielding substitute-mothering of Dr. Stanley. She pleaded:

> I feel wretched to add to your burdens, but you could *never* do so much for me in any other way as helping me again with Dorothy. You see she is uncommonly intuitive and I have been so distraught this winter that she and her training have suffered. I am sorry. Please help me get her back to sweetness and quietness again and thoughtfulness and good manners.
>
> As Rose says, "You have to speak right firm to her!" Please try to make her tell her faults. . . .
>
> She has, I'm sure, resented the fact that I've had no time for her. She needs reading and every night wanted to read to me—partly to stay up and partly to get the story too.
>
> Please love her for me—into sweetness again—but *please* be strict with her. Papa, you have no idea what a lasting impression your severity and companionship meant to me. Won't you *please* help to impress Dorothy too.

She added her concern that Fred Horowitz, who had escorted Dorothy on the long train ride from Washington to Los Angeles, and the Walkers had "become disillusioned as to what it meant to care for a child of six."[58] She urged her parents to help Fred learn to like Dorothy again, for Mabel was considering marriage with her long-time friend and associate.

Fred Horowitz, who had been Mabel's faithful stand-in with her parents, was also, as he expressed it, "crazy about her."[59] During much of the 1920s, they enjoyed her parents, shared investments, and considered marrying. Mrs. Walker loved Fred as a son and encouraged any signs of a marriage. Her letters to Mabel were full of his kindness and care.

During Mabel's first winter in Washington, when rain and floods inundated San Gabriel and cut telephone service for a week, Fred drove out to check on the Walkers. When his car mired in the mud he rented another, determined to get through. Mrs. Walker reported, "That is the kind of faithful friend Fred Horowitz is."[60] When the chicken dust touched off his asthma, Fred persevered and helped set thermostats for the brooders. Mrs. Walker exclaimed, "It was just as though we had adopted him and *we love him for it.*"[61] In the summer of 1923, when Horowitz visited the Walkers after his vacation, Mrs. Walker lyricized: "He is a magnificent looking man. Tall and big [with] his dark hair and eyes and his fine sensitive mouth. He is tanned now and it is really becoming." She envisioned Mabel smiling and saying, "Mama is sure dippy about Fred," and admitted "I guess I am but so is your Papa."[62]

Horowitz not only helped the Walkers arrange for the subdivision of their property but shared his excitement over his real estate ventures and offered investment suggestions. While he was making $10,000 a year in his law practice, Mrs. Walker observed, he could have made $25,000 in real estate.

Through Willebrandt's visits to California and Horowitz's to Washington and through letters, they tried to keep their close relationship. Willebrandt was the more faithful correspondent and worried when she did not hear from him. In her Christmas letter to her parents, she reflected on her marriage and her friendship with Fred:

> My nature with my dear friends is garrulous. I open the door and invite them right into my thoughts and heart. He doesn't. He locks his closest friends outside and when outside one wonders what goes on within. When you sit beside a friend like a deep pool you wonder whether lovely caverns of philosophy and reasoning and pouring springs of spiritual faith keep it pure or whether it's just a rocky container with no surprises worth the diver's trouble and risk! Of course you, Mama, always see what you want to see where you can't see anything! But I just say I don't know! I never again will build my faith in the existence of *anything* unseen since I built and lost on the evidence of something interesting behind an implacable mental exterior in A.F.W. The torture was too nasty to live around when there was no intellectual contact or intimacy—like fishing in a frozen sea. But I couldn't stop fishing.

She ended; "Where a life is so fine and pure or withal virile as his, there's got to be a hidden spring—and it's a shame for him to keep his friends outside!"[63]

Five months later, in May 1923, she sought news of Fred from her mother: "I know he's making lots of money. I always knew he'd do that, but *is* he storing up things in his personal and intellectual and spiritual life to 'retire' on when he gets old besides money?"[64] Still later, Mabel wrote home:

> I am trying so hard to get hold of myself. I try to read my lesson [Christian Science] but I am all shattered. I weigh less than I have for 15 years. I know I am at fault. I am in danger of losing my contact with God. I have permitted my study of science to re-volve too much about Fred. We've studied together. He has a lovely spiritual understanding and force and has helped me more than you can know or guess and it breaks my heart to have him turn aside from the best side of himself or stultify his spiritual powers. I want him to be happy, manly, fine and a leader as he can be. Mama, won't you hold me and won't you hold Fred in loving thought when you study your lessons.[65]

Her anxious mother immediately wrote to Fred, quoting Mabel's letter and questioning: "I wonder if you are standing at the crossroad of your spiritual life?" She urged him to "follow the road that leads to life."[66]

Separated by distance and different careers, they temporarily drifted apart. Mrs. Walker wrote of Fred's increasing attention to their friend Winnie Ellis. She worried that Mabel might be drawn to an eastern marriage and warned:

> I hope you will be very careful should you decide to marry. Some way I do not believe you would be happy to change into a cold eastern woman who simply loved to wield power. To be sure you might marry a man who would be an aristocrat by birth and training who would surround you with an atmosphere of culture and if you would be happy in that atmosphere I would rejoice in your happiness; but if your heart was in the west, if the west called you, it seems so foolish for you to attempt to make *yourself* over, to "change inside." . . .
> Back here among your friends who really love you for your-self might bring you more real happiness than some other place without *real* friends. If you could be happier with the compan-ionship of a husband I would love to see you marry, but re-member this, there are many fine *western* men.[67]

In the autumn of 1924, Fred Horowitz journeyed to Washington to try to settle their future. Mabel reported home: "He's so much more mature than he used to be, has so much greater self control and thinks a lot more. For all of these things I love him more dearly. But our aims and interests and mode of life are widely divergent I fear."[68] She did believe that for the first time he "really *saw*" her life and career. Before, he had been "superior" and held her work "in a kind of contempt." She was grateful that he knew the "magnitude of my *power* and the graceful things in the life" around her. She tried to persuade him to leave his practice and undertake some important prosecutions for the Justice Department, worrying that "the most deadly characteristic one can harbor is lack of interest—or a feeling of self-satisfaction."[69] During Coolidge's election celebration in November 1924, she feted Fred and managed to introduce him to the president. Fred left only more determined to find a way to end their separation. He set the next year as a trial period.

In the summer he met Mabel in Michigan to see Dorothy and to be part of her decision on the adoption. In November he asked her to reach a decision on marriage. Mabel's response was frank and poignant:

> The year is up and you rightly ask for a final reply. I do not question your demand. . . . For several months I have increasingly known that it must be as it is—I am *afraid*; I cannot feel sure that your love and satisfaction with our marriage will last in spite of the strain social conditions and other circumstances out of my control will put upon such a relationship as ours. In fact I feel so brokenheartedly sure that however high and sure your faith is now it will not survive the storms into which we head.
>
> White butterflies—out to sea! Perhaps you won't understand —now. . . . You haven't in the past, but . . . for you and I there will always be the dearest tenderness and oh, I give you if you care to take, a love that's more than possessing.
>
> . . . this year for me has been more hard than I think you know, to love an expanding "you" increasingly and yet increasingly feel I dare not trust it—dear, dear, good night.[70]

They decided to persevere in their old relationship. In May 1926, Mabel opened a Los Angeles office with Fred and an associate, George F. Baker. She urged her parents not to put any interpretation on it. She just wanted to practice with Fred because they combined the qualities that could make a great law firm and because she liked "the idea of returning to what I left."[71]

Seeing Fred at her Christmas visit home in 1926, she again mused on the possibility of marriage, writing to her parents en route to Washington:

> . . . if my marriage could be a private affair in my life the way it was for a man. . . . Unfortunately the things I most prize are tenderness and intellectual challenge. I don't seem to find *both* in any one so far. There's been but one I could care enough for to think it thru, I think you both know whom I mean and yet after much thrashing it out I'm certain his friendship means more to me than his possession. And with all the strains such a marriage would induce I fear the high quality of friendship and comradeship would die. So that is decided. Indecision wrecks me. . . . If we are of the calibre I think there will be no interruption in the finest part of an association filling now nearly 12 years of my life.[72]

The decision brought "a great inner peace of mind for I know so surely *what* I want." She wanted the capital to have a home and children and to protect against physical disability in the future. She also knew she would never be content to "marry that capital." She explained: "It has been a sort of inferiority complex I've had always over making money and for the sense of victory it would give me, I want to make it myself—especially since there's no such thing as getting it out of a clear sky with no donor attached!"[73] Finally, she concluded, it was not fair to Fred to just let things drift.

Fred visited Washington in the spring of 1927 to hear Mabel argue a case before the Supreme Court and returned the following March for the inauguration of Herbert Hoover. Again, Mabel and he discussed marriage. This time the failure of some Horowitz investments complicated the issue, particularly the failure of the Chateau Marmont, which he had built on Sunset Boulevard. Mabel's friends Winnie Ellis and Laura Jane Emery had invested in it and partially blamed Fred for their loss.[74] They charged that he did not live up to his agreements. Mrs. Walker urged Mabel to keep her faith in Fred. Her father, in a rare letter, reviewed the entire relationship, writing:

> You seem to complain and be puzzled why Fred had not been more frank or definite of late. By way of clearing the situation, do you realize how many times you have slighted or even snubbed his attentions? In the press of business or your habitual mad rush from one angle to another you may not have realized your apparent indifference or slight when he had come all the way to Washington.[75]

Winnie had alleged that Mabel had "found fault" with Fred's religion and name. Her father admonished: "Stop and think, whether he is not justified after these rebuffs" in being cautious. He urged her to discuss their differences and finally reach an understanding.

In the difficult spring months of 1929, when Mabel was considering her resignation, she won an appointment for financially beleaguered Fred Horowitz as a special prosecutor in some Texas mail fraud cases for the Justice Department. In her own frustration after the draining campaign of 1928, she again considered and finally decided against marriage to Fred.[76] Writing to Mabel earlier, Maud Hubbard Brown had presciently observed: "I've never seen a man yet that was in your class—maybe there is one, but he's never met me. I've wondered if you ever did meet one whose qualities you really admired—outside of your dad."[77]

While trying to maintain her family life and grappling with her own marriage dilemma, Mabel Walker Willebrandt also lived a full professional and social life. One of her oldest California friends, Laura Jane Emery, concluded: "Truth is, I think, she never belonged really to any one. She belonged to her *career*. Through her success she paved the way for other women lawyers. They all, indeed, owe her a great debt. For us, her friends, we cherish her friendship."[78]

As Willebrandt built a network of women's organizations in the struggle to establish Alderson and Chillicothe prisons, she also worked consistently to advance the careers of women lawyers. Her major vehicle was Phi Delta Delta, the women's legal fraternity. The fledgling group had gradually built chapters in the Midwest and East, a slow process, since there were less than a dozen law schools in the United States with the requisite five women students to initiate a chapter. Willebrandt developed strong friendships with founders Georgia Bullock, municipal court judge in Los Angeles, and Sarah Patten, who married Professor Frank Doherty, Willebrandt's political mentor. Other friends included Litta Belle Hibben, who married law professor Kemper Campbell, in whose office Arthur Willebrandt clerked for a brief time, Myra Dell Grether Collins, Winnifred Ellis, and judges May Lahey and Orfa Jean Shontz.[79]

In 1922, with fourteen chapters and more than 180 members, including "nearly all of the well-known women lawyers in the country," Phi Delta Delta chose Mabel Walker Willebrandt as national president. In the midst of her other responsibilities, she characteristically worked hard to expand the organization and to promote the Phi Deltas. Readying for the 1924 convention in Washington, where she had arranged to take over the national headquarters of the General Federation of Women's Clubs for the Phi Delta meeting, a weary Willebrandt wrote home: "I dread it—the girls seem awfully *young* to me now and I'm out of touch with their college but I'll try to make it a success."[80]

Always ready with her encouragement and support for those willing to work for an education, Willebrandt launched the Phi Delta Delta endowment fund for scholarships. For those who had completed their degree, the Phi Delta Delta leadership was alert to opportunities. Louise Foster, in her third year at the George Washington School of Law, responded to a call from Willebrandt to the Zeta chapter asking if there were any members who wanted a position in the Justice Department. Foster interviewed for the job, secured the congressional backing that Willebrandt noted was essential, and began to work. Serving in Willebrandt's division, she also became editor of the Phi Delta Delta magazine and was able to supply her with introductions to Delta members in other parts of the country on her Justice Department trips.[81] In 1926, when she went to receive an honorary degree and to give an address at the dedication of the new building of the University of Southern California College of Law, Willebrandt made certain to build room in her crowded schedule of speeches and meetings for a session with the two Los Angeles Phi Delta chapters. In that same year, as she left the presidency, grateful Phi Delta Delta members voted her honorary president for life.[82]

At the 1928 convention, Willebrandt, her good friend and new national president Grace Knoeller, and Louise Foster initiated the first Phi Delta Delta breakfast at the American Bar Association convention. Phi Deltas were instructed to invite their partners from the ABA dance to the fraternity's eight o'clock breakfast the next morning. Their more distinguished male colleagues were targeted. When Willebrandt discovered that neither she nor Grace Knoeller had invited Dean Roscoe Pound, she instructed Knoeller, at 6:00 A.M., to call him up. A sleepy and somewhat disgruntled Pound was roused, soothed by Willebrandt, and snared for the breakfast.[83]

While the breakfast was one effort to integrate women lawyers more fully into the male network, Willebrandt worked hard to ensure a good attendance by the outstanding Phi Deltas at the convention, always held in conjunction with the ABA annual gathering. Typical was her exhortation to Judge Georgia P. Bullock: "I think it is a real duty for women who are holding high positions to come to the American Bar Association, so as to accustom the leading men lawyers to the fact that women lawyers holding splendid positions, or particularly successful in practice, are not 'queer.' . . . You owe it to yourself to come and to the younger girls for the inspiration you would be to them. By this time your subpoena has arrived—please obey it."[84]

While she was president of Phi Delta Delta, Willebrandt was active in other professional groups and a popular and frequent lecturer on women and the law. In 1924 she chaired the Committee on Criminal Law and Criminology of the Women Lawyers' Association. She joined Judge Florence Allen of Ohio in giving the 1923–24 series of law lectures at the Brooklyn Institute. In one address, "Some Observations of Women and the Field of Law," she tried to summarize her advice and cautions. Particularly, she warned women against entering the study of law when too young or inexperienced. The most successful lawyers were those who had taught, been secretaries, or held positions in business. A young woman professional had to sell herself; that took maturity and experience. Above all, she stressed her own formula: diligence, character, and "work, work, work." On the back of the text she scribbled a note reflecting her own experience: "When you reach a place of measurable success in business or professional life, the curiosity makes you like being a circus performer walking a tight rope at the top of the tent, and every step of the trip is a fight against insistent influences that try to sidetrack you, minimize your worth and make you angry."[85]

She later generalized her advice for women in a spirited article in the February 1930 issue of *The Smart Set*, "Give Women a Fighting Chance!" She took the offensive in the first sentence, asserting: "Women have no fair chance in the business world yet. To say that they have is just 'Pollyanna talk!'" Observing that "the world has too long regarded woman primarily in the light of her sex value to the race and to men," she compared the path to success for boys and girls:

> A boy must just do the job well, and develop personality.
> A girl must do the job well and develop personality. PLUS—
> Break down skepticism about her ability.
> Walk the tight-rope of sexlessness without loss of her essential charm.
> Keep up an impersonal fight against constant efforts to sidetrack her.
> Devote extra work and thought to making an opportunity out of every little opening.

Make the hard choice between giving up children and home-life in order to advance, or having them in the face of increased prejudice.

And lastly, maintain a cheerful and normal outlook on life and its adjustments in spite of her handicaps.

Career and home were possible, but only if the husband gave up the time-worn theory, "my wife mustn't work for another man." It was that attitude and the subsequent "imprisoning" of an educated, experienced woman in an apartment, with no outlet for her energy or ability, that led to divorce. She argued that "those women who are quietly, unostentatiously and successfully combining marriage and career are real pioneers. It is cruel that the world should exact of the girl who tries to climb up in business or profession the sacrifice of home and children."[86]

On the job, a woman would certainly face "the lash of intangible prejudices," but she must not give up. "There is nothing more futile than the impotent anger of a weak man who cannot fight, unless it is the anger of a woman whom the world will not let fight." In occupations usually reserved to men, women had to maintain a "discriminating balance between womanly charm and professional strength and aggressiveness."[87] She ended with a formula for success:

Handle money, control its investment, as well as its expenditure.

Be charming but impersonal in office and conduct.

Take when desired, both marriage and business life, and dispel criticism by making both successful.

Live at all times up to the high plane of being the "exceptional woman."

Refrain from argument on the woman question.

Keep a sense of humor.

Love people, especially the men, in spite of their foibles.[88]

She acknowledged that the woman who succeeded was "bound to look back with yearning and perhaps with regret at dead hopes—the boy she loved but rejected because in his masculine egotism he demanded without understanding her free spirit's sacrifice—the children she might have had—the companionship she missed." It would be a long road, but the next generation would find it easier because of the "exceptional women who brave ridicule, and because of the men who stand by them in braving it too."[89]

She accepted as many invitations to speak before women's and professional groups as possible, speaking to the WCTU, League of

Women Voters, the National Woman's party, the Women's Section of the American Bankers Association, and at Vassar and Wellesley. In May 1925, she particularly relished addressing the student body of Columbia Law School, since "they've never permitted women at the law school, and do not yet."[90]

Beyond bringing competent women into the Justice Department, Willebrandt tried to spur women's progress in other areas of government service. She became a good friend of Civil Service Commissioner Helen H. Gardener and joined her effort "to keep the inspiring types of women in the offices that count."[91] Her approach is reflected in a letter to the IRS solicitor A.W. Gregg: "I am not trying to press the suggestion other than to just put them at some post where if they make good you will have an opportunity to know it and advance them on merit only. After all, about all any of us who are ambitious and willing to work want is an opportunity." She then specifically urged his appointment of Annabel Matthews, stressing her dignity, reliability, brains, discretion, and poise.[92]

She was equally tenacious in fighting for equity and recognition of merit in the lower echelons. When the special attorney White Miller was preparing the Savannah case he requested a "male" stenographer, though a "reliable female" would probably charge half as much. Willebrandt wrote back approving a stenographer, male or female. Miller responded: "Prefer man for this particular work pending which may arrange differently for future service." The approval was made for a male or female at the same rate for either of $1,800 per annum.[93]

While working for the advancement of women in the profession, Willebrandt continued to support women's issues from her position in the Justice Department. She backed a League of Women Voters measure to transfer the Interdepartmental Social Hygiene Board to the Justice Department. She urged approval of the transfer by Attorney General Daugherty explaining that the board, which dispatched undercover agents to collect evidence on venereal disease and prostitution to prod local officials to action, did not deal in maudlin sympathy over the "fallen women" and their "rescue" but accepted prostitution as a fact. The board had been effective in wartime and could continue to help communities. She reassured Daugherty that she had "no political ax" to grind. She was not a member of the League of Women Voters and added: "I do not particularly sympathize with quasi-political bodies organized along sex lines. I have no political friends on the Social Hygiene Board. My views are prompted by the fact that I came in contact with the postwar work of this Bureau in Los Angeles, and I pronounce it good. I am further not unmindful that when I go before women's organizations, it is a talking point I can effectively and conscientiously use."[94]

She viewed her major triumph in the area of women's issues as the changed position of the Justice Department on the legal question of community property in California. Again persuading Daugherty, she summarized her "years of labor without any remuneration" fighting with women's organizations in California for revisions in the community property law. The *Blum* v. *Wardell* decision of the Supreme Court of California had finally upheld the right of husbands and wives to file separate income tax returns and accepted the position that the wife did have a vested interest in the community property during marriage. If the Justice Department chose not to fight but accepted the Wardell decision, the federal government might have to return taxes "to the tune of several million dollars," but it would safeguard the inherent property rights of the wives of California. In October 1924, Willebrandt wrote to her mother: "Hurrah—the most wonderful news. The A.G. has today just shown me his concurring opinion upholding my Com. Prop. opinion. Isn't that a vindication of all those years of work that I spent on the Community Property Question in California. . . . His opinion, constantly refers to mine of March 8th and ends by reaffirming and reissuing it. . . . Aren't you just happy with me tonight? I feel you *must* know how gratified I am." The fiscal magnitude of her accomplishment was noted in a later *New York Times* article that suggested the decision would cost the Treasury Department $77 million.[95]

Once women had full legal rights, Willebrandt believed that they should and would "make it on their own." In a *New York Herald Tribune* interview, she stressed: "Sex is not the barrier; it is temperament. There are weak sisters among the men just as there are among the women." Women should lead the way in ending sex discrimination in business and the professions: "Not by mannishness, that only confesses weakness. It is preposterous because it is parody; but professional women . . . can lead by accepting and insisting on a fair field for all, with no particular favors to the fair."[96]

Willebrandt was painfully aware of the problem of being a successful woman in a generally male profession and the difficulty of following her advice in achieving a "balance between womanly charm and professional strength and aggressiveness." She recounted her experience in addressing the Women's Bar Association and their guests, the men of the New York Bar Association, in March 1922. She particularly enjoyed the evening because she sat next to Judge Learned Hand, "a most likeable individual," but she exclaimed in frustration: "These doggone Easterners seem to think that a woman can't get over the 'girlie girlie' stuff." At the end of her remarks when she was working her way down the long line of handshakers,

> a little man came rushing up to the front of the table. His head just came to the top of it, since I was standing on the platform. He reached his hand up and said, "I do want to shake hands with you because I just mustn't leave without telling you that you have the most wonderful eyes I have ever seen in a human head. They are perfectly wonderful."
> I guess about that time my eyes were expressing a few things at him because he quickly exclaimed, "Oh, don't misjudge me. I'm an old man with four daughters of my own, and am president of the Brooklyn Bar Association of 1100 members, but I have never seen such remarkable eyes as yours."
> I was a little surly, I guess, because I said very promptly, "I wish my eyes would do the talking in these after dinner speeches, I'm not very strong for doing it myself."

The press account described the "beautiful picture" she made in "a black spangled gown," and noted she "laid a silken scarf aside as she arose to speak." Her remarks were then reported. Willebrandt grumbled: "Why the devil they have to put on that 'girlie girlie' tea party description every time they tell anything a professional woman does, is more than I can see."[97]

Adding to her discomfort, Winnie Ellis's sweetheart had sent violets to Willebrandt before her speech which she "would just as soon wear" than "as get up and sing a song at the beginning of my speech." She exclaimed, "Why the devil they can't when they ask me to do something professional, treat me like a professional man, I don't know. Any pride I might have had in the speech I delivered was well toned down by the 'beautiful eyes and the silken scarf and violets.'"[98]

Her annoyance and frustration were particularly acute because her wardrobe was a key device in her effort to identify her professional and personal roles. In the office or in court appearances, she dressed in dark, tailored suits with a carefully selected blouse softening the effect. For her Supreme Court appearances, she added a black pin-striped suit, observing with a chuckle as she joined her male colleagues in their matching pinstripes, that she was now "in uniform." On the job, her dress was to be both businesslike and feminine. At home, she changed the image. Novelist Frances Parkinson Keyes, arriving to interview Willebrandt for the series "Homes of Outstanding American Women" reported "in her own home she changes to dainty and exquisite dresses, soft drapes, with a flower, at waist or shoulder." Keyes exclaimed: "How lovely she looks!"[99] Willebrandt obviously tried to establish clear divisions. Violets at home or worn at a dance were perfectly acceptable; she had no intention of wearing them for a professional occasion.

Yet her official and social life inevitably merged. She described the last dinner meeting of the "Baby Cabinet" at the end of the Coolidge administration, when all twenty-seven men paid "the loveliest tributes" to their lone woman colleague. Willebrandt responded: "For 7 years I have sat with you. The spirit that made you take me in, making me at all times without mawkishness feel one of you has been fine. It has not always been easy, I know full well, not without sacrifice for your inclination and convenience, but it has not gone unnoticed by me, nor unappreciated. You have been generous and sportsmanly and I thank you."[100]

A single woman in an official, highly publicized position, Willebrandt faced "some awkward moments." Socially, this was compounded by her role in prohibition enforcement. She was careful to note that at Senator Spencer's party at the Amsterdam Hotel only gingerale was imbibed. Occasionally, she would be invited to a private dinner party where cocktails were served. While this violated the spirit of the law it was not against its letter. Throughout the life of the Eighteenth Amendment, however, Willebrandt did not drink. Much more complex was the question of her status as Mrs. Willebrandt. When she first arrived in Washington, she was separated from her husband; in 1924 the separation ended in divorce. Publicly, in the many interviews and stories on Willebrandt, Arthur Willebrandt is generally mentioned only through the University of Southern California years. He then disappears altogether or is a shadowy presence somewhere in California. Her friends in California were aware of her situation. In Washington, Willebrandt, in demand as an attractive woman and engaging guest, had a wide circle of male friends and colleagues and willing, congenial escorts. From evenings at the opera to dances at the elegant Sulgrave Club near Dupont Circle, she managed to achieve a social life of circumspection and fun.

Good friends and good conversation equaled a good time for Wil-

The "baby cabinet" of undersecretaries and assistants gather with their lone woman member.

lebrandt. In her friends she cherished loyalty, intelligence, generosity. She abhorred "lounge lizards" and small talk, observing: "When I listen to the prattle that a child of a few years could duplicate that most people call friendly conversation, I thank God for friends like the many I have, capable and interested to talk about the subjects of the day."[101]

During Christmas week 1922, she had dinner with the editor of the *Christian Science Monitor* and his wife. The next week she visited Justice and Mrs. Brandeis for tea. The writer Anne Hard poured. It was, Willebrandt exclaimed, "a den of radicals! Horrors!" In March she had lunch with Mary Roberts Rinehart, Mrs. Herbert Hoover, and Mrs. George H. Lorimer, wife of the editor of the *Saturday Evening Post* and "a live wire in Republican politics." One Thanksgiving, she was forced to choose between invitations to dinner from Chief Justice Taft and Justice Brandeis.[102]

Her White House visits increased through the decade. Just after Christmas 1924, she was among forty guests enjoying a musical evening with the Coolidges and reported "being in a transport of delight" at the concert. Within a month, she recorded: "Really I've been invited to the White House so often lately and all the officials are so fine to me that I can't help having a grudging enjoyment of it all. I know I've earned it, for I received *less* recognition from official Washington" in earlier years. Two years later she enjoyed impressing a California friend, Florence Woodhead, and one of her first clients by taking them to the south entrance for a White House reception, an entrance reserved for Supreme Court justices and cabinet and subcabinet officers.[103]

Willebrandt liked to entertain, but her apartment and limited budget made it difficult. For companionship, protection, and economy, she generally shared her home with women friends. In her first two years in Washington, she had been joined by her Phi Delta Delta friend Winnifred Ellis. Later, when Willebrandt shared a generous two-story shingle house on 18th Street near Columbia Road, N.W., with fellow professionals Annabel Matthews and Dr. Louise Stanley, there was finally room to entertain, if she could find the time. One February, she decided at least to be "at home" for her friends. She explained to her parents:

> So many people asked when they could call that I put it in the paper I would be at home on the three Thursdays for the balance of this month. After testifying at the Judiciary Committee on

increased penalties for violations of the Volstead Act that are also
violations of the 18th Amendment, and working on a tax brief I
dashed up home at the last minute to be "at home." I had not
sent out any cards. It had just been in the newspaper that my
friends might call, and Rose was right when she said, "I guess
there'll be plenty here all right." I thought there wouldn't be
more than one or two, but they just piled in on me. Late in the
afternoon, when a good many of them were gone, Lady Isabelle
Howard, of the British Embassy came up and stayed over half
an hour just talking with me. . . . I was much embarrassed by
Dorothy coming in and saying to me, "Mother, dinner is ready
when this lady goes." And then turning to Lady Isabella, she
said, "Why don't you go home.?"[104]

Though occasionally, when it was still manageable size, she would
have the staff of her division to dinner, she preferred small affairs at
home. In March 1925, she entertained the wives of the justices of the
Supreme Court, several of the "nicest Senators' wives and some intel-
lectuals." She believed that the occasion went well but confided: "social things throw me in a panic. I'd give anything if I could have a *home*
and not mind the cost of just modest little groups for entertaining. For
there are so many people who I'd love to know personally and inti-
mately here—Many of real intellectuality, whom to know is to be
enriched and broadened. . . . But I have to let the overtures they make
go by for I can't keep them up. It wouldn't take so much money if one
had *time*, but not having that I can't afford to push the friendships."[105]

She extended her entertaining through her parents. Friends journey-
ing to California were invariably invited to the Walkers for an afternoon tea or dinner. Willebrandt carefully arranged the events from
Washington. Her thoughtfulness and attention to detail are evident in
her letter to her parents in May 1925 before the visit of the superintendent of prisons, Luther White.

Mr. White is a phi beta kappa from Dartmouth College, is a
discriminating reader, and has a wide acquaintance among
worth while people but is the simplest person in the world. He
is, however, a voracious smoker so do not forget to invite him to
smoke when you have him out for dinner. He'll have his own
cigarettes, but seeing none of you smoking may refrain and a
mark of your hospitality will be an early suggestion for him to
smoke when and as he pleases. . . . Ask Fred to bring him out in
the late afternoon when the twilight colors are so lovely on the
mountains. He can visit Winnie in midday where there's
shade![106]

Willebrandt loved to dance, particularly "if the man would really help to lead." In New York on department business, she joined Senator Seldon Spencer's party in the evening, having "two fat dances" with the Missouri senator on the Amsterdam Hotel roof and "more fat dances" later at the Plantation in Harlem. In a busy social and official season in January 1927, Willebrandt faced a dancing party almost every night. "Practically none of the time have I gotten to bed before two or three o'clock," she wrote to her parents, "except two or three evenings when I was able to fall asleep in front of the fire. . . . but I enjoyed it in spite of everything." After one dinner dance, she returned to the office and "worked most of the rest of the night on a brief."[107]

Willebrandt had grown up respecting the simple dignity and naturalness of her mother and father, yet like her mother she sometimes felt at a loss dealing with a particular kind of old money or old family. After a difficult speech at Wellesley, she reflected:

> Why is it certain things undermine me so—sap my self-confidence and put me into a perfect complex of inferiority. It's always to do with *money*. Wealth and family and social position make me shudder and want really to get in bed and cover up my head. I rebel so that some have them all without effort. I know the rebellion is wasteful & perhaps wicked, but I can't conquer it tho sometimes I ignore it and keep it from showing. It's pain and has always been. I remember suffering from it terribly when we first moved to K.C. . . .
> Their imported clothes, their soft voices, always repressed and proper, their scholastic conversations distress me so—and prevent all my best qualities from showing. I *contract* all over.[108]

Gradually, she tried to cut back her social engagements, confessing that pressure increased rather than diminished in spite of the fact that she kept "eliminating, eliminating, and eliminating," and finally accepted "practically no invitation except those from people that I just thoroughly like and regard as intimate friends or where I want to establish on the basis of intimate friendship." Her Easter letter to her parents in 1929 indicated her lack of success. She described breakfast as "elaborate formal and fine" at the home of the editor of the *Washington Post*, Ned McLean. In the afternoon she had tea with a new member of the Federal Farm Board from Minnesota. While she was writing in the evening, Annabel Matthews was preparing for some company downstairs—"eternal company!"[109]

From California, Willebrandt had the constant support of her family. Her mother had encouraged her: "Mabel, this is *one time* in your life *one wonderful time*. Grasp every moment and live it to the fullest." Weekly letters from her mother were full of pride and happiness at her accomplishments, though increasingly they revealed anxiety at her schedule. "There is only so much flesh and blood will stand," she warned.[110] Willebrandt relied heavily on this support and reported on her work, which would "surely cause you pride." She also sometimes felt that her parents were "too far away and Dorothy too young to have joy in my thoughts. We all want to feel our success *for* somebody."[111]

In 1927 she again urged her parents to join her on a Chautauqua tour, but had to settle for a vacation with them at Yellowstone Park. But in 1928 she persuaded them to come to Washington, drive through New England with her, and then join her at the Kansas City Republican National Convention. Willebrandt shared her life and schedule. Her parents visited her office, met Senators Curtis and Smoot and Speaker Nicholas Longworth, among others, watched Willebrandt appear before the Claims Committee to argue for an additional $40,000 for her division, and lunched in the Senate dining room with Victor Berger, the Milwaukee editor, and Congresswoman Florence Kahn of San Francisco. On her birthday, May 23, Willebrandt invited her staff and Attorney General Sargent to dinner. After the New England tour, the Walkers and daughter settled in at Kansas City for the convention. David Walker mingled with the disgruntled agricultural representatives, eavesdropped among the milling politicos, and visited Willebrandt's headquarters. He reported: "It was marvelous to see the system work she was so quietly planning and ably handling that finally swung the convention results just as she planned and desired."[112] But Willebrandt's achievement in aiding and securing the nomination of Herbert Hoover for president led to her participation in the 1928 campaign and the most desperate year of her life.

CHAPTER SIX

Political Campaigns in the 1920s

They left me in No Man's Land!

MABEL WALKER WILLEBRANDT
1928

No other woman has ever had so much influence upon a Presidential campaign as Mrs. Willebrandt has had upon this one.

The Gentleman at the Keyhole
"Where Duty Lies," *Collier's*,
October 27, 1928

*P*OLITICS in the 1920s has traditionally been assessed as an "unfortunate interregnum," "the Shame of the Babbitts," a decade when the progressive, imperial presidencies of Roosevelt and Wilson degenerated into the ineptitude and corruption of the Harding administration and the inactivity of Calvin Coolidge. The contemporary critic H.L. Mencken exasperatedly observed that Nero at least fiddled while Rome burned; Coolidge only snored. The triumphant "Golden Glow" of business prosperity and the alleged revolution in manners and morals dwarfed the significance of political concerns. Only belatedly, after World War II, did historians reassess issues and leaders and conclude that the political history of the 1920s is a most exciting historical frontier.[1]

Yet while new studies have upgraded Harding's effectiveness, depicted Coolidge as a master image politician, affirmed Hoover's progressive credentials, found women, blacks, and social workers experiencing the "seedtime of reform," the dominant political reality is reaffirmed. Cultural issues divided Americans. Immigration restriction, the Scopes "monkey" trial, revivalists' crusades, blue laws, Klan rallies, and the dry crusade were the anxious assault of rural, Protestant, old-stock America on the worrying reality of the census data of 1920. For the first time, more Americans lived in cities than in the countryside. The specter of dominating city machines and an urban, wet, immigrant citizenry fueled a series of rearguard actions. Political campaigns still mounted some old progressive battles on agricultural, labor, tariff, and power issues; Republican incumbents stressed prosperity and peace, but the fiercest battles were waged on cultural lines.[2]

Entering office as a progressive Republican and emerging by 1928 as "the embodiment of Prohibition," Mabel Walker Willebrandt was a significant participant in the increasingly turbulent campaigns. Loyal to the party, still hoping for the reward of a federal judgeship, avidly sought after as the highest ranking woman in government, she was repeatedly on the hustings. Her loyalty and fierce commitment and competitiveness in the 1928 battle would ruin her public and political career and devastate her private life. She was in the fight of her life.

Willebrandt's first major foray was in the congressional race of 1922. Progressive disaffection with the Harding administration promised a difficult Republican year. Fulfilling a personal commitment, she worked hard for the reelection to the Senate of her sponsor, Hiram Johnson. In October, she spoke for the Republican cause at meetings of the League of Women Voters in Minnesota and Ohio. At a Youngstown, Ohio, rally sponsored by the Women's Branch of the Republican party, she commended the leadership of Harding and Daugherty, the "greatness" of the GOP candidates, and reminded the newly enfranchised women: "It has been the Republican party that has looked after the health and welfare of the American household." Republican legislatures had labored for minimum wage laws, mothers' pensions, compulsory school laws; nationally, they had sponsored the Pure Food and Drug Act. A comparison of the Democratic and Republican records, she asserted, confirmed that the Republicans stood for "the ideals in which women are largely interested—the preservation of the home, safeguarding the educational and other rights of childhood, promotion of business and the establishment of economic security."[3]

Though the Republicans still controlled the new Congress in 1923, Willebrandt worried about the disarray in party ranks and assessed the strong showing of the progressive candidates of both parties. She wrote to her parents in March that if the labor unrest and progressive trend continued, "Harding has not the slightest chance of election." The party machinery remained firmly in the hands of "the ostrich-like reactionary elements," but only a progressive would "rally the tides of discontent surging away from Republican standards." While Harding might finally assume some leadership, she was doubtful that he would withstand the Republican insurgents' pressures to withdraw to prevent a Democratic victory. Indeed, she concluded, Harding, loving "the quiet life more than the White House" and faced with his wife's illness, might be content with retirement.[4]

Expecting a leadership change, she discussed her own future with the national committeewoman Mrs. Harriet Tayler Upton, particularly the possibility of appointment to a federal judgeship in California. Upton and Harry Daugherty concluded that with the unsettled political situation they "could not afford to shelve" her in a position where they would lose her campaigning in 1924. Complaining that this only added "complexity to an already complex situation," Willebrandt wrote that once she was certain that Harding would run again and left to her own "selfish desires," she would resign and build her private practice. She dreaded the prospect of a Harding campaign, unless the Democrats were "fools" in their nomination. Loyalty, "a matter of personal primary obligation," might force her to remain, but if Harding withdrew and Hoover was the candidate she had no such compunction, observing: "I owe nothing to Hoover and I do not have personal respect for him enough to do any campaigning."[5]

The sudden death of Harding in August 1923 and the presidency of Coolidge increased her dilemma. In November, Hiram Johnson announced his candidacy for president. Willebrandt believed that if he were nominated he could win and finally "unsaddle the party machinery."[6] She lamented his early announcement, since Coolidge could use his December message to Congress to "take the wind out of progressive sails." Again, she hoped that she might be spared the campaign by a judicial appointment. Her mother, responding to her dread of campaigning, urged her to "think a long time" before agreeing to the effort. If she won the judgeship, "well and good"; if not, she could come home and fight for "any true cause" among her California friends.[7]

In June 1924, Willebrandt had an opportunity to witness the selection of the Democratic opposition. William Jennings Bryan, "a fine cordial friend," gave her tickets to the national convention in Madison Square Garden. She watched his "dramatic and splendid figure" addressing the 18,000 delegates and spectators who "had been raised to fever pitch by the Catholic and Jewish gallery demonstrations for Al Smith, and the incendiary speeches for him from the platform delivered in as great intolerance of the K.K.K. as it was accused of representing toward them." Bryan was met by boos and cat-calls from "the Murphys and O'Learys" in the galleries, but he swung the vote for "temperance of judgement"[8] and avoided outright condemnation of the Klan in the Democratic platform.

Willebrandt judged it a good platform, particularly "the plank that about makes me a Democrat to wit: 'That capital and resources of the country shall be conscripted in times of war as well as the youth are for armies.' I think that would do more to stop future wars than anything else. It would *enlist capital* on the side of peace and largely take the profits out of wars."[9]

Leaving the Democrats, she boarded a train to Toronto for a convention of social workers. She was in a sober mood on the journey home to Washington. Riding through Pennsylvania, she reflected on the beauty of the countryside and the grim life of the coal miners living in the company houses straggling up the hillsides. Describing the scene, she wrote: "the earth all about is so lovely, yet they who work underground can have but a few tired hours of it. When will we learn sense and make manual labor of such deadening kinds short enough in hours to permit some fullness of life outside. Six hours is enough—and it is coming—but so slowly." She wondered "if all our fussing or speeches or agitation enter the womb of life *or* hurry its travail of progress." If the workers had limited working hours, would they leave the company houses, "*would* they move into the daisy patches?"[10]

As the 1924 presidential contests formed, Willebrandt's sympathies were clearly with the LaFollette-Wheeler Progressive ticket. An alliance of farmers, labor, Socialists, and reformers, the Progressives attacked the dominance of business, the conservatism of the courts, and the insensitivity of the two major parties to the concerns of workers. In "an attack of radical urge," Willebrandt reported, "every fiber responds to their campaign." Her preliminary assessment was that LaFollette would "make hay" against two Wall Street men. He would hurt the Republicans more than the Democrats. If he were successful enough to throw the election into the House of Representatives, she feared a victory by Democratic candidate John W. Davis. Though Davis was "an honorable and high type man," she thought his internationalist foreign policy was "very dangerous."[11]

At the Republican convention at Cleveland, Coolidge easily turned back the challenge of Hiram Johnson. Willebrandt was philosophical and looked for his good points, concluding that he was a typical New

Englander with "all of the good qualities and all of the liabilities." Though certainly not a dramatic candidate for the hustings, he was "steady, patriotic and sane, and above all a Christian man with high ideals."[12] Like a good soldier, she enlisted for the campaign, hoping for support in return. In September, she reported to her parents: "The Pres. has sent to confer with me tomorrow—Don't worry, that *doesn't overawe me*! But I *shall* put in an oar about some things for women in the way of US atty opportunities as well as for proper Prohibition handling of investigations."[13]

Once committed, her campaign schedule, combined with Supreme Court cases and office demands, was hectic. On October 16 and 17 she spoke at Springfield and Kansas City, Missouri; on the 22d, in New York City; on the 31st, at White Plains, New York; then Baltimore, West Virginia, and back to New York. She turned down engagements in Detroit, Toledo, Indianapolis, Cleveland, and Texas. In the last week in October, La Follette's camp tried to make an issue of her letter, critical of weak enforcement of prohibition, to the Law Enforcement League of Philadelphia. Obviously, the Progressives charged, Coolidge was responsible for this poor record. However, no issue, real or contrived, was able to stop the Coolidge victory. Willebrandt noted: "Coolidge is in and everyone is wondering what will happen next. Probably *nothing*—as per Coolidge!"[14]

In the next three years, she developed a correct, uneasy relationship with Coolidge.[15] She remained respectful of his integrity, exasperated by his caution, frustrated in her judicial hopes, and finally puzzled with other Americans as to the meaning of his cryptic 1927 pronouncement that he "did not choose" to run for reelection in 1928. Willebrandt believed it would develop that he was "playing a deep game."[16]

By 1928, Willebrandt was a seasoned campaigner, in demand as a speaker on prohibition and law enforcement and women's issues. Though her patron Hiram Johnson still referred to the leading Republican candidate Herbert Hoover as "the Great One," she had developed a friendship with the Hoovers in the Washington years that enabled her now to support this fellow Californian. She explained, "I do not regard Hoover as a spectacular man, but he is by all odds nearer a man of the people than can be gotten anywhere else." The choice of the Republicans was between Hoover and "some accidental demigod" who might emerge at the convention and who would be controlled by the financial interests.[17] In spite of Hoover's trickle-down theories and possible lack of vigor in prohibition enforcement, she believed he was marvelously efficient, had a good home life, and vision. Working herself up to it, she concluded that she was "really enthusiastic for his election."[18]

By early February, Willebrandt was a committed Hoover advocate. Hearing a rumor that Hoover had sent money to a Georgia organizer who "ought to be in the penitentiary," she loudly protested to one of Hoover's assistants, Walter Brown, and succeeded in funneling the funds to black committeeman Ben Davis. Davis, she argued, stood by his word, and "decent white folks could work with him."[19] Dinner with a young southern couple alerted her to Klan activities that were helping Hoover to make inroads into the solid South vote. She reported to Hoover's campaign leaders on Klan efforts to organize Louisiana for Hoover behind a New Orleans leader. Willebrandt took advantage of that dinner contact, observing, "Well, I made hay while the sun shone rapidly and in detail getting a great many practical suggestions and arranging for a good deal of work in Alabama, Mississippi and Florida."[20] On another level, she delivered the report of a friendly New Jersey federal judge who had spent a weekend with J.P. Morgan, Jr., observed his chilly reaction to Hoover, and made the suggestion that the candidate might woo the financier with a hint that he might consider appointing Dwight Morrow, Morgan's colleague and friend, as secretary of state.[21]

Willebrandt's endorsement of Hoover made headlines in April. Responding to a letter from Mrs. Ella A. Boole, national president of the WCTU, who asked if Hoover was an adequate prohibitionist, she wired, "he is the answer to those who said prohibition cannot be enforced."[22] Anti-Hoover Republicans and Democrats gleefully pointed out the logical implication that the Coolidge administration and perhaps her own department were currently failing. Was Willebrandt implying that she had been hamstrung? The Democrats suggested calling her before a Senate committee to testify, while the *Washington Post* noted that the Senate might reject that proposal, since Mrs. Willebrandt was "a very forceful person and might perhaps tell of the handicaps prohibition enforcement encounters in certain communities, a narrative that might have its embarrassments for members of Congress."[23] She curtly dismissed the minor tempest, asserting that "no honest construction of her words would impute criticism to Coolidge."[24]

In June, accompanied by her parents, Willebrandt arrived in Kansas City as a California delegate for Hoover at the Republican National

Convention. In a bout of preconvention campaigning, she spoke to a group of Stanford alumnae, the Women's Law Enforcement Committee, and presided at a Hoover mass meeting. The *New York Times* described her as "unexpectedly effective" and the "feminine feature" of the convention. Willebrandt commented: "I'm having a splendid time."[25] In recognition of her Hoover commitment, her campaigning, her prohibitionist credentials, and her possible influence on the women's vote, the Republicans named her the chairman of the credentials committee, the first woman to head a committee at a Republican convention. With sixty contested delegates and a stop-Hoover movement to contend with, it was a job that was more than window dressing.

Hoover was a dogged but uninspiring campaigner, and he spoke as infrequently as possible. As one contemporary observer noted, he "had no oratorical ability whatsoever!" His speeches in printed form proved "rhetorically cumbersome." He had lost in every primary where he contested a favorite son: Norris in Nebraska, Lowden in Illinois, Watson in Indiana, Goff in West Virginia. He had won in Ohio, but only when its favorite son, Senator Frank Willis, died just before the election. Yet his records on war relief and as food commissioner and secretary of commerce and his assiduous work for southern delegates brought him to the convention well ahead in the delegate count. Opponents Frank Lowden, Jim Watson, and Senator Charles Curtis of Kansas forged an uneasy alliance to try to stop his victory on the first ballot. There was also lingering uncertainty whether a draft-Coolidge move would emerge.[26]

Willebrandt, as permanent chairman of the credentials committee, conducted a marathon twelve-hour session. When the meeting adjourned at three in the morning, the judgment of the national committee had been followed in every contested case. Only in the Texas dispute was a minority report filed. Hoover was the heavy winner. With four hours' sleep, Willebrandt delivered the majority report to the convention. Focusing on the female phenomenon, the *New York Times* described her as "fresh and unruffled." Dressed "in her straight two-piece black georgette frock with crisp white collar and cuffs, her eyes clear and bright," she presented her report "in a clear resonant voice which carried to the utmost confines of the hall." *Time* magazine's language was saltier, citing her as "shapely, smartly dressed, full of vitality," speaking with a "strong voice and finishing with plenty of stingo." Watching from the gallery, her proud father reported that her ten-minute speech was a "marvel for clearness, logic, enunciation and articulation." It "captivated the crowd and carried her point." Later, during the victorious Hoover demonstration, she was seen as she was "jubilating near the platform in an evening gown with orchids quivering on the shoulder strap."[27]

A triumphant Willebrandt left the convention early for business in Chicago; her excited parents returned to California. She was immediately back in the press of official duties, some of which would also involve her in two major issues of the campaign.

For the first time since the Civil War, the Republicans hoped to make inroads into the Democratic bastion of the South. Black supporters were still generally loyal but blocked by poll taxes, grandfather clauses, and community pressures from casting a significant vote; southern whites, however, affronted by the candidacy of wet, Roman Catholic, Tammany Al Smith, might bolt to the GOP. The case of Perry Howard was closely watched for Republican intentions. Howard, a black Republican national committeeman from Mississippi and a former U.S. assistant attorney general, stood accused of "trafficking" in offices and soliciting money from federal office holders. Suspicions had been aroused in 1921 and charges lodged in 1925. Though Assistant Attorney General William Donovan urged that the case be sent to the grand jury, no action was taken except to try to persuade Howard to resign. When he declined, he was suspended. The charges stayed in the news with House and Senate calls for the report of the Justice Department's investigation and a request from the National Civil Service Reform League for some action by the attorney general.[28] Willebrandt reviewed the charges and recommended to the attorney general that "in the best interests of the service" Howard be dismissed. She cited investigative reports that disclosed that under Howard as national committeeman, postmasterships and other appointments in Mississippi were generally sold for money. Additionally, the files revealed that in 1925, while still in the Department of Justice, he received $5,000 from the Pullman Company in payment for his services—at a time when the Pullman porters were trying to win wage increases.[29]

When the Justice Department decided to prosecute Howard, Willebrandt journeyed to Biloxi to present the government's case in *United States* v. *Howard et al*. She won an indictment from the grand jury in July 1928. Howard's supporters charged that she had "used her feminine wiles and glamor" and denounced the indictment as "a Republican set up to win votes." Facing strong local opposition, Willebrandt arranged for a special assistant to the attorney general to aid the U.S. attorney in preparing the case. The date of the trial became an issue. The *New York Times* reported that Willebrandt expected an early trial. When there was still no date set in October, Willebrandt argued against a long continuance at a departmental conference, claiming she was tired of allegations that the trial was politically motivated as an attack on a black Republican to win southern white votes.[30] But the trial was not begun until well after the election. In March 1929, the U.S. attorney urged that the case be dropped, since the Biloxi community obviously did not want to try Howard and he was having great difficulty in developing a jury. Still insisting on prosecution, Willebrandt understood his problem in getting an unbiased jury and wired: "Use your best judgment. I'll back it up. I can't do any more."[31]

She was fully involved with the more significant campaign issue of prohibition. Willebrandt, having won the Biloxi indictment of Howard, had to fly to meet a commitment to speak before the annual meeting of the American Bar Association in Seattle. In her address, "The Government as Client," she challenged the audience of 1,500 lawyers on their tendency to excuse violations of the prohibition law, reminding them that their professional oath to uphold the Constitution made the government their first client. She wrote to her father about the reception:

> I had made up my mind to be sincere and talk about the danger of scoffing at law in the encouragement it gives crime in great cities. I knew it wouldn't be popular because the Bar Association is a drinking bunch and most of them had been to Vancouver that day. I went thru with it. I felt an adamant psychological wall as I spoke, but at the end about a third, maybe half the audience were with me and rose cheering. The rest had guilty consciences I guess. But many said afterward it was right and I felt it was myself and am glad I talked that way.[32]

Her remarks may have brought some discomfiture to her colleagues, but her actions brought banner headlines following the New York City padlock raids on twenty Broadway nightclubs and restaurants on the night of Al Smith's nomination by the Democratic National Convention in Houston. The *Washington Times* sensationalized Mrs. Willebrandt's "society manhunt with Federal officers armed with subpoenas scurrying hither and yon over Long Island and Park Avenue, dragging into court such society night club habitues as they could lay their hands on." The *Washington Herald* noted that Mrs. Willebrandt was in "sole command" as her dry army launched this latest campaign. Another "firecracker was tossed in the explosive liquor clean-up" at the report that Mrs. Willebrandt had evidence that would involve prominent New Yorkers in a nationwide conspiracy. If the first witnesses grilled did not provide enough evidence, the *Washington Times* reported, she had a reserve list of 5,000 known night-club patrons. The *New York Times Magazine* spotlighted "The Woman Behind the Night Club Raids," while the hostile *New York World* ran a poem, "Lines to Be Engraved on a Padlock":

> A girl I try to hate & can't
> Is Mabel Walker Willebrandt
> Her comely brow and nice expression
> Reflect so poorly her profession
>
> The others of her noxious craft
> Display (when they are photographed)
> The warped, the mean—vicious faces
> Of those who like to snoop in places
>
> . . . .
>
> At risk of sounding ungallant
> To Mabel Walker Willebrandt
> I hope that after March they'll get her
> A job that suits her features better.[33]

The Democrats predictably lashed out. Congresswoman Mary Norton of New Jersey complained that Mrs. Willebrandt was "using her office for political effect," and insisted that an eighth-grade child could see through the timing of the raids. In Washington a conference of New York Republican leaders huddled with Hoover and Willebrandt, prompting more accounts of the raids "engineered" by Mrs. Willebrandt. Speaking to the waiting press after the meeting, she was "plainly annoyed" by deductions that Hoover had called her "to account" and heatedly stated: "It is preposterous that Mr. Hoover or any other candidate for a high and dignified office . . . would presume to control a public officer in the discharge of official duties. Hoover had not done so." Her actions had not even been discussed.[34] In September, however, when Democratic Chairman Raskob charged that Willebrandt was planning raids in Albany the day of Smith's acceptance speech, she did confer with Hoover on the proper response. He told her not to worry.[35]

Behind the scenes in the New York situation, she acted to stop the Republican chairman, Hubert Work, from withdrawing forty men from their patrol of New York breweries at the request of state politicians. Pointing out that the men were civil service employees, she suggested the dangers of a possible press leak of an action that demonstrated "the most questionable political tactics."[36]

In September, after both candidates had made their traditional acceptance speeches, the campaigns were officially launched. Though Hubert Work had observed earlier, "Prohibition is not an issue, being merely a local matter and will not be allowed to enter the campaign," judged by the frequency with which prohibition was used in speeches and releases, it emerged as one, second only to prosperity.[37] The *New York Times* commented that Smith, in choosing the businessman John J. Raskob to dent the Republican prosperity issue, had ensured that prohibition would be more central in the campaign. But the contrasting positions of the two candidates and Smith's telegram to the Houston convention guaranteed that prohibition would be central in the campaign rhetoric. Responding to the dry-enforcement plank of the party, Smith wired:

> It is well known that I believe there should be fundamental changes in the present provisions for national prohibition. . . . while I fully appreciate that these changes can only be made by the people themselves through their elected representatives, I feel it to be the duty of the chosen leader of the people to point the way which in his opinion, leads us to a sane, sensible solution of a condition which, I am convinced, is entirely unsatisfactory to the great mass of our people.[38]

Specifically, Smith recommended fixing a higher maximum alcoholic content in beverages, to be set by the states, and an amendment restoring liquor control to the states while guarding against a return of the saloon.

The Republican platform pledged the party and nominees to "the observance and vigorous enforcement" of the Eighteenth Amendment, but there was full discussion by Hoover's advisers as to how that should be translated in the campaign. Senator Borah wanted to press for a state dispensary system. Assistant Attorney General William Donovan, Christian Herter, and other eastern Republicans believed that Hoover could win the industrial states only by taking a "less closed position" on prohibition. Mrs. Willebrandt represented to Hoover "the millions of women who had been through the non-Prohibition days" in rural and urban areas. Hoover explained that he "had promised all the women's organizations that he wouldn't move against prohibition." He believed that all the states west of the Mississippi would vote dry "anyway." The three campaign rules he issued to his followers seemed to waffle on the issue: (1) conduct a clean fight; (2) do not mention Smith's religion; (3) follow the lead of the community on prohibition.[39] It could be translated as be dry with drys and moist with wets. The marginal areas that would be testing grounds were the border states, Texas, Florida, and the mountain states.

Willebrandt, already a proven campaigner in the key border states and the Midwest, was dispatched to Ohio in September. She was apprehensive. En route she wrote to Chairman Work: "I seem to be a sort of storm center. In the minds of many I guess I personify 'Prohibition.' Apparently there is much difference of view as to campaign tactics on prohibition—and as a consequence diversity of view on whether I harm or help." She noted that she had promised three speeches in September and had been told by Congressman Newton of the Speakers Bureau at Chicago headquarters that he would book her for three weeks in October. She asserted: "However it is too hard work, and I'm too tired and obliged to work too hard to keep my official duties performed when I absent myself for speech-making to go to *sure* states or to little women's luncheon meetings." She cited pressure to speak in New Jersey, Massachusetts, and New York but observed, "still the view prevails in some quarters that I am an unwelcome speaker." She concluded:

> I have no desire except to help. But I refuse to be haggled over and thus contribute to the indecision and confusion of a hard campaign. Consequently, I am stating my reasons, and notifying you that I am withdrawing from any participation in the campaign. Please wire Congressman Newton that my name is to be withdrawn from speakers' lists. You can merely say that press of official duties makes it impossible for me to accept any speaking engagements whatsoever.[40]

It was in this frame of mind that she arrived at Springfield, Ohio, to speak to a conference of two thousand Methodist ministers. She began by reviewing the long, successful campaign of the Methodists to achieve the "state of mind" that won the Eighteenth Amendment. There were still "wilful sections" that did not accept the law. The worst area was New York City, ruled by Tammany and its underworld connections. As Tammany's governor, Smith had signed the state measure repealing its responsibility for enforcement; Tammany had "reared him, gave him power. Tammany's desires were his conviction." Smith's pledges of enforcement notwithstanding, she wondered whether he would preserve, protect, and defend the Constitution. On the other hand, the Methodists could have intelligent, courageous, systematic, and consecrated leadership from Hoover. As an engineer he was used to confronting "the impossible." Methodists had an opportunity by electing Hoover to prove that "obedience to law can be secured." She charged, "No citadel was ever taken by a general who said it could not be done." Enforcement must be in the hands of those who believed in it.

She sent the pastors forth with the plea to preach the message: "There are two thousand pastors here. You have in your churches more than six hundred thousand members of the Methodist church in Ohio, alone. That is enough to swing the election."[41] It was a thundering challenge and a sharp attack on Smith as the candidate of Tammany and organized crime. Not once did she mention his religion. But for the Methodist audience, the plea for action forged the religious connection.

The speech was reported fully in the *New York Times*, but it was not until two weeks later that Smith, angered by a growing "whispering campaign" on his religion, stung by the presence of burning crosses as he approached Oklahoma City for a major address, decided to face the religious issue directly. Willebrandt's speech to the Methodists capped his decision. Against the advice of his managers and before a tense local audience, he made a nationwide broadcast appeal to "look at the record" and excoriated the introduction of religion into politics.

In a ringing address he reviewed his record in state reorganization, budget methods, increased support for public education (the subject of "the most insidious, the most stupid and the most wilful of lies spread"), public health, water power, agriculture, and appointments. He cited the vicious intolerance of the pamphlets issued by the Klan's *Fellowship Forum* and the whispered stories of his drunken driving on Broadway and appearing so drunk at the New York State Fair that it took two men to drag him from the rostrum. He reminded his audience that he did not drive and certainly drunk or sober could not navigate on Broadway at the alleged speed of fifty miles an hour. Then, in a sober note, he stated that religious intolerance and the use of religion in the campaign had been denounced by the Republican National Committee. But no one had disclaimed responsibility for Willebrandt's exhortation to the Methodists. He remarked, "There's sep-

GIVE THIS LITTLE GIRL A GREAT BIG HAND

Talburt's cartoon in the *Washington News,* September 25, 1928, depicts the public furor after Willebrandt's address to the Methodist ministers.

aration of church and state for you," and speculated on the reaction if a member of his Albany cabinet appeared before a convention of Roman Catholic clergy and made such a statement. No Catholic, he concluded, should vote for him because of his religion; but if anyone believed he were better qualified and voted against him because of his Catholicism, he challenged, "he is not a real, pure, genuine American."[42]

Willebrandt had urged the Methodists on in the dry fight; Smith urged his audience to reject religion in politics and had not mentioned prohibition. Together the two speeches made the linkage that formed the major cultural divisions of the campaign. Catholic, wet, Tammany-urban Smith versus Protestant, dry, rural Hoover. Willebrandt's position in the Republican administration and Smith's nationwide address brought the religious issue into the open. Smith believed the gauntlet had been hurled; he responded with his own challenge.

Stunned, Willebrandt left Washington in a growing press barrage to speak to another Methodist group on September 23 at Lorain, Ohio. "The Assault on Prohibition in the Presidential Campaign" was designed to answer Smith's charge and if possible to defuse the religious issue. In a stinging speech, she stressed again the fifty-year battle of the Methodists for prohibition; a struggle that "never asked a man's church or his party if his acts and utterances were against liquor." Thirty-one national organizations, including two Catholic groups, had joined in the final nondenominational effort for the amendment. She reported they had recently regrouped in Washington and vowed to vote against Smith as "the servant of the saloon and the liquor traffic interests." She repeated a Methodist statement celebrating the "spiritual and moral achievement" of the Eighteenth Amendment, concluding if a defense of that victory from "a Tammany politician's unwarranted attack" be politics, "then make the most of it."[43] Smith, she charged, was hiding behind his church, "afraid to come out and face the record that he has made as a champion of the liquor traffic." Dry and Catholic, Senator Thomas Walsh of Montana found no such Methodist opposition. Had he been the candidate, her Springfield speech would not have been made. She scored the religious issue as a "wolf-wolf cry" that attempted to avoid the wet, Tammany charges. Reviewing the successes in law enforcement in closing the open saloon, routing rum row, eliminating "old drunks from gutters" and liquor-bred poverty, she concluded that no thoughtful leader could safely propose that the American people abandon efforts to secure observance of the law.[44]

Two days later, she gave an address, "It Can't Be Done," at a Presbyterian gathering in Warren, Ohio. Again, she centered on prohibition, the Tammany wet record, and Smith's signing of the repeal of the New York State enforcement law. Picking up a reminder in the Democratic southern press that Tammany had stood by the South in the travails of Reconstruction, Willebrandt, in a low point in the speech, cited the *Encyclopaedia Britannica* article on Tammany with special emphasis on the Tweed days of corruption. With a play on the "whispering campaign" and statements that Smith had reformed Tammany, she concluded "I want to say far above a whisper, that I doubt it." Conversely, Hoover's record showed that enforcement could become a reality. His wartime meatless days could be extended to the cocktail-less days in prohibition. She stressed his "amazing spiritual leadership to make each law-abiding household want to do its bit. Governor Smith says it can't be done. With Herbert Hoover we know it can be done!"[45]

From Warren, Willebrandt telephoned Hoover headquarters to report. The Lorain speech, she said, had been treated "marvelously" by both wet and dry presses in Ohio, but this good impression was threatened by the Associated Press release from Chicago that the Republican committee there repudiated her speech; she asked that the press release be recalled. She foresaw "a whole flock of editorials probably saying Mrs. Willebrandt is going to kick over the traces."[46] What she sought was a statement from Hubert Work that there was no effort by the Republican committee to recall her or her speeches. She asserted, "I have suffered much humiliation at the hands of the wets at Headquarters—that doesn't matter to anyone but me except that I do not want to lose the good effect of what has already been said."[47]

National headquarters did issue a flat statement explaining that "Mrs. Willebrandt was obviously, on this occasion, not speaking under any political organization and directly made her own advance release of her speech. A clerk in the Chicago office not knowing it had been released" issued another, which was recalled to avoid confusion and duplication.[48] It was not a ringing affirmation. The press persisted. *Time* reported a conversation with Chairman Work:

Q. What is Mrs. Willebrandt's status?
Dr. W. I don't know. She is sort of free lance.
Q. Do you approve of the speeches she has made?
Dr. W. . . . . I have not read them all so I cannot answer.[49]

On September 27, Willebrandt dispatched a blistering letter to Work with a copy to Hoover, charging that the "lack of backing" from his office was augmenting the intolerance-religious issue. She observed caustically, "I have had too much experience in too many campaigns ever to be a 'free lance.'" She had maintained silence after the Springfield speech to avoid the "public spectacle of disorder in our own ranks by giving out the truth." She reminded him in detail, "I have not made a single speech that has not been arranged through your own office," and pointed out her letter en route to Springfield asking to be relieved from further campaigning. Her Springfield speech had been reviewed at her request by J. Francis Burke, a Roman Catholic and counsel of the Republican National Committee, in an effort to avoid any remark that could be construed as anti-Catholic. He suggested some additions but assured her there was nothing offensive; three days before its release it was given for review to others in Work's organization. Still, on orders from Work's office, the Speakers Bureau in Chicago released it "with a note disclaiming responsibility for its statements." Democrats had certainly not missed such an opportunity for attack. This had been followed by the Lorain imbroglio. If Smith's tactic was to divide and disorganize the opposition, she concluded that Work had certainly cooperated.[50]

Not counting on action from Work, Willebrandt took the train to Chicago, avoiding the press until she had finished a two-hour conference with Congressman Walter Newton, chairman of the GOP Speakers Bureau, and James William Good, "Hooverizer of the West." When eager reporters asked what her "auspices" were, she referred them to Newton. He announced, "Mrs. Willebrandt certainly has been speaking under the auspices of the Speakers Bureau of the Republican National Committee."[51]

Contacted by the press in Washington, Hoover commented that he "would rather not discuss the matter." Privately, after the Springfield speech, he had asked Willebrandt to keep the last fifteen days of the campaign open, since the "best speakers" might be needed to counteract Smith. Privately he also condemned Smith's remarks on her as "barbaric."[52] Publicly, he kept his counsel.

Press rhetoric covering the controversy matched the intensity of the party debates. The usually staid *Independent* editorialized, "Mrs. Willebrandt Runs Amuck," and asserted, "No event in the Presidential campaign has been more fatuous or less in keeping with fair play than the proselytizing of Mrs. Mabel Walker Willebrandt in the organization of the Methodist Episcopal Church." A September 27 *New York*

Times editorial urged Hoover as engineer in chief to get her off the track. The *New York Daily News* more colorfully described her as leaping from church conference to church conference demanding that the churches go into politics and complained that "no one in authority puts brakes on her ninety-seven horsepower tongue." The hostile *New York World* noted, "This lady who has dwelt in perfect happiness in the midst of numerous scandals involving hundreds of millions of dollars in Washington is still shocked at some things Tammany did sixty years ago." She was "the perfect symbol" of the Republicans.[53] In its September 29 issue, the *Literary Digest* reviewed the press furor over "Mrs. Willebrandt's Appeal to the Methodists." The *Springfield (Massachusetts) Union*, a Republican daily, charged that the speech associated the issues of the campaign with the interests of a religious denomination. The dry press responded that Mrs. Willebrandt had properly spoken only on prohibition, which Smith had already made an issue. A Methodist Indianapolis organ, *The National Enquirer*, called her the "Joan of Arc" of prohibition. A Plainfield, New Jersey, paper set the idea to rhyme:

> Snarling foes will not unnerve her
> As they scorn her from the Dark
> May the Grace of God preserve her
> Prohibition's Joan of Arc.

The *New York Times* cited a supporter's characterization of her as "Deborah—a woman of God carrying a great message."[54]

Beyond editorials and poetry, the press quoted angry Democratic and Republican politicians who wanted her silenced. Attorney General Sargent's office was deluged with wires and letters to call her home. Senator Edwards, a New Jersey Democrat, condemned her Springfield speech as "a disgrace to the Justice Department." Congresswoman Norton denounced her campaign as one of "contemptible injustice." The New York Democratic congressman Emmanuel Cellar threatened to bring her conduct in office before the House of Representatives. John W. Davis, the 1924 Democratic nominee, broadcast an angry appeal for an official rebuke to Mrs. Willebrandt.[55]

Eastern Republicans joined in the cry. A conservative New York Congressman, Hamilton Fish, Jr., demanded that Willebrandt be recalled to her duties at the Justice Department. "Ohio Republicans" wired Sargent to "muzzle & silence this new mud slinger." Former Maryland congressman John Philip Hill, a militant wet, urged that Willebrandt be ordered to cease and desist. Not surprisingly, the

Women's Committee for the Repeal of the Eighteenth Amendment also wired their demand that Mrs. Willebrandt remain on duty at the Justice Department and not be allowed to campaign.[56]

Wet and dry religious leaders issued their denunciations or support. The Reverend John Roach Straton, a dry campaigner energetic in his use of the religious issue, gave tribute to Willebrandt from the pulpit of his Calvary Baptist Church in New York. He indicated that he was considering inviting "that brave little woman down in Washington" to speak in his church, since he hated having the Methodists monopolizing a "good thing." The Reverend Henry Van Dyke, a moderate Presbyterian who pleaded for religious tolerance, condemned the "female firebrand."[57]

Though he did not issue any statements to the press, Hiram Johnson vented his anger at Willebrandt in a bitter letter to his progressive friend Harold Ickes. He had brought Willebrandt from a "position of obscurity and penury" to her Washington post, he asserted, but she soon "took on the complexion of her environment. . . . As I have observed of women in politics, she became at first anxious for publicity, and then her greediness for it made her perfectly mad. She out Coolidged Coolidge and out Daughertyed Daugherty. Her ambition increased with the prominence she achieved." He charged that she had become "one of the most determined of reactionaries." His conclusion, however, revealed the real source of his discontent. No one loyal to Hiram Johnson could join the Hoover forces, and, Johnson asserted, "there is no more intimate supporter of Hoover than Mrs. Willebrandt."[58]

Unaware of this estrangement, Willebrandt phoned her old friend Frank Doherty in Los Angeles. She asked, "Surely you and Sarah do not believe these things of me!" At his reassurance, she broke into an expensive long-distance "cry," later writing: "What satisfaction my weakness would cause a lot of folks who thought I was 'leathernecked'! I do enjoy a real, clean fight, political, legal or otherwise, but most of us have a vulnerable spot where we can really be hurt, and the charge of religious intolerance found mine."[59]

More personally devastating was the news break on her divorce, picked up September 27 by the *New York World* and other dailies and noted nationally in *Time* magazine. The story broke the "mystery" of how her 1924 divorce had been so quiet. The complaint filed in Los Angeles had used the middle names of both Arthur and Mabel, citing: "Willebrandt, Frank against Elizabeth." The action had been quietly handled by Willebrant's lawyer friend Elizabeth A. Kenny and an interim decree granted by default by her friend Judge Harry A. Holzer. The story detailed Arthur Willebrandt's complaint that "on or about the first day of January, 1916 the defendant [Mrs. Willebrandt] disregarding the solemnity of her marriage vow, willfully and without cause, deserted and abandoned the plaintiff." Reporters tracked down the plaintiff at the Huntington Park vine-covered cottage where he lived with his mother. An unwilling interviewee, Arthur declined political comment, suggesting: "Mrs. Willebrandt has been very successful so far, so why not ask her about this." He refused any statement on the divorce except to say it came "in the usual manner when two people cannot get along in their work." He now hoped "to completely divorce himself from Mrs. Willebrandt's public life as he divorced himself from her personally." In Washington, a distraught Mabel Willebrandt collapsed in tears at this latest press assault. Pronouncing it "just too much," she rode with a friend through the Washington night sobbing uncontrollably.[60]

Now letters on the divorce came into her office and Attorney General Sargent's. An anonymous postcard to Sargent asked, "why permit a divorced woman to fly about the country preaching politics and morals in the ME churches? Better give her the air." A New York businessman wrote her: "To judge from the story of your life as given in the press, you seem to be one of those women with a heart like a stock ticker that does not beat over anything except money and publicity. When you found your husband could not give you enough of these you deserted him. That is your conception of a marriage vow. . . . As to Methodism, it may be as good a vehicle as any to land some people in Heaven, but I have grave doubts that it will ever get you there."[61]

Facing a heavy case load in the Supreme Court and buffeted by the press, Willebrandt was dispatched again to campaign in Kentucky, South Dakota, Minnesota, and finally Los Angeles. She showed the text of her speeches to Attorney General Sargent, conferred with Hoover before leaving, and secured an Associated Press release that she was speaking under the direction of the Republican National Committee. She was not going to address any church groups.[62]

Her first address on this final swing was "Answering the Charge of Bigotry," delivered October 8 in the dry, mountain country at Hardinsburg, Kentucky. In a brief speech, she immediately brought up Smith's charges that she introduced religion as an issue and again claimed: "I know it was not Governor Smith's religion that prompted this unsportsmanly attack." She quoted from a letter from P.H. Callahan, a Kentuckian and leader of the Association of Catholics Favoring Prohibition. He had found no criticism in her speeches of the Catholic church or the religion of Smith. Other Catholic leaders from the Irish priest Father Mathew to Pope Pius X and Cardinal Mercier were cited as supporters of prohibition. Opposition to Smith, she concluded, came not from his religion, but his stand on immigration, his Tammany allegiance, and his attack on the Eighteenth Amendment.[63]

That same evening she addressed an Owensboro, Kentucky, audience, "Seeing the Real Issues Through Democratic Smoke Screens." She warned of the political showman and the demagogue who appealed to emotions. Thinking voters should focus on the real issues; the religious issue was "a lie dressed up and waved around like a red herring." For the first time in her addresses she developed the Republican positions on inland waterways, agriculture, the protective tariff, and continued prosperity. She asserted, "Not many farmers will want to leave the solution of their problem in the hands of a man who has never lived on a farm . . . who was plainly in a fog on the whole subject." Smith was trained in city streets, "having spent his life holding offices within the gift of the Tammany organization."[64]

Speaking at Hopkinsville, Kentucky, on October 9, she again stressed a variety of issues but centered mainly on immigration, threatening that a Democratic victory "would mean drowning out prosperity in the cheap labor of foreign centers." Tammany had voted consistently against immigrant restriction; Smith was proposing to change the quota allotments based on national origin and would thus allow an "unprecedented increase in the number of unemployed." While Republicans believed in immigration restriction, she denied that this was "in a selfish sense." Reviewing wage differentials in Europe and America and the prosperity of the American workers, she stressed the need to select carefully the new immigrants for physical, moral, and mental readiness for citizenship.[65] Though she ended with a statement on prohibition, she was clearly diversifying her speeches.

During the last week in October she spoke at Wheeling, West Virginia; Nashville; and St. Paul, Minnesota (where she was matron of honor at the wedding of Laura Volstead).[66] Her last major address was given at home at the Philharmonia in Los Angeles on November 3. It was an unusual and controversial political address. Clearly, she was trying to sum up the issues and her positions; midway she paused and reflectively spoke of Christianity, love, the Sermon on the Mount, before ending on the religious issue in the campaign. First, she rehearsed the reasons for her opposition to Smith.

> It is my conviction that it would be nothing short of disastrous for this nation to elevate to the Presidency of the United States a Tammany-trained politician with his Tammany connections proudly acknowledged, who has had no international experience, who has had no contacts with that vast section of our country west of the Mississippi River, who as Governor of the Empire State, has never been able to win the agricultural counties of his home state, and who, for the political effect of winning the support of anti-prohibitionists in both parties, made a false political gesture in the form of an assault on one part of the Constitution of the United States. I am convinced that the inevitable result of this leadership would be destructive of our national prosperity and an unprecedented increase in lawlessness.[67]

She then introduced the religious theme and the irony that Christians hated one another in the name of Him who commanded, "love one another," concluding: "Christianity without love is a mockery of Christianity—a barbarous ritualism. It is not the joyful unselfishness of St. Francis of Assisi and John Wesley. It is the Christianity of Ivanhoe that glorified a dumb Rowena and persecuted a glorious Rebecca. It is no Christianity at all." The Sermon on the Mount might yet bring a united Christendom, but the Christianity of "mere creeds and ceremonials" was dying from lack of love. Instead there was intolerance and bigotry.[68]

Turning to the attack and "needed truth" on the religious issue and the Eighteenth Amendment, she relied primarily on the quotations and suggestions sent to her by Hayward Kendall on October 8 from Cardinal Mercier, Pope Leo XIII, Cardinal McCabe, Pope Pius X, Archbishop Spalding, and Archbishop Ireland, asserting that all were supporters of prohibition. She recalled the tumultuous reception nineteenth-century America afforded to the Irish apostle for abstinence and prohibition, Father Mathew, quoting the welcome of Henry Clay, Sam Houston, and William Ellery Channing. Prohibition had a long tradition, she argued, in America and in the Roman Catholic church. "Loyalty to prohibition," she concluded, "is not disloyalty to the Catholic Church . . . but loyalty to God, America, Humanity and the great Catholic leaders who conceived it and fought to make it a blessed reality." When she had fought those Catholic politicians who "sought to mis-lead their co-religionists into the belief

Addressing a friendly crowd at Temple City in 1928. *Below*, broadcasting in the final days of the 1928 campaign. Photograph by Underwood and Underwood.

that loyalty to prohibition is little short of heresy," she had been attacked as a bigot.[69]

The American was "the most tolerant" on earth, but he could be roused when called a fanatic or bigot for his loyalty. Now "all of these elements which have debauched our literature and the stage, which jeer at sobriety and chastity, and are threatening the very foundations of our national life," were "aligned with the Tammany candidate and with the social froth and dregs in opposition to the Eighteenth Amendment." Hoover's toleration, kindliness, and idealism would bring Protestant, Catholic, Jewish, and racial groups to new and higher levels of life and tolerance.[70]

It was a long, powerful, impassioned address. Critics rightly noted that she had not distinguished between support for temperance, abstinence, or legal prohibition among the churchmen quoted. She plainly had little time for preparation and no time to check her limited sources. She believed that prohibition, not religion, was the issue; yet the clustering of Tammany, wet, Catholic, immigrant, urban perceptions of Smith made the linkage indissoluable. Her Catholic defense of prohibition kept religion and morality central in the wet-dry fight.

The dilemma was obvious in her November article for *McCall's* magazine, "The Republican Platform—Viewed by Mrs. Mabel Walker Willebrandt." Paired with Democratic spokeswoman Mrs. Henry Morgenthau, she listed the reasons for women to vote Republican. She began with an image from nature, which immediately demonstrated the inextricable issues: "Spiritual and material fields in America lie fallow, awaiting a wise husbandman." Again, she stressed the issues of prohibition, the tariff, agriculture, inland waterway system, and prosperity. Particularly, for the women, she noted Hoover's international experience and the need for peace, concluding: "The spiritual undertone of Mr. Hoover's acceptance reveals that he would receive the nation's highest office with a deep sense of consecration." He was the "trustworthy candidate."[71]

On election day the issues of prosperity, prohibition, religion, agriculture, race, waterways, government organization, character of the candidate, and party loyalty produced the Hoover victory. In an impressive voter turnout of 70 percent, Smith won 15,016,000 votes, more in a losing cause than any other previous challenger but well short of Hoover's 21,392,000 total and 444 electoral votes. Hoover won Virginia, North Carolina, Florida, Texas, and the border states.

Contemporaries and historians have labored to establish which were the most telling issues. Prohibition and prosperity were certainly major determinants, but in 1928 prohibition and religion "were knitted together." In his quantitative analysis, *Prejudice and the Old Politics*, the historian Allan J. Lichtman noted that this fusion of the two issues was fostered by the "unleashing" of Willebrandt. But Protestants were more likely than Catholics to favor prohibition and "the most resolute Protestant drys were likely to be among the most vocal opponents of the Catholic Church. The Prohibition controversy also enabled Protestant leaders to join in the campaign against Al Smith without openingly initiating religious animosity." Hoover's tactics were to remain above the battle, sending his surrogates into the more sensitive skirmishes, yet he remained in control of all of the fine details of his campaign and, Lichtman concludes, was quite "willing to exploit the tensions of his society."[72]

Willebrandt had done what she had been asked by Hoover and the party, but the intensity of her defense of prohibition and then herself and the ensuing controversy roused speculation on her future. In late November, the *New York Times* reported that she might leave the Justice Department to lobby for dry organizations. Syndicated political columnist Frank Kent, citing Willebrandt as the "most notorious woman in America," asserted that "perhaps the biggest of the littlest problems that will face Mr. Hoover is what to do with Mrs. Mabel Walker Willebrandt." A *New Yorker* article in February, "Mrs. Firebrand," asserted that her coveted judgeship would be hard to win from her political enemies in Congress, noting that she never "sympathized with the easy give and take of politics and cultivated a certain pride in the aversion that most politicians have for entering her office." Yet, "the personification of a national phenomenon" could hardly be expected to return to the obscurity of private law practice.[73] The dry *Christian Herald* ran a full-page ad urging Willebrandt's appointment to full charge should the recommended shift of the prohibition enforcement forces be moved from the Treasury to the Justice Department.[74]

At home for her first Christmas in eight years, Willebrandt dispelled rumors in Los Angeles that she was planning to resign. But she, too, was anxious about the future and wired Hoover's assistant, Lawrence Richey, that she was ready to come to Washington any time Hoover wanted to confer. When she returned to the Justice Department in January, she kept in close touch with Richey and Congressman Newton on appointments and patronage.[75]

Early in February, Hoover wired her for an assessment of five candidates for the post of attorney general. On February 8, she wrote a precise, forceful, six-page response. First, she outlined the qualities she believed most essential. Hoover's attorney general must be a *"doer"* who could "inspire faith," an executive with the ability "to put morale into indifferent men." He must be politically astute, experienced in political tactics, and ready to "wrestle with political influence in the Department of Justice" and in the U.S. attorneys' offices. Merely a good lawyer, especially one untrained in dealing quickly with political forces, would never succeed. She cautioned against an attorney general of "powerful *personal* ambitions." A "lesser legal light of unquestioned and unselfish loyalty" would be much safer. Tactically, she urged that "haste *must be made*," but quietly and carefully, until a majority of senators were won for the appointment. Hoover's choice for attorney general, she concluded would *"make or break"* his administration.[76]

With that introduction, and aware that she was the candidate of the dry forces for the position, she made her assessment. Of the five names Hoover listed, she devoted her most precise attention to two: Solicitor General William D. Mitchell and William J. Donovan, assistant to the attorney general. To Willebrandt, Mitchell's strength was "a mind like a steel trap, clear, clean, cool and logical. He was of the highest personal character." However, Mitchell had neither understanding of nor any interest in politics and was "almost utterly wanting in administrative capacity or interest." On the dry issue, he was "not a prohibitionist" and was rather "impatient of the whole prohibition question." Finally, Mitchell was "traditionally and staunchly a Democrat."[77]

Donovan's strengths were his "administrative and executive ability, clear scintillating mind, well-trained and most engaging personality." Ambitious, forceful, and impulsive, Wild Bill used "gate crasher tactics" but was "so pleasant people are rather glad he crashed in!" To Willebrandt, his appointment would be a mistake for two reasons: "the prevailing notion (whether justified or not) that at the last campaign when things were hot he had the greatest opportunity to serve, and failed to rise to the opportunity" and that he was "risky on Prohibition." His appointment would "destroy the faith of those who worked hardest to win the election for Hoover." Still, Willebrandt reasoned, his administrative qualities would make him a better candidate than the much abler lawyer, Mr. Mitchell.[78]

She wrote only briefly of three other candidates: J.W. Davis of Iowa, Judge Dietrich of Idaho, and Walton Miller of New York. Her own candidate was not on Hoover's list, John J. Parker, U.S. judge on the Fourth Circuit. Parker understood politics, would be satisfactory to the drys, was a progressive representative of the New South. He would bring not only "legal attainments and a fine mind" but also the "flaming enthusiasm of a young man eager to make the Administration a success."[79]

Her letters to her parents in February and March trace her continuing concern about Hoover's choice. On Washington's Birthday, she reported, Hoover called her in the evening. After asking, "Anyone on the line?" he apologized for not having her to his house to talk, but that would raise comment and speculation. Then he announced: "I just wanted to tell you the new Attorney General is a friend of yours. I say that because maybe when you see him you might not think so but he is and we want you to stay on . . . at least for a while. It will be best for you. You deserve the recognition it will mean and the work deserves it and needs you." A stunned Willebrandt agreed to "stay awhile" but wanted to discuss it with him and the new attorney general before deciding anything further. She wrote to her parents: "Taken all together, I was intensely *hurt* that he asked me that way. It is part and parcel of the *many* backstairs methods he adopted of dealing with me and with the drys during the campaign. The courteous thing would have been for him to ask me to come to his house to talk to me face to face. I think it goes to prove the thing I have feared, and my instinct has told me long ago—that fundamentally he doesn't feel on a level with women nor deal with them as men." That he communicated the decision with just a phone call and patronizing comment hurt "bitterly." She ended: "The real truth is that he *needs* to have me stay for a while, but instead of saying so frankly he put it that *I* needed it—as tho he were doing me a great favor." She wondered how she could "go through the next few months."[80]

Hoover's choice for attorney general bypassed both the drys' candidate, Mabel Walker Willebrandt, and the antiprohibitionist assistant attorney general and hard campaigner William ("Wild Bill") Donovan. Instead the selection was Solicitor General William D. Mitchell. A Democrat, neither wet nor dry, he was supported by Chief Justice Taft and Senator Borah. Dean Roscoe Pound of Harvard called him the best fitted candidate to be appointed to the post in thirty years.[81] Clearly, Hoover had opted to remove the prohibition controversy from the Justice Department with this above-reproach appointment.

At the end of March, Willebrandt wrote her parents that while she was "working just like mad," she was frustrated with Mitchell's organization and leadership. She reported: "I feel just as tho I had been pushed out on a limb, can't get down and no way back because of the heavy responsibility—the wretched thing is that I personify prohibition. The anti Hoover forces wish to break him on prohibition and to do that any pretext is seized upon to discredit me."[82]

Two such pretexts were seized in March and April. First, reporters broke the story of her use of a "spy" to gain evidence on Warden John Snook at the Atlanta penitentiary. The warden resigned, but Attorney General Mitchell was reported to be opposed to the practice. He ordered all of the undercover men out of prisons, particularly condemning the practice of federal courts' issuing of fraudulent papers in committing the agents to prison. Willebrandt defended the results of the undercover work and declared that it was the only way to procure difficult evidence on dope smuggling and the responsibility of prison officials. In April, the *Philadelphia Sunday Transcript* complained that she had used women as government spies in assignation houses and on the Montreal-New York train to confiscate liquor supplies. Neither was a major story, but they did keep her in controversial headlines.[83]

By May, Willebrandt believed that events were moving to a crisis. Hoover told her that he did not think he could achieve the movement of the prohibition forces from the Treasury to the Justice Department. She wrote of her frustration to her parents: "I can do very little to improve things. If he'd only let me resign or give me work other than prohibition."[84]

Feeling politically deserted and frustrated in her work, Willebrandt again seriously considered marriage with Fred Horowitz, but once more her misgivings about marriage itself rose and stopped her. Her mother, trying to be helpful, encouraged her to marry Fred and wrote to her reviewing the political situation:

> We of course were sorry that you are in such perplexity and we realize your reluctance to quit before finishing your task. The way it looks to me is that it will take many years to really finish the job even under the best of cooperation. If Pres. Hoover is really sincere in an earnest wish to enforce prohibition he can but see that under the present line up it can not be done. It does seem that if he truly wanted to help you he would have allowed you to pass on the man who was to be your chief. If he fears the foes of enforcement to such an extent as to be timid about coming out in the open and boldly using every means at his command then of course in order to play in with the W.C.T.U. and the church

crowd he will do everything possible in a persuasive way to keep you where you are, for as long as you are there it will soothe those who do not realize how you lack authority to do what you might do. I believe if you could only not try to solve it yourself and trust God fully *you would be given the understanding*.

Mabel wrote in the margin of the letter of her decision "like a flash of light to resign *whether* or *no*."[85]

On May 26 she wrote to Hoover informing him that she had been offered the post of Washington counsel for the Aviation Corporation. Citing the challenge of the growing field of aeronautical law, she asked to be relieved of her duties by June 15. She expressed her genuine "regret" at leaving the connection with the accomplishments of his administration but noted her seven long years of service and her desire to seize this opportunity. "To have had a small part in your election will always be a source of great satisfaction to me and in my own behalf the way I have served my country best." She reviewed her contributions in the area of prisons, and stated that her division was up to date in tax work; prohibition would be safe under his leadership.[86]

Hoover wrote a letter of regret, which the *New York World* characterized as "the warmest praise given by this Administration to any public servant leaving office." He acknowledged: "I cannot, however, allow the opportunity to pass without an expression of the indebtedness of the American people and of the Government for so many years of effective public service. The position you have held has been one of the most difficult in the Government and one which could not have been conducted with such distinguished success by one of less legal ability and real courage." From Texas, where she was receiving an honorary degree from Baylor University, a still loyal Willebrandt responded, "I am deeply touched at the dignity and strength of your tribute. I pray I may live to merit it and still serve you."[87]

Editorial tributes and sighs of relief at her departure were mixed with speculation over why she had resigned. The *New York Times* believed Hoover still wanted her but "could not prevail upon her to stay with such a lucrative offer." In a friendly article that denied friction between Willebrandt and Hoover or Mitchell, the *Washington Herald* stressed her disappointment at not being appointed to a federal judgeship. The *Seattle Times* asserted that she was piqued at realizing that if the prohibition forces were transferred to Justice she would not be placed in charge. The most searing interpretation was offered by a *Chicago Tribune* correspondent, Arthur Sears Henning. He cited

Mitchell's blocking of Willebrandt's ambition to be "generalissimo" of all the prohibition forces. He had wanted to accept her pro forma resignation tendered at the beginning of the new administration, but since that would have aroused the drys, he "edged" Willebrandt out by denying her control and allowed "nature to take its course." Not only did Mitchell "foil" Willebrandt in her prohibition work, but he had also stopped the undercover work in the prisons and, according to Henning, dissatisfied with her Supreme Court work, had cut back on her case load. It was the most brutal assault of her career and only partially assuaged by the letters of support both public and private from Ella Boole, Justice Stone, and WCTU chapters.[88]

On the eve of her departure Hoover entertained her at a White House dinner, publicly displaying his support. Privately, he responded to a nomination of a Massachusetts woman to fill her post by writing tersely: "It is not proposed to again put a woman in the position of having to deal with criminal elements, their supporters and the wet press throughout the United States. A woman may be appointed in the Department of Justice, but for some entirely different position."[89]

Personally, Willebrandt tried to prepare for the future while closing down her office and her old life. She wrote her parents that she was "very uncertain about this year" and worn by the fatigue of meeting people and playing a part. "I'm so tired by the time I've said 'fine' 'fine' all day every day." Still thinking of possible marriage, suggesting alternatively that her parents might come East to be with her, she reached out for emotional support, writing: "I *have been* trying terribly hard. And I succeed fairly well outwardly—all the time playing a part. But at *home*—the human animal doesn't want to play a part."[90]

On June 30, the *New York Times* reported that Mrs. Willebrandt "Quits office quietly" and that she would issue a statement to the press in a short time, again raising speculation on why she had resigned.[91] Her answer was given partially on August 5 as she moved to set the record straight and fulfill her last effort at prohibition enforcement. Her story, *The Inside of Prohibition*, was syndicated in more than twenty major dailies. She refused to be left in "No Man's Land." With her version of the record stated, she moved to put her new life together.

CHAPTER SEVEN

Private Practice, Private Life

You have no idea how hard I worked on that aviation case.

MABEL WALKER WILLEBRANDT
1931

*L*EAVING the Justice Department in June 1929, Willebrandt launched a private legal practice that in its pioneering and diversity almost rivaled the challenges of her eight years in public service. Her experience in Washington, her connections with the administration, her success in the federal courts brought clients anxious for expert representation in the tangle of bureaucracy and regulation of the Hoover and early New Deal years. With clients in the aviation and radio industries, Willebrandt won judgments in two landmark cases in the emerging field of air law. She entered the field of international claims, pressing the case of Alaskan colonizers against the Soviet Union. Building on her Justice Department experience, she became a sought-after tax lawyer in income and estate cases. Her California connections remained strong as she served as Washington counsel for Metro-Goldwyn-Mayer and advised her old friend Louis B. Mayer and a veritable galaxy of his directors and stars. As she began her transition to private practice, however, prohibition kept her in the headlines. Representing Fruit Industries, Ltd., an organization of California grape growers, Willebrandt was heatedly accused by prohibitionists of consorting with the enemy.

In 1929, the California grape industry experienced the problems in overproduction, low prices, and sluggish market that had plagued major American commodities through much of the decade. Vintners and wine grape growers had fought hard against prohibition, first in state campaigns in California, and then in a losing national effort. Braced for disaster when the Eighteenth Amendment was ratified, they found instead a boom. Thirsty Americans, particularly in the East, took advantage of a provision in the Volstead Act that allowed a homeowner to produce up to 200 gallons of wine a year for family consumption. With a healthy market, prices of wine grapes rose in the early part of the decade. By 1927, however, overproduction brought sharp declines. Vintners who had worked for repeal, or at least a modification to permit the manufacture of light wines, intensified their efforts. Conferences with California presidential candidate Hoover won his assurance that he would see that "something was done" for the grape industry.[1]

Hoover's major instrument to relieve and reorganize American agriculture emerged from a special session of Congress in the spring of 1929. A five-member Federal Farm Board was created with the mission and funds to work for market stability through organizing the producers of the major commodities. Agriculture was to be "rationalized" and brought into the prosperity of New Era economics that manufacturing had enjoyed in the 1920s.

California grape growers were quick to organize. Vintners had already formed the California Vineyardists Association; raisin grape growers joined in the Sun Maid Raisin Growers cooperative; table grape producers organized in the California Fruit Exchange. In late July, L.S. Tenny, vice-president of the Vineyardists Association, appeared before the new farm board to detail the incorporation of the Federal Grape Stabilization Corporation, formed by the organizations of the wine, raisin, and table grape producers to control the national market. Tenny, who was president of the new amalgam, stressed the urgent need for farm board funds. Between 14,000 and 16,000 of the growers were "absolutely broke" and facing foreclosure. A $300,000,000 industry was imperiled. The requested loan of $7,700,000 would enable the Grape Stabilization Corporation to buy up a surplus 100,000 tons of grapes, hold them off the market, protect prices, and begin to establish centralized control.[2]

With this industry-wide organization in place, the subsidiaries continued to work for stability and expansion in their own market areas. The Vineyardists Association was particularly active. Led by Paul Garrett, producer of Virginia Dare Tonic and other wine grape by-products, vintners and producers formed a new marketing cooperative, Fruit Industries. Donald Conn, the executive director and public relations expert, was also the manager of the Vineyardists Association. Conn, in an early discussion with the head of the Federal Farm Board, Alexander Legge, was advised that he had "better get the best available counsel."[3] Legge's suggestion was Mabel Walker Willebrandt. Paul Garrett already knew Willebrandt through his dealings with the Justice Department and its review of his tonic product. All the officers of Fruit Industries accepted the need for a skilled Washington lawyer, and Conn contracted with Willebrandt for her representation for five years.[4]

Fruit Industries developed and marketed nearly thirty different grape by-products. Grape jellies, juice, breakfast syrup, candy, cooking sauces, and concentrated grape drinks were produced. Experiments with combined fruit beverages were aimed at tapping into the billion dollar soft drink industry. Fruit Industries, Virginia Dare, and Guasti all produced tonics, selling a large volume of their wine base to patent medicine perunas. The most controversial of the by-products was a grape concentrate, which, when water and yeast were added, fermented into a very acceptable wine. The concentrate was delivered directly to the consumer, and after the fermentation process, a service man returned to rack the juice off the barrels, filter it, and bottle it, adding attractive labels to identify the product as Port, Muscatel, Sherry, Burgundy, or Sauterne.[5] In May 1927, Donald Conn, representing the Vineyardists Association, asked for a Justice Department ruling on the legality of selling the grape concentrate to individual consumers. Assistant Attorney General Willebrandt assured him it was a "strictly legal product."[6]

Fruit Industries was eager to work with the Federal Farm Board to expand its markets. In August 1929, a delegation led by Donald Conn, T.T.G. Gregory, their California counsel, and Secretary Walter Taylor submitted an application for a loan of $2,500,000 to purchase marketing facilities and to aid in merchandising their commodities. Willebrandt testified that the grape concentrate was perfectly legal. In mid-October the board approved a loan of $1,000,000. A minimum of $50,000 was to be used for research. Twelve million dollars in common stock were to be made available to growers not members of the original cooperative. The board stipulated that the plants were to be operated in strict conformity with the Volstead Act.[7] On February 1, 1930, Fruit Industries approached the farm board for a loan of $1,500,000. Again, after stressing the need to expand the membership of Fruit Industries, the board responded favorably.[8]

Armed with these farm board funds, Fruit Industries launched a nationwide campaign. Paul Garrett marshaled his sales force, the best in the wine business.[9] He personally discussed the projected selling campaign with Dr. E.C. Dinwiddie, one of the authors of the

Eighteenth Amendment. Dinwiddie not only accepted the sale of concentrate as legal but also Garrett's argument that it would be easier to safeguard against abuses if the sales were controlled by one organization. He agreed to be one of a board of three referees on all questions of prohibition related to Fruit Industries. The decisions of the referees would be binding on the sales organization and "guide the distribution of fruits and concentrates toward the promotion of temperance." For the two other referees, Garrett proposed Mrs. Lenna Yost, legislative superintendent of the WCTU, and Mrs. Mabel Walker Willebrandt. Further to strengthen this screening by three known dry supporters, Garrett asked the farm board to provide a government stamp of approval by making the appointments. Skillfully sidestepping the issue, the board noted that the proposed committee would "No doubt . . . be a fine thing," but some other way would have to be found "of putting your program over." The farm board had no authority to participate in prohibition issues. It had "enough problems without taking on questions of that character."[10]

Donald Conn, Walter Taylor, and Willebrandt appeared before the board on July 22, 1930. Conn reviewed the progress of Fruit Industries, citing its 75 percent control of plants handling grape byproducts. Sales in the last fiscal year totaled approximately a million gallons of concentrate. He predicted that Fruit Industries would produce more than two million gallons in 1930–31, using 80,000 tons of grapes. Willebrandt reaffirmed the legality of the concentrate. The prejudice against it, she asserted, came from improper methods of distribution, which in some cases resulted in a partial fermenting of the concentrate before delivery. "From the standpoint of a prohibitionist," she insisted, "it was a distinct advantage in enforcement for eighty or eighty-five percent of the grapes of California to be under the control of one agency."[11] The farm board responded in August and October with additional merchandising loans.[12]

One of the first markets targeted for a "hard test" was Chicago. Fruit Industries purchased a plant, dispatched a Californian to organize the distribution, and bought trucks and cars for the winemakers to service the concentrate in Chicago homes. The first opposition came from local teamsters, who balked at this new nonunion operation and demanded an accommodation. But it was the alleged opposition of Al Capone at this incursion into his territory that made headlines. On November 19, the San Francisco *Call-Bulletin* reported that local attorneys for Capone had been meeting with the California grape growers, independent of Fruit Industries, to arrange a market a rival concentrate in Chicago and Brooklyn. Negotiations were abruptly terminated, the *Call-Bulletin* speculated, either when the growers appointed Ralph Merritt, a close friend of Hoover, as one of their counsels, or when Willebrandt appealed to Assistant Attorney General O'Brien to investigate the Capone threats. A Fruit Industries press release sparking the furor had been issued by Conn on November 13 in Chicago. Part protest, part promotion, it cited the opposition of the bootleggers and racketeers:

> Fruit Industries is the only agency of the California Grape Control Board engaged in marketing grape by-products. One of its many commodities is Vine-Glo,—a pure California fruit juice. Of course, those who are engaged in the unlawful distribution of illegal liquors resent any plan of industry action to conform with the law.
>
> Vine-Glo is now being sold by four hundred druggists in Milwaukee. It will next be introduced in Chicago, then at New York and other important centers. It represents a new and great innovation to assist agriculture and gives the American public a fine beverage, strictly within the law. It is sold by the highest class of our merchandisers—the corner drug store.
>
> . . . Fruit Industries—backed by government funds—conducting all of its activities according to law will take its chances with the racketeers. It will protect the law, itself, its agencies, and its customers.[13]

The *Chicago Tribune* editorialized dryly: "There may be a wine publicity agent hiding in this story somewhere."[14] The *Washington Post* agreed, citing the "Grape Juice Hubbub" as "the greatest publicity hoax that has been put over in this country in a long time, and it is beginning to get on the official nerves." The *Post* asserted that this was "just about the climax of the harassment the officials have suffered at the hands of that creature of Mrs. Mabel Walker Willebrandt, the California fermentable grape industry." The Capone story was "a masterpiece of work, the work of a psychologist." If Capone were interested enough to interfere, the thirsty consumer might rightly conclude that the product "must be something good."[15]

Highly disturbed, Willebrandt tried to spike the publicity. She denied asking the Justice Department for protection for Fruit Industries and urged Conn to shut down public comment as much as possible. Agreeing with the *Post*, Willebrandt argued that allegations of racketeer attacks created the unfortunate impression that Fruit Industries was "stooping to compete with bootleggers." Fruit Industries should emphasize that it was marketing "nothing of any more prohibition relationship than sugar, corn syrup or fresh fruit." Constant inquiries certainly were irritating to government officials. She wired the prohibition director, Colonel Amos Woodcock, to express her concern. Conn, also denying he had asked for federal help, insisted that the story was planted by "insidious wet propaganda," traceable to Hearst and the brewers.[16] He issued a news release emphasizing the nonalcoholic content and the legality of Vine-Glo.[17]

Willebrandt pursued her own campaign, sending the *Washington Post* clipping and a pointed column from the *San Bernardino Evening Telegram* to C.C. Teague of the Federal Farm Board, Attorney General Mitchell, Colonel Woodcock, and Mrs. Yost with an explanatory note. The San Bernardino column, interspersing poetry and prose, focused on Willebrandt's role in assuring the government that the Fruit Industries product was legal. Typical was the paragraph: "My earlier impression that Mabel was a corker has been slightly shaken by the assurance from the correspondents who are writing the prohibition stories from Washington that grape juice left uncorked becomes wine. It may therefore be that Mabel is, after all, an uncorker."[18] To fellow attorney Ralph Merritt, Willebrandt wrote that "most of the storm of publicity seems to have multiplied and hypothecated here in Washington. Anything you can do to get everybody to smile pleasantly and say nothing will be appreciated."[19] She warned the leaders of Fruit Industries that the publicity "is the kind of thing that will arouse the drys against us."[20]

The drys were aroused. Dr. Clarence True Wilson, general secretary of the Methodist Board of Temperance, lamented: "We were so used to leaving everything to Mrs. Willebrandt who represented our side for years that our eyes were not opened to the fact that she is now attorney for the grape industry." In December, to protect Fruit Industries and to reassure the drys, Willebrandt spoke for two hours behind closed doors to the Methodists' National Temperance Council. She insisted that she was as dry as she had been when assistant attorney general. Other drys were loyal in their support. Norma C. Brown, vice-president of the Flying Squadron Foundation, sympathized that the dry complaints must be "a crown of thorns" for Willebrandt, who had suffered so much for the cause. Another concluded, "Well, no matter what it is, it is right, because she did it."[21]

In January, Willebrandt spoke to 450 Anti-Saloon League members in Washington and received a standing ovation. The *Washington Post* reported, "Mabel Walker Willebrandt may now be engaged in trying to help the California grape growers by putting potential wine into American homes, but she is still the heroine of the drys." The ovation she received when she rose, "attired as usual in an attractive gown," exceeded "for spontaneity and lustiness the one given to Amos W.W. Woodcock." Willebrandt spoke briefly "with her usual vigor," affirming her conviction that there was "no weakening of the American people on the Eighteenth Amendment," for "underneath the policy, . . . underneath the purpose of the voters, there is an irresistible upward reaching, a spiritual flame that can't be argued with. . . . Last night's meeting dispelled notions that Mrs. Willebrandt's popularity with the drys is on the wane."[22]

Advertisements for Fruit Industries were now cleared by Willebrandt. In March, the McCann-Erickson Agency produced full-page advertisements headed "The Truth about Vine-Glo and Fruit Industries, Ltd." and stressing that Fruit Industries was an organization operating under the California Grape Control Plan. The sale of its product did not violate any law; it was a "sincere attempt to solve a serious agricultural problem. . . . Vine-Glo is not a ballyhoo for wine." Eight varieties were available: Port, Virginia Dare, Tokay, Muscatel, Claret, Riesling, Burgundy, and Sauterne. Twenty-five-gallon kegs sold for $65.00; five-gallon kegs were priced at $16.50. All carried a guarantee of satisfaction or money back.[23]

To meet the expense of setting up a nationwide merchandising operation, Fruit Industries requested additional Federal Farm Board funds through the autumn of 1930 and the following spring. Conn explained that "obviously outgo was substantially greater than income on that phase of operations." Willebrandt appeared several times before the board with Ralph Merritt. In August, the board approved a $500,000 advance for operating capital, but with two important stipulations: Fruit Industries must immediately discontinue all retail business and conduct its operations as a manufacturing distributor, and it must discontinue all objectionable advertising.[24]

These strictures represented a gathering storm of protest by drys and a review by government officials. In April 1931, a New York grape concentrate plant was raided. The prohibition director, Woodcock, criticizing the ads for the concentrate, now concluded that the sales in their present form were illegal. The next month, the *St. Louis Globe Democrat* ran an article headlines "Grape Products Wary of Missouri," alleging that Willebrandt had wired Fruit Industries to keep out of the state while officials pondered the legality of the concentrate. The story provoked Willebrandt's vehement denial and statement that it was "unauthorized, unwarranted and untrue." Meanwhile, in Washington, the District Retail Druggists Association advised its members to discontinue sales of the grape concentrate, suggesting that while the letter of the law might be upheld, the spirit was not.[25]

By the end of the summer the situation worsened. A distributor of a wine brick concentrate, Vino Sano, was raided. Vino Sano executives protested that they were prosecuted while Willebrandt's Fruit Industries' client was not. They telegraphed Willebrandt to ask her to defend them.[26] The humorist Will Rogers reviewed the current legal status in a syndicated letter:

> Here is what the prohibition director decided about this pressed grape bricks you have been reading so much about.
> They will turn to wine if handled properly, but it's not illegal to buy 'em. We will have to prove that he was going to handle 'em properly. Well, that's fine, 'at-a-gal, Mabel, and I hope you get the government loan. By the way, a few sample bricks would reach me at the above address. Only, mind you, for paving and heaving purposes. I got a cat on my back fence, I want to throw 'em at. Of course, if they turn to wine before I hit him I will be disappointed and humiliated beyond words because the cat don't like wine. Send instructions what to do in case I make up with the cat.[27]

On the defensive, Fruit Industries sought counterpublicity. Asked to approve an effort to get an article in *The Saturday Evening Post*, *Colliers*, or *The New Yorker*, Willebrandt wired the public relations manager, "That would be perfectly splendid—go to it." A friendly editorial in the *Minneapolis Sunday Tribune* argued, "The ribald satisfaction of the wets and the prayerful regret of the drys because Mrs. Willebrandt as a lawyer has clients whom she would have opposed as assistant attorney general are not particularly well-founded."[28]

There was a lull in press attention until October, when Fruit Industries won a million dollar loan from the farm board. Senator Royal Copeland of New York charged that Willebrandt was being "paid off" for helping Hoover. Not only, he asserted, had she succeeded in obtaining $20 million (an exaggeration) from the farm board but the concentrate that she represented had escaped prosecution. A zealous Denver district attorney charged in the *Rocky Mountain News* that he would prosecute the concern "with which Mrs. Mabel Walker Willebrandt has a job" and he hoped that she would appear as defense counsel. An indignant Willebrandt caustically wired him to "check his facts." She had no connection with any so-called wine brick sellers. Fruit Industries did no business in Colorado.[29]

But the federal government was moving to test the legality of Fruit Industries' products in Missouri and California. In November 1931, in a ruling against the Ukiah Company in Kansas City, the federal district court ruled that the grapes themselves must be delivered to the consumer. On November 4, Donald Conn made the announcement from Willebrandt's Washington office that Fruit Industries would abandon the sales and service of Vine-Glo, since the court decision cast doubt on their legality. The company would continue to sell a grape concentrate for soft drinks. The *New York World Telegram* noted that the Fruit Industries' decision had come after Willebrandt had made several calls at the White House during the week.[30] The *Washington Times* suggested that the matter had been brought to a crisis when young Allen Hoover wrote his father a kidding letter about the "wine juice salesmen" at Harvard. The president was reported to be "much aroused."[31] The *Washington Post* asserted, "The abandonment of the chemical nursing service signifies the collapse of one of the most audacious adventures in national sophistry in the history of the world."[32] The wet *Baltimore Evening Sun* perceptively editorialized in "Back to Gin":

> The discovery that grape juice left to the laws of nature would presently evolve into a potable beverage with enough alcoholic content to be slightly stimulating, but not enough to instigate battle, murder and sudden death, was indisputably an excellent thing for the grape juice business. But it had at least one advantage for the country, as well—it offered formidable competition to gin as the national tipple. By aid of the grape concentrates, a good many thousands of Americans were in a fair way to become wine drinkers, instead of gin drinkers.

For the ordinary American, "it was back to the juniper-juice and alcohol."[33]

Fruit Industries' action had been voluntary. But in March 1932, the prohibition director, after reviewing the Ukiah decision, made it mandatory. The *Washington Daily News* reported, "Woodcock Puts Ban on Willebrandt Wine." Fruit Industries struck back with a ringing charge of "betrayal." Donald Conn charged that in adopting this policy the government was reversing years of support; the farm board had lent them in excess of $10 million. He also cited the support of Herbert Hoover for the sale of grape concentrates when he had been secretary of commerce and the legal opinion of Willebrandt when she had been assistant attorney general. Both Conn and Willebrandt were hesitant about the betrayal story developed by the public relations manager, but finally, Willebrandt, "always suspicious of newspaper people," was won over. She changed a few words, but finally approved it.[34]

The beleaguered Fruit Industries' leaders appeared before the farm board with a reorganization plan and a proposal to refund its debt, since, as Willebrandt and others reported, the growers' organization was in "desperate straits." In May they reappeared, negotiating for the sale of the concentrate in the export market.[35] Legislatively, Willebrandt and the grape growers intensified efforts to modify prohibition to allow the sale of wine. The intransigence of both drys and wets was formidable. The distillers' viewpoint was clearly stated by Representative Charles Linthicum of Maryland, leader of the House wet bloc: "Congress will never agree to a change in the prohibition laws that favor one industry."[36] Repeal of prohibition ended the controversy, but wine consumption lagged. California vintner Antonio Perelli-Minetti reminisced: "The opening of a saloon . . . killed the dry wine market overnight and that was a pitiful thing."[37]

Why Willebrandt, fresh from the wounding campaign and wet-dry wars of the 1928 campaign and able to choose from a broad range of clients, should elect to represent Fruit Industries was puzzling to friends and foes. She was always careful never to take a case for the distillers; her close friends urged her to be as circumspect with the vintners. She responded wearily and somewhat cryptically only that she would work to make her family and friends proud of her action.[38] Her decision seems to have been finally based on her loyalty to Hoover, to California, and, paradoxically, to the dry cause.

Hoover's intense economic and political interest in the grape industry is clear. His consistent foe, Hiram Johnson, always ready to criticize "the Great one," claimed that the grape stabilization organization was in place before the legislation creating the farm board was passed. He believed that lawyer T.T.C. Gregory had "privately perfected" the organization after "some weeks of consultation with Hoover." More easily documented is Hoover's persistent effort to persuade C.C. Teague, a major grape growers' organizer, to serve on the Federal Farm Board. He refused to accept two polite rejections.[39]

In April 1930, with the grape industry still in decline, an analyst from Stanford University urged fellow Californian, Interior Secretary Lyman Wilbur, to secure Teague's help with balky California banks, for "the chief and the administration have a large stake in this grape plan."[40] That same month, the *Baltimore Sun* noted the political consequences of "anything like a prolonged collapse in the grape industry." It "would tend to destroy this crucial voting bloc's last lingering faith in prohibition as a boon to grape growers. It would also impair seriously their faith in the farm rehabilitation powers of their dry fellow grape grower and Californian Herbert Hoover." The question was whether the Federal Farm Board could with a "little delicate assistance from the Prohibition Bureau" rehabilitate the $100 million grape industry.[41] Hoover would certainly have thought of the value of Willebrandt in such a rehabilitation effort. Her loyalty to him and, ironically, her continued loyalty to a cause she had defended so energetically would explain her defense of this new client.

With the repeal of prohibition in 1933, she worked with Fruit Industries to develop a plan for the liquidation of inventories and surplus plants and to begin new pooling arrangements that allowed the organization to repay all but a small part of the facility loan to the government and to put it "on a going concern basis."[42]

While old issues and causes continued to haunt Willebrandt, she was exhilarated by new challenges. In resigning from the Justice Department to become the Washington counsel of the Aviation Corporation, Willebrandt found an opportunity to pioneer in the field of aeronautical law and the federal legislation and regulation for the infant industry.

Willebrandt always gloried in flying and whenever possible traveled on government mail flights to meet the demanding business of the Justice Department. On one of these flights to Boston, when her plane ran out of oil and barely managed to limp onto the runway, the *New York Times* reported that Willebrandt emerged wearing her government regulation one-piece aviator suit over knickers, gray stockings, and a black knitted jacket, cheerfully announcing to a reporter that she had enjoyed the flight "thoroughly." In July 1928, the American Bar Association arranged to fly her to Seattle to address their convention. "I'm so happy over flying west," an excited Willebrandt wrote to her parents. "Soon it will be the way I'll always go and it's joyous to start so now."[43] En route, she detailed the beauty and the rigors of the flight to her father:

the plan was to leave Chicago at evening but weather reports said low fog "ceiling" so we delayed the take off until 10:00 P.M. The pilot was Lee. . . . They wouldn't have let a greener man go at all. Lee tried but after a few miles out of Chicago had to land at an emergency field. . . . it was too dangerous to fly so close to the ground just escaping tree tops as he was obliged to do. Well we waited and tried a few miles and came down again. This continued till 8:00 A.M. Not yet 50 miles out of Chicago we tried, but it started to rain and we came down in a farmer's field. . . . in 10 minutes Fords and Dodges darted from every direction and I guess 10 cars came out to the field. Most of the farmers were in overalls and many barefoot. I climbed out of my cabin and was standing on the wing talking to the pilot whose "pit" is 6 feet back. These farmers were curious, looked the plane all over and me too. It started to rain hard but they wouldn't leave. They were going to see that plane rise! Many crawled on the wet grass under the wings and stuck it out. There we sat til 11:00 A.M. from dawn. At 11 it cleared a little and the pilot rose and we started West in earnest, 16 hours late! . . .

Late afternoon at Cheyenne, Wyoming, we followed the sunset. Never have I seen anything lovelier. Banner sculptured volcanic buttes all lighted mauve and purple and rose. At Rock Springs, Wyoming, it was dark, but the winking lights were placed across the Wassach range, high and wide, so we pushed on. It was eerie, the plane climbed to 9000 feet or more and over black canyons, the motor thudded from one winking light to another, finally from a great steep height swooping out of the mouth of a canyon into view of Salt Lake City. . . . I do not think there can be (anything) so beautiful as that gem studded valley set in the center by the lighted capitol dome, all reflected in the Lake at its feet with black silhouette peaks on all sides.[44]

On her return flight from the Seattle convention, with "Mr. Boeing, the owner of this whole air line," and two other passengers, the engine suddenly "cut out" at 5,000 feet over rough mountains. Willebrandt described: "Boeing who was sitting with me went white as a sheet, saying 'it's engine trouble—but don't be afraid, he can land the plane somewhere.'" The pilot glided and "side-swiped" to land in a field twenty miles away. Airborne again after some repairs, the plane began to miss on two cylinders at 6,000 feet. On landing at San Francisco, Willebrandt confessed: "Loss of sleep and an hour in mid-air behind that engine had given me a fit of nerve and all I did for 3 hours of beautiful scenery was to count the beats of that engine and watch for a possible landing spot 8,000 feet below. I was terribly ashamed of

Arriving in Boston in 1929 in a government regulation flying suit, Willebrandt is obviously unfazed that the plane had run out of oil just before
touching down at Boston.

myself not to be able to control my feelings, but really suspense is more wearing than disaster."[45]

Her excitement in flight was not dampened long. A year later, while flying to Boise, Idaho, for the Aviation Corporation, Willebrandt complained of "caution artists" (who, she said, were usually easterners or Bostonians). She particularly chafed at the caution of "a Harvard product" who delayed the flight from Cheyenne, by "the best case of worked up caution psychology by a Bostonian on a pilot I ever saw." She commented disgustedly: "All the real western men who fly this country . . . just smiled back of their hands. This flying game is knowing your country, your ship, and having guts. Caution artists don't belong in it anymore than croakers do in a Christian Science Church."[46]

Aviation provided the incentive for a frustrated Willebrandt to leave the Justice Department. In her letter of resignation, she cited the "real challenge" offered by the Aviation Corporation, adding: "We are on the threshold of rapid expansion of air traffic. The law throughout the forty-eight states and the Federal Government is in the making."[47] Her letter of agreement set as a special charge, besides handling legal matters referred to her by general counsel of AVCO and its affiliates, "to make a survey of existing laws and procedures in aviation." Her retainer was $20,000, but "should a program to advance the interests of commercial aviation be adopted as a result of the survey, this will be made the subject of a further agreement on compensation."[48] Willebrandt's AVCO contact was its lobbyist Hainer Hinshaw, active in Republican headquarters during the 1928 campaign. Her good friend Walter F. Brown was the new postmaster general, czar of air mail contracts. As a loyal campaigner, her access to Hoover remained open. AVCO had a strong, well-connected Washington advocate. To Willebrandt, AVCO brought the challenge of a new field of law, the promise of financial security, and release from an increasingly intolerable situation in the Justice Department. Accepting the offer, she wired Hainer Hinshaw: "God Bless You."[49]

As an industry, aviation entered the 1920s almost totally free. Planes, pilots, carriers, and flying schools needed no license. The air was open to all. The war had stimulated aircraft manufacturing and the postwar years were dominated by promotion, barnstorming, and erratic development.[50] Willebrandt, in her first year with AVCO, helped in some promotional trips. She was a passenger on AVCO's first regularly scheduled air-rail transcontinental trip, carrying a bottle of water

Willebrandt and Amelia Earhart, 1930. *Below,* Earhart (fourth from right) and Willebrandt with a delegation promoting air travel, 1930.

from New York's mayor, Jimmy Walker, to the mayor of Los Angeles. In July, she journeyed to Cincinnati and Boise. Nine months later she arranged some publicity for AVCO's affiliate Eastern Air Express, Inc., and promoted a South American tour of Pan American Airways to coincide with her vacation. Willebrandt referred to this as "selling tickets."[51]

The promotional efforts reflected the problems of an industry struggling with the chaos of the marketplace and overwhelming competition from rail and bus companies. The size of the planes and limited terminal and field facilities meant that aviation posed no immediate interstate threat in passenger or freight traffic to other carriers. While it did not share in Coolidge prosperity, the industry did begin to organize. The Aeronautical Chamber of Commerce was formed in 1921. Later, the energetic secretary of commerce, Herbert Hoover, helped to form the National Aeronautic Association. The major stimulus to government promotion of air commerce was the challenge hurled by General William "Billy" Mitchell to the Coolidge administration's military policy and budget. To deflect the storm of publicity roused by Mitchell's fight for an air force, Coolidge named a blue-ribbon board, headed by his close friend Dwight Morrow, to make recommendations on air navigation and the air industry in America. Reporting in 1925, the Morrow board urged the federal government to "progressively extend the air mail service" and "meet the need for air ways and air navigation facilities." The resulting legislation, the Air Commerce Act, established an assistant secretary of aeronautics in the Department of Commerce and ordered that department to encourage air commerce and commercial aviation.[52]

More immediately significant legislation was the Air Mail Act of 1925, or the Kelly Act. In contracting for domestic air mail service with commercial carriers, the Post Office Department was also given a mandate to "encourage commercial aviation" and to work for federal airway development and regulation. The second assistant postmaster general was to construct a coordinated transcontinental air service. With this incentive, Henry Ford began building airplanes, announcing, "I feel it is now or never to get hold of commercial flying and make a success of it."[53]

In the competition for air mail revenue, AVCO pressed Willebrandt into service for its affiliate PAIC (Pittsburgh Aviation Investors Corporation). At stake was the designation of PAIC-owned Butler Field as the air mail stop for Pittsburgh and a $100,000 appropriation for lighting the runways. The competition was the Curtis-Keys group, who controlled the current mail stop at Bettis Field. Both interests pressured the second assistant postmaster general. Hinshaw wrote Willebrandt that they would "have a fight worthy of our mettle." He reassured an anxious PAIC executive, George Hann, that "a certain pressure will be brought to bear on Postmaster General Brown that "should be fruitful."[54] Willebrandt confirmed Brown's interest in the development of the Pittsburgh airport and noted that she was "greatly encouraged" at his promise to speed up the matter. With Hinshaw, she reviewed their joint objectives: to arrange a conference between the second assistant postmaster and Hann; "to keep Brown's mind clear on the cooperative spirit of our crowd in working this out"; and to keep the matter "pushed as much as possible." This would be done through phone calls and contacts with the postmaster general's office.[55] Willebrandt was in charge of the Washington arrangements to bring Post Office and Commerce Department officials to the dedication of the new Butler Field.[56]

The first wave of competition for air mail contracts following the Kelly Act ended in 1929. As the initial four-year contracts were about to expire, Postmaster General Brown, a man with a mission and vision, was determined to forge a rational, efficient air mail system and simultaneously to fashion a viable commercial aviation industry. To Brown, the air mail business was "like a kennel at feeding time." He sought new legislation freeing him from the fetters of competitive bidding and allowing him through negotiation or extension of existing routes to build a grid of four major east-west routes and eight major north-south patterns. He recommended that air mail payments be made to the carriers on the basis of capacity and space for the mail cargo rather than by pounds carried.[57] Basically, he attacked the old system in which government contracts were awarded to those businesses which could bid low because of poor equipment, cost-cutting measures, short-term investment, and weak safety records. His candidates for the four east-west routes were the largest, most experienced, and most soundly financed carriers. AVCO and its operating subsidiary American Airways were targeted by Brown for the southern route.

When Willebrandt joined AVCO in 1929, it was just two months old. Organized primarily as a holding and development corporation by Lehman Brothers and W. A. Harriman, Inc., the two million shares of common stock it offered on the market netted the new corporation approximately $35 million. By the end of the year, the Aviation Corporation acquired ownership or a controlling interest in Universal Aviation Corporation: Southern Air Transport, Inc.; Colonial Airways Corporation; Interstate Air Lines, Inc.; Embry-Riddle Aviation Corporation; Fairchild Aviation Corporation; and Alaskan Airways, Inc. In January 1930, American Airways, Inc., was formed, eventually incorporating into its organization all of the other operational affiliates. At its height, AVCO had eighty subsidiaries. It represented, on the basis of total mileage, perhaps the largest air transportation system in the United States, but its 9,000-mile collection of routes was "utterly incoherent." In its first ten months of operation, AVCO registered a deficit of $696,727. Like Postmaster General Brown, AVCO wanted stability and predictability.[58]

Willebrandt began her major work for the firm with a strategy breakfast session on June 27, 1929. The discussion introduced her to the sweep and complexities of the law and regulations for the air industry. Reviewing the field were the AVCO general counsel, William Dewey Loucks, of the New York firm of Loucks and Cullen; Hainer Hinshaw; George Hann; Talbot Freeman, of the National Aeronautical Association; and Cletus Keating, an expert in admiralty law. The task, as Freeman indicated, was "to decide the things we ought to go after." It was a rapid and intensive introduction for Willebrandt. Keating urged that in the areas of jurisdiction and liability, the aviation industry would find a workable model in admiralty law.

Willebrandt, the neophyte, asked the essential questions. If a federal statute extended the limited liability granted to ships of the sea to air ships, would not the industry face the same state court tests that had dogged the young railroad industry? Would admiralty jurisdiction best be extended to aviation through a constitutional amendment? How could federal law so limit liability that state tests would be precluded? And, she observed, "the minute Congress passes that act, it is going to put jurisdiction somewhere to pass rules and regulations—and rates—interpreting that act."[59] In a spirited discussion of rate regulation and the danger of state action in the absence of congressional initiatives, Loucks, underscoring Willebrandt's importance to AVCO, asked if she had talked to the president about this air legislation. "Not recently," she responded.

Again taking the lead in the discussion, Willebrandt urged that the industry "take advantage of the air-mindedness of the country." AVCO and others should agree on minimum and maximum objectives. What the industry wanted, she believed, was a law, providing a single judiciary, and "a simple proceeding that has established precedent to make it certain from the time it starts." A constitutional amendment might take three years for passage; an act of Congress would be swifter, if not surer. The breakfast ended with a legislative blueprint. AVCO would press for admiralty jurisdiction, limited liability, interstate regulation of traffic, and certificates of necessity (federal license). Willebrandt and Keating were charged with drafting the legislation.[60]

Called in to consult on this legislative initiative was T.T.G. Gregory, Willebrandt's old friend and colleague who had represented the California grape growers. Gregory warned of pending legislative proposals and pressed AVCO to have its own measure when congressional debate on air regulation began. He recommended that some skillful person with proper contacts keep in constant touch with this situation in the House, the Senate, and the administration; he "knew of no one who could more skillfully handle its many phases than Mrs. Willebrandt, who not only has all of the necessary contacts but who herself would be a strong factor in molding a program."[61]

The bill that emerged from this groundwork was the McNary-Watres Act, drafted by Walter Brown and Second Assistant Postmaster Warren Glover, aided by Willebrandt and former assistants in the Commerce and Post Office departments, William P. MacCracken, Jr. and Paul Henderson. The measure called for a new air mail rate scale based on cubic feet of space rather than pounds and the elimination of competitive bidding for contracts. The Post Office Department would negotiate air mail contracts without advertising for bids. The postmaster general could extend or consolidate routes when he believed the public interest would be served. Essentially, Brown would have a broad initiative to mold a coherent air mail system and to organize the airline industry on national lines.[62]

It was this power that raised opposition in Congress and to some extent in the industry. Particularly vehement in his opposition was Clyde Kelly, the "father" of the Air Mail Act of 1925. Willebrandt worked hard for passage. Testifying before the House Committee on the Post Office, she orchestrated the AVCO support at the hearings. In the crucial April deliberations in Congress she went "to everyone in Washington that had, in any way, anything to do with this bill." Both she and MacCracken had "been working on Clyde Kelly," with the result that, after winning modification on competitive bidding, he asked for few amendments.[62] One lobbyist for an AVCO affiliate reported to his headquarters that if the Post Office Department and other people interested in the bill worked with the energy and effectiveness of Mrs. Willebrandt, "it would make all the difference in the world getting this legislation through."[63]

After intense lobbying by the Post Office Department and the industry, the final measure passed in April 1930. The Watres Act changed the terms of contract bidding. Awards were to be made to the lowest "responsible" bidder who had owned an air line operated on a daily schedule of at least 250 miles for a minimum period of six months. Brown added a proviso that the line must have night flying experience.[64] The Aeronautical Chamber of Commerce concluded that the act was responsible for the most important fundamental changes in the air transport picture during 1930.[65]

The new legislation rewarded the major pioneering lines that had demonstrated successful operations with mail and passengers. By the end of 1930, lines with mail contracts, responding to new incentives on cubic feet of space, all carried passengers. The president of AVCO, Graham Grosvener, estimated that its operating subsidiaries would benefit by $100,000 additional revenue monthly. Estimating a yield of $3 million under the new law, Grosvener urged, in April 1930, that every effort be made to win these awards. Commenting on the night flying proviso, a *Baltimore Sun* correspondent noted that AVCO had an advantage, since only two airlines, both with political connections, qualified: American Airways, represented by Willebrandt, and TWA, where Herbert Hoover, Jr., was a chief engineer.[66]

Not wasting any time in organizing his system, Postmaster Brown issued invitations to representatives of the major carriers for a May meeting in his office. Here he outlined his transcontinental routes and invited cooperation and agreement. He wanted only one operator carrying both mail and passengers on each route. He suggested that the representatives discuss and agree on the organization of routes in a separate meeting. After adjourning to an adjacent hotel, the operators' conference achieved only minor agreements, reluctantly reporting to Brown that they could do no more. Anticipating this impasse, Brown implemented his planned transcontinental routes, favoring the major operators. AVCO's American Airways was awarded the southern route. AVCO was then pressured by Brown to buy out rival Southern Air Fast Express and to work out an agreement with Delta. When the

A mid-career portrait of Willebrandt in her office in the Shoreham Building, Washington, probably in the late 1930s.

system was completed, American, TWA, United, and Eastern carried 89 percent of the mail.[67]

The outraged cries and charges of conspiracy, favoritism, and maladministration by the small independent lines stirred congressional hearings, but there was no reversal of policy. By 1933, when Brown left the Post Office Department, the Watres Act had remarkably accomplished his purposes. It was the last year that air mail revenues exceeded passenger revenues.[68] A new fleet of larger planes, encouraged by the cubic space allocations of the act, was bringing greater safety and regularity to the industry.

The airlines looked forward to the new administration of air-minded President Franklin Roosevelt. Contrary to expectations, however, the New Deal introduced economy measures that cut the postal rates awarded carriers. A reorganization in the Commerce Department downgraded the special position of aeronautics. Worst of all for the airlines was an investigation of ocean and air mail contracts by a special committee of the Senate, chaired by Willebrandt's friend Hugo Black of Alabama. Responding to the continued allegations by the independents, the Black committee investigated the May 1930 meetings of the operators in the "spoils conferences." The Alabama *Mobile Times* speculated, "Mr. Black's inquiry may reach Teapot Dome proportions."[69] Investigators subpoenaed the records of the aviation companies, probing for political influence and favoritism. They developed a small file of Willebrandt-Hinshaw letters, labeling them "political contacts." Though Willebrandt was never called by the committee, Hainer Hinshaw was questioned sharply. The star witness was Walter Brown, who testified frankly on his policies. He had worked to develop a strong system of both air mail and commercial aviation and he had no apologies.[70]

Black and his committee charged, "The control of American aviation has been ruthlessly taken away from the men who could fly and bestowed upon bankers, brokers, promoters and politicians sitting in their inner offices, alloting among themselves, the taxpayers' money."[71] As a result of the hearings and a judgment of fraud by the Post Office Department solicitor, Postmaster General James Farley canceled air mail contracts with all the major carriers who were part of the spoils conferences. A disastrous experiment of carrying the mail by the army was initiated. In one week, twelve pilots plunged to their death, bringing Roosevelt his first major loss of public support.

New federal legislation, the Black-McKellar Act, passed in June

1934. Described as "a hodgepodge of conflicting ideologies," it stressed competitive bidding, economic regulation, and air mail awards.[72] Commercial aviation was not specifically promoted. Holding companies who had participated in the spoils conferences were to receive no contracts. *Aviation* magazine summarized the carnage: "Seldom are turning points in history as clearly defined as was that marked by the cancellation of the airmail contracts in February last. An entire industry in rapidly accelerating motion collided with an immovable object. . . . Everything came to a full stop."[73]

Faced with lower air mail rates and heavy equipment costs, an American Airlines (a change of name from American Airways had won it contracts) executive, C.R. Smith, reported to a congressional committee in 1935 that relief legislation was very badly needed. Between 1934 and 1936, carriers lost more than $3,500,000.[74] Relief was several years in coming. When it did, through the creation of the Civil Aeronautics Authority (CAA) in the Civil Aeronautics Act of 1938, Willebrandt did not testify before the congressional committees. Now the chairman of the Committee on Aeronautical Law of the American Bar Association, the first woman ever appointed to chair an ABA committee, she was deeply involved where she had started—in working to define and develop this new field of law.[75]

The Committee on Aeronautical Law of the American Bar Association had been working with the National Conference of Commissioners on Uniform State Laws since 1922. In 1930 the committee reported on the Watres Law and noted its continued study on uniform state law. It particularly noted the Swetland case in the federal district court, Northern District of Ohio, involving one of the most important and vexing questions in aviation law, the control and ownership of airspace. Was flight over private property without the permission of the property owner, trespass? The old common law maxim, *Cujus est solum, ejus est usque ad coelum* (whose the soil is, his it is all the way to the heavens) was at issue.[76] Willebrandt filed an amicus curiae brief for the Aviation Corporation in the Swetland case (*Frederick L. Swetland and Raymond H. Swetland v. Curtiss Airports Corporation, Ohio Air Terminals, Inc., and Curtiss Flying Service, Inc.*) in the U.S. Court of Appeals for the Sixth Circuit in 1931.

Her forty-nine-page brief reviewed the law of trespass "over" property from the Justinian Code through Coke's Institutes and Blackstone's Commentaries. She cited forty-five cases in challenging the district court decision that enjoined as trespass any flights under a

500-foot ceiling over the Swetlands' country home. She directly challenged the maxim *Cujus est solum, ejus est usque ad coelum*, arguing that "there was no such thing as aerial trespass because there is no such thing as ownership of unenclosed air space. It is *res communis*—or free to all." The district court, she asserted, had confused the law of trespass in this instance with the law of nuisance.

Tracing the maxim through the Justinian Code, she concluded that it applied only to the right of the property owner to the use of his land free from anything attached to and projecting out from adjoining property. The Justinian Code affirmed air as *res communis* as did the early English writers. She cited George Dawson's *Origo Legum* of 1694, detailing an imagined case of a man flying with artificial wings over the earth (even to the moon). He would have free use of the air in his journey, unless he built pillars to erect a sky house. Then he would have to obey the law of the soil.[77] Citing Blackstone on *res communis*, Willebrandt observed: "The coming of the airplane does not need the making of new law to meet new conditions as so many thoughtlessly assert; it simply needs the uncovering of what the law has always been." There was no danger to aviation if the courts restrained careless flying or flights that constituted a nuisance, but to "apply the ancient *coelum* maxim loosely and conclude that flight at any height is a trespass," besides being bad law, would seriously retard all aviation development. Using a Bible analogy she recalled that the Children of Israel, weary of worshipping an unseen God, built an image as a reminder. Over time the image became the reality. The "image" of *cujus est solum* had also become accepted as reality. Its original meaning should now be restored. "There is no property right in air space," she concluded, "but unreasonable use of superincumbent air space may constitute a nuisance." It was not trespass. The appendix bristled with further proofs, citing cases from Henry VII's reign.[78] In its landmark decision, the court of appeals agreed with her basic argument. The Swetlands were granted an injunction against low flights over their property from the adjoining flying school and airport, but the grounds were nuisance, not trespass. Both sides essentially achieved their objectives; neither appealed.

In the annual report of the ABA Committee on Aeronautical Law, Willebrandt's argument was cited "as the clearest discussion of the history, import, scope, and authority, of the maxim 'cujus solem est' which has been written since aviation discussion began." The significance of the case was underscored in an article in the *Air Law Review* noting that to a greater extent than any other case, this settled the law relating to air space.[79]

Within two years, Willebrandt had become one of the leaders in this fledgling field. When New York University formed a new national organization, the American Academy of Air Law, she was one of the major figures invited to join its "galaxy of aviation leaders." She was on the editorial board of the Air Law Review and also active in the legal and legislative research service of the Aeronautical Chamber of Commerce.[80] In April 1932 she contributed a major article to the new *Journal of Air Law* on federal regulation by "Certificates of Convenience and Necessity."[81] As the chairman of the ABA Committee on Aeronautical Law in 1938, she spoke at the annual convention of the National Association of State Aviation Officials on the need for a uniform aviation liability act and more broadly on legislation needed in aviation. Reviewing the first ten years of aviation history, Willebrandt observed that the industry's "doleful predictions" of legal trouble from "ground minded" lawyers had not been borne out. Uniformity of law was now accepted as essential and the establishment of the new Civil Aeronautics Authority was a major step in achieving that goal. The changing field of aviation needed continuing flexibility. She ended with Justice Holmes's advice on applying existing law to new conditions: "The Constitution of the United States should ever be regarded as the bark of a living tree and ever be applied as to permit of expanding life within."[82]

Willebrandt headed the ABA Committee until 1942; during that time she cooperated with the CAA and studied the implications of its decisions and the need for further federal and state legislation. Nine short years after her entry into aviation law, she held the ABA's most important post in this new field. Her accomplishments had been made in the face of her increasing hearing disability and while she was also remarkably pioneering in a parallel field of air law—the radio.

Willebrandt's education and immersion in radio law was as rapid as her introduction to aeronautical law. Three months after leaving the Justice Department, she issued a short-notice dinner invitation to her aviation colleague Hainer Hinshaw. Explaining that the radio expert Martin Codel and his wife would be there, she urged: "I want you & Martin Codel to educate me on Radio, the pleadings, opinions, rather, of the Hazeltine case have come. They're full of the most terrible language—grid and plate circuit neutralization and multistage amplifiers, etc., etc. It's over my head. Other times I've been confronted with things over my head, and somehow the Lord has helped me through. Won't you again be His agent?" She ended, "Codel is a radio nut. Help me draw him out while covering my own ignorance—will you?"[83]

The Hazeltine case involved Willebrandt's client, the radio manufacturer Atwater Kent. It introduced her to the complex patent issues in the industry. Her other major radio client, the Johnson-Kennedy Radio Corporation, involved her in a central issue of federal regulation of the airwaves. As in aviation, Willebrandt addressed the central legal questions of the new industry and the new field.

Radio, like aviation, was "developing the rules of the game" in the 1920s. Stimulated during World War I, radio had a rapid and chaotic commercial growth as newspapers, churches, universities, cities, and manufacturers pressed to win their share of the ether. The major impetus for expansion came from the pioneer radio manufacturers like Atwater Kent, Zenith, RCA, and electrical companies, who were anxious to build markets for their products. In 1923, half of the 550 stations in operation were associated with these businesses.[84]

Complicating and retarding expansion was the war-extended authority of the navy. The first federal radio law in 1912 gave the navy unrestricted control of frequencies needed for its sea operations; in 1920 this control extended from 187.5 to 500 kilohertz. As radio developed and expanded, both the Post Office Department and the Department of Commerce, believing as always that they should promote business order out of chaos, challenged the navy control. Secretary of Commerce Hoover hosted annual radio conferences bringing technical, scientific, and managerial leaders together to set an agenda for development. Working with private industry and the new National Association of Broadcasters, Hoover built a powerful groundswell for comprehensive federal legislation.[85]

Concerns about possible monopolies by American Telephone and Telegraph (AT&T), General Electric, Westinghouse, and the new giant Radio Corporation of America (RCA), the emergence of network broadcasting with the inauguration of the Red and Blue networks by the National Broadcasting Company (NBC), and problems in overlapping frequency use that threatened a true "Tower of Babel" finally resulted in the Radio Act of 1927. Philosophically, the act affirmed that the electromagnetic spectrum, like the lands and the forests, was a valuable natural resource. It also accepted that radio broadcasting by its nature was interstate commerce. Specifically, the

Radio Act established a new regulatory agency to bring order to the air waves. The Federal Radio Commission (FRC) was to classify stations, assign bands of wavelengths, determine equitable geographic distribution, regulate interference, and develop guidelines for chain operations to prevent monopoly. To underscore its new authority, all existing licenses were repealed; 18,000 corporations and organizations would have to petition for new licenses.[86] Reviewing the FRC's mandate, one of the first commissioners vented his frustration over the virtual impossibility of discriminating between the conflicting public service claims of "grand opera and religious services, of market reports and direct advertising, or jazz orchestras and lectures on the diseases of hogs."[87] Adding to the difficulties, Congress set an initial limit of one year on the FRC's legislative life and then neglected to vote any appropriations. Death claimed two of the first five appointees. A year later Congress extended the term of the commission and passed the Davis Amendment to the 1927 Radio Act, which required a survey of the five geographic zones and the equal distribution of broadcasting facilities within them. In a 1929 decision, the Supreme Court unanimously affirmed the congressional power to regulate this new interstate industry.[88]

Willebrandt entered radio law in the patent area. An inventor, Louis A. Hazeltine, had perfected the first neutrodyne receiver in 1923, allowing tuning and frequency amplification. Reception was now free from oscillation (squeals and whistles), and tuning could be logged for resetting to the same stations. The Hazeltine Corporation licensed and provided engineering support for licensees using the neutrodyne receiver. Having its "own inspired engineering staff," the Atwater Kent Manufacturing Company chose not to seek a Hazeltine license. It made its own adjustments to achieve neutralization and then pioneered in producing the first "unicontrol" of several tuned circuits. Hazeltine was unimpressed and charged an infringement of patent by Atwater Kent (and other firms). He won an injunction against the Kent company in a decision in the Federal District Court for the Eastern District of New York. Kent appealed and lost in the circuit court of appeals by a two-to-one margin. When Willebrandt was called in to review the appeal in September 1929, Kent and his attorneys, the Philadelphia firm of Neave and Philbin, were preparing a petition for a writ of certiorari to the Supreme Court, a move denied in January 1930. Successful in its infringement suit, the Hazeltine Corporation sued Atwater Kent for damages in the Third Federal District Court in

Philadelphia, charging that he was personally responsible. Willebrandt was again consulted. Eventually Kent paid $680,000 in 1934 as back royalties and signed a license for use of the neutrodyne receiver.[89] In none of these cases did Willebrandt represent Kent in court. She advised him and worked with his attorneys in the appeal procedures and in the final monetary settlement. It was a good education into this highly technical field, providing early experience that she effectively utilized in one of the major test cases involving federal regulation of the air.

In 1931, another client, the Johnson-Kennedy Radio Corporation, operating station WJKS in Gary, Indiana, petitioned the FRC for assignment of a frequency band then used by two Chicago stations, WIBO and WPCC. Willebrandt represented WJKS from the FRC hearings in April 1931 through the successful Supreme Court argument in 1933. Developing her case before the FRC's chief examiner Ellis A. Yost (the husband of her old friend and WCTU leader Lenna Yost), Willebrandt argued that WJKS should have the award (1) because it performed a valuable public service in the multiethnic city; (2) because there was no full-time, clear channel station in Indiana, a state that was 20 percent under quota while Illinois was 49 percent over quota; (3) because by operating at its present 1,300 kilocycles it received interference from station WFBL, Syracuse, New York; and (4) because the Radio Act as amended in 1928 and 1930 stated that the petitioner must name the stations it wished to replace. WIBO and WPCC of Chicago, sharing frequency 560, she argued, could be replaced without a serious loss of service to listeners in the Chicago area.

Two other radio stations were represented at the FRC April hearing. The attorney general of Ohio represented the Ohio State University station, WEAO, and claimed that the frequency change of WJKS would interfere with WEAO broadcasts. WISJ of Madison had also shared frequency 560 with WIBO and WPCC but had temporarily been awarded 780 kilocycles. Its operators worried that if the assignment did not become permanent, it would be left with nothing.[90]

The hearings were replete with technical arguments on what constituted interference, the angle of radiation of a high frequency versus a low frequency, the programming of Chicago stations that might provide a similar service should WIBO and WPCC lose their licenses, and the financial investment of the backers of WIBO. Willebrandt hammered hard on the public service aspects of WJKS and the equal distribution of radio service mandated by the Radio Act of 1927 and the amendments of 1928 and 1930. In the sometimes heated exchanges with the examiner and other attorneys, Willebrandt's hearing difficulties were occasionally evident, necessitating repetition from a questioner not in her immediate vision. It did not damage her presentation or argument, but it underscored her difficulties in a physical situation where her eyes could not help to inform her ears.[91]

After more than 800 pages of testimony and argument, Yost, obviously unmoved by his friendship with Willebrandt or her argument, ruled against the Johnson-Kennedy Radio petition. On review, the Federal Radio Commission unanimously reversed his ruling on the basis that WJKS rendered "an excellent public service." That decision was appealed by WIBO's owners, Nelson Brothers Bond and Mortgage Company, to the District of Columbia Court of Appeals. The appeals court ruled three to two that the "facts furnish no legal basis" for the commission's decision, which was "in a legal sense arbitrary and capricious."[92]

In the *Federal Radio Commission, Johnson-Kennedy Radio Corporation, Intervener* v. *Nelson Brothers Bond & Mortgage Company*, the FRC and Willebrandt for WJKS tested the regulatory powers of the agency in the Supreme Court. In April 1933, Willebrandt was once more in the familiar court, this time facing her old Justice Department colleague, former solicitor general James M. Beck, who represented WIBO. Her brief posed the essential question of whether the Federal Radio Commission had the power under the statutes in the interest of greater public service to transfer the facilities of broadcasting stations WIBO and WPCC in an over-quota state to station WJKS in an under-quota state. Because the court of appeals decisions had stressed the "facts" of the case, she presented a detailed defense of the "facts" of the WJKS public service. In Gary's population of nearly one million, 60 percent were foreign born; 90 percent were involved in the steel industry. WJKS was the only station in Gary. Its particular contribution was in its weekly foreign language and ethnic music programs featuring local Hungarian, Italian, black, Mexican, Russian, Polish, and Irish talent. Eight to fourteen hours of programming each week were devoted to these broadcasts. They stimulated pride in racial origin and community and instructed in American citizenship. Special steel-mill accident-prevention talks were aired. Every noon the Radio Chapel hour was produced. On Sundays, Baptist, Presbyterian, Methodist, Catholic, and Salvation Army services were broadcast. The station had equipped Gary police cars with radios and the police could interrupt to broadcast at any time. Gary was a twenty-four-hour community; it needed a twenty-four-hour station.[93] Conversely, the FRC had concluded that both WIBO and WPCC could leave the air without depriving any major audience. WIBO, with its heavy reliance on NBC network programming, could be covered wholly or partially by other stations in Chicago; WPCC was dependent on programming by its founder the Reverend Mr. O'Hair. His independent church was not connected with any regular denomination. The Moody Bible Institute station in Chicago broadcast exclusively religious programs that could replace WPCC. Finally, she noted, the FRC had accepted the WJKS contention that it faced objectionable interference from WFBL in Syracuse, New York. By moving to 560 kilocycles, WJKS would be free of such interference.

The Federal Radio Commission had made the assignment to WJKS on two grounds: first, it would achieve more equitable distribution of the broadcasting facilities with the fourth zone (Illinois, Wisconsin, Minnesota, North and South Dakota, Nebraska, Kansas, Missouri, and Indiana), since Indiana was 20 percent under and Illinois 49 percent over quota and there was "no one single full-time regional or clear channel station" in Indiana; second, "public interest, convenience and/or necessity would be served by the granting of this application."[94] Finally, Willebrandt argued, whereas the "facts" supported WJKS, WIBO, which had so impressed the appeals court by its claim of loss of financial investment, had submitted no "facts" certified by accountants to substantiate this.

The Federal Radio Commission, she argued, was clearly following both the facts and the law, specifically the Davis Amendment, which, in conjunction with FRC General Order No. 92, set the classification and rating of the value of radio facilities and published the quota results. In effect, every licensee in over-quota areas was warned, "watch out! Your area is using more facilities than it has any right to under the law and some of you will have something taken away from you, if applications are made from areas having less than the law gives them." General Order No. 102 mandated that plaintiffs in under-quota areas had to name the licensee whose facilities it "desired to capture." The FRC could then judge better between their respective services. If the appeals court decision were allowed to stand, it would be impossible for the FRC to carry out the directive of Congress to maintain a fair and equitable allocation of the broadcasting facilities throughout the country.[95]

Chief Justice Charles Evans Hughes wrote the opinion of the Court, May 8, 1933, upholding the contentions of the Willebrandt argument and concluding that the commission's finding of fact rested on substantial evidence.[96] The Court determined that the Federal Radio Commission could "legally determine the number, location, and activities of all stations." It affirmed that the "regulation standard of public interest, convenience and necessity were not vague and did not involve unlawful delegation of legislative authority."[97] For the first time the Supreme Court upheld the power of the commission to regulate broadcasting.[98]

Willebrandt embarked on still another new legal venture in the first years after leaving the Justice Department—the field of international claims. She represented her friend Carl Lomen, "the Reindeer King" of Alaska, in his claim against the Soviet government for spiriting away his small colony from the disputed territory of Wrangel Island. One hundred miles north of Siberia, Wrangel Island, described by Lomen as "the maverick land of the Arctic" and "a wasteland of misery and tragedy," had been claimed at one time by Great Britain, the United States, and the Soviet Union.[99] In 1920, the well-known Arctic explorer and developer Vilhjalmur Stefansson, alert to the future strategic importance of the island to air travel over the Arctic route, pressed the British to assert their claim. A man of action, Stefansson sent a party two years later to raise the Union Jack. The Lomen family firm outfitted this colonizing effort and the subsequent futile rescue attempt. When a relief mission finally arrived in 1923, it found one lone Eskimo. The British still hesitated in pressing their claim, and a frustrated Stefansson asked Carl Lomen if he would like to relieve him of Wrangel Island. Always open to new adventure and already involved in the Wrangel missions, Lomen first consulted Secretary of State Charles Evans Hughes, who hailed the Lomen overture as "the first concrete American move" made for Wrangel. "Personally," he stated, "I say go and hold it. The only claim the Russians could advance would be one of contiguity and that would not hold in international law."[100]

In 1924, the Lomens took over from Stefansson, assuming responsibility for the colony, which had been reestablished in the 1923 rescue mission. Lomen immediately dispatched fourteen more Eskimos, a white Alaskan, and ten reindeer to reinforce the colony's leader Charles Wells and twelve Eskimos. Contracting an old whaling vessel to make the run to the island, the Lomens were soon as frustrated as Stefansson. Severe Arctic ice and storms twice forced the whaler to turn back to Nome, and the new colonizers never reached the island. Meanwhile the Lomens received the disturbing news that a Soviet icebreaker, the *Red October*, had removed Wells and the Eskimos and transported them to Vladivostok, leaving the Soviet flag behind on Wrangel.[101]

Rushing to Washington to win the aid of the State Department, Lomen found officials solicitous but unwilling to take any action. His impatient friend, Mabel Walker Willebrandt, tried to help him sway the department and chafed at the "petty minded politicians" who could not "see the value of holding [the island] from the overreaching claims of the Bolsheviks."[102] The Red Cross forwarded $1,600 to the State Department to help with the tortuous arrangements to return the interned colonizers. A flurry of press accounts reactivated discussion of the conflicting American and British claims. Meanwhile, Willebrandt intensified her efforts to help Lomen, taking him to see Secretary of the Navy Curtis Wilbur, Secretary of State Kellogg, and finally President Coolidge. She talked with the general counsel of the State Department and the chairman of the Senate Foreign Relations Committee. Assured by the general counsel that the Lomens had a valid claim, the family engaged Willebrandt to keep pressing it. In 1933, she urged Carl Lomen to organize his evidence and prepared for a six-week cruise to Russia. (Not unexpectedly, she had to cancel the trip when an important case came up in June.) Twenty-six years later she finally won a settlement of $32,000 from the Soviet government for her old friend.[103]

Willebrandt was brought into another Alaskan crisis by Lomen and Stefansson in November 1929. Two American fliers, Colonel Ben Eielson and Earl Borland of Alaskan Airlines, an AVCO affiliate, crashed near North Cape, en route to recover furs from an ice-bound steamer, the *Nanuk*. They were experienced pilots and it was assumed that they survived on the ice, since they were close to Siberian territory and to a Russian icebreaker. Willebrandt, urged to intervene by Lomen and Stefansson, worked with her usual energy to persuade Washington to ask the Soviets' aid. On December 23 she journeyed to the White House, then reached Secretary of the Interior Dr. Ray Lyman Wilbur. While sympathetic, he talked of red tape and generally responded with "a lot of baloney." She had more luck with Senator William Borah, who talked with representatives of the Soviets in

Washington and cabled Moscow. Willebrandt then rushed off to meet a Soviet representative to draft a cablegram to Moscow and to give him a map from Stefansson. By four o'clock, Willebrandt reported to Stefansson, "Interior Department got pepped up over the fact that Borah was acting while they parlayed." Interior pressed the State Department into action. Stefansson wired Willebrandt, simply, "Bully for you."[104] Her whirlwind twenty-four-hour effort, winning such rapid action from two departments in Christmas week, was remarkable testimony of her powers of persuasion when six months out of office.[105]

Willebrandt was less successful in helping Carl Lomen in his continuing conflicts in the 1930s with the Interior Department and its Reindeer Committee. Lomen had journeyed to Alaska with his father in 1900 in the wake of the Klondike gold strikes. His father, a lawyer, had intended to leave his practice only "for the summer," but he remained in Alaska and was appointed to a federal judgeship in Nome in the 1920s. Carl and his brothers discovered their gold in the reindeer industry. Willebrandt first met Lomen in 1922, beginning a fifty-year friendship that survived her rejection of his proposal of marriage. Instead she introduced him to Laura Volstead, daughter of Congressman Volstead, and was matron of honor at their wedding in 1928.

The Lomens' problems began at the end of the 1920s and the onset of the depression. After years of developing their herd, establishing packing and transportation facilities, and promoting their product, the Lomens shipped about 30,000 reindeer carcasses annually to mainland markets. Their success roused the opposition of livestock interests in California and other states. More serious were the charges of a former superintendent of reindeer that the Lomens, in the mingling of the Eskimo and Lomen herds, were unfairly claiming Eskimo deer, and that when they did purchase from the Eskimo, they did not pay a fair price.[106]

The charges, hotly denied by Carl Lomen, were repeated in missionary magazines. Interior Secretary Wilbur, deluged with more than five hundred letters of protest, set up a special Reindeer Committee to hold hearings on the charges and to make recommendations for the future of the reindeer industry and how the Interior Department could best meet its responsibilities to the Eskimo. Willebrandt did not appear at the February and March sessions of the committee, but she did write a note to Secretary Wilbur congratulating him on "the very fine Committee you appointed to look into the Alaskan reindeer situation. Sometime may I tell you more about it? I left a message for you the other day."[107] In April, when Attorney General Sisson, a committee member, sent her a copy of the final report, which generally upheld Lomen but did not settle the future actions of Interior, she wrote to Lomen, "Looks like 'buck passing' to me! . . . Are you satisfied?"[108] Two years later, she still monitored the situation for him. Writing of an alleged tirade against the Lomen Reindeer Corporation by "the new man in charge of Indian Affairs," she thought Lomen might like "to lay his ear to the ground and check up on it." After ten investigations the Interior Department, under the leadership of Secretary Harold Ickes, finally decided to buy out the whites in the industry. The reindeer were to be the sole preserve of the Eskimo. After almost forty years in Alaska, the Lomens ended their reindeer adventure more than $410,000 in debt.[109]

Throughout the Washington years, Willebrandt attracted a broad range of clients in federal income and estate tax disputes. Though her experience in the Justice Department and with the ABA Special Committee on Federal Taxation spared her the rapid immersion demanded by the new aeronautical and radio fields, she recognized the unusual demands put on this practice by the endless changes and refinements and interpretations in federal tax law. Addressing the Nebraska State Bar Association in December 1932, she reflected on her change from advocate of the tax collector to defender of the taxpayer: "In those days the treasury department was my client, and I was inspired and zealous with a patriotic fervor to insist that the taxpayer must fully and completely meet his tax obligations to his country." While her own income was small, she did not feel the burden. In private practice, she found her "patriotic fervor" gradually changing from "protection of the government to the protection of the taxpayer."[110]

Citing a particular concern at the burden of taxes in the hard depression years, she noted the anomalous situation: "Citizens are taxed the most when they can afford to pay the least. Such a situation, of necessity, leads to widespread discontent." Since citizens did not have the immediate recourse of turning the rascals out or of achieving a referendum on a single tax measure, their major ally in the struggle against unsound taxes was the lawyer, whose bulwark was the Constitution. Willebrandt urged, "The lawyer must keep his balance, and, with the Constitution as his shield, fight the encroachment of illegal taxation and unconstitutional spending."[111] It was not an easy task.

She suggested several approaches. As usual, all were direct and advocated with energy and forcefulness. First, she argued that a recent Supreme Court decision overturning a section of the Revenue Act of 1926 (that any property given within two years prior to death would be taxed as part of the decedent's estate) was "capricious and unconstitutional." It might signal the end of the judicial hands-off policy on taxation matters. Lawyers should seek injunctions and more confidently press the constitutionality of these measures.[112]

In more detail, she urged her Nebraska colleagues to use their "legal reasoning" to build new procedures to fight Congress on new, excessive expenditures. Lawyers should shift the congressional emphasis from "getting more income to working on outgo." The new bureaus and boards being launched had to be paid for. Using her knowledge of the Bureau of Home Economics that she had gained from its director, Louise Stanley, her former housemate, Willebrandt noted that the bureau had been established in 1887 with a $10,000 appropriation. In 1932, it spent $283,000 on bulletins about making jellies and children's rompers. In was dubious, she argued, that these activities fell into the category of powers delegated to the federal government by the states. Lawyers needed "a good dose of courage . . . to apply the constitutional yardstick, and lay it down on the laws before they are passed." She concluded that "a check on the mad rush of Congress to spend is the fundamental solution for high taxes" and suggested that the taxing power of the Sixteenth Amendment, which she had been so instrumental in defining through Supreme Court tests, should now be balanced by a constitutional amendment to limit taxes and so rein in congressional spending.[113]

Willebrandt again counseled lawyers one year later at the American Bar Association's first tax clinic at the national convention at Grand Rapids. In 1934, she served on the ABA Committee on Federal Taxation, working with the Ways and Means Committee of the House and the Senate Finance Committee to win changes in estate taxes.[114]

One of her more spectacular estate cases involved a foray into Dutch law to save the widow of a Royal Dutch Shell executive more than a million dollars in taxes. Bereaved and bewildered, the woman had been advised by her lawyer at Goldman Sachs investment company that she would owe at least that sum in taxes on the Shell stock and other holdings. She turned to Willebrandt for a second opinion. In

typically thorough and practical fashion, Willebrandt contacted officials of the Dutch consulate in San Francisco for a briefing on Dutch
law and discovered that at the pledge of the marriage vows in Holland,
the husband's property automatically becomes his wife's and the wife's
holdings automatically belong to the husband. A surviving spouse
cannot inherit what she already owns. After the case, Goldman Sachs
flew her from California to New York to give a seminar to their legal
staff. Willebrandt's advice to the chagrined lawyers and to her friends
in California was succinct: "If you marry again, marry a Hollan-
der."[115]

Willebrandt's work in estate tax and inheritance cases was always
marked not only by an extraordinary mastery of complex legal
technicalities but by her full sensitivity to the human dimension of
each case. When she drew up a will, it was a model of precision graced
by language richly conveying the care and affection of her client for the
surviving family or friends. In one case, particularly reflective of this
combination of expertise and compassion, she represented a young
man who had befriended and comforted a lonely woman in the last
months of her life. When the woman gratefully made a bequest of
$38,000 to him, the will was challenged by her niece with the charge
that he had exerted undue influence. Willebrandt won his case and
inheritance with the telling argument that "undue kindness is not
undue influence."[116]

Willebrandt's clients in tax and regulation matters also benefited
from her wide professional and social contacts with both Republican
and Democratic leaders. Her hard-won connections and wide circle of
friends were almost unmatched in Washington, where contacts are so
vital. Reflecting on the changing of the guard in 1933 to Roosevelt and
the brain trusters, she noted: "How well I knew them, Wallace, Tug-
well, Tommy the Cork, Moley and Cohen. I never liked any of them,
altho all—including the ubiquitous Eleanor were outwardly nice to
me and never discarded and used me as did the 'new' Republicans
under Hoover. They were at all social gatherings and so was I." In spite
of the "ubiquitous" reference, Willebrandt invited Mrs. Roosevelt to
her receptions at the Sulgrave Club and was invited to the White
House to tea. Willebrandt later wrote admiringly of Mrs. Roosevelt's
example as an "invitation to courageous and sincere living to us all."
Frances Perkins, whom she also respected, was her Georgetown
neighbor. Admiral Ross McIntire, Roosevelt's physician, was her
physician and friend.[117] Politically, she had determined to avoid all

public comment in the wake of the searing campaign of 1928, but in 1930 and 1932, when Hoover asked her support, she loyally and briefly spoke out, in spite of his and the party's abandonment of prohibition in the 1932 convention. Her major address, "The Creed of a Bewildered Citizen," confronted the desperate condition of the country but warned against turning to political renegades, quacks, mountebanks, false prophets, or "unprepared blatherskites" in our "mental panic."[118]

Yet Willebrandt found much to recommend in Roosevelt's energetic, broad-gauged attack on the depression in the first New Deal. Though she sometimes chafed at the tangled bureaucracy and complained that the brain trusters were out "to wreck the country," she applauded the liberalism articulated in Roosevelt's 1935 state of the union message. She wrote expressing her support after that address and two others: his 1938 Labor Day speech and his brief remarks opening the New York World's Fair in April 1939. All three messages demonstrated a concern for national unity, respect for the Constitution, the need for spiritual values; all contained his definition of liberalism.[119]

Writing to him in September 1938 of her gratitude for his "courageous stand for liberalism," she added her belief that he was using his high office "to accelerate ideals, and to put down the fears that inhibit attempts at bettering the life of the average man." She shared her favorite Justice Holmes quote that the Constitution was "like the bark of a living tree—essential to the nation's growth. . . . it should always be construed to permit expanding life within." When her Republican friends accused Roosevelt of "cutting through the constitution with a sharp knife," she reminded them that "that is the approved way, when a tree is 'bark bound' to save both bark, and growth of the tree!" America needed "leaders with steady nerves, and open minds, unafraid of receding horizons, and willing to undertake the labors of path making through new economic and legal frontiers." Roosevelt was clearly pleased, writing on the top of the letter, "Mac—to prepare very nice reply."[120] Six months later, against a gathering world crisis, she wrote again, commending his appeal for peace at the opening of the New York fair and focusing "world thought back again on the sweetness and beauty and opportunity of living under a tolerant democracy growing in social and economic responsibility for its citizens, such growth directed by a constitution interpreted as guiding principles, not as stop signs."[121]

These letters affirming her support for Rooseveltian liberalism, broadly conceived, are flanked by others commending the president on his judicial appointments. Clearly, Willebrandt not only remained a progressive but also still cherished some hope for a judicial appointment.

Hoover never encouraged that ambition. During the heated 1928 campaign, *Time* had speculated that Hoover might appoint her to a federal judgeship but commented that since she was the controversial "personification of prohibition, . . . few Senators are sufficiently 'noble in nature and far-reaching in purpose' to approve putting Mrs. Willebrandt on a bench of Justice."[122] Certainly, she could not count on the endorsement of her own senators, Shortridge and Johnson, in 1929. Hoover, soon after he became president, wrote to Attorney General William Mitchell, "I should like very much to appoint a woman to a distinguished position if I could find a distinguished woman to appoint."[123] He filled an opening on the Ninth District Court in Southern California by appointing Willebrandt's friend, Judge Harry Holzer. When a Supreme Court vacancy developed in the spring of 1930, a *Christian Science Monitor* editorial suggested that it was time to consider the appointment of a woman. Two were eminently qualified: Judge Florence E. Allen of the Supreme Court of Ohio and Mabel Walker Willebrandt, whose "proved legal talents, her wide legal experience and her appearances before the Supreme Court in behalf of the Government have all adequately tested her abilities."[124] Hoover considered neither. Though he appointed forty-four judges to the district and circuit courts of appeal and two justices to the Supreme Court, Hoover never appointed a woman to the federal bench, nor did Attorney General Mitchell ever recommend one.[125]

When Roosevelt began to make his appointments to the Supreme Court after the tumultuous court-packing battle of 1937, Willebrandt's letters commending his choices reveal the kind of judge she would have liked to have been. Delighted with the appointment of Hugo Black, she listed her reasons for her own choice of Black to prosecute prohibition cases: "incorruptible courage, studiousness, resourcefulness and fairness." She added: "true he has not yet proved his judicial temperament, but he has the foundation of character and industry on which true judicial temperament must rest and I would prefer to see an advocate gradually grow into a jurist than to hope for a jurist out of one without courage enough to make enemies. Can't Black's critics remember that Brandeis was once opposed for lack of judicial temperament?" Roosevelt's acknowledgment was brief but warm, with a handwritten postscript: "I hope to see you when I get back."[126] Five months later when Roosevelt named Stanley Reed for the next vacancy, Willebrandt again wired her support and pleasure that a former Justice Department colleague would be appointed. In February 1939, before Roosevelt made his next nomination, Willebrandt sent a four-page letter suggesting the qualities she thought most important for the post. She wrote in the midst of an intense lobbying effort for the appointment of a woman, Democratic judge Florence E. Allen. Willebrandt urged the choice of a woman but argued that the candidate should be a "real intellectual liberal," and a Republican.

Liberalism was her major criterion. She reviewed Roosevelt's contributions, observing: "Your 'forgotten man' was not a mere campaign slogan. You have put into the legal structure of this country more *ideas* than it has received since perhaps the days of Jefferson and Lincoln. These ideas are planted; a certain number will survive in spite of everything." The major safeguard, however, in the reactionary regime that was sure to follow, was the Supreme Court. "The court's greatest service," she contended, "is not now, but will come a few years hence." She reviewed her own struggles as a progressive in a conservative regime, "constantly chafing at the red tape, and the 'Mellon type' of reactionaries who feared to sweep the cobwebs lest the legal roof fall in!" Her experience then demonstrated that "it was the vital *force* our liberals, Holmes and Brandeis, and later, Stone, exerted on the entire judicial system . . . that lifted the *idea* of the law out of its formalism and procedural wastes." She urged:

> *First*, therefore, whether he is a Republican or a Democrat, from the East or West, a man or a woman, the one you choose, above all else, should be a real intellectual liberal—
> With if possible, the humanity of Brandeis, the realism of Stone, and the originality and understanding of Holmes—
> If that's too big an order, just at least find one whose mind won't "jell" when encased in a Supreme Court robe!

She rejected the advice that the candidate should already be serving on the lower bench. She believed he should not bring "already acquired judicial habits (which he is bound to take on anyhow), but the largest possible amount of vitality and vivid concepts from active professional life." Similarly, she argued that geography should not be a major consideration. "The vital thing is to find one with an unquenchable thirst for growth."

Her second criterion was that of party. She hoped that he would demonstrate his bipartisanship by appointing a Republican.

Finally, she urged that he appoint a woman.

> For, Mr. President, it will be years and years, if ever, before we have a Chief Executive like you with enough courage and independence to do it.
>
> I can't bear to see this opportunity go by.
>
> I don't want an unqualified woman named, but would gladly see, not the First, but the Second Suggestion waived in such good cause. For I do believe the major blocs of our people rightfully should be represented on the court. We feel a Jew should be there.
>
> Yet women have by far the largest stake, as a group, in the preservation of industry and advancement of the welfare of the nation. They actually own 40% of the real estate, 60% of *all* of our national wealth, a majority of the corporate securities, and are purchasers of 89% of all goods retailed. They bear the men who fight the wars, and they do have a viewpoint that, if expressed by an intelligent womanly woman, would surely only richen the court's interpretive powers.
>
> Furthermore, while the Justices now on the court would not likely *seek* a woman associate, they would welcome and respect her.
>
> All, *except* Justice McReynolds. He feels so strongly on the subject, he might resign.
>
> But that wouldn't be an unsurmountable loss!

She suggested that he just send the name to Congress "suddenly with a brief statement" of his reasons, to try to minimize the prolonged debate that might curb the support of some in Congress. She ended with a ringing plea.

> Whether it would astonish or gratify, I do think it is *right* to appoint a woman. I hope you think so too.
>
> You have my unstinted admiration, and faith in, and gratitude for the legal and economic ideas you have given. It is because I believe a woman appointed by you should, and would defend these ideals thoughtfully and wisely, and with all her heart in the councils of the court,—as well as for other less worthy reasons of my own pride in women's work, that I urge you, if you can, to appoint a woman in this vacancy.

Roosevelt sent his response on March 21 with the "Hope that the nomination of Honorable William O. Douglas, which I sent to the Senate yesterday, will meet your approval."[127]

Throughout the hectic 1930s, Willebrandt found time to encourage women, particularly young women professionals. She added two Phi Delta Delta colleagues as associates in her Washington office; she took the daughter of her old friend from law school, Myra Dell Collins, into her home for a brief time while she studied medicine at George Washington University;[128] and she sponsored a concert for Dorothy's piano teacher, the accomplished pianist Rose d'Amore. In 1934, Willebrandt backed the aviator, Jacqueline Cochran in a race to Australia. Attracted to Willebrandt because of her known interest in aviation, the beautiful Cochran asked her sponsorship because she was determined that no one could say that "some man" advanced her funds because of her looks. Willebrandt immediately responded, "Well, of course, I'd be delighted to do it," and put up part of the needed $20,000, charging no interest.[129] In a more professional connection, Willebrandt represented Cissy Patterson in her complicated negotiations with William Randolph Hearst to win control and finally ownership of the *Washington Herald* and the *Washington Times*.[130]

Youth found in Willebrandt a lively, challenging, and generous companion. Between sessions of the court, her table at lunch was frequently crowded with young lawyers.[131] John Sirica and his partner, starting their criminal law practice in a small office on the same floor in the Shoreham Building as Willebrandt, were given full access to her large, legal library. Willebrandt presented Sirica, as she did many others, to the Supreme Court. When he was embroiled in the major criminal case of his young career, Willebrandt, consistent in her opposition to the government's use of wiretapping, contributed a major argument to his brief, attempting to demolish the eavesdropping evidence that was the basis of the prosecution's case.[132] Willebrandt also found time to pursue some of her own interests. She took flying lessons and planned vacation trips to South America, Mexico, and even Russia. She began to indulge what the *Christian Science Monitor* described as her "gay, fun-loving side that gets too little exercise."[133] A sought-after guest, Willebrandt was described by the society editor of the *Washington Herald* as an "ornament" to the president's annual dinner for the Supreme Court in 1932, and always dressed in excellent taste. Willebrandt's "smooth hair, her facile manners, her engaging wit," the editor added, were an attraction at any gathering.[134]

With the income from her prosperous practice, she purchased a comfortable three-story home on Dumbarton Street in Georgetown. Its gracious living room provided a warm setting for intimate afternoon teas. A Willebrandt dinner invitation to the Supreme Court

Willebrandt at Jacqueline Cochran's table at the tenth anniversary banquet of the Ninety-Nines, an organization of pioneer women aviators. Cochran is center, front, facing camera; Willebrandt is left, rear.

justices was invariably accepted by all nine of them and their spouses. An experienced, accomplished hostess, she was meticulous in the seating arrangements that might interest each justice. She hosted her large receptions and dinners, concerts, and Dorothy's debut at the nearby Sulgrave Club.[135]

The most spectacular of her receptions were those combining her Hollywood friends with her Washington associates. In 1935, fresh from a private California screening of the MGM production of *Naughty Marietta*, directed by her friend and client Woody Van Dyke and starring another client, Jeanette MacDonald, Willebrandt proposed a Washington world premiere. If Louis B. Mayer would agree to the opening in Washington, Willebrandt would help him draw up the guest list. On March 8, 350 Hollywood and Washington luminaries congregated for dinner and the screening. The guest list included two Supreme Court justices; Senators Black, Borah and George, and thirty-two other senators and representatives; the Russian, Austrian, and Greek ambassadors; the owner of the *Washington Post*; and Secretary of the Interior Ickes and others of the Roosevelt administration. At a small party at Willebrandt's Georgetown home after the premiere, Nelson Eddy and Woody Van Dyke organized a sing-along, culminating with choruses of "Auld Lang Syne" at four in the morning. Van Dyke and Eddy helped the last guests find their way home by commandeering a milk wagon and galloping off singing through the streets of Georgetown.[136]

Five years later Willebrandt entertained Jeanette MacDonald at the Sulgrave Club after the star's address to the Women's Press Club. Presiding over the tea table were Mrs. Hugo Black, Mrs. Harlan Fiske Stone, Mrs. Henry Wallace, Mrs. William MacCracken, Jr., and Mrs. Thurman Arnold. Mrs. Carl Lomen, Mrs. Donald Richberg, and others mingled with such politicians and diplomats as Representative Joseph Martin, Senator William King, and Stanley Hornbeck of the State Department.[137]

In her personal and professional life, Willebrandt was sustained by the continuing support of family and friends in California. Willebrandt shared an office in the Union Bank Building in Los Angeles with Fred Horowitz and a San Bernardino lawyer, P.N. McCloskey, in the firm of Willebrandt, Horowitz, and McCloskey. Horowitz, who had been heavily involved in real estate development in the 1920s, was hit hard with the onset of the depression. His most ambitious project, the construction of the handsome Chateau Marmont on Sunset Boulevard, had been completed in 1929. With its Vermont slate roof, copper piping, and luxuriously tiled baths, the Spanish style apartment house was one of the most elegant in Hollywood. Every unit, according to the *Los Angeles Times*, was "a young palace."[138] Willebrandt had helped to choose the furniture and fabrics and even to push the chairs into place; she also publicized the new building to her friends. Her old friends Laura Jane Emery and Winnie Ellis had invested in the Chateau Marmont; they like Horowitz, were caught in the crash. Overextended and offered "a deal he couldn't refuse," a reluctant Horowitz consolidated his holdings and sold the Marmont. Part of the purchase price was a 3,600-acre ranch at Lake Hodges in Escondido. Willebrandt, delighted at the rough beauty of the property, became part-owner of the 4-S ranch.[139]

She dispatched the Walkers to help make the ranch and guest quarters warm and habitable. They immediately introduced white leghorn chickens and purchased horses and cattle. In the summer, Willebrandt sent Dorothy in the care of Grace Knoeller to the Walkers, urging: "I do hope that you will be stern with her this summer. I am convinced that the only chance of development is stern, constant observation so that she can get away with nothing—coupled, of course, with love and affection. . . . If Papa would *PROMISE* me and you would *PROMISE* that you would let *papa* make *her toe the mark* (I remember how he used to be stern with me)."[140]

Dorothy (or Mabel Jr., as she liked to be called) and her grandparents thrived. Clad in cowboy boots to protect against the "wall-to-wall rattlesnakes," Dorothy mounted her pony and set off alone to ride through groves of eucalyptus trees, chase wild horses, and explore. Her grandfather introduced her to the chicken business, giving her a white leghorn hen with an option on three others.[141] Mrs. Walker wrote reassuringly to Willebrandt that Dorothy "ought to be in a place where there is space for her to play and to develop naturally and be able to raise animals . . . where she is needed to do things and help save someone else because she loves them and knows that they love her." She added, "Your girl will surprise you in ten years."[142]

Dorothy stayed for the school year in Escondido, enjoying herself thoroughly, since she was ahead of the class in most subjects. Her teacher proudly sent her poems to the superintendent of schools of San Diego County. She played the lead in the class play and sang a solo. It was a short, glorious year.[143]

In 1933 and 1934, Willebrandt and Horowitz made plans not only to

Myrtle and David Walker, 1930.

sell the 4-S ranch but to divide all of their real estate holdings and assets and to end the association of Willebrandt, Horowitz, and McCloskey. Their practice had always been divergent. They dissolved the firm and finally drifted apart.[144]

Willebrandt brought Dorothy and the Walkers to Dumbarton Street. Dorothy, who loved being a "wild Indian," was sent to the nuns of the Sacred Heart to be toughened up academically and trained to be a lady. Willebrandt brought her ever-active father into her office to help with personal correspondence and to have him nearby for advice. While the family settled into Washington life, Willebrandt searched for another country haven.[145]

On Sunday outings, the family, sometimes joined by Grace Knoeller, set out to explore the backcountry roads of Maryland and Pennsylvania. Mrs. Walker, anxious about Willebrandt's heavy work schedule, urged her to find a country place near the mountains "which are lovely as a dream," where she could "go weekends and see growing things and ride a horse and row a boat."[146] In 1935, they finally found a 516-acre tract nestled into the foothills of the Blue Ridge Mountains near Fairfield, Pennsylvania. Mrs. Walker and Knoeller were dispatched to bid for the property, since Willebrandt feared her name would drive up the price. Walker Fields was hers for $5,000.[147] Once again, the Walkers would have their chickens, a garden, and the rich countryside.

Willebrandt found a manager for the farm in her direct way. Driving north from Washington, she was impressed with the way a young black man was plowing a cornfield. Stopping her Cadillac, she approached the startled worker with the observation, "Looks like you're taking an interest in what you're doing." He responded, "That's what you're supposed to do," adding that he liked to have the furrows straight when the big officials from Washington drove by. Willebrandt asked if he could recommend someone to manage her Pennsylvania farm. He sent a candidate, but the next year Willebrandt found him again and asked if he would now come to Walker Fields himself. He accepted, and Calvin Claggett joined the Willebrandt household with Mary, his wife; he remained for more than twenty-five years.[148]

Aided by her friends Laura Jane Emery, Grace Knoeller, and others, Willebrandt energetically began transforming the old farmhouse and work buildings into a comfortable place where family and friends could gather. With her father and Claggett, she also made it a working farm. The chickens were joined by hogs and sheep. One of the lawyers

Walker Fields, near Fairfield, Pennsylvania. *Below,* Willebrandt on her favorite mount, Miss Queen, with her parents and Dorothy, at Walker Fields, 1937.

in her office gathered the Department of Agriculture bulletins on the care of sheep and the best soil conditions for raising barley, wheat, corn, and alfalfa. In 1938, she imported prize Holsteins from the Carnation Farms near Seattle, Washington. A dairyman was engaged to tend the herd, which grew to seventy registered Holsteins. Willebrandt's Saturday routine at the farm included a session with Claggett on the crops and livestock and with the dairyman on the butterfat content of the milk produced by the Holsteins. In the afternoons, she and Dorothy would ride around the farm on horseback, Willebrandt on her favorite mount, Miss Queen. Dorothy reveled in these rare moments alone with her mother. Generally, guests joined the family on weekends as Willebrandt extended her entertaining from Washington to Walker Fields. Officials from Fruit Industries, lawyers, judges, senators, and congressmen learned the route winding through Emmitsburg and the Maryland countryside. A trunkful of overalls and shirts was kept for guests. Men slept on cots in the screened sleeping porch; the women lodged in rooms in the main house or in the small guest house. On Sundays, Rosa Gainer and Mary Claggett would cook a fried chicken dinner for perhaps fifty or a hundred guests. Pick-up baseball games, riding, swimming in the nearby stream, singing around the piano, or just good conversation made a weekend at Walker Fields a pleasant interlude for tired Washingtonians.[149]

If Walker Fields was a haven for Willebrandt, she hoped that it would be a restorative second home for the Walkers in the warm spring and summer months. Always concerned about her father's propensity to overwork, she was increasingly anxious about her mother's high blood pressure. Certainly, Mrs. Walker's health was precarious. In January 1938, after a pleasant family Sunday drive, she was suddenly stricken on the return to Dumbarton Street.[150] She died in a matter of moments. It was three months short of the Walker's fiftieth wedding anniversary.

After taking her home for burial with the Eaton family at Powersville, Missouri, David Walker wrote his family and friends: "We always congratulated ourselves that our lot in life had been as well as it was. No wealth, but ordinary needs of life supplied and with it blessed with good health and an abundance of good friends everywhere we chanced to be."[151] Always supported and encouraged by her mother, and always urged to deepen her spiritual life, a grieving Willebrandt recounted that as she lay sleepless, the night her mother died, she looked up and saw "the most beautiful cloud you could imagine, rose

Christmas at the farm, 1937. Laura Jane Emery is in the background.
Trixie was one of a long line of Walker–Willebrandt dogs.

tinted cloud, and Mama said to me, 'Mabel, don't worry, I'm all right.'"[152]

David Walker continued to go to the office with Willebrandt each morning, but increasingly her practice and interests centered in California. With the coming of the war in December 1941 and the rigor and uncertainty of transcontinental travel, Willebrandt decided to sell the Dumbarton Street house and move into an apartment on Connecticut Avenue. The next year, in an even harder wrench, Willebrandt auctioned off her Holstein herd and sold Walker Fields.[153]

CHAPTER EIGHT

Hollywood and the Red Scare

. . . you will always be an unforgettable example of courage
among the timid; of grace under pressure; of integrity among the
hypocrites; of morality among the point shavers, and of brains
among the dim-wits.

FRANK CAPRA to Mabel Walker Willebrandt
at her retirement, January 1962

*A*LWAYS a westerner in spirit,
Willebrandt gradually moved family and practice home to California.
Although she maintained an office in Washington until 1959 and continued to represent major clients in federal tax and regulation cases,
increasingly most of her clients, old and new, were Californians. Such
companies as 20 Mule Team Borax joined the wine industry in retain-
ing her as their chief legal counsel. Her reputation as one of the best tax
lawyers in the country kept her one of the busiest attorneys in Los
Angeles. Increasingly she directed much of her legal skill and her time
to "the industry" in that one-industry town, Hollywood.[1]

Willebrandt's most powerful Hollywood client was Louis B.
Mayer. In the 1920s when he first met her, his MGM studio boasted a
galaxy of directors and stars that included Erich von Stroheim, King
Vidor, W.S. Van Dyke, Ernst Lubitsch, Clarence Brown, Greta Gar-
bo, Norma Shearer, John Gilbert, Wallace Beery, Marie Dressler,
Ramon Navarro, and Francis X. Bushman. Mayer, the quintessential
self-made man, was the architect and master of the most powerful
studio in the fast-growing new media.

Temperamentally attracted to the hard-driving and the powerful,
Willebrandt liked and respected Mayer. It was mutual. In New York
on government business in 1927, Willebrandt wrote to her parents
after seeing the Ziegfeld production of *Rio Rita* as the guest of Mayer,
"Louis will do most anything for me and is truly anxious to see me
appointed Judge." But Mayer, conscious of her valuable influence in

Washington, also advised her to stay at her Justice Department post, for "only lately did California begin to feel" her.[2]

Mayer and Willebrandt were also linked through politics and the friendship of Ida ("Kay") Koverman. As secretary to Herbert Hoover before he entered politics, Koverman helped to organize his first campaigns in California. She met Willebrandt through these efforts and possibly met Mayer through Willebrandt. In 1927, although she still supported her old chief, Koverman joined Mayer's staff as his political adviser, secretary, public relations expert, and discoverer of stars. Through Koverman, the ambitious Mayer, already at the top in cinema production and anxious for larger political arenas, made substantial contributions to the Republican party and built his contacts with Secretary of Commerce Hoover.[3]

On the eve of the 1928 Republican convention, Willebrandt and Koverman maneuvered to have Mayer among those seconding the nomination of Hoover for president. Mayer would not only bring his money but could woo his friend William Randolph Hearst for the Hoover camp.[4] At the last minute their careful groundwork was sabotaged by adverse publicity from a California fraud case. Mayer, though only a peripheral figure, was featured prominently in all but the Hearst papers and was considered too tarnished to be publicly linked with the candidate. Still, he worked loyally to win Hearst for Hoover and served as treasurer of the Republican National Committee for California. He was rewarded by being the first overnight guest of the new president in March 1929, just as the equally loyal Willebrandt was rewarded by an invitation to the first White House luncheon.[5]

After Willebrandt resigned from the Justice Department, her work with Mayer intensified. Throughout the 1930s, her notice in the Martindale-Hubbard lawyers directory prominently cited her representation of Metro-Goldyn-Mayer. As in radio and aviation, she was the specialist in federal regulation and tax matters for MGM and sometimes assisted in public relations in Washington. Her efforts ranged from a modest request to an assistant secretary of state to arrange a welcome by the Mexican authorities for Mayer, "a public spirited citizen of high repute," to an attempt to extricate writer-director Edmund Goulding[6] from the toils of British justice so that he could return to labor in the MGM vineyard. On a more personal level, Willebrandt represented Mayer's brother Rudolph when he was charged with obtaining money under false pretenses in Maryland. He had solicited funds there for a motion picture that was never produced. Willebrandt journeyed to Baltimore, engaged the city solicitor, her old friend Simon Sobeloff, to work with her as assistant counsel, and proceeded to win over both the State attorney and the judge by her charm, eloquence, and sense of concern for the "hapless investors." Her insistence that they be compensated earned an unusual stetting of the criminal case by an agreement to settle the civil claims.[7]

Generally, Willebrandt's work for Mayer was in the area of taxes. In 1940, with the IRS vigorously investigating Hollywood producers Joseph Schenk and Darryl Zanuck, Willebrandt advised MGM producer Billy Goetz and the Mayer family trust so well that they not only avoided fines but in Mayer's case received a $48,000 refund. She shared her satisfaction at the outcome with her father: "When all the smoke clears away I think this is going to put our clients in a lot better position than the clients of Mr. Burns and Jimmy Roosevelt, . . . because their clients are either going to be indicted or are being heavily soaked with taxes."[8] In 1951, she fought a federal tax provision that would prevent horse breeders like Mayer from claiming a depreciation or write-off of stable losses. Arriving in Hollywood to consult with Mayer and to seek the lobbying help of Koverman, Willebrandt found an irate Mayer berating Koverman and threatening to dismiss her. Hedda Hopper reported the confrontation and Willebrandt's warning: "Mr. Mayer, we have to work day and night to keep this tax measure from passing. I need your cooperation and Kay's too. I will tell you right now that unless I can have her help with yours and unless you keep her on the payroll, we won't possibly win." Mayer "swallowed hard" and subsided, agreeing that she could have anything she needed. The measure failed by one vote in the Senate-House conference. To ensure the retention of Koverman, whose health was increasingly precarious, Willebrandt quietly waived her fee to Mayer for one year. Since the sum sometimes reached $75,000 it was no small gesture for the money-conscious Willebrandt.[9]

Mayer's friendship and backing and her own tax expertise brought Willebrandt star clients. She advised Jean Harlow, Clark Gable, Jeannette MacDonald, and Grace Moore. Though she frequently lost patience with the Hollywood moral climate, she also found strong and engaging friends in Jeanette MacDonald and her husband, Gene Raymond, Grace Moore, and others. Whenever MacDonald or

Backyard cookout with Hollywood clients and friends. Willebrandt standing first row, second from the right, next to Ginger Rogers's mother.

Moore came to Washington, Willebrandt invariably entertained her at the Sulgrave Club. She described Grace Moore as "undoubtedly the most effervescent, completely madcap person I've ever known."[10]

Given her respect for strength and decisiveness, it is not surprising that Willebrandt's staunchest friends and certainly her most numerous Hollywood clients were the screen directors. She worked with MGM directors W.S. Van Dyke, flying buff Clarence Brown, flamboyant Rouben Mamoulian, and young George Sidney, but her two closest friends were Leo McCarey and Frank Capra. The two seemed, as one critic observed, "to go together like ham and eggs." Capra's films *Mr. Smith Goes to Washington, Mr. Deeds Goes to Town,* and *State of the Union* mirrored the faith of Willebrandt and McCarey in the individual and their intolerance of fraud and corruption. McCarey's *Ruggles of Red Gap, Going My Way,* and *Bells of St. Mary's* spoke to the moral sense of Capra and Willebrandt.[11] Both directors were tough professionals and optimists, uncompromising in their ideals.

It was Capra who contracted with Willebrandt to represent the screen directors in their confrontation with the producers in 1938. Threatened with a National Labor Relations Board (NLRB) hearing and facing the producers' counsel, Wild Bill Donovan, the directors wanted an attorney with strong Washington connections and experience. Capra stated that his "first meaningful action as the new president [of the Screen Directors Guild (SDG)] was in acquiring the wisdom, experience, and brilliant legal talents of that great lady of the law, Mabel Walker Willebrandt." She arranged a date for the NLRB hearing, an action that won the promise of new negotiations from the producers. At issue was recognition of the fledgling guild as the bargaining agent. Other demands included contractual acceptance of the director's right to make or approve the first cut of the picture, to know all contractual obligations before signing on a film, to be consulted in casting, and to know and approve of the utilization of any second unit. The work week was to be limited to sixty hours and six days.[12]

In spite of new negotiations and new bargaining teams, the talks remained stalemated. The Producers Association having just yielded in contracts with the Screen Actors Guild and Screen Writers Guild was reluctant to bow now to the directors. Frustrated, Capra and the directors agreed to strike by February 16 and to boycott the Academy Awards ceremony if the producers remained intransigent. Willebrandt telegraphed their ultimatim to the Producers Association with the promise that if there was no positive response, the guild would act.

The next day, SDG had an agreement recognizing it as the bargaining representative.[13]

These organizational fights were merely a prelude to the tensions of the 1940s. As it had in 1917, Hollywood went loyally to war in 1941. Frank Capra directed the Why We Fight series for the Office of War Information; stars joined the military services and traveled with the Stars Over America Tours to raise more than $838,000,000 for the war effort. The industry churned out war films and reaped high profits from their traditional entertainment features. In 1946, when the industry produced such high quality productions as *How Green Was My Valley* and *Citizen Kane*, its $1,750,000,000 gross was the highest in history. But the 1940s also brought the attorney general's attack on the "blind" booking practice, which locked distributors into the entire annual product of the major studios. By 1948, the Justice Department launched an antitrust suit to divorce production from exhibition.[14] The beleaguered industry simultaneously girded itself to confront competition from the rapidly expanding television industry, increased foreign competition, and the violent jurisdictional labor disputes that spawned a wave of strikes. Willebrandt was kept busy with guild matters.

In October 1948, *Variety* reported that the eastern division of the Screen Directors Guild was fast rivaling its "big brother" unit in Hollywood.[15] SDG faced a major jurisdictional dispute with the Radio and Television Directors Guild (RTDG) over which one should organize the new television directors and assistant directors. SDG organized a Film Advisory Council, which dispatched Executive Secretary Vernon Keays and Carol Post to New York to spearhead a major organizational campaign in March 1950. From Washington, Willebrandt cautioned SDG that it might be on the verge of a NLRB fight. While working to recruit new television directors for SDG, it must not "let those boys down" who had already joined. In September 1950, the two guilds tangled on the West Coast over which one should represent the directors at the Los Angeles ABC affiliate KECA. SDG argued that it was empowered to represent those who "directed action that moved across the screen." Insisting that it was first on the ground, RTDG filed charges of unfair labor practices when the KECA directors voted SDG as their bargaining agent. RTDG contended that SDG was "employer dominated." Willebrandt shot back at the NLRB hearing that RTDG was "Communist dominated" and guilty of fraud. SDG won this battle, but the fight went on.[16]

Negotiations involving the television industry continued throughout the 1950s.[17] The guild won a contract with ZIV, a major producer. In 1958, with Frank Capra again as president of the Screen Directors Guild of America, as it was now known, discussions with RTDG intensified. Capra credited Willebrandt with providing oil to take the squeaks out of the wheels, working to eliminate egos, and generally fighting to keep the talks on the issues at hand.[18] However, another ten years elapsed before a merger finally created the new Directors Guild of America.

Meanwhile, Willebrandt advised the guild on tax, incorporation, and contract matters. One major contribution was winning a complicated contract dispute in *Heindorf* v. *SDGA* in 1956. Her adversary was the well-known Hollywood attorney Martin Gang. Heindorf, a musical director at Warner Brothers wanted "Musical Direction" as his screen credit on a Warner's production. The Screen Directors' contract with Warner Brothers stipulated that only a film director could have the coveted "director" title. In a triumphant letter to the 900 guild members, Willebrandt explained her successful motion to dismiss the case "on the grounds that Mr. Heindorf could not legally drag SDGA into court to defend a contract to which Mr. Heindorf is not a party; that SDGA's contract is valid as carrying out the purposes of collective bargaining negotiations for members, and that neither in Mr. Heindorf's pleadings nor in Mr. Gang's 'Opening Statement' had a 'justiciable controversy' been set up." The executive director of SDGA, Joseph Youngerman, later explained it more simply: "If A has a contract with C, and B has a contract with C, B's contract with C does not entitle it to interfere with A's contract with C."[19] Two days of arguments had ensued before the judge ruled for the guild, finding "nothing illegal in a company such as Warner Bros. granting a concession to one, such as screen credits, which will prevent it from granting an equal concession, or a similar concession, to another." He found no restraint of trade involved. Court costs were assessed to Heindorf, since "the plaintiff has no right to bring the defendants in question into court." The action was dismissed. A happy Willebrandt wrote to her friend Grace Knoeller: "I won it . . . I thot you'd enjoy the fact that I threw Gang, Kopp & Tyre (very pinko law firm) out of court on *law alone*. The Judge, tho a fine Judge, apparently doesn't like women—or me, I don't know which. He *hated* to rule but is such a good lawyer he did on the legal point. . . . They may appeal, if so, I'll beat 'em again!"[20]

Willebrandt cherished the guild and its members and was generous with her time and advice. Cautioned by the guild's vice-president, Al Rogell, that she was not keeping track of her time, she replied, "Oh, the hell with that!" She stayed in the background at guild functions and generally worked quietly and hard to keep its highly creative artists in harmony. Called by Rogell, "Our guiding light, our glue, our coherence," Willebrandt was devastated by the rift that nearly destroyed the guild during Hollywood's agony with the Red Scare.[21]

Red hunts were not new to Hollywood. In 1940, the Dies Committee launched a series of closed hearings on the motion picture industry, and five years later, the House Un-American Activities Committee chairman John Rankin, announced: "The information we get is that this [Hollywood] is the greatest hotbed of subversive activities in the United States. We're on the trail of the tarantula now, and we're going to follow through. The best people in California are helping us."[22]

Indeed, Californians were tracking subversives. Under the chairmanship of California senator Jack B. Tenny, the Joint Fact-Finding Committee of the legislature had begun energetically in 1941 to pursue suspected Communists in public schools and universities. It culled names from newspaper stories in the West Coast paper *The People's Daily World* and from the Dies Committee reports and expanded its investigations to zoot suited rioters, the Hollywood Writers Mobilization, and the CIO. Senator Tenny asserted that Congressman Rankin was "guilty of understatement in his announcement that Hollywood is full of reds."[23]

Threatened by outsiders, Hollywood's instinctive reflex was to circle the wagons and argue that it was cleaning its own house. In 1944, the directors Sam Wood and Clarence Brown and the producer Walt Disney, backed by Hearst, launched the Motion Picture Alliance for the Preservation of American Ideals. "Dedicated to turning off the faucets which dripped red water into film scripts," the alliance vigorously fought the impression that the industry was "made up of, and dominated by, Communists, radicals and crackpots." Cecil B. DeMille formed his own DeMille Foundation pledged to flush out Communists in government and Hollywood.[24] These self-defense measures did nothing to forestall the congressional or California investigations. In 1947, both state and federal committees focused on communism in Hollywood.

The federal probe began first. In May, a three-man subcommittee of the House Un-American Activities Committee (HUAC) quizzed labor figures and thirteen actors, producers, and directors. Most were friendly witnesses, including Willebrandt's friends and clients Leo McCarey and Louis B. Mayer. Mayer spent much of his testimony defending the MGM war drama *Song of Russia* as just a love story that happened to be set in the country of a wartime ally.[25] If Willebrandt advised him, it was quietly, behind the scenes. She was not present at the hearings. Similarly, she was absent at the sessions of the full HUAC in Washington in October. Described by columnist Max Lerner as an attempt "to track down the footprints of Karl Marx in movieland,"[26] these were the most widely publicized hearings of the widely publicized career of HUAC.[27] Forty-five Hollywood witnesses were subpoenaed. Again, Mayer and McCarey were friendly witnesses. Sam Wood opened the sessions with what *Time* magazine described as "a thunderclap," asserting that the Screen Writers Guild was "controlled by Communists" and that the Screen Directors Guild had a strong pro-Communist bloc, which included his subpoenaed colleague, director Edward Dmytryk, the only SDG member of the "Hollywood Ten."[28]

Willebrandt did not represent Dmytryk, Mayer, or McCarey. Her presence is more obvious in a Screen Directors Guild statement issued early in October 1947. Willebrandt's style is evident in the language of the italicized passages:

> 1. Official investigations into the political beliefs held by individuals are *in violation of a sacred privilege guaranteed* the citizen in this free Democracy.

. . . .

> 5. If any threat to our constitutional government is presented by subversive elements within the country, the machinery for combating and *overcoming such is already in existence: namely, our law enforcement agencies and the courts. To assume the prerogative of those properly designated bodies amounts to charging them with incapability of maintaining law and order, and, in the light of their splendid records, such a charge is completely unwarranted.*
> 6. *As Americans, devoted to our country and the Constitution, which is its spiritual shape and form, we hereby resolve to defend the reputation of the industry in which we work against attack. . . .*[29]

Clearly torn between her detestation of a coercive government and her genuine concern at the threat of communism, Willebrandt saw her first responsibility as protecting her client. As always, she was a determined, tenacious representative.

Hollywood's circling of the wagons grew more desperate. In December, fifty film executives wrangled for two days at the Waldorf-Astoria in New York and then agreed to fire the Hollywood Ten cited for contempt of Congress. In the "cleaning our own house" tradition, they also vowed not to "knowingly employ a Communist" and repeated their conviction that "nothing subversive or un-American has appeared on the screen." *Time*'s analysis of the Waldorf declaration perceptively noted box office concerns and reported that MGM had slashed its payroll 40 percent in the previous week.[30]

In Hollywood, the guilds met to determine their response to the Waldorf decision. When the Screen Directors executive board met on December 2, the session was stormy. Rising to urge an SDG protest at the firing of Dmytryk, the director Robert Rossen was soundly booed.[31] Reluctantly, the guilds acquiesced to the Waldorf declaration and then faced the grim reality of lengthening blacklists of suspected reds and pinks.[32] The virulently anti-Communist publications *Counterattack* and *Red Channels* relentlessly supplied new candidates for investigation. In Sacramento the Tenny Committee issued its new lists of those "within the various Stalinist orbits."[33] By 1949, Los Angeles County adopted a loyalty oath program; a year later, Governor Earl Warren pressed for a still stronger oath for state employees. As nine of the Hollywood Ten began to serve their sentences in June 1950, North Korea invaded South Korea.[34] The Red Scare was now fueled by the headlines and long frustration of war.

That summer the Screen Directors Guild embarked on a course that nearly destroyed the organization and almost ended Willebrandt's long association with it. This time she was not on the periphery but played a leading role.

Cecil B. DeMille was the first to sound the alarm. In the absence of the guild's president, Joseph Mankiewicz, who was in France, he called the vice-president, Al Rogell, to report a phone call from "some very important people" in Washington who warned that unless Hollywood made an overt move, "something that would put the brakes on," it might face an onslaught from the powerful red-hunting senator Joseph McCarthy. Respecting DeMille's known Washington contacts, Rogell consulted Willebrandt and Frank Capra, a member of the guild's board. Deciding that McCarthy might indeed target Hollywood, the ad hoc group determined to head him off by drafting a non-Communist affidavit for their membership. To Rogell, it was strictly a matter of self-defense. He explained that if any director was a member of the Communist party, all he had to do was resign. The next day he could sign the affidavit asserting he was not a party member. The important issue was to avoid another Washington intrusion into the movie industry.[35]

Called into session by Rogell in August, the guild's executive board voted to hold a referendum on the recommendations that all members be required to sign a loyalty oath and specifically deny adherence to the Communist party. All new applicants for membership already had to sign such an oath. Rogell issued the statement to the press: "We, the Screen Directors Guild of America, as representatives of one of the world's greatest industries, must make our position known to America and to the world on behalf of this industry. We sincerely hope and know that all guild, unions and other motion picture organizations and affiliates will follow our move."[36]

Mabel Walker Willebrandt drafted the oath. The *New York Times* reported on August 27, "Loyalty Oath Issue Raised in Hollywood" and noted that the directors' union-shop contract could mean that the non-Communist affidavit might be regarded as a condition of employment. The story carried Willebrandt's clarification that the Taft-Hartley Act allowed a union to prescribe its own rules for membership. It also specified that in spite of a union-shop contract, "no union may coerce any employer into denying work to anyone for any breach of union regulations other than failing to pay dues or initiation fees."[37] It remained to be seen how the oath would be interpreted.

Meanwhile, thoroughly alarmed by calls from friends and directors that Rogell and DeMille were attempting a "take over," and not reassured by Rogell's explanatory overseas phone call, Mankiewicz returned from France in the first week of September challenging both the oath and the referendum. Though he had promised Rogell to make no statement to the New York reporters, in an interview with columnist Dorothy Manners he did question why the oath was seen as such an emergency measure and why the ballots were signed and not secret.[38]

On home ground at a meeting of the executive board, Mankiewicz set off what one colleague described as the "hottest firecracker that has exploded in Hollywood in years."[39] The majority of the board, now described by the *New York Times* as right wing, supported a resolution authorizing the executive secretary to mail the loyalty oath to the membership, which had voted approval of it by a resounding 98.6 percent in the recent referendum. The board then passed a constitutional by-law requiring members to sign the oath. Mankiewicz declared that as a guild officer he had already signed the oath mandated by the Taft-Hartley Act and had no intention of signing this added guild document. In sharp disagreement with the board's majority, he ordered Executive Secretary Vernon Keays to call a general meeting of the membership. By the end of the meeting of the board, however, he was persuaded to delay this move.[40]

After the confrontation with Mankiewicz, the board acted. Guild members were mailed a ballot to vote in the recall of Mankiewicz. A 650-word telegram followed, signed by Al Rogell, Clarence Brown, Cecil B. DeMille, Frank Capra, and others, accusing the president of dictatorial conduct. A shaken and angry Mankiewicz, whose own ballot was delayed as were those of some of his supporters, met with friends at Chasens Restaurant. He rounded up 25 members in good standing to join in calling for a restraining order from the court. A phonathon waged by the Mankiewicz group won the agreement of 106 members, almost enough to block the recall move, not to sign their ballots. On Saturday, a working day for the guild staff, Mankiewicz tried to get a membership list from Executive Secretary Keays only to find the office locked and Keays nowhere to be found. On Monday, he finally secured the list and ordered a mailing calling an emergency meeting of the membership. Meanwhile, his supporters, represented by attorney Martin Gang in a court hearing on their motion for a restraining order, accepted Willebrandt's proposal to defer any count of the recall ballots pending the general membership meeting. In the interim, peacemakers worked feverishly but futilely to head off the confrontation.[41]

The climactic general meeting convened Sunday, October 22, in the ballroom of the Beverly Hills Hotel at 7:30 in the evening. "The most tumultuous evening in Hollywood" extended for the next seven and a half hours. Five hundred members jammed the hall. The most prominent members of the guild took turns addressing the group from the stage and the floor. Mankiewicz began with a detailed, eloquent report to the membership. Rogell made the board majority's rejoinder, followed by DeMille, who reviewed Mankiewicz's actions and then veered into a guilt-by-association litany, ticking off the Red-front organizations of the opposition. In the midst of the booing and hissing that erupted, Don Hartman rose to decry "paper-hat patriots who

stand up and holler, 'I am an American' and contend no one else is."
Peacemaker William Wellman urged Mankiewicz to try for a recon-
ciliation. John Ford and George Stevens then questioned Vernon
Keays's actions in allegedly deleting fifty-five names from the mailing
list for the recall petition. Ford asked the membership to recall the
recall and to empower the board to destroy the ballots. Following
William Wyler's call to depose the board, Ford moved the board's
resignation and recommended that Mankiewicz form an executive
committee of past guild presidents. Rogell, seeing Mankiewicz's support and seeking peace, seconded the motion. Passed overwhelm-
ingly, this motion was followed by the dramatic tendering of resignations by the board members, one by one. Exhausted and emotionally
drained, Willebrandt rose and offered her resignation also, since she
had been engaged by the outgoing directors. Her brief speech was met
by a motion, unanimously approved, that she be retained as counsel
pending the decision in an upcoming "cat fight" with the NLRB. She
agreed to stay on until a successor could be chosen.[42] The marathon
session ended at 2:20 A.M.

In the aftermath, Mankiewicz, having made his point, asked the
members to sign the loyalty oath voluntarily. A *Variety* editorial urged
that the matter be ended "right now, when Hollywood continues to
need all the professional knowhow of its seasoned producers and
directors."[43] The guild survived, though the scars and divisions were
not easily healed. The new executive secretary, Joseph Youngerman,
later observed: "Mabel helped us to survive." Punctiliously loyal, her
professionalism and generous service to directors on both sides of the
issue saved her for the guild. But, Rogell reported, she never got over
it, "it was that much of a blow."[44]

As the Red Scare rolled on, Al Rogell was blacklisted. Asserting he
had been a loyal Republican all of his life and believing that some of the
other directors were at the root of the attack, he sought the advice of
Willebrandt, asking, "Why the hell don't we publish the real reasons
for the oath?" Perhaps sensing it would only rekindle the controversy
and acrimony, she cautioned, "Let the fires die down; let the fires blow
over." It took Rogell a year to extricate himself.[45]

Against a background of a new round of HUAC Hollywood hearings in 1951, Willebrandt's client and old friend Frank Capra also faced
a blacklist. Agreeing to help the California Institute of Technology on
a Defense Department project, he found his security clearance in-
explicably delayed. Relieved of his papers and documents, a troubled

Capra traced the problem to an old review by Lee Mortimer of his *State of the Union*, which accused him of peddling "some peculiar" political thinking. The "artful trickster," Mortimer charged, had hawked propaganda that "would not seem out of place in Isvestia."[46] Capra had immediately rejoined that Mortimer was completely "off his nut." But the question was how to fight this old attack. In his autobiography, Capra told of his wife's urging him to "call Mabel" and Willebrandt's swift and aggressive response. She advised: "Fight hard, Frank. Fight with truth, but fight with passion. Get *mad*! Now, fast. Tell all your children. They must not hear about it from some other source. Second. Work hard; work fast. Dig for facts and figures—all the figures; your donations, activities for the past twenty years. Who your friends are, a list of character references. And hit hard. Be wrathful. It's your world that's being destroyed not theirs." In ten days, Capra had compiled his facts and affidavits, including one from Willebrandt. A State Department request for his services at a film festival in India and its subsequent investigation and intervention helped in demolishing the suspicion. By January 14, 1952, he had his top secret clearance.[47]

Willebrandt's fight continued. A Russian promoter, claiming he had smuggled film footage of the revolution out of Russia, brought the print to Willebrandt in 1951. After Rogell screened it for her, she concluded, "You've got to show this to people here." Rogell agreed to help and wove a narrative line for the disjointed film clips. "It was," he reported, "grainy as hell." When there was a gap, he put in some smoke. He combined it with captured film in the United States military archives of the German war effort. Willebrandt, who "hated Communism with a passion as she hated Nazism," was anxious to show the similarities between Hitler's Germany and Stalin's Russia. Her original idea was to have either former president Herbert Hoover or General MacArthur introduce the narrative, telling a story to children, with the general theme that there is "no such thing as a little bit of dictatorship." On reflection, she decided that it should not be narrated by anyone in politics and engaged journalist Quentin Reynolds for the task.[48] Released through Hallmark Productions, the forty-two-minute feature was titled *Halfway to Hell*. *Variety*'s review, reported that the majority of the footage was surprisingly clear. Quentin Reynolds's narration of the story line kept the interest high and "emotions aroused." It should, concluded *Variety*, "satisfy those who like such film fare rough. . . . A shocker not for the squeamish."[49]

In addition to expending her time and money on this film warning, Willebrandt spoke of her concern at the Communist threat. She addressed her fellow members in the Ebell Club in Los Angeles in November 1952, asserting: "There is no greater challenge to the American women now than helping in the resistance to Communism. It's not a pleasant subject to study, but all of us *should become informed* as to the methods now being used by Communists to infiltrate our government offices, our schools, our clubs, and our public press." One way to be informed was to subscribe to the weekly open letter *Counterattack*, which gave "names, and events and instances of the efforts of Communists to infiltrate into Radio, Television, the legal profession, civic and cultural clubs, and government agencies." As an example of what women could do in the fight against subversion, she cited her friend Ruth Shipley, controversial head of the Passport Division in the Department of State. Shipley, she noted, was "utterly courageous." During the Spanish Civil War she had been alerted by the report of three hundred missing American passports and surmised they were being used by communist spies. "She was right!" concluded Willebrandt. She urged the Ebell members to help Shipley by being alert and forwarding to her or to the FBI the name of any Communist or fellow-traveler planning to go abroad.[50]

Six months later she wrote to her friends Laura and Carl Lomen of the great excitement in Hollywood of the renewed HUAC hearings. This time HUAC focused on infiltration in the schools. Willebrandt found the testimony alarming but hoped that it might "jolt the public into less complacency on these matters." She commented on recent headlines:

> Good old Senator McCarthy! He certainly does not mind sticking his neck out, does he? But I'm betting on him. Everyone thot he had ruined himself when he attacked Lattimore and Lattimore then published a book "Trial by Slander" which had a wide circulation and created much sympathy for him, and for a while we thot it would lose the election for Senator McCarthy. But the Senator was certainly vindicated when two years later the true facts came out and constituted evidence on which a grand jury indicted Lattimore.[51]

She still worried about Communist infiltration into the Screen Directors Guild. Writing to the Lomens, she reported on the election of a new, "very fine Bd. . . . But the Commies were at work. I was amazed to see 3 suspects nominated—but fortunately they didn't get elected, so we are to have a good conservative American group to work with next yr."[52]

In her law practice, Willebrandt's concern about communism merged with her strong commitment to family and care for children. In the same Ebell Club speech in November 1952 in which she extolled Shipley and the work that women could do, she raised another issue, urging members' efforts to change the court procedures in custody cases. She asserted: "The custody of the children is disposed of more casually than the property rights of the spouses" in divorce cases. Usually, she explained, a brief custody agreement was included in the agreement settling property; the judge generally made no investigation. If there was a hearing, charges were aired and the "papers have a Roman holiday over the filth." The proceedings could "scar the sensibilities of the children." Women should work for uniform laws in this area, particularly urging that the judge hold private hearings and base his decision on the children's best interest. Adoption matters, she argued, were private; custody battles should be also.[53]   Willebrandt made this plea in the aftermath of a tumultuous three-week custody hearing in Los Angeles Superior Court. The actress Dorothy Comingore, an unfriendly witness in a recent HUAC hearing, sought custody of her two children and back child-support payments from her ex-husband, Richard J. Collins, a friendly HUAC witness and Willebrandt's client. Collins, who had had the children with him for three years, testified he was certainly not liable for all of the support payments claimed and charged that Comingore was an unfit mother, since she associated with persons of doubtful loyalty to the United States.[54]

In her examination of Comingore, Willebrandt raised the question of the kind of persons the children would socialize with, should she win custody. Comingore's response was heated: "Good people. I would assume the people I know are loyal, patriotic Americans. Good people are people who don't hurt other people. They are people who have responsibility to themselves, to their neighbors and to their country, and who do not conduct themselves [she addressed Willebrandt] as I have seen you conduct yourself in this court." When Willebrandt asked directly whether the children would associate with Communists, Judge Caryl Sheldon interrupted to observe that the "good people" as Comingore defined them could not be Communists. Willebrandt then asked if Comingore had once said that HUAC members "had entered into an organized conspiracy to destroy my country and my people and my people's rights." The actress replied that she had, adding that she had walked "an honorable picket line outside the Federal building a month ago" during the committee hearings.[55]

Comingore's attorney, William B. Estman, who had been ejected from the recent HUAC hearings, objected and charged Willebrandt with misconduct for attempting to introduce evidence that the actress had taken the children into the homes of disloyal Americans. "A very noisy clash" ensued, with Willebrandt heatedly protesting, "Never in all my 30 years at the bar have I been charged with misconduct." Judge Sheldon sustained the objection, while declaring that introducing evidence was not misconduct. At the recess, a livid Willebrandt challenged Estman, "Now let me tell you young man I am not going to take charges of misconduct from you." Estman, obviously enjoying himself, rejoined, "Well, it's in the record. What are you going to do about it?" But Willebrandt carried the day and the case. Custody was awarded to Collins. It was the kind of publicized legal battle she always strove to avoid; it was particularly painful because it involved the two children trapped in the middle.[56]

Three years later she was embroiled in a similar case in the California First District Court of Appeal. Again, she argued the father's side in a custody case; again the issue involved the Communist convictions and connections of the mother. In the divorce proceedings the mother, Barbara Smith, won custody of her young daughter and son. In the summers, the children visited their father, Walter Smith, in Utah. Both Smiths subsequently remarried. A renewed custody battle arose when the daughter, Amanda, during one visit with her father, indicated that she wanted to stay with him rather than return to her mother. He kept her until the mother arrived and spirited her back to California. Willebrandt's client faced a contempt citation for violation of the custody decision; he sought exoneration of that charge and final custody of the children. Again, the charge was that the mother was unfit.

Willebrandt's brief detailed the contrasting environments of the two homes. Side by side, page after page, she traced the comparison. Barbara Smith Taylor's new husband was a black day-laborer who was "mostly unemployed." For nine hours each day, while the mother worked, she left the children with a baby-sitter. Private investigators retained by Willebrandt reported dirt on the floor, dirty dishes, wet diapers, and the smell of urine in the baby-sitter's residence. Five months after Smith married Taylor they had a child.

Amanda had become a thumbsucker, and on her last visit to her father in Utah she had arrived with a black eye from school. Additionally, the brief argued, Barbara Smith Taylor subscribed to *The People's World*, viewed as the West Coast version of *The Daily Worker*. She had declined to answer in a previous trial whether she was a member of the Communist party, the California Labor School, Inc., the Committee for a Democratic Far Eastern Policy, or the Civil Rights Congress. Willebrandt noted that the earlier trial judge in awarding custody did not "shut his eyes to the fact that the Communist newspaper with all its slanting of current events along the Communist Party line was constantly in her home available to Amanda, a child who reads a lot." Willebrandt concluded that the "communistic tendency raises a red flag for the court to consider." The record, she concluded, demonstrated that the mother was a person of "warped and bitter outlook, indifferent to her parents, to her country and to the need of these children for a normal, moral upbringing."[57] On the other hand, Walter Smith was a war veteran, decorated in battle, and a music teacher. His home with his in-laws, who were prominent in the Mormon church, assured Amanda good schooling and a moral, stable environment. Most telling, Amanda wanted to be there. Again, Willebrandt carried the day. The children were reunited with the father and permanent custody granted to him.[58]

While attacking possible Communist influence head-on in her legal practice, Willebrandt generally worked quietly behind the scenes in the traditional area of politics. In the 1940s she maintained her contacts with Roosevelt, briefly writing of her appreciation of his steady war leadership, but her personal energy was directed to Republican candidates and leaders. Her office in the Title Insurance Building in Los Angeles was just down the hall from her old friend and political mentor Frank Doherty; her friendship with Ida Koverman, "Mrs. Republican" of Southern California, and Louis B. Mayer, and her continuing access to Herbert Hoover made her a valuable ally and advocate for party candidates and causes.

In California Republicanism in the 1940s, Earl Warren dominated as no one had since Hiram Johnson. Like Johnson, he expected and demanded personal loyalty from those in the ranks. Like Johnson, he soon turned his attention to national affairs. Willebrandt astutely accepted Warren's state leadership, while continuing her loyalty to Hoover. Increasingly, however, she was attracted to and supported the presidential aspirations of Robert Taft, respecting his rugged in-

Willebrandt speaking at Nome, Alaska, 1946.

tegrity, unfailing honesty, impatience with government bureaucracy and waste, and tough anti-Communist stance.

Though not a delegate to the Republican convention in 1940, Willebrandt attended and worked for Taft's support. At the final stampede to Wendell Willkie, the California delegate vote for Taft rose from 7 to 22; Willkie garnered only 17 votes.[59] Four years later she was in Chicago for the convention and her daughter's wedding, carefully timed to coincide with the Republican gathering. Again, though not a delegate, she supported Taft. It was a Dewey year, and the best that she and alternate delegate Ida Koverman could accomplish was to work for the vice-presidential bid of Governor Bricker of Ohio.[60]

With the Dewey-Bricker defeat in 1944, Taft finally emerged as the front-runner for 1948. Now, however, Governor Earl Warren's candidacy posed a major challenge. It was time for caution among California Republicans. Willebrandt, approached for her support for Taft, responded to her Ohio friend Katherine Kennedy Brown: "I know you are well aware of my deep admiration for Bob Taft and of my earnest backing of him all through the convention at Philadelphia when Wendell Willkie was nominated. California Republicans are milling around, and until I am a little more certain of the views of Senator Knowland and Governor Warren, I wish to make no public statement. I'm sure you understand the wisdom of that policy. I shall, however, keep in touch with you, and watch developments closely."[61] In January 1948, when Taft heard that Warren had invited Willebrandt to be a delegate, he urged her to accept, since she was "strong for him."[62] She did not. The California delegation was a handpicked Warren group; delegates were not to think of any other choice.[63]

Doherty did work with Taft's men when they arrived in the spring to get endorsements from movie figures and their participation in short radio spots, "Why I'm for Bob Taft, American." Willebrandt's friends Clarence Brown, Clark Gable, Hedda Hopper, Sam Wood, and Leo McCarey all gave their aid. Through her contact with Doherty and her friendships in the Hollywood community, Willebrandt was almost certainly quietly involved.[64]

But 1948 was another year of frustration for Taft supporters. Again it was a Dewey convention; Warren capitulated and agreed to join the ticket in the vice-presidential post. In Los Angeles, Willebrandt loyally supported the party, issuing a rare public statement in the last week in October. The *Los Angeles Times* headlined: "Noted Woman Attorney Urges Dewey Election." Her press release was a summary of the political qualities she had valued since the candidacy of Hiram

Johnson. She stressed that Dewey and Warren had made their way up "by hard work and honest living." Each was a "distinguished fighter against crime and graft that weaken democracies." Each had shown his capacity in administering a large state government. Neither had become rich in office. Both had "been strong and wise enough in the true values of life to live normally, and to maintain an ideal Christian home and family." They were, she concluded, "partners in integrity" who would not only win international respect but would "clean out fumblers, duplicities and the riff-raff in government." They would "get a dollar's worth of good government for each dollar of taxes."[65]

The stunning victory of Truman over the Dewey-Warren ticket prompted a poignant request from Willebrandt to Herbert Hoover. Reflecting on twenty years of Democratic dominance and conscious of Hoover's possible influence with Truman, since he had undertaken, at the president's request, his monumental survey of the bureaucracy, Willebrandt again raised the question of a federal judgeship, writing:

> Could you have it in your heart to recommend me for appointment to the Circuit Court of Appeals for the 9th Circuit (California) to President Truman?
>
> I'm 59; my daughter has her own family; my Father is 88; I have enough to live on, but I am alone. There are twelve or fifteen years ahead of me that I'd like to devote to something worth while in my profession.
>
> I'd try to be a good Judge and make you proud of me.
>
> I do have the experience qualification. I am respected at the bar. I've made a modest success of the practice of law; have both tried and argued cases in many jurisdictions of the Federal Courts, and have had the privilege of appearing before the Supreme Court of the U.S. more often than any but two or three lawyers in the country.
>
> Our friend, Wm. Mitchell, would, I think, tell you whether I am a real lawyer.
>
> Of course, the President would not normally name me, a woman, and a Republican. Roosevelt only appointed New Dealers and personal friends. As a result practically all Federal Judges are Roosevelt Democrats. But, *this* President might *like* to demonstrate that he now represents *all* the people, might take pride in appointing a woman and a Republican if you put it up to him.
>
> I'm sure it could only be brought about through you.
>
> With admiration, and gratitude for your friendship, . . .[66]

Hoover, who had so bitterly disappointed her twenty years before but who had kept her loyalty throughout, scrawled across the top of the letter: "My dear . . . I would do anything for you. But my relations with the man you mention would do you more harm than good. I will inquire for a better proposer."[67] There is no evidence that he did. Even had he tried, it was highly unlikely that the embattled Truman would make so controversial a choice when trying to hold the Democratic party together.

The plea to Hoover marked one of the lowest points in Willebrandt's political involvement, but as usual she rebounded. Once again, she rallied to support Taft. In November 1951 she wrote to him of her enthusiasm for his "courageous campaign," adding "I wish I were in a position to do more but be assured I am putting in every effort possible in this confused and misguided state of California."[68] With mounting charges of corruption in the Truman administration, she advised Taft to reveal another side of his character.

> There is one side of you I wish the American people could get a glimpse of. It is the tender, considerate, understanding and spiritual well-spring of your intrinsic character. It cannot come from you right now because aggressive fighting on national and international and military and economic issues is the role in which you are cast at this time. But I feel a great mass of people, otherwise inarticulate, yearn for a leader with essential Godliness in his character and if some of us could assemble facts along that line it would stir support from many who cannot and do not understand the larger issues.[69]

Taft agreed that more "emphasis ought to be laid on the spiritual issues" and indicated he would try to work something out "on that line."[70]

In March she again wrote him a letter of encouragement: "You are doing the greatest job in history. Don't let anything discourage you and do be careful of your health. . . . I am doing everything I can and keeping in touch with your headquarters in the hope I can do more."[71] California, however, was again Warren territory. Frank Doherty realistically assessed the situation for Taft. As in 1948, he advised the senator not to seek California delegates but instead to win support as a second choice should Warren falter. Hollywood figures such as Louis B. Mayer, Hedda Hopper, John Ford, and Leo McCarey helped to organize the national Citizens for Taft Committee. Willebrandt's name was not included in this listing nor in the Lawyers for Taft group.[72] As in 1948, she attended the convention and worked hard for Taft. When his last, heartbreaking effort ended in Eisenhower's triumph, she wrote him: "I want you to know that I've worked with all my might for you in 1940 at Philadelphia, in 1948, and again this year, and *I would do it all over again*. One of the things that I admired most was the valiant spirit you both [Senator and Mrs. Taft] displayed. True character comes out in the face of unjustified attacks and disappointment. Remember always my deep friendship and admiration, and hope that an opportunity may come to express that friendship again."[73] She particularly lamented that Taft had not succeeded, for America might then have had a Theodore Roosevelt administration not afraid to stand up to "the old bandit" Khrushchev.[74]

With Eisenhower the nominee, she still loyally supported the party ticket. At his election in November, she spoke to her fellow members of the Ebell Club in Los Angeles on women in government and urged them to press for the appointment of women to significant posts in the new administration. Specifically, she recommended that Eisenhower recognize that women were "full 50% partners, by naming them to assistant cabinet positions in each department and nominating women for the federal judiciary." With the Republicans finally in power, her own prospects for appointment to the coveted judgeship were hurt by her age and perhaps her support of Taft.[75]

She was not sanguine about the Republican future. Remaining on the sidelines in the 1960 struggle, she wrote of her distrust of Nixon. He was, she believed, "too small of soul. . . . You know my affinity for the underdog, and I *tho* a life time Republican, find myself more and more secretly rooting in my heart for Kennedy. As I think you know, I just do *not* like Nixon; I do *not* trust him. I think he just plays his luck for Nixon." In a campaign that must have brought back memories of 1928, she reflected on the strong anti-Catholic feeling against Kennedy, observing: "Catholics do *not* vote *as* Catholics."[76] Thirty-two years after being the storm center in the religious issue of the Smith campaign, she quietly rooted for his co-religionist and hers. Eight years earlier she had been baptized into the Roman Catholic church. It was one of the several major changes in her private life in the California years.

Facing the increasing illness of her father and the loss of his companionship, Willebrandt found strength and comfort in her new faith. Her decision had been forming for some years. It seemed to be made, finally, as had all of her spiritual choices, on the basis of simple conviction rather than from a reasoned dogmatic position. Faith was an affair of the heart and the will, not the mind. The life of the law was concrete, logical; her life of the spirit was a matter of belief. Willebrandt's early faith simply followed her mother's. She grew up in the Christian church, nourished by a belief in the immanence and love of the God she saw in the prairie fields and sky. Later, asked about a turning point in her career, she related a Kansas City experience. At thirteen, ill with whooping cough she opened her bible to the passage "Ask and ye shall receive. Knock and it shall be opened to you." Henceforth, she explained, she saw God as a "partner"; if she would do her part, He would do His.[77]

She found her faith most easily in the experience of God in nature and in others. Writing to her parents at Christmas 1924, she reflected on the happiness of two young Salvation Army workers recently married in New York: "They must love each other more because they love God together. I do not say these things idly or 'soulfully' to discuss religion. I have thought a great deal about such things lately. And it has come to me that those lives most deeply moving mine are all ones who love God. . . . And, if my blessed parents, our home had given me nothing more than the certainty that the love of God makes me invincible, it would have made life wonderful."[78]

Her mother's comforting and supportive letters during the difficult Washington years always echoed this sense of confidence, partnership, and the immanence of God. In the midst of the Harding scandals, she urged: "Remember Jesus says always 'Fear not.' Remember how the storm blew the ship around and the disciples were afraid and Jesus looking *higher* than the seeming discord said 'Peace! Be still!' and the winds obeyed His voice. . . . The spirit of God will guide you in *all* your *ways* and *lead* you into that which is for your good. Fear not, just be still and know God. Remember His promises, 'I will in no wise fail thee, neither will I in anguish forsake thee.'"[79]

In 1925, after adopting Dorothy and feeling the need to attach herself to a church, she chose her mother's new allegiance to Christian Science. The Christian Science faith that "all things are possible with God," the emphasis on Christ's life rather than his words, the conviction of a harmonious universe, the certitude of God's healing presence, were all congenial to Willebrandt. Her faith in the healing power of Christian Science was not strong. For a cure for her ears, she turned to the latest in medical science as well as to prayer. In 1935, driving home from a Sunday outing with her parents, Willebrandt, impatiently passed a slower driver on a hill and smashed into an oncoming car. Her mother suffered severe head injuries, her father emerged cut and bruised, and Willebrandt fractured her arm. All were treated in Washington County hospital in Maryland, but as soon as Willebrandt was released, she rushed to call a Christian Science practitioner.[80]

Typically, her slow journey to Catholicism began with a person, not dogma. Her good friend Grace Knoeller invited a young priest from her Pennsylvania hometown to come to the Walker farm from his nearby post at Mount St. Mary's Seminary in Emmitsburg, Maryland. Willebrandt, in her usual way of getting others to talk, drew out Father Robert McCormack on his priesthood and his faith. Over the next years he visited often and a strong friendship grew out of the inevitable discussions and sometimes vigorous arguments. Willebrandt did follow some of his reading suggestions. By the time she was ready to receive formal instruction in Catholicism, she was home in California.[81] She found her instructor in a fashion reminiscent of her discovery of Calvin Claggett in a Maryland field. She drove her "big, black car" to the yard of the beautiful old Mission San Gabriel, which she passed every day on her journey to and from her office in Los Angeles. Entering the walled garden area next to the church, she walked up to a startled priest sweeping the path, engaged him in conversation, and liking his simplicity, asked him to undertake her instruction. Taken back by this formidable, elegant, determined woman, he tried to send her to someone "grander," but was faced down by Willebrandt and yielded.[82] For her baptism, she returned to her original guide, Father McCormack, now stationed at St. Gregory's Church in Baltimore. In 1952, just before the Republican convention, she called her friend John Sirica, asking if he would be her sponsor but warning that she wanted a simple, quiet ceremony and "none of that Clare Boothe Luce stuff."[83] Two years later, with a delay caused by the death of Father McCormack and by her father's illness, she was confirmed at Mission San Gabriel.[84]

While in some aspects it was a long road from Christian Science to Catholicism, for Willebrandt there were obvious links. She wrote of the "*desire* to *pour* out one's heart in prayer" shared by every Christian and the "readings" and prayers that churches provide. The Catholic church, she observed, "is very rich in books of prayers. Their approach tho, to which I'm *not* fully educated is much rote repetition."[85] The faith in the saving presence of God, the confidence of the church that it was Christ's instrument, and the emphasis on good works were familiar and comforting. The uncompromising anti-Communist stand, the sense that the church "stood" for something, would attract

Portrait of Willebrandt in the 1950s inscribed "To my Father more loved and more admired with the passing years. Mabel." Photograph by Harris and Ewing.

Willebrandt. Perhaps most appealing, however, was the long tradition and history, the endurance of Catholicism represented so visibly by Mission San Gabriel. Her essential faith was perhaps best summed up in a short Christmas essay written in the painful aftermath of the 1928 election campaign. She began with a reference to the giant redwoods of the Pacific, "Our Western Christmas Trees." They had stood in the high Sierras for four thousand years, "linking the centuries by their life." They were there when Christ was born. She reflected:

> Today they stand the world's greatest, oldest Christmas trees, symbol of the living faith with which the life of Christ has filled the world.
> That living faith is the sap that has nourished civilization and will develop our individual lives. . . . they fulfill the law of all life; they stand sturdily in simple soil. They push unerringly upward.
> Each of us can do no more. We can root ourselves sturdily in the soil of simple living, honest toil, friendliness to folk about, truth in daily dealings. And with the hope that rises in every heart we can push our thought and aspirations unerringly upward to the blue heaven of lofty purpose and the sunlight of an understanding of God's law.[86]

While Willebrandt was finding a spiritual home, she faced increasingly sharp breaks in her haven of family. In 1940, a bitter family dispute erupted. The *Los Angeles Times* ran the headlines: "Willebrandt Suit Aired," "Former Chum in Property Suit," "Poet Seeks Recovery of Temple City Home from Former Official." The public squabble ended the thirty-year friendship of Willebrandt and Maud Hubbard Brown. The story unfolded in Los Angeles Superior Court. Maud who had bought a home in Temple City before returning to China with her three sons in 1926, had deeded the property at 133 South Cloverly Avenue to Mr. Walker for safekeeping. When she returned in 1935, separated from Brown, who had been convicted of embezzlement at an American court in China, she met with Willebrandt, to whom Walker had in turn deeded the property. Willebrandt agreed to pay Maud $2,600 and assume the mortgage payments.[87] The Browns could live in the Cloverly Avenue house until the property was sold. In her testimony in 1940 Maud Brown denied that any such agreement had been made. She claimed that the property was rightfully hers. She emphasized that she considered herself a member of the Walker family, and as substantiation cited the volume of her poetry, "The Flowering Pagoda," which she had dedicated to Willebrandt. She added that she always followed Willebrandt's advice and had most recently accepted it in obtaining her divorce from J. Ward Brown. A furious Willebrandt, who had arranged for her old classmate Myra Dell Collins to handle the complicated matter of extricating the felony papers from war-torn China and arguing the divorce case, countered Brown's claim by introducing a 1938 letter in which Maud asked "nothing better than to forget him completely," and ended by writing off all men as "a lot of bums—that's all."[88] For Willebrandt, who prized family privacy, it was particularly anguishing to have her eighty-year-old father involved in a court procedure. She worked out a settlement. Maud would have an opportunity to recover the property by reimbursing her for paying off the mortgage; meanwhile Willebrandt would retain the title.[89]

Her father, as he had always been, remained the most important person in her life. In January 1942, Dorothy was away at college and David Walker, chafing at city living, left for the new family retreat, a ranch Willebrandt had purchased in the desert at Indio, California. Walkersands replaced Walker Fields. "Batching" it from January to July, Walker supervised repairs to the house and put in the crops. A vegetable garden yielded lettuce, beans, turnips, onions, beets, and sweet corn; a new batch of chickens supplied poultry and eggs.[90] A Mexican family was brought in to manage the date crop. In 1943, when Willebrandt moved to California, Indio remained a haven on weekends and vacations, but her major year-round home was with her father in Temple City.

With signs of his gradual failing, Willebrandt worked some vacations into her schedule, determined to make the most of the time she had left with him. In 1946, she arranged an energetic trip to Alaska's Mount McKinley National Park, Fairbanks, and Nome. The next year they relaxed in the Hawaiian Islands.[91] It was their last major journey. After a series of small strokes and increasing arteriosclerotic problems, David Walker needed a relative, friend, or nurse in attendance. In August 1954, Willebrandt chanced a rare business trip to Europe, carefully arranging with her secretary Olive Morgan to send her cables every other day. During the weekend of August 15, while she was en route from Milan to Madrid, her father fell and fractured his hip. Belatedly receiving word of the accident, Willebrandt made frantic efforts to fly home. Just before departing, she was informed that her father was dead. In Los Angeles, she made arrangements, and then, joined by Olive Morgan, her Eaton cousins, and her long-time friend Laura Jane Emery, took his body home to the rolling fields and the small cemetery outside Powersville, Missouri. Dorothy flew from Alaska to be with her mother. At the graveside, the minister spoke briefly, using her favorite text, 2 Tim. 1:7, "For God hath not given us the spirit of fear; but of power, and of love, and of a sound mind." He then read two of Mrs. Walker's poems, entitled "Faith" and "Prayer."[92] After the service, those from the small village who had known her father and mother came quietly forward, sharing her grief and relating what her parents had done for them, how her mother had nursed their baby or her father had harvested their grain. Overcome with her loss, Willebrandt found their comfort "healing" but wrote to her good friend Grace Knoeller: "It was a bitter cup and still is to have had him suffer from carelessness and not to be able to reach him to love and comfort him after he was hurt and say goodbye." She refused to see the nurse who had been in charge when he had fallen.[93]

With the death of her father, Willebrandt increasingly devoted her attention to Dorothy and her young family. Dorothy's upbringing had involved a stormy clash of wills. Willebrandt and her daughter had radically opposed views of what she would be. Dorothy was happy to be a tomboy and yearned to live on a farm and become a veterinarian. Willebrandt was determined that she would not work for self-discipline and grace but that she would be a young lady. Dorothy studied piano. At eighteen she had a coming-out party complete with Meyer Davis and his orchestra and a glittering host of Washington lawyers and leaders at the Sulgrave Club. She was first sent to college at Bucknell, where the retired Mary Belle Harris could keep an eye out for her. After Dorothy applied her familiar weapon of passive resistance, she transferred to Wheaton College in Illinois. Though chafing at the abundance of rules that were part of the Christian missionary heritage of the school, she enjoyed her classmates, particularly one older theology student, Hendrick Van Dyke. In the summer of 1944, she and Hendrick, who had been accepted at Princeton Theological Seminary, were married. The site was Chicago, close to their college friends, and the locale of the Republican convention. Willebrandt's Washington and Hollywood friends could also attend. As usual, Willebrandt supervised all of the arrangements, choosing Dorothy's dress and selecting Rose D'Amore, her piano teacher, as maid of honor. She designed and sewed Dorothy hats to match every dress in her trousseau. Hedda Hopper reported the event.[94]

Willebrandt's involvement did not end there. She helped Dorothy find an apartment in Princeton, suitable, as Hendrick observed, for one she assumed would be no less than the pastor of New York's finest Presbyterian church. Furniture was sent from the farm in Pennsylvania. Dorothy and Hendrick tolerated their splendor for the first few months and then rebelled at apartment living and in true Walker fashion "set out for the territory," trading their proper address for a small rustic cabin on a nearby farm. Willebrandt and her father arrived to spend Thanksgiving with the young couple. Appalled at the simple, spartan, drafty surroundings, Willebrandt kept silent, betraying her emotion only by grimly cracking nut after nut from the bowl on the dining-room table. But Dorothy and Hendrick's declaration of independence was accepted. Willebrandt continued to send treats, tickets for New York shows, furniture, and generous Christmas presents. When the Van Dyke sons began to arrive, she thoroughly enjoyed her role as grandmother, albeit at long distance, since Hendrick's posts ranged from rural Maryland to Seattle, Alaska, California, and Oregon.[95]

Willebrandt dispatched cards and presents to the three young boys, David, Pieter, and Jan Christopher, on Easter, Valentine's Day, Christmas, and the Fourth of July, interspersed with short, newsy letters, very much adult to adult. David, the oldest and her father's namesake, was particularly cherished. When his difficulties in mathematics were traced to a slight learning disability, she arranged with Dorothy and Hendrick to send him to a private academy. In her take-charge manner, she paid the bills and also ordered that the grades be sent to her rather than to the annoyed parents. Her letters to David were full of encouragement, stressing the value of education. She urged him to get the best preparation he could, for without education "one is held back from getting a good job and being independent . . . that I know!" When he was sixteen, she wrote from Texas, sending him pictures of the Trinity University campus and offering to "make a deal" that if he made good grades she would save the money and send him there. Since it was a leading Presbyterian university she was certain Hendrick would approve.[96] On her birthday in 1962 she wrote a particularly poignant note to young David: "I'm writing this on my birthday. I am old, but you are young. I hope you have a useful life as your namesake, my dear Papa, had, because he worked hard, looked ahead and was always fine and true."[97]

As she grew older and her health worsened, Willebrandt reminisced in her letters to Dorothy. Appreciating Dorothy's closeness and concern after David Walker's death in 1954, she wrote, "I realized so many times how grievously I failed you." She dismissed her disappointment at Dorothy's school record and now was "full of pride" at the "usefulness of her life."[98] On Mother's Day she wrote a note: "For Darling I could never find a card that would say what is in my heart. For I want you to know that every memory you have given me throughout all your life is precious—rewarding and cherished as the golden threads throughout the years too wasted on law and other things that tarnish."[99]

She shared her warmth and loyalty with her extended family, particularly Calvin and Mary Claggett. Before Willebrandt sold the Pennsylvania property, Claggett, who had managed the farm so well, was involved in an accident that certainly helped to determine her decision to leave Pennsylvania. Driving home one evening he struck and killed a man walking along the dark county road. Terror-stricken at the possible consequences of local justice for a black man, the usually steady Claggett drove to Walker Fields and kept his counsel. Willebrandt, checking accounts with him, perceived that he was obviously deeply troubled and asked her good, gentle friend Grace Knoeller to try to find out what was wrong. Claggett recounted the tragic accident and then reported to the police. Willebrandt secured his defense attorney and appeared as a character witness, pointing out his years of responsible service. When Claggett was found guilty of involuntary manslaughter and sentenced to a Pennsylvania prison, Willebrandt was outraged. She "never forgave" Pennsylvania justice.[100] After the farm was sold, she brought Mary Claggett to Walkersands at Indio. When Calvin Claggett was released, he was brought to manage the California ranch quickly learning the methods of harvesting dates. He drove Willebrandt back and forth from Indio to the office in Los Angeles, joining her other friends in urging her to cut back her killing schedule. If only, he urged, she would take no phone calls at the ranch and leave her work in the city.[101]

With the death of her father, Willebrandt determined to move out of the homes they had shared together. She sold the ranch at Indio to her neighbors, Jacqueline Cochran and Floyd Odlum, and established the Claggetts temporarily in a house in Indio, though "outraged" at the prices charged to a black couple, and finally on an acre of her Indio land.[102]

Willebrandt brought Minnie Wells, now widowed, and her daughter Mabel to Fullerton, California, and bought them a small house. With a little help from Willebrandt, Minnie and Mabel could be independent.[103]

She moved both home and office. Selling her house in Temple City, Willebrandt bought a lovely ranch home in the West Hollywood hills with a sweeping panorama of Los Angeles to the south and east. Her new office at 9110 Sunset Boulevard was a few blocks away. Her friend Laura Jane Emery came to live with her again after Emery's small house was burglarized. The nephew of another friend and client moved in while finishing his studies at the University of Southern California. Willebrandt, who always loved to entertain, enjoyed being hostess to visiting Washingtonians such as Grace Knoeller, Knoeller's sisters, and John Sirica. She particularly enjoyed a party for twenty of her "young friends," all those she had worked with and helped as they began their own businesses. She kept in touch with Carl and Laura Lomen, working hard to get two of Carl's articles published in *Reader's Digest* to raise his spirits after he was struck down by a series of strokes. Increasingly, as her own health deteriorated from years of overwork, she cut back her social and work schedule.[104] She was determined to end her trial work. After she lost a case in 1956, that involved a pregnant woman's losing her baby as a result of being struck by a car, Willebrandt, decrying the verdict for the insurance company as "one of the worst miscarriages of justice during all my law practice," hoped that her friends would declare her "mentally incompetent if I ever take another piece of actual litigation again."[105] Of course, she did.

Her last case, involving a twenty-two-million-dollar estate, was argued in February 1962, in St. Louis. She made the journey with a broken wrist and with the apprehension of her doctor. She described her cast from wrist to elbow in a letter to a grandson and told him, "I'll be a funny sight, but I don't give up. . . . I've got to make my argument just that much better."[106] To Grace Knoeller she wrote: "Did I tell you about that Judge in St. Louis? He's pretty cute! 8 lawyers had told him 5 different interpretations of the will, and 8 different things to do in his decree. So after we had all written 3 big briefs, 'opening,' 'supplemental' and 'answering,' he asked each counsel to write 'Findings of Facts and Conclusions of Law.' . . . I'm the only one who tore down the middle and said the trustees were wrong in not appealing to Equity for 37 years. So everyone thinks I, an outsider, am a bounder. I doubt if the Judge goes my way. He *lives* with all the others and the

Trustees, who are big shots in St. Louis! Anyway I gave them something to think about, and, I think to fear some."[107]

She looked forward to the end of the case and her practice, writing to Knoeller that she was happy to have no one call with the legal problems and other demands that "go with practicing law. I can hardly wait to send out the notices—goodbye to law—desk vacant." Her actual card a few months later showed a vacant desk, an open door, and a happy Willebrandt dashing toward a waiting ship and airplane with a smiling sun beaming down on the scene.[108] She looked forward to rest, reading, and travel, but she had not stopped soon enough. She had written the briefs for the St. Louis case between hospital visits. Rapidly, she was just "giving out."[109]

Throughout, her ears had continued to be a source of frustration and difficulty. In 1945, after years of seeking help, Willebrandt became one of the first patients to undergo the new surgical procedure of Dr. Julius Lempert. Awakening in a New York hospital the morning after surgery, she clearly heard the rumble of a passing truck. Recuperating with her father and Grace Knoeller at Indio, she was full of wonder at hearing a bird sing in the early desert morning. She celebrated at a small party for Dr. Lempert at the Sulgrave Club, sharing her happiness with old friends, Chief Justice and Mrs. Stone, Admiral and Mrs. Ross McIntire, and others.[110]

Unfortunately, the cure was only temporary. A second operation left her with only minimal improvement in hearing and permanent difficulties in maintaining her balance. The embarrassment of leaving a party or cocktail lounge or of simply walking and suddenly lurching from side to side was acute. She usually contrived when in trouble to hold on to a friend, but could sometimes hear the whispers of those who did not know her that she was drunk. Her unsteadiness caused her to fall frequently.[111] Leaving the home of the executive secretary of the Screen Director's Guild, Joseph Youngerman, she fell into his bushes and hurt her ankle. She recounted to a grandson an experience of being blown over by a big wind and fracturing her wrist. In May 1961, struggling and hopping to jump out of a dress with a balky zipper, she lost her balance and "flew like the man on the trapeze feet in the air, my feet hitting several things enroute and kerplump!" Thinking she was only bruised, she crawled into bed. After six days of pain, she called the doctor and was hospitalized with six badly cracked vertebrae.[112]

Her heart and lungs were failing. After a bout of tests, she wrote to Grace Knoeller, "Well, I lived through it, came (droopingly), saw (painfully) and *conquered* the worst bunch of tests you could imagine! I'm all right too—well relatively, just a bit too many years—somewhat too few, (if *any*) rest periods—much too much tensity etc. etc. plus *all* the things Doctors are wont to say when they want to cover up their lack of knowledge of what's wrong with a *tired* mind with no objective! I knew it all along."[113] Part of the diagnosis was emphysema. She had smoked fairly heavily, but now cut back to "a reasonably moderate rate." She noted that her doctor did not believe that smoking was the cause but attributed it to either a chemical in the smog or her five previous bouts with pneumonia. She confided to Knoeller: "I puff and gasp for breath. And (what I hate worse) is that I have little ambition to travel or do anything except *sit*." (She wrote this from St. Louis while completing her trial brief.)[114]

In 1962 she closed her office, sold the West Hollywood home, and moved to an apartment. Then on doctor's orders to protect her lungs, she moved to a small home in Riverside. She journeyed to Mayo Clinic in Rochester, Minnesota, for a complete diagnosis. There were new medicines but no remedy. From Riverside in November 1962, she wrote a long letter to Grace Knoeller explaining why she had not corresponded sooner: "I truly have practically no energy. Can you imagine me so? I sit, or lie in bed, and think of nice things to do—what I would enjoy or things I *should do*. Always I plan them for tomorrow morning!" She detailed her day with a lawyer's cool objectivity: "About 10 A.M I start putting on my harness (brace with iron stays). I have to lay it out on the bed—lie into it, slipping arms in the straps and buckle 9 straps and adjust the tightness of each, fasten, stand, take deep breaths, readjust brace straps." Her secretary Olive Morgan arrived two days a week about eleven o'clock for dictation. By four o'clock her back and shoulder "hurt so I just rebel at sitting at the desk any-more;" she walked outside if the sun were shining. The hardest thing, she wrote Knoeller, was the "mental lassitude. . . . What I can't understand is that once I was an eager person with interests, plans, and even if I felt bad I was conscious of and wanted to meet obligations. Now I'm not, I just don't *care* any more. I'm mentally a perfect beach comber, dozing in the sunlight, interested only in not being bothered and in no one cutting off my sunlite!!! Where I *used* to do many things in a day—lots of diversified interests—now I have a *full* busy!! day if there is *one* task to be completed—like ordering wood for the fireplace or sewing hooks on a skirt. To also write a letter on that busy day is unthinkable!! So it's put off till tomorrow." One day, planning to drive to Los Angeles and stay with a friend, she got only as far as the Mission Inn in Riverside. Immobilized by a sudden angina attack, she put nitro under her tongue and waited alone in the lobby until the pain passed an hour later and she could cautiously drive home.

At the end of this precise, detailed analysis of her health, Willebrandt energetically discussed the political debacle of Nixon's 1962 gubernatorial race and his famous TV capitulation. Now, she hoped, he would have to work for a living. Clearly her illness had not, as she feared, changed her personality "into a cipher."[115]

Five months later, on April 6, 1963, after weeks of severe pain, she died of lung cancer in the small Riverside home. A good lawyer, she left all in order: the will was drawn up; personal gifts were wrapped and addressed to friends; daughter, foster sister, Minnie Wells, and the Claggetts all were well housed and taken care of. For the requiem mass at nearby St. Francis de Sales Church, her daughter suggested her mother's favorite verse for inclusion in the eulogy, 2 Tim. 1:7: "For God hath not give us the spirit of fear; but of power, and of love, and of a sound mind." She suggested that the reading be extended to include 2 Tim. 4:7: "I have fought the good fight, I have run the race, I have kept the faith."[116]

It was the epitaph Willebrandt had chosen for her father, and one she would surely have elected herself. Earlier she had mused: "These 70s are funny and need adjustments just *like adolescence* did. At 72 I'm making that adjustment and finding as friends die the long shadows that lengthen are not black; they're just deep green cool, and it's good to rest in them from the long strenuous race."[117]

It was a rare moment, for Willebrandt seldom looked back and had never paused in the race. Her motion was always forward, her vision to the future, her courage ready for the new challenge.

Notes

ABBREVIATIONS

AVCO	Aviation Corporation, New York, N.Y.
Black Committee	Senate Special Committee on Air-Ocean Mail Contracts, 74th Congress
BOP	U.S. Bureau of Prisons
CWHP	California Wine Industry Oral History Project, Bancroft Library, University of California, Berkeley
DA	U.S. Department of Agriculture
DGA	Directors Guild of America
DI	U.S. Department of the Interior
DOJ	U.S. Department of Justice
DVD	Dorothy Van Dyke
FCC	Federal Communications Commission
FFB	Federal Farm Board
FRC	Federal Radio Commission
GFWC	General Federation of Women's Clubs
HHP	Herbert Hoover Papers
LAT	*Los Angeles Times*
MWW	Mabel Walker Willebrandt
MWWP	Mabel Walker Willebrandt Papers
SD	U.S. State Department
SDG	Screen Directors Guild
SPCS	South Pasadena City Schools
USC	University of Southern California
WJCC	Women's Joint Congressional Committee

PROLOGUE

1. *New York Times*, Oct. 26, 1928; "The First Legal Lady of the Land," *Literary Digest* 76 (Mar. 31, 1923): 41, "America's Portia," *New York Herald Tribune*, July 1, 1928; Martin, "Mrs. Firebrand," *New Yorker*, Feb. 16, 1929; Kent, cited in *New York Times*, Dec. 31, 1928; The Gentleman at the Keyhole, "Where Duty Lies," *Collier's*, Oct. 27, 1928.

2. MWW memorandum to Alpheus Mason, Jan. 31, 1951, box 83, Stone Papers.

3. Jacqueline Cochran, interview with author. Prison citations are in ch. 4.

CHAPTER ONE

1. DVD, interview with author, Oct. 20, 1978; Mrs. Walker, MWW's mother, to MWW, July 1923, MWWP. The Willebrandt papers were given by Mrs. Van Dyke to the Manuscript Division of the Library of Congress, spring 1980, but had not been processed when I was doing my research.

2. The history of Grandma Alton and Grandma Eaton was traced by Mrs. Walker when MWW was interested in the DAR (MWWP). "Dolly's" maiden name is unknown. The gravestone of Thomas Eaton in the Powersville, Mo., cemetery indicates that he served in Co. F, 7th Mo. Cav. Vol. *History of Adair, Sullivan, Putnam, Schuyler Counties, Missouri*, 497, relates Civil War activities; the *Illustrated Historical Atlas of Putnam County, Missouri* is also helpful.

3. W.H. Lowry to MWW, Feb. 18, 1938, MWWP.

4. Mrs. Walker's autobiographical sketch, MWWP. For Kansas conditions see Dick, *Sod House Frontier, 1854–1890*, 129, and Farmer, "Economic Background of Frontier Populism," 406–47. For a fine study of frontier women, see Jeffrey, *Frontier Women*; a helpful anthology is *Let Them Speak for Themselves*, ed. Christine Fischer.

5. McNeal, *When Kansas Was Young*, 161. See description of January blizzard in Stratton, *Pioneer Women*, 92.

6. Dick, 228; Farmer, 416.

7. McNeal, 171–72. A follow-up to this incident was related by Strakosch in "A Woman in Law," 190. Strakosch, visiting Mrs. Willebrandt's office in the Justice Department, recounted MWW's finding a letter from her mother to President Benjamin Harrison pleading for justice. The ambushers had been arrested, tried, and found guilty in 1891, but the decision was reversed on a technicality and a new trial ordered. The trial had not been held and Mrs. Walker pleaded for action. For MWW's persistence in the case, see Hoover to MWW, Apr. 26, 1926, file 23-19, 14, box 4892, DOJ; MWW to parents, Sept. 23, 1926, and MWW to J.E. Hoover, Feb. 9, 1927, MWWP. MWW had asked for further data on the Sam Robinson case.

8. Fred Walker to MWW, Oct. 17, 1921; D.W. Walker, "Paternal Ancestry of Mabel Walker Willebrandt," and D.W. Walker to Margaret W. Peterman, Apr. 17, 1937, MWWP.

9. D.W. Walker, "Retrospective of Seventy-Five Years Concerning Local History," MWWP.

10. D.W. Walker to Emma Ganaway, Oct. 5, 1928, MWWP. See also file of teaching certificates and recommendations, MWWP.

11. D.W. Walker, "Paternal Ancestry of Mabel Walker Willebrandt" and certificate file, MWWP. In 1889, there were 733 weekly papers in operation in Kansas (Stratton, 197).

12. Strakosch, 190.

13. Ise, *Sod and Stubble*, 211.

14. D.W. Walker, in his journal, "My Trip," April 9, 1928, describes leaving Kansas with three-month-old Mabel, MWWP. DVD remembers her grandfather's describing his run for the Cherokee strip in April 1889; if so, he was unsuccessful twice and it would have meant that he left Mrs. Walker when she was eight months pregnant (DVD tape to author, Nov. 1981).

15. Hicks, *Populist Revolt*, 30–32; see also Hewes, *Suitcase Farming Frontier*. An obituary article in the *Kansas City Star*, Apr. 4, 1963, indicates that Woodsdale had disappeared from maps and postal guides by 1915. Hugoton, located in one of the world's largest gas fields, survived.

16. Certificate file has testimonial, MWWP.

17. Strakosch, 190.

18. Certificate file, MWWP; "Facts in Mrs. Willebrandt's Life," manuscript, MWW file, *LAT*.

19. *Lucerne Standard*, n.d. (clipping in MWWP).

20. DVD interview with author, Oct. 20, 1978. For more information on the Cherokee run see McReynolds, *Oklahoma*, 299–301.

21. D.W. Walker to Herbert H. Smock, Feb. 18, 1931, MWWP.

22. Dick, 417.

23. *Blackwell Times*, Nov. 1, 1893 (clipping in MWWP).

24. Strakosch, 192.

25. Jennie C. Walker to Olive Morgan, MWW's secretary, Feb. 11, 1964, MWWP.

26. Strakosch, 194, and "Who's Who—and Why," 74. *Plat Book of Putnam County Missouri* shows the 80-acre tract in York Township, 66–67 north, ranges 21–22 west, pp. 22–23. MWW's mother wrote to her on July 12, 1924, about how she would raise the poor children in the city if given the opportunity and described what she had apparently followed in raising Mabel (MWWP).

27. "Facts in Mrs. Willebrandt's Life," MWW file, *LAT*.

28. MWW, "First Impressions," 222.

29. "Facts in Mrs. Willebrandt's Life," MWW file, *LAT*, and interview with the Walkers in the *Kansas City Star*, June 15, 1928.

30. Strakosch, 192. David Walker always drank his coffee out of his saucer whether in Washington or California society (DVD to author, Nov. 1981).

31. Articles of Agreement between the Chicago Orphan Asylum and David and Myrtle Walker, MWWP.

32. The certificate file, MWWP, contains a testimonial from the cashier of the Powersville Bank.

33. DVD, interview with author, Oct. 20, 1978; unpublished essay by DVD, "Interview with a Failure," Dec. 28, 1970.

34. *Hoyes Directory of Kansas City*, 1903, lists the Walker address as 1006 Cherry

Street. They moved in 1904 to 2617 East 11th Street, out of the immediate downtown area (The Commercial Club, ed., *Kansas City Illustrated, 1901*, p. 3; Walker interview in *Kansas City Star*, June 15, 1928).

35. Minnie Hickstein Wells and her daughter, Mabel Wells, interview with author. Mrs. Wells remembers her happiness with the Walkers—"a real Christian family"—who treated her like one of their own daughters. Mr. Walker's description of Maud is in a letter to DVD, Sept. 1938 (MWWP). See also Mrs. Walker to MWW, Sept. 1924, MWWP.

36. Kansas City Manual Training High School, *Courses of Study, Requirements for Admission*, pp. 7–19, 114–15 (available in the Missouri Valley Room, Kansas City Public Library).

37. The St. Louis trip is discussed in *The Nautilus* (quarterly of Manual Training School) 7 (Mar. 1904): 5–6, 31–32; for a picture of the class officers for 1906, see *Nautilus* 8 (June 1905): 98.

38. MWW to parents, Christmas 1924, MWWP.

39. Admission form for Park College, Jan. 24, 1906, submitted by MWW, Park College Archives.

40. Eggleston, *Park College Centennial Sketches*, 19.

41. *Narva*, 1906, the Park College yearbook, provides a picture and listing of members of the academy class of 1908. MWW and Maud are listed but were not in the picture. Statistics in the 1906 *Narva* also indicate that one student from this class was "fired." Maud Brown wrote to MWW, Dec. 10, 1923, of their Park classmates (MWWP). L.M. McAfee is described in Joseph E. McAfee, *Mid-West Adventure in Education*, 51.

42. J.E. McAfee, 87–88.

43. MWW, "The College Student as an Immediate Citizen," Conference of College and University Students, April 5–6, 1924, MWWP.

44. MWW to Kingsley W. Given, May 14, 1942, and biographical sketch of MWW by Kingsley W. Given, Park College Archives; DVD tape to author, Nov. 1981.

45. Martin, "Mrs. Firebrand," 23.

46. *Buckley Enterprise*, Aug. 23, 1907, and a New Year's greeting from the Buckley Bank (clipping and flyer in MWWP).

47. "Facts in Mrs. Willebrandt's Life," MWW file, *LAT*; D.W. Walker to DVD, Sept. 1938, MWWP; D.W. Walker recommendation, May 9, 1911, in MWW's dossier, Office of the Superintendent, SPCS.

48. See Mr. Walker's recommendation, MWW file, SPCS, and "Who's Who—and Why," 74. Hard, in "America's Portia," indicates that the knife-wielding student became a solid citizen and a faithful correspondent with MWW. MWW's family scrapbook in DVD's possession shows the basketball team posed in front of the Buckley Bank and picnic romps at Duck Lake.

49. Kingsley W. Given biographical sketch, Park College Archives; DVD interview with author, Oct. 20, 1978; and Grace Knoeller, interview with author, June 1980.

50. MWW to parents, Christmas 1924 and Mar. 31, 1923, and MWW to mother, Mar. 22, 1923, MWWP.

51. Powell, *Arizona*, xiii; MWW wrote of the challenge to her parents, July 26, 1926, MWWP.

52. "The Consumptive's Holy Grail," *World's Work* 20 (Dec. 1909), 12333; also Collins, "Tuberculosis," in *Encyclopedia Americana* (Int. ed.), vol. 27 (Danbury, Conn.: Americana Corp., 1978), 193–202. For a contemporary sense of the dread of tuberculosis see "The Spectator," *Outlook* 95 (May 7, 1910): 1618, and Thomas S. Carrington, "The Evolution of the Lean-to," *Survey* 22 (July 17, 1909): 553–54.

53. Atwood, "Where Friendly Help Counts," *Spirit of the Missions*, May 1909, pp. 393–9.

54. Ibid. The Phoenix Historical Society checked the *Phoenix City Directory* for 1910 and 1911 and found no listing for Arthur or Mabel Willebrandt.

55. Buchanan, ed., *Phoenix*, 80–82 and 13.

56. Hopkins and Thomas, Jr., *Arizona State University Story*, viii–ix and 50.

57. Ibid., 141–65.

58. Ibid., 177.

59. Ibid., 171–78.

60. MWW, "First Impressions," 222. Years later, her adopted daughter recalled her mother telling her of considering an abortion, but Arthur Willebrandt, dispatched to seek out an abortionist, returned home without any contact (DVD, interview with author, Oct. 20, 1978).

CHAPTER TWO

1. Fogelson, *Fragmented Metropolis*, 190–91 and 213–18.

2. Ibid. See also Mayer, ed., *Los Angeles*, and Schiesl, "Progressive Reform in Los Angeles under Mayor Alexander, 1909–1913."

3. George E. Mowry's *California Progressives* provides the best account of the development of the reform movement.

4. MWW file, SPCS.

5. Ibid.

6. Ibid.

7. Ibid.

8. Ibid.

9. Ibid.

10. A picture of the Lincoln Park school is available at the new Arroyo Vista School, built on its site; Strakosch, "A Woman in Law," 192.

11. The current principal of Arroyo Vista noted the streetcar location, as does Fogelson, 164; Grace Knoeller, interview with author, June 5, 1978.

12. "The First Legal Lady of the Land," 41; Strakosch, 192.

13. MWW, "First Impressions," 266.

14. Strakosch, 192–94.

15. Catalogue, 1912–13, College of Law, USC, 208–209. The 1913–14 catalogue describes the women's room, 219.

16. Judge May Lahey, interview with author, July 1978. The founding of Phi Delta Delta is described by Annette F. Hunley, "Early History of Phi Delta Delta,"

Sarah Patten Doherty, "Sowing the Seed of Phi Delta Delta," Litta Belle Hibben Campbell, "A Tribute to the Founders of Phi Delta Delta," *Phi Delta Delta* 5 (Nov. 1973): 4–11, and the *Daily Southern Californian*, Nov. 6, 1912 (Clipping Book 2, Bullock Papers).

17. For curriculum and fees see 1912–15 USC College of Law catalogues.

18. Commencement Program, 1915, College of Law, USC, lists Arthur Willebrandt as a graduate. Material on the divorce is in MWW file, *LAT*. Arthur Willebrandt eventually returned to teaching, earning a bachelor of science and a master's degree in education in 1926 and 1928 at USC; the *Los Angeles Directory* lists MWW's addresses and schools and offices; she first shared a home with Evelyn Costello, who followed her as assistant police court defender (Grace Knoeller and Paula Knoeller Gore, interview with author, July 7, 1978).

19. MWW to father, Oct. 1, 1924, MWWP.

20. MWW, "Give Women a Fighting Chance!" 25.

21. Myra Dell Collins, interview with author; MWW to father, Nov. 29, 1924, MWWP; O'Neill, in *Divorce in the Progressive Era*, traces the emergence of "mass divorce" and high incidence of divorced or single women among major reformers.

22. MWW to father, Nov. 29, 1924; MWW to mother, Nov. 28 and Dec. 10, 1924, MWWP.

23. Strakosch, 194; Myra Dell Collins, interview with author.

24. The drawn-out decision to form the police court defender's office can be traced in the Los Angeles City Council Records, vol. 100, no. 1462; vol. 102, no. 2839; vol. 103, no. 463. The post was originally unsalaried. In a letter to Donald J. Schippers on Jan. 25, 1966, Pope notes that a salary of $75 was finally paid to her successor (file 7, box 4, no. 752, Pope Papers).

25. *Annual Report, Police Department, 1917*, p. 25.

26. Robinson, *Lawyers of Los Angeles*, 249; *Annual Report, Police Department, 1917*, p. 28. For 1916–17, the squad reported 462 arrests, 429 convictions, 41 cases dismissed. Entrapment is noted in one complaint to the city council by Police Court Judge Thomas P. White, Los Angeles City Council Records, vol. 109, no. 2161. Los Angeles vice crusades were part of a nationwide movement. See Roy Lubove, "The Progressive and the Prostitute," *Historian* 24 (May 1962): 308–30.

27. *Los Angeles Record*, Dec. 25, 1914 (Clipping Book 2, Bullock Papers); *Los Angeles Express*, n.d., and *Los Angeles Evening Herald*, Jan. 12, 1916 (Clippings of Interest, Bullock Papers).

28. Strakosch, 196; Grace Knoeller, interview with author, May 10, 1978.

29. Strakosch, 196.

30. F.K. Ryan to MWW, Aug. 23, 1924, MWWP.

31. Grace Knoeller and Paula Knoeller Gore, interview with author, May 1978; DVD, interview with author, July 28, 1979; MWW to parents, April 21, 1925, MWWP.

32. James H. Pope to Donald J. Schippers, Mar. 23, 1966, file 7, box 4, Pope Papers.

33. Ibid.

34. St. Johns, *Honeycomb*, 19; Johns, *Victims of the System*.

35. Los Angeles City Council Records, vol. 108, no. 1233.

36. Fred Horowitz, interview with author, July 23, 1979; MWW, "The Inside of Prohibition," *Washington Evening Star*, Aug. 5, 1929.

37. Cited in Hard, "America's Portia."

38. Ibid.; James Pope to Donald Schippers, Dec. 31, 1965, file 6, box 4, Pope Papers.

39. Strakosch, 194.

40. Ibid.

41. *Annual Report, Police Department, 1918*, 5–6. The report noted that military commanders approved this operation. During the first five months of the program, 257 women were examined and 205 sent to Los Feliz; Los Angeles City Council Records, vol. 108, no. 1703.

42. MWW to father, n.d. (probably summer 1918), MWWP.

43. Frank Capra, interview with author; Fred Horowitz, interview with author; O'Donnell, "Can This Woman Make America Dry?"

44. Robinson, 294–95; Judge May Lahey, interview with author; Myra Dell Collins, interview with author; the 1920 *Los Angeles Directory* lists officers of the Women Lawyers' Club and the Professional Women's Club.

45. Strakosch, 196; Alice A. Winter, "First Lady in Law," *Ladies' Home Journal* 42 (June 1925), 39.

46. MWW, "Some Observations on Women in the Field of Law," undated speech, MWWP.

47. See 1920 *Los Angeles Directory*; "Facts on Mrs. Willebrandt's Life," MWW file, *LAT*.

48. "Who's Who—and Why." There is disagreement on the date Willebrandt actually appeared before the legislature; she cites 1920 in a memorandum to Daugherty, Dec. 29, 1923, MWWP. See also editorial, "The Community Property Act," *Sacramento Union*, Jan. 7, 1921. Published records of the Senate and House do not indicate her attendance. Also see Hichborn, *Story of the Legislative Session of the California Legislature, 1921*.

49. MWW to father, n.d. (probably summer 1918), MWWP. David Walker is listed in *Who's Who in Finance*, ed. John W. Leonard (New York: Joseph & Sefton, 1911), with the information: "started a bank in March 1907 and does a general banking business, with loans and insurance." A representative of the Buckley Bank attended the Michigan Banker's Association meeting from 1908 to 1921, according to the Annual Convention Report of the Michigan Bankers Association. Since the Buckley Bank was not chartered by the state, there is no official record of the exact date of its collapse. From correspondence between MWW and her parents, it seems to have occurred in the spring of 1918. At any rate the Walkers were in California by January 1920.

50. Mrs. Walker to MWW, Feb. 16, 1925.

51. "Facts of Mrs. Willebrandt's Life," MWW file, *LAT*; Myra Dell Collins, interview with author.

52. D.W. Walker to editor, *Temple City Times*, Dec. 12, 1940 (clipping in MWWP); MWW, "College Student as an Immediate Citizen," Conference of Colleges and University Students, Washington, April 5–6, 1924, MWWP; "Inside of Prohibition," *Washington Evening Star*, Aug. 5, 1929.

53. MWW, "Some Observations on Women in the Field of Law," MWWP.

54. MWW, "Popular Government and Public Commissions."

55. Mowry, 215–16; Hichborn, 15.

56. Mowry, 275–88; Burner, *Herbert Hoover: A Public Life*, 153; Hichborn, 250–58; Rogin, "Progressivism and the California electorate."

57. Jensen, "Annette Abbot Adams, Politician"; Frank Doherty to Hiram Johnson, Feb. 17, 1921, box 33, pt. 3, Johnson Papers.

58. Frank Doherty to Hiram Johnson, Dec. 6, 1920, and Feb. 17, 1921, box 33, pt. 3, Johnson Papers.

59. Hiram Johnson to Frank Doherty, June 24, 1921, box 33, pt. 3, Johnson Papers; Robinson, 168.

60. Hiram Johnson to Frank Doherty, June 28, 1921, box 33, pt. 3, Johnson Papers; MWW to Mrs. Katherine Edson, Sept. 3, 1921, Edson Papers.

61. Frank Doherty to Hiram Johnson, June 28, 1921, box 33, pt. 3, Johnson Papers; Strakosch, 196; James Pope to MWW, Oct. 10, 1927, MWWP.

62. Frank Doherty to Hiram Johnson, June 29, 1912, box 33, pt. 3, Johnson Papers.

63. Hiram Johnson to Frank Doherty, Aug. 4, 1921, box 4, pt. 3, and Frank Doherty to Hiram Johnson, Aug. 18, 1921, box 33, pt. 3, Johnson Papers.

64. Harry M. Daugherty to Warren G. Harding, Aug. 27, 1921, Calif—E, reel 199, Harding Papers.

65. Hiram Johnson to Frank Doherty, Sept. 7, 1921, box 4, pt. 3, Johnson Papers.

66. MWW to father, n.d. (probably summer 1918), MWWP.

67. MWW to Alpheus Mason, Jan. 31, 1951, box 83, Stone Papers.

68. Virginia Kellogg Mortensen, telephone interview with author; Myra Dell Collins, interview with author.

CHAPTER THREE

1. Giglio, *H.M. Daugherty and the Politics of Expediency*, 124–25.

2. MWW, "Inside of Prohibition," *Washington Evening Star*, Aug. 5, 1929; Erwin N. Griswold, interview with author.

3. MWW, *Inside of Prohibition*, 10.

4. Sinclair's *Prohibition: The Era of Excess* provides good general background.

5. MWW, *Inside of Prohibition*, 27.

6. Sinclair, 200.

7. *Baltimore Observer*, Aug. 9, 1924; Sinclair, 202–204.

8. Gusfield's *Symbolic Crusade* provides background, as does Burnham's "New Perspectives on the Prohibition 'Experiment' of the 1920's"; Kyvig, *Repealing National Prohibition*, xii–xv.

9. MWW, *Inside of Prohibition*, 15.

10. MWW speaking on law enforcement to the City Club, *Los Angeles Times*, Sept. 11, 1924, and MWW, "The Department of Justice and Problems of Enforcement," address to the Citizenship Conference, Washington, D.C., Oct. 14, 1923,

speech file, MWWP; reprinted in *Law vs. Lawlessness*, ed. Fred B. Smith (New York: Revell, 1924). See also MWW, *Inside of Prohibition*, 111–12.

11. Merz, *Dry Decade*, 67; MWW to mother, Oct. 13, 1926, MWWP; also see Steuart, *Wayne Wheeler, Dry Boss*, 172–73 and 179–80; MWW, *Inside of Prohibition* 32, 198–99.

12. MWW to Mason, Jan. 31, 1951, box 83, Stone Papers; MWW, *Inside of Prohibition*, 152.

13. Schmeckebier, *Bureau of Prohibition*, 45–49; MWW, *Inside of Prohibition*, 116–17.

14. Steuart, 170–71; MWW to Mason, Jan. 31, 1951; box 83, Stone Papers.

15. MWW, *Inside of Prohibition*, 200–203, 63; MWW to Mason, Jan. 31, 1951, box 83, Stone Papers.

16. MWW to Mason, Jan. 31, 1951, box 83, Stone Papers; MWW, Inside of Prohibition, 140.

17. Cartoon in MWWP; U.S. Department of Justice, *Annual Report of the Attorney General of the United States*.

18. MWW to parents, Apr. 4, 1924, MWWP.

19. *New York Times*, Nov. 3, 1924.

20. Ibid., May 5, 1923.

21. Ibid., June 27, 1927; Wayne Wheeler to MWW, June 22, 1924, file 44-4-2-3, Mail and Files Div., DOJ (this file has not been accessioned by the National Archives); MWW to parents, May 18, 1923, MWWP.

22. MWW, "Department of Justice and Some Problems of Enforcement."

23. MWW, "Will You Help Keep the Law?" 73.

24. MWW, "Smart Washington after Six O'clock," 10.

25. MWW, "Half or Whole-Hearted Prohibition," 17.

26. For details of the case see O'Donnell, "Can This Woman Make America Dry?"; *New York Times*, Aug. 17, 1923.

27. MWW memorandum to Acting Attorney General Seymour, Apr. 11, 1923, and MWW to Director Burns, Apr. 5, 1922, file 5-647, Special Corres. no. 2, DOJ.

28. MWW memorandum to the Attorney General, Sept. 20, 1922, file 5-674-1 and MWW memorandum to Acting Attorney General Seymour, Apr. 11, 1923, file 5-647-2, DOJ; clippings from Savannah newspapers, July 6 and July 9, on the trial, file 5-647-2, DOJ.

29. Assistant U.S. Attorney Donnelly to MWW, July 12, 1922, MWW to Jones, July 17, 1922, Assistant Attorney General Crim to J. Meyer, U.S. Attorney, Charleston, Aug. 2, 1922, MWW to Carl A. Mapes, Solicitor, Bureau of Internal Revenue, Oct. 29, 1922, file 5-647, DOJ.

30. MWW to Mapes, Oct. 29, 1922, MWW to Judge Holland, Jan. 19, 1923, MWW to Crim, Jan. 11, 1923, file 5-647-1, DOJ.

31. MWW to U.S. Attorney Boatright, Mar. 20, 1923, MWW to David H. Blair, Apr. 28, 1923, file 5-647, Spec. Corres. no. 2, and Blair to MWW, May 4, 1923, file 5-647, DOJ; MWW to parents, May 18, 1923, MWWP.

32. MWW to White B. Miller, May 17, 1923, file 5-647, Spec. Sec. no. 3, and Agent F.L. Daily (alias for Franklin Dodge) to MWW, file 5-647, Spec. Sec. no. 5, DOJ. For sheriff's role see Buckley to MWW, Feb. 9, 1923, file 5-647, Spec. Sec. no. 3, and MWW to Woods, July 18, 1923, file 5-647-4, DOJ.

33. MWW to parents, Aug. 11, 1923, MWWP; MWW to Golding and Graham, Aug. 11, 1923, file 5-647-2, DOJ.

34. MWW to Blair, Aug. 20, 1923, MWW to Elmer Irey, Sept. 14, 1923, file 5-647-1, MWW to White B. Miller, Aug. 20, 1923, file 5-647-3, and MWW to Allen, Miller, and Pagan, Aug. 11, 1923, file 5-647, Spec. Sec. no. 5, DOJ.

35. MWW to Edward J. Brennan, Aug. 19, 1923, file 5-647, Spec. Sec. no. 5, and MWW to Miller, Aug. 29, 1923, file 5-647-1, DOJ.

36. MWW to Burns, Oct. 12, 1923, file 5-647-2, and MWW to Miller, Aug. 29, 1923, file 5-647-1, DOJ; MWW to father, Sept. 2, 1923, MWWP.

37. MWW to mother, Nov. 25, 1923, MWWP; MWW to Miller, Nov. 28, 1923, file 5-647-2, DOJ.

38. MWW to Attorney General Daugherty, Dec. 11, 1923, file 5-647-5, and press release, file 5-647, Spec. Sec. no. 3, DOJ. Willebrandt was generous in praise and in trying to help those who had worked so hard in the case. In June, she wrote to Secretary of the Treasury Mellon recommending Treasury agent Allen for a post on the Board of Tax Appeals, file 5-647-2, DOJ.

39. MWW to Holland, Mar. 28, 1924, file 5-647-3, DOJ; MWW, "Inside of Prohibition," *Washington Evening Star*, Aug. 10, 1929; correspondence of Miller and MWW in file 5-647 provides details of the tax negotiations. The final settlement of $140,000 was reached in Feb. 1929.

40. *Mobile Register*, Nov. 14, 16, 21, 23, and Dec. 19, 20, 21, 1923; Hamilton, *Hugo Black: The Alabama Years*, 109.

41. *Mobile Register*, May 1, 1924; Hamilton, 190; Dunne, *Hugo Black and the Judicial Revolution*, 107–109.

42. MWW to parents, Sept. 23, 1924, MWWP. Congress passed a measure, Apr. 21, 1924, to increase federal appropriations to the Coast Guard, Public Law 103.

43. Charles S. Root to Lawrence Richey, Mar. 21, 1924, Subject File, Prohibition Enforcement, box 237, Presidential Papers, HHP; MWW, *Inside of Prohibition*, 220–29; see also Merz, 87; MWW to William Howard Taft, Feb. 9, 1928, reel 299, series 3, William Howard Taft Papers. Also MWW to parents, Nov. 18, 1923, and Mar. 26, 1924, MWWP.

44. Root to Richey, Mar. 21, 1924, Subject File, Prohibition Enforcement, box 237, Presidential Papers, HHP.

45. Coffey, *Long Thirst: Prohibition in America 1920–1933*, pp. 29–30, 44–46, 102; Harold Orcutt to MWW, n.d., file 23-1907, William Harrison to Harry M. Daugherty, Jan. 5, 1922, James Clark to H.M. Daugherty, Aug. 9, 1921, and Daugherty to Clark, Oct. 26, 1921, file 23-1907-1, DOJ, Suitland. Records of prohibition cases, RG 60, DOJ, are in both the National Archives, Washington, and National Archives and Records Service, Suitland, Md.

46. MWW, "Inside of Prohibition," *Washington Evening Star*, Aug. 10, 1929.

47. Coffey, 103–104.

48. See opinion of Judge Peck, *U.S.* v. *George Remus, et al.*, no. 2142, U.S. District Court, Southern District of Ohio, in file 23-1907, DOJ, Suitland; Thomas Morrow to MWW, May 27, 1922, and memorandum to MWW, July 26, 1922; MWW to Attorney General, May 17, 1922, MWW to R.T.D. Dickerson, Oct. 3, 1923, and MWW to Attorney General Stone, Sept. 25, 1924, file 23-1907, DOJ, Suitland.

49. MWW to parents, Jan. 2, 1923, MWWP.

50. Coffey, 129; Daugherty to A.E. Sartain, Mar. 5, 1924, and MWW to A.E. Sartain, Mar. 11, 1924, file 23-1907, DOJ, Suitland.

51. Giglio, 136; George Remus to Harlan Fiske Stone, George Remus to MWW, Aug. 6 and 25, 1925, and MWW to Solicitor General, Sept. 10, 1925, file 23-1907, DOJ, Suitland. Remus was also involved in the Jack Daniels Distillery case noted by MWW in "Inside of Prohibition," *Washington Evening Star*, Aug. 6, 1929. Subsequently the Department of Labor moved to deport him. Memo from R.L. MacCutcheon to MWW, June 16, 1927, file 23-1907, DOJ, Suitland. The press noted the murder of Mrs. Remus by her husband (*Cincinnati Times Star*, Oct. 6, 1927, and Coffey, 214–18, 222–29). Willebrandt fought the Brookhart Committee on giving Mrs. Remus immunity in the Jack Daniels case in return for her testimony before the committee (MWW to Harold Jones, June 11, 1924, file 23-1907, DOJ, Suitland).

52. MWW, *Inside of Prohibition*, 43.

53. Merz, 159–60, gives some background details on padlocking, as does John Kohler, *Ardent Spirits*, 147–48; E.C. Yellowey to MWW, July 14, 1923, William Hayward to MWW, Oct. 18, 1923, and John H. Clark to MWW, Mar. 10, 1924, file 23-014-51-1, DOJ, Suitland.

54. MWW to John H. Clark, Mar. 27, 1924, file 23-014-51-1, DOJ, Suitland. Willebrandt wrote of her dissatisfaction with the New York consent decree to the Attorney General, June 8, 1926, file 23-014-51, DOJ, Suitland.

55. Walker, *Night Club Era*, 64. MWW to Prohibition Commissioner, Dr. J.M. Doran, Feb. 25, 1929, file 23-014-51, DOJ, Suitland.

56. MWW to Attorney General Sargent, Aug. 2, 1928, file 23-51-448; MWW to David H. Blair, Aug. 22, 1928, DOJ. Accounts are in the *Washington Post*, Aug. 21 and 23, 1928.

57. MWW to Sargent, Aug. 21, 1928, file 23-014-51, DOJ, Suitland.

58. MWW to Sargent, Aug. 23, 1928, file 23-014-51, and MWW to Norman Morrison, Aug. 29, 1928, file 23-014-51-2, DOJ, Suitland.

59. MWW to Charles H. Tuttle, Aug. 26, 1928, file, 23-014-51, DOJ, Suitland; Merz, 152; MWW, *Inside of Prohibition*, 169–70. The volume of correspondence on the padlocking episode was so heavy that Willebrandt sent a form letter to acknowledge those that expressed support. See also U.S. Department of Justice, *Annual Report of the Attorney General, 1929*.

60. MWW to her parents, May 11, 1924, MWWP.

61. Kohler, 147–48.

62. MWW to parents, May 11, 1924, MWWP. The *Louisville Courier Journal*, May 9, 1924, noted that Willebrandt was the first woman to practice in that federal district court.

63. MWW to parents, n.d. (obviously 1925), MWWP.

64. MWW to mother, June 2, 1925, and MWW to parents, May 28, 1925, MWWP.

65. MWW to parents, Sept. 29, 1925, MWWP; A.E. Bernstein to MWW, May 22, 1925, and M.D. Kiefer to MWW, May 27, 1925, file 23-3257, DOJ, Suitland; *Columbus Evening Dispatch*, June 4, 1925; *Cleveland Press*, June 5, 1925; *Cleveland Plain Dealer*, June 11, 1925; MWW to Attorney General, May 6, 1926, file 23-3257,

DOJ, Suitland; MWW to White Miller, Apr. 25, 1925, file 5-647-4, DOJ; MWW to parents, Apr. 24, June 4 and 15, 1925, MWWP. U.S. Attorney Bernstein wrote to Willebrandt that one of the jurors stated that her participation was one of the leading factors in winning the verdict, June 20, 1925, file 23-3257, DOJ, Suitland.

66. MWW to Al F. Williams, Feb. 21, 1925, and June 17, 1924, S. Kaliski oath, Apr. 23, 1924, Senator Curtis to Stone, Dec. 6, 1924, Stone to Rush Holland, Jan. 20, 1925, Al F. Williams to Attorney General, Feb. 12, 1925, and memorandum for files from agent Frank Buckley, Apr. 11, 1925, file 23-29-7, DOJ, Suitland.

67. MWW to Attorney General Sargent, Feb. 18, 1926, file 23-29-7, DOJ, Suitland.

68. *Kansas City Capital* and *Kansas City Star*, Feb. 20, 1926 (clippings in file 23-29-7, DOJ, Suitland).

69. MWW to Attorney General Sargent, Feb. 25, 1926, file 23-29-7, DOJ, Suitland.

70. MWW to White B. Miller, Apr. 27, 1925, file 5-647-4, DOJ.

71. Distributed letter from A.H. Post, Superintendent of the Anti-Saloon League of Missouri, to "Dear Friend," May 16, 1925, file 23-42-26, DOJ; "The Booze Ring's Last Stand" a broadside reprint of an editorial, *Atlanta Mission Express*, n.d., file 23-42-26, DOJ, Suitland.

72. *St. Louis Globe Democrat*, May 26, 1925 (clipping in file 23-42-26, DOJ, Suitland); MWW to parents, May 27 and 28, 1925, and MWW to mother, June 2, 1925, MWWP.

73. *St. Louis Globe Democrat*, May 28, 1925; MWW to parents, May 28, 1925, MWWP.

74. The correspondence in file 23-42-26, DOJ, Suitland, contains the exchanges between Dyott and MWW regarding the three trials and appeals. The final decision, Oct. 1933, by the department is in Frank M. Parrish to the Attorney General, Oct. 7, 1933, file 23-42-26, DOJ, Suitland.

75. Libel trials are reported in the *New York Times*, June 19 and 22, 1930. Nations's statement was carried by the *Los Angeles Times*, Aug. 28, 1929; MWW's statement was reported in the Aug. 14, 1929, column in the series "Inside of Prohibition," *Washington Evening Star*. The passage is not included in her book, *Inside of Prohibition*.

76. MWW, *Inside of Prohibition*, 118–19; agent Alf Oftedal to MWW, July 26, 1926, MWW to Attorney General Sargent, Dec. 22, 1926, and the Green statement (in an interview with agent Oftedal), July 23, 1926, file 23-11-163, DOJ, Suitland.

77. MWW to Mason, Jan. 31, 1951, box 83, Stone Papers.

78. Ibid.

79. Ibid.; MWW to parents, Christmas 1924, MWWP.

80. MWW to Mason, Jan. 31, 1951, box 83, Stone Papers; *New York Times*, Dec. 16, 1924.

81. MWW to Mason, Jan. 31, 1951, box 83, Stone Papers; MWW to parents, Christmas 1924, MWWP.

82. MWW to parents, Christmas 1924, MWWP.

83. MWW to Mason, Jan. 31, 1951, box 83, Stone Papers; *Literary Digest*, Nov. 15, 1924, pp. 14–15.

84. *Literary Digest*, Nov. 15, 1924, pp. 14–15.

85. MWW to Mason, Jan. 31, 1951, box 83, Stone Papers.

86. *Literary Digest*, Nov. 15, 1924, pp. 14–15. On Feb. 8, 1925, MWW wrote to her parents of her disappointment of losing Stone in the Department of Justice and of not being able to work with him to carry out the program he had started (MWWP).

87. MWW to U.S. Attorneys, July 22, 1925. Correspondence on this survey is in file 44-4-2-3-1, Mail and Files Div., DOJ.

88. MWW, *Inside of Prohibition*, 239.

89. "Portia in Wonderland," *American Mercury*, July 1929, 332–38.

90. MWW to parents, Mar. 9, 1926, MWWP.

91. MWW reports in U.S. Department of Justice, *Annual Report of the Attorney General of the United States* for 1923, 1925, 1928.

92. MWW to mother, Aug. 2, 1923, and MWW to parents, Feb. 2, 1927, MWWP.

93. *New York Times*, July 30, 1924. She cites her office's 1929 record in "Inside of Prohibition," *Washington Evening Star*, Aug. 5, 1929.

94. *Cunard Steamship Co., Ltd. et al.* v. *Mellon, Secretary of the Treasury*, 262 U.S. 100 (1923).

95. MWW to parents, Jan. 2, 1923, MWWP.

96. 262 U.S. 100 (1923).

97. MWW to Citizenship Conference, Oct. 14, 1923, Washington, D.C., speech file, MWWP.

98. *Washington News*, May 18, 1927.

99. *Marron* v. *U.S.*, 275 U.S. 192 (1927).

100. *U.S.* v. *Carroll*, 267 U.S. 132 (1925). MWW discusses this case in *Inside of Prohibition*, 239.

101. *Roy Olmstead et al.* v. *U.S.*, 277 U.S. 438 (1928). MWW wrote of her opposition to wiretapping in *Inside of Prohibition*, 231–38. She was so strongly opposed to it that she contributed a major section of a brief for one of John Sirica's major criminal cases (Judge John Sirica, interview with author).

102. *James Everard's Breweries* v. *Dry Prohibition Director of the State of New York, et al.*, 265 U.S. 545 (1924); *Donnelly* v. *U.S.*, 276 U.S. 505 (1928); MWW to Anna B. Hail, file 44-4-2-3-3, Mail and Files Div., DOJ.

103. MWW's appearances before congressional committees were covered by the *New York Times*, June 20, 1924, Apr. 3, 1925, May 2 and 28, 1926; MWW, *Inside of Prohibition*, 250–63.

104. MWW, *Inside of Prohibition*, 282–84.

105. Ibid., 285–87; MWW to parents, Mar. 31, 1929, MWWP.

106. MWW, *Inside of Prohibition*, 297–99.

107. Ibid., 300–301.

108. Burnham, "New Perspectives on the Prohibition 'Experiment' of the 1920's," 60.

109. MWW to mother, Oct. 6, 1924, MWWP.

110. Burnham, 59–68. Kyvig has the fullest and most recent assessment of the repeal movement.

111. MWW to Mason, Jan. 31, 1951, box 83, Stone Papers.

112. U.S. Department of Justice, *Annual Report of the Attorney General of the United States, 1929*, p. 29; MWW to parents, Mar. 31, 1929.

CHAPTER FOUR

1. Freedman, *Their Sisters' Keepers*, 145–46; Bates, *Prisons and Beyond*, 9–40; Filo, "Reclaiming Those Poor Unfortunates," 266.

2. Gibson, "Women's Prisons," 210–33; Freedman, 110–21; Bates, 9–40.

3. Memorandum from Votaw to MWW, n.d., file 4-9-01, box 659, BOP. A summary of the issues is in the 1922–24 report of the Committee on Institutional Relations, General Federation of Women's Clubs, GFWC Archives.

4. Gibson, 210–33; Freedman, 110–47; MWW, "Inside of Prohibition," *Washington Evening Star*, Aug. 5, 1929; St. Johns, *Some Are Born Great*, 224–25.

5. Gibson, 210–33; Harris, *I Knew Them in Prison*, 237. For general background see Eugenia Lekkerkerker, *Reformatories for Women in the United States* (The Hague: J.B. Wolters, 1931).

6. Votaw, "Memorandum for the Attorney General," Jan. 11, 1923, file 4-9-01-3, box 659, BOP; Harris, 260, notes that the drive had been launched for a federal prison for women in 1910 by Mrs. J. Ellen Foster. She believed that Willebrandt heard Foster speak on the issue in Los Angeles.

7. MWW to parents, Jan. 2, 1923, MWWP; Margaret A. Smith to Mrs. Walker, Feb. 16, 1923. See Special Sec., Bills, Hearings and Unrecorded Memos, file 4-9-01, box 657, BOP, for hearings on Mount Weather Bill. MWW to Mrs. Arthur Watkins, National Congress of Mothers, Jan. 22, 1923, file 4-9-01, box 659, BOP. Reports of the "Lookout" Committee of the WJCC, monitoring the progress of the women's prisons bills and correspondence, box 1, WJCC Papers.

8. Minutes of Feb. 16, 1923, meeting of the WJCC, box 1, WJCC Papers. MWW to Lida Hafford, Mar. 21, 1923, Julia K. Jaffray, National Committee on Prisons and Prison Labor, to MWW, Mar. 21, 1923, MWW to Mrs. Edward F. White, Apr. 12 and 30, 1923, MWW to Anna Gordon, President, WCTU, Aug. 29, 1923, MWW to Mrs. Russell Tydon, President, Women's National Farm and Garden Assoc., Aug. 29, 1923; M.F. Cunningham, League of Women Voters, n.d., sent MWW the list of women's organizations and leaders; MWW wrote to M.A. Smith on the bottom of the Cunningham letter, "This is fine—go at it" (file 4-9-01, box 660, BOP).

9. Filo, 265–70.

10. Ibid., 275–80; Margaret A. Smith to Mrs. Walker, Feb. 16, 1923, MWWP; for stories on the women's prison drive see *General Federation News*, May, June, and July 1923.

11. Proceedings of the conference are detailed in GFWC pamphlet "Federal Prisons," box 7, Presidents' File, Alice Ames Winter, GFWC Archives; Harris, 261; MWW to mother, n.d., MWWP.

12. MWW to mother, n.d., MWWP.

13. MWW to Senator Charles Curtis, Dec. 12, 1923, and MWW to Rep. George S. Graham, Dec. 15, 1923, file 4-9-01, box 660, BOP.

14. MWW testified on HR 685, HR 2689, and HR 4125 before the House Judiciary Committee, 68th Congress, 1st sess., Dec. 5, 1923 (Special Sec., Bills, Hearings, file 4-9-01, box 660, BOP).

15. *New York Times*, Nov. 18, 1923;MWW to Votaw, file 4-9-01, box 660, BOP.

16. Resolutions in file 4-9-3-15, BOP; MWW to Rep. Israel Foster, Jan. 29, 1924, file 4-9-01, BOP; minutes of Jan. 1924 meeting, box 1, WJCC papers; Georgia Bullock to MWW, Mar. 28, 1924, and MWW to Bullock, Apr. 19, 1924, file 4-9-01, and Carl W. Barnett to MWW, Jan. 25, 1923, file 4-9-01-2, box 660, BOP.

17. Lida Hafford to MWW, May 26, 1923; MWW to Frederick Gillett and Hatton W. Sumners, May 28, 1924, file 4-9-01, box 659, BOP; Report of the Department of Public Welfare of GFWC, 17th Biennial Convention, GFWC Archives.

18. MWW to Rep. Graham, May 28, 1924, and MWW to Julia Jaffray, June 5, 1924, file 4-9-01, box 659, BOP.

19. Letters from West Virginia in support of the site are in file 4-9-3-15, BOP. See W.W. Smith to Harlan Fiske Stone, June 6, 1924; Governor E.F. Morgan to H.M. Daugherty, Jan. 12, 1924; Goff to Votaw, June 26 and July 2, 1924; R.E.L. Allen to Secretary Work and Stone, Aug. 5, 1924; Dudding to Votaw, Aug. 5, 1924; Crawley to Slemp, Aug. 14, 1925, file 4-9-3-15, BOP. A letter to MWW in Mar. 1924 indicated preliminary lobbying for Alderson (MWW to Mrs. E.S. McCullough, Mar. 20, 1924, file 4-9-01-2, box 660, BOP).

20. MWW to General Hines, Aug. 17, 1924, file 4-9-01, box 660, BOP; Votaw to Stone, Oct. 11, 1924, West Virginia Industrial Farm Commission to MWW, Sept. 1, 1924, Crawley to Slemp, Sept. 5, 1924, Yost to MWW, Sept. 18, 1924, file 4-9-3-15, BOP.

21. Judge Mary O'Toole to Dudding, Sept. 19, 1924, MWW to T.L. Woodson, Nov. 15, 1924, MWW to Crawley, Nov. 17, 1924, Crawley to E. Chase Bare, Nov. 18, 1924, file 4-9-3-15, BOP. Filo, in ch. 6, writes of the drive for Alderson.

22. MWW to Stone, Nov. 17, 1924, MWW to Hubert Work, Nov. 26, 1924, Crawley to MWW, Dec. 12, 1924, MWW to Stone, Jan. 10, 1925, Engineer's Report, John P. West, file 4-9-3-15, BOP.

23. Stone to MWW, Jan. 17, 1925, and MWW to Stone, Jan. 21, 1925, file 4-9-3-15, BOP; Water Supply Report, Jan. 24, 1925, file 4-9-03, box 658, BOP.

24. MWW to parents, Jan. 29, 1925, MWWP.

25. Harris, 251, 267, 272; MWW to Attorney General, Feb. 7, 1925, file 4-9-01, box 658, BOP.

26. *New York Times*, June 4, 1926; Mrs. John D. Sherman to Attorney General Sargent, Apr. 15, 1926, file 4-9-03, box 658, BOP.

27. Harris, 254–55, 262, 74.

28. *New York Times*, Nov. 28, 1928.

29. Harris, 248–49.

30. Harris, 262. On MWW's resignation, Harlan Fiske Stone wrote to her on April 26, 1929: "I shall never forget that if it hadn't been for your energy and resourcefulness at a critical moment, we probably would still be struggling to get a federal women's prison" (Stone Papers).

31. Votaw memorandum to MWW, n.d., Special Sec., Bills, Hearings, file 4-9-01, box 659, BOP. Groups with representatives at the meetings were the Benevolent Protective Order of Elks, Federal Council of the Churches of Christ in

America, International Association of Civitan Clubs, Loyal Order of the Moose, National Catholic Welfare Conference, National Council of the Protestant Episcopal Church. The hearings of the House Judiciary Committee, 67th Cong., 3d and 4th sess., Nov.-Dec. 1922, HR 12123 (Serial 42), file 4-9-01, box 659. MWW's testimony indicates some early hearing difficulties (see hearings, pp. 29–30).

32. Votaw memorandum to MWW, n.d., Special Sec., Bills, Hearings, file 4-9-01, box 659, BOP.

33. Hearings for HR 2869, HR 685, HR 4125 (Serial 1), 68th Cong., 1st sess., pp. 10–18, file 4-9-01, BOP. MWW also corresponded with leaders of organizations to rally support. See MWW to Charles Barnett of the Federal Council of the Churches of Christ in America, Nov. 11, 1924, and Barnett to MWW, Nov. 13, 1924, file 4-8-0-1, BOP.

34. MWW memorandum to Attorney General, May 2, 1925, and MWW to Secreretary of War, May 20, 1925, 4-8-3-15, BOP.

35. MWW memorandum to Senator Walter George, May 14, 1925, and MWW memorandum to the Attorney General, July 28, 1925, file 4-8-3-15, BOP.

36. MWW to Attorney General, July 28, 1925, file 4-8-3-15, BOP. On Aug. 8, 1925, Lord advised Acting Secretary of War Davis that if legislation establishing a military construction fund was enacted, a working balance would be required to permit beginning of construction (file 4-8-3-15, BOP). See also Davis to Attorney General Sargent, Aug. 14, 1925, Luther G. White to Attorney General Sargent, Aug. 27, 1925, and Executive Order 4283, Aug. 14, 1925, file 4-8-3-15, BOP (the file also contains telegrams to General Hines of the Veterans Bureau opposing the Chillicothe site), Howard Jones to MWW, Aug. 20, 1925; Sargent letters to Davis, President of the Senate, and Nicholas Longworth, Sept. 18, 1925, on the choice of a site, and MWW memo to Attorney General, n.d., file 4-8-3-15, BOP.

37. MWW to parents, Apr. 15, 1923, MWWP. She also described in that letter a trip she had taken to Stone Mountain on a moonlight drive with the prison doctor: "The Ku Klux Klan often build fires and gather on the top of the mountain. The Klan is very strong throughout the South, more than we in the north or west can realize."

38. MWW to Votaw, Aug. 7, 1923, and Acting Director, Bureau of Investigation, to Attorney General, Oct. 14, 1924, file 4-1-4-89, BOP.

39. MWW to parents, Christmas 1924, MWWP; Stone to MWW, Oct. 14, 1924, and MWW to Stone, Oct. 21 and 27, 1924, file 4-1-4-89, BOP.

40. Stone to MWW and Donovan, Nov. 20, 1924, urging them to work closely together, file 4-1-4-89, BOP.

41. *New York Times*, Dec. 17, 19, and 20, 1924.

42. MWW to parents, Christmas 1924, MWWP.

43. Ibid. The *New York Times* covered the trial on Feb. 10, 11, and 19, 1925. Heber Votaw resigned on Jan. 21, 1925, citing ill health. Stone praised him for help in reorganizing the executive force at Atlanta Prison (*New York Times*, Jan. 22, 1925). Sartain was convicted and sentenced to serve eighteen months at Atlanta.

44. MWW to parents, Christmas 1924, MWWP. MWW reviewed the Atlanta affair in a long memorandum to Alpheus Mason, Jan. 31, 1951 (box 83, Stone Papers). In June, MWW went to Atlanta and interviewed George Remus, who was

to testify on prison favoritism (*New York Times*, June 25, 1925); MWW to parents, Feb. 15, 1925, MWWP.

45. U.S. Penitentiary, Atlanta Ga., *Annual Report, 1925*; *New York Times*, Apr. 4, 1925; R.R. Treadway to Sargent, July 9, 1926, a "citizen" to Sargent, Nov. 24, 1926, MWW to Hammack, Sept., 1926, Senator Alben Barkley to MWW, Dec. 1, 1926, file 4-1-4-89, BOP.

46. MWW to John W. Snook, Oct. 7, 1926, file 4-1-4-89, BOP.

47. *Atlanta Life*, July 2, 1927 (clipping in file 4-1-4-89, BOP). Snook threatened to sue for libel. Snook to Superintendent of Prisons Conner, July 2, 1927, Mrs. R.R. Treadway to Calvin Coolidge, Sept. 20, 1927, U.S. Attorney Clint W. Hager to MWW, Aug. 24, 1927, MWW to Hoover, n.d., Hoover to MWW, Nov. 10, 1927, file 4-1-4-89, BOP.

48. Warden John W. Snook to Senator William Borah, Sept. 25, 1928, box 281, Borah Papers.

49. MWW to parents, Aug. 21, 1928, MWWP.

50. Snook to Borah, Oct. 4, 1928, box 281, Borah Papers.

51. MWW to Snook, Oct. 18, 1928, ibid.

52. MWW to Snook, Nov. 1, 1928, ibid.; the *Atlanta Constitution*, Oct. 11, 1928, reported on Senator George's interest.

53. MWW to parents, Mar. 31, 1929, MWWP.

54. Ibid.

55. Snook to Borah, Mar. 7, 1929; in a letter to Snook on Mar. 3, 1929, MWW had moved to rescue the planted prisoner and to secure his release; MWW to Snook, Mar. 14, 1929; Snook to Mitchell, Mar. 10, 1929; Borah wrote to Mitchell, Mar. 12, 1929, after Snook wired him alleging he was being forced out due to opposition to the "spy" system, box 281, Borah Papers.

56. Snook to Borah, Mar. 19, 1929.

57. *Birmingham Age Herald*, Jan. 22, 1929, and *Atlanta Constitution*, Mar. 18, 1929 (clippings in box 281, Borah Papers).

58. MWW to parents, Decoration Day 1926, MWWP.

59. Ibid. The *New York Times*, Apr. 25, 1926, reported an investigation at Leavenworth and on July 22, 1926, reported on mismanagement at Leavenworth. U.S. Penitentiary, Leavenworth, Kansas, recorded overcrowding in the prison in its *Annual Report, 1926*. See also MWW to Annabel Matthews, June 26, 1926, folder 6, box 1, Matthews Papers; MWW to parents June or July 1926, MWWP.

60. *New York Times*, Sept. 26 and Nov. 10, 1926; MWW to parents, Aug. 21, 1928, MWWP.

61. MWW to parents, Apr. 15, 1923, MWWP.

62. Ibid.

63. Ibid.

64. Pamphlet, "Federal Prisoners," p. 11, box 7, Presidents' File, Alice Ames Winter, GFWC Archives.

65. Lewisohn, "A Programme for Prison Reform," 423–25; see also Lewisohn, "Prisons and Prison Labor," and Disque, "Prison Progress."

66. MWW to Votaw, Sept. 1, 1923; MWW to Mrs. A.A. Bourne, editor, *Bergen County Republican*, Apr. 28, 1924 (clipping in file 4-4-15, BOP).

67. MWW to parents, Feb. 12, 1928, MWWP. For story on White appointment, see *New York Times*, Mar. 25, 1925.

68. MWW to Mitchell, wire, May 6, 1929 (copy to Richey in box 21, Executive Department, Justice, Presidential Papers, HHP). See also Stone to MWW, Apr. 26, 1929, box 30, Stone Papers, and MWW to parents, May 24, 1925, on importance of prison work: "I have so much wanted to show real development of the prison work before leaving this post" (MWWP).

69. MWW, *Inside of Prohibition*, 10. A review of all of Willebrandt's cases in *United States Reports*, 1921–29, indicates her increased role later in the decade. MWW to parents, May 27, 1927, described her victory in the Sullivan tax case, "Fred heard me argue the big tax case in the Sup. Ct., and wasn't it wonderful last Monday to have the decision written by Holmes and a unanimous court" (MWWP). See *Taft* v. *U.S.*, 278 U.S. 470 (1929); *Bowers, Collector* v. *Kerbaugh Empire Co.*, 271 U.S. 170 (1926); *Helmich, Collector* v. *Missouri Pacific RR Co.*, 273 U.S. 242 (1927); *Heiner, Collector* v. *Colonial Trust Co., Exec.*, 275 U.S. 232 (1927); *Edwards* v. *Chile Copper Co.*, 270 U.S. 452 (1926); *Helmich* v. *Hellman*, 276 U.S. 233 (1928); Hard, "America's Portia."

70. DOJ, *Annual Report of the Attorney General, 1926*, p. 64 (hereafter, *Annual Report*).

71. See particularly, DOJ, *Annual Report, 1924, 1926*, and *1928*; *Inside of Prohibition*, 10; MWW to parents, Feb. 14, 1928, MWWP.

72. MWW to parents, Feb. 14, 1928, MWWP.

73. Ibid.

74. MWW to James G. Kinsler, June 1922, file 59-1-69, DOJ, Suitland.

75. MWW to Edwin A. Olsen, May 4, 1925, file 5-23-18, DOJ, Suitland,

76. MWW to parents, Feb. 14, 1928, MWWP.

77. MWW to parents, Christmas 1922, MWWP.

78. Giglio, 118–25.

79. Ibid., 126.

80. See *Facts of Record and Editorials Concerning Impeachment Proceedings at Washington against Hon. Harry M. Daugherty*, n.p., n.d., a collection of congressional testimony, speeches, and press clippings for background of charges.

81. MWW to parents, Christmas 1922, MWWP.

82. Ibid.

83. Ibid.

84. Ibid.

85. MWW to parents, Mar. 28, 1923, MWWP.

86. Ibid.

87. MWW to mother, May 13, 1923, MWWP.

88. MWW to parents, May 18, 1923, MWWP. She added, "Sure enough," the defendant had applied for a passport to Europe and had the trial been delayed he would have left the country.

89. MWW to parents, June 19, 1923, MWWP; in a letter to her parents on Aug. 11, 1923, MWW writes of the death of Harding (MWWP).

90. See Mason, *Harlan Fiske Stone*, 142–44, and Giglio for Brookhart Hearings; Wheeler's version of the hearings in his *Yankee from the West*, 9; Mrs. Walker to MWW, n.d., MWWP.

91. Mason, 188. See also MWW to Mason, Jan. 31, 1951, box 83, Stone Papers. U.S. Senate, 68th Cong., 1st sess., Resolution 157, Investigation of the Attorney General, XI, 3193–240.

92. MWW to parents, Mar. 30, 1924, MWWP.

93. MWW to parents, Apr. 4, 1924, MWWP; *New York Times*, Apr. 24, 1924.

94. MWW to parents, Feb. 19, 1927, MWWP; *New York Times,* Feb. 18, 1927.

95. MWW to Mason, Jan. 31, 1951, box 83, Stone Papers.

96. MWW to parents, May 11, 1924, MWWP; MWW, *Inside of Prohibition*, 140; MWW to Mason, Jan. 31, 1951, box 83, Stone Papers; MWW to parents, Mar. 19, 1925, MWWP.

97. MWW to parents, Mar. 19, 1925, and n.d. (probably Mar. 1926), MWWP.

98. MWW to parents, Aug. 11, 1923, MWWP.

99. MWW to parents, Sept. 21, 1924, MWWP. Her secretary, Margaret A. Smith, wrote to Mrs. Walker, Oct. 11, 1922, "Everybody loves her and she is held in such high regard by the Attorney General and all the other Assistants" (MWWP).

100. MWW to mother, Oct. 1, 1924, MWWP.

101. MWW to parents, Feb. 12, 1928, MWWP. Margaret A. Smith had wired MWW, Aug. 28, 1922, "everything running smoothly in your division," file 44-4-2-3, Mail and Files Div., DOJ. When Erwin Griswold came into the department under Hoover, he noted that Willebrandt's division was one of the best administered (Griswold, interview with author).

102. Upton, *Random Recollections*, ch. 27. MWW to parents, Aug. 16, 1923, MWWP.

103. MWW to father, Sept. 2, 1923, MWWP.

104. MWW to mother, Nov. 12, 1923, MWWP.

105. MWW to mother, Nov. 25, 1923, MWWP.

106. MWW to parents, Dec. 6, 1923, MWWP.

107. Maud Brown to MWW, Dec. 19, 1923, MWWP.

108. Mrs. Walker to MWW, Dec. 11 and 25, 1923, MWWP.

109. MWW wire quoted in Frank P. Doherty to Hiram Johnson, Dec. 15, 1923, box 33, pt. 3, Johnson Papers.

110. MWW to mother, Jan. 25, 1923, MWWP.

111. MWW to parents, Feb. 9, 1924, MWWP.

112. Frank P. Doherty to Hiram Johnson, Nov. 8, 1923, box 34, pt. 3, Johnson Papers; Mrs. Walker to MWW, Dec. 2, 1924, and Jan. 5, 1925, MWWP.

113. *New York Times*, Jan. 11 and 19, 1925. In a letter to her parents, Jan. 29, 1925, MWW commented that Coolidge yielded to the opposition that argued that in spite of rapid progress the time was not yet right to appoint a woman to the federal bench (MWWP). Judge A.F. St. Sure of San Francisco won the post. The *Los Angeles Times*, Feb. 15, 1925, reported that MWW had been seen as a compromise candidate and had been called to the White House but soon after her departure Senator Shortridge had called on Coolidge to renew his support of St. Sure; the article went on to say that MWW had been a storm center of controversies over the dismissals of U.S. attorneys. Hiram Johnson to Harold Ickes, Sept. 29, 1928, box 33, Ickes Papers; *New York Herald Tribune*, Jan. 11, 1925.

114. Mrs. Walker to MWW, Feb. 16, 1925, MWWP.

115. Frank P. Doherty to Hiram Johnson, Feb. 18, 1925, box 34, pt. 3, Johnson Papers; MWW to parents, Mar. 19, 1925, MWWP.

116. MWW to parents, Mar. 19, 1925, MWWP.

117. Ibid.

118. MWW to parents, Apr. 10, 1925, MWWP.

119. MWW's interest was shown in a wire from her assistant Howard Jones to MWW, June 24, 1926, while she was on the Chautauqua circuit, file 44-4-2-3-3, Mail and Files Div., DOJ; MWW to parents, Decoration Day 1926, MWWP.

120. MWW to parents, June 1926, MWWP; *Los Angeles Times*, n.d. (clipping in MWW file, *LAT*).

121. Frank P. Doherty to MWW, July 24, 1926, box 34, pt. 3, Johnson Papers.

122. MWW to parents, Dec. 1926, MWWP.

123. Ibid.

124. Frank P. Doherty to Hiram Johnson, Feb. 8, 1927, box 34, pt. 3, Johnson Papers.

125. MWW to parents, Mar. 14, 1927, and Easter 1927, MWWP. The *Washington Post*, May 10, 1927, indicated that MWW was being considered for the northern California post.

126. MWW to parents, Sept. 31, 1927, MWWP.

127. MWW to parents, Jan. 25, 1928, MWWP.

CHAPTER FIVE

1. Mrs. Walker to MWW, n.d., May 19, 1923, and June 5, 1924, MWWP. MWW asked her mother to keep her letters, since she did not have time to keep a diary and was writing them as a "sort of running history of events" and "her letters might sometime keep me from the penitentiary by proving an alibi. Who knows?" Unfortunately, her mother destroyed most of them in the wake of the Nations case and at the request of MWW, who wanted to be rid of Washington once and for all (MWW to Mason, Jan. 31, 1951, box 83, Stone Papers).

2. Mrs. Walker to MWW, Dec. 10, 1924, Mar. 23, 1925, MWWP.

3. Mrs. Walker to MWW, Sept. 24, Dec. 7, 1921; Mrs. Walker to MWW, Aug. 30, 1923, MWWP.

4. Mrs. Walker to MWW, July 2, 1924, Oct. 9 and 11, 1924, and Oct. 16, 1924, MWWP.

5. Mrs. Walker to MWW, Jan. 9, 1925, Jan. 5, 1925, and n.d. (probably 1925), MWWP.

6. Mrs. Walker to MWW, Dec. 2 and Nov. 24, 1924; Mrs. Walker to MWW, n.d. (probably Nov. 1923), MWWP.

7. Mrs. Walker to MWW, Oct. 11, 1924, and n.d. (probably Nov. 1924); Minnie Hickstein Wells to Mrs. Walker, Nov. 21, 1923; MWW to mother, Nov. 25, 1923, MWWP.

8. MWW to parents, Aug. 15, 1925, MWWP. In an interview with the author, Mrs. Ira Wells and Mabel Wells recounted how Willebrandt had settled the Wells on a farm in Missouri. When Mr. Wells died, she brought Mrs. Wells and Mabel to California, buying Minnie a house in Fullerton for her lifetime. Both Wellses remember Willebrandt's kindness and generosity and her sense of family.

9. MWW to mother, Nov. 25, 1923, MWWP. Willebrandt's scrapbook contains photographs of the Willebrandt's journey to Maud's graduation from Park College and their vacation in Michigan (in possession of DVD).

10. Maud Brown to MWW, Dec. 10, 1923; Mrs. Walker to MWW, n.d. (probably autumn 1924), MWWP.

11. Mrs. Walker to MWW, n.d., and Oct. 11, 1924, MWWP.

12. Mrs. Walker to MWW, July 21, 1925; MWW to mother, Sept. 1925, MWWP.

13. MWW to parents, June 9, 1925, MWWP.

14. MWW to parents, Dec. 1926, MWWP. On April 15, 1927, Maud Hubbard, back in China, wrote to MWW asking her to try to book her on the Chautauqua circuit so that she might have "some kind of harvest of the present interest in China and my gift of gab. . . . There was a time when I wouldn't have done that, but I'm beginning to realize you have to use what you can to arrive, and I should take care that you needn't be ashamed of me!" (MWWP). Maud Brown did complete a volume of poetry, entitled *The Flowering Pagoda*, printed in China. Below the dedication "To My Sister Mabel Walker Willebrandt" was a poem:

> I never shut the door on hope
> In darkness and despair,
>   But that I heard your love, which stood
> In patience knocking there.
>   I never sank in seas of things,
> But you stretched out a rod,
>   And drew me, somehow, back at last,
> To the green isles of God,
>   Beloved, if my little light
> Burns steadily or true
>   It is because I kindled it
> At the red flame of you.

15. MWW to mother, Aug. 29, 1923, MWWP.

16. MWW to mother, Oct. 1, 1924, MWWP.

17. MWW to mother, Oct. 3, 1924; Mrs. Walker to MWW, Oct. 11, 1924, MWWP.

18. MWW to Fannie French Morse, Dec. 4, 1924, file 4-9-0, BOP; MWW to mother, Dec. 3, 1924, MWWP.

19. MWW to parents, Jan. 2, 1923, MWWP.

20. MWW to mother, Mar. 22, 1923, MWWP.

21. Ibid.

22. Mrs. Walker to MWW, Aug. 20, 1923; MWW to father, Sept. 2, 1923; MWW to parents, May 11, 1924, MWWP.

23. Grace Knoeller, interview with author, Oct. 1979.

24. MWW to parents, Christmas 1922, MWWP.

25. Mrs. Walker to MWW, n.d., MWWP.

26. Mrs. Walker to MWW, Oct. 3, 1924, MWWP.

27. MWW to parents, July 14 and Aug. 15, 1925, MWWP.

28. MWW to parents, Aug. 2, 1925, MWWP.

29. Mrs. Walker to MWW, July 21, 1925, MWWP.

30. DVD, interview with author, Oct. 20, 1978, and tape, Nov. 1981.

31. Ibid.

32. MWW to parents, Aug. 2, 1925, MWWP.

33. MWW to parents, Aug. 26, 1925, MWWP.

34. MWW to parents, Aug. 15, 1925, MWWP.

35. MWW to parents, Aug. 2, 1925; MWW to mother, Feb. 15, 1924, MWWP.

36. MWW to parents, Aug. 15, 1925, MWWP.

37. Ehrenreich and English, *For Her Own Good*, 201–207.

38. MWW, "First Impressions," 39.

39. Ibid., 219.

40. Ibid., 226.

41. Ibid., 229.

42. Ibid.

43. Hohman, *As the Twig Is Bent*, 29 (copy marked by MWW in the possession of DVD).

44. Ibid.

45. Ibid., 35.

46. DVD, interview with author, Oct. 20, 1978.

47. See Hohman, 134–36, and MWW notations in margins (in the possession of DVD).

48. Aldrich and Aldrich, *Babies Are Human Beings*, 60, 83–84 (copy marked by MWW in the possession of DVD).

49. MWW to parents, Apr. 21, 1926, MWWP; Hohman, 47–48, (copy marked by MWW in the possession of DVD).

50. Notation is in Hohman, 79 (in the possession of DVD). On Dorothy's schooling see Constance Tuthill to MWW, May 18, 1927, and MWW to parents, July 23, 1929, MWWP.

51. DVD, interview with author, Oct. 20, 1978.

52. MWW to parents, Oct. 28, 1927, MWWP.

53. MWW to parents, Apr. 2, 1926, MWWP.

54. MWW to parents, May 30, 1926, MWWP.

55. MWW to Annabel Matthews, June 26, 1926, folder 6, box 1, Matthews Papers.

56. Ibid. Grace Knoeller and Paula Knoeller Gore, interview with author, summer 1979.

57. MWW to parents, July 26, 1926, n.d., and summer 1926, MWWP; DVD, interview with author, July 28, 1979.

58. MWW to parents, n.d., and spring 1929 (in the possession of DVD).

59. Fred Horowitz, interview with author.

60. Mrs. Walker to MWW, Dec. 22, 1921, MWWP.

61. Mrs. Walker to MWW, n.d. (probably 1923), MWWP.

62. Mrs. Walker to MWW, Aug. 30, 1923, MWWP.

63. Mrs. Walker to MWW, autumn 1923; MWW to parents, Christmas 1922, MWWP.

64. MWW to mother, May 13, 1923, MWWP.

65. Mrs. Walker to Fred Horowitz, n.d. (in the possession of DVD).

66. Ibid.

67. Mrs. Walker to MWW, Oct. 11, 1924, MWWP.

68. MWW to parents, Nov. 11, 1924, MWWP.

69. Ibid., MWW to parents, Nov. 24, 1924, MWWP.

70. MWW to Fred Horowitz, Dec. 2, 1925 (in the possession of DVD).

71. MWW to parents, Aug. 24, 1926, MWWP.

72. MWW to parents, Dec. 1926, MWWP.

73. Ibid.

74. Mrs. Walker to MWW, Mar. 23, 1929, and Apr. 1 and 13, 1929, MWWP.

75. Mr. Walker to MWW, Mar. 30, 1929, MWWP.

76. MWW to parents, May 8, 1929. O'Neill in *Everyone Was Brave*, 140, concludes that "success as a public woman was almost always secured at the expense of the family claim." See also Stricker, "Cookbooks and Law Books."

77. Maud Brown to MWW, Dec. 10, 1923, MWWP.

78. Laura Jane Emery to Grace Knoeller, June 2, 1965 (in the possession of Grace Knoeller).

79. Hunley, "Early History of Phi Delta Delta."

80. MWW to parents, June 30, 1924, MWWP; *Women Lawyers' Journal* 13 (June 1, 1924): 3, and 13 (Oct. 14, 1924): 14.

81. Louise Foster, interview with author, Feb. 1981.

82. MWW to parents, itinerary of trip, 1926, MWWP.

83. Grace Knoeller, interview with author, summer 1979.

84. MWW to Georgia Bullock, June 14, 1926, Memory Book No. 2, Bullock Papers.

85. MWW, "Some Observations on Women in the Field of Law," undated speech in MWWP. She also noted: "It takes years to learn that the only way to play politics is not for your friends or your supporters but by the rules of right."

86. MWW, "Give Women a Fighting Chance!", 24.

87. Ibid., 26 and 107.

88. Ibid., 107.

89. Ibid.

90. After she spoke before a group of university women in Oct. 1924, MWW wrote to her parents, "Their pride in me and my work was a blessing." (MWW to parents, Oct. 27, 1924, MWWP). See other letters MWW to mother, Oct. 24, May 5 and 8, Sept. 25, 1925, MWWP. Requests for Willebrandt appearances are in file 44-4-2-3, Mail and Files Div., DOJ; the *Los Angeles Times*, Feb. 12, 1926, covered her University of Southern California schedule; dedication program is in the archives, USC.

91. Helen H. Gardener to MWW, June 1925, file 44-4-2-3, Mail and Files Div., DOJ.

92. MWW to A.W. Gregg, Apr. 17, 1925, folder 11, box 1, Matthews Papers.

93. White Miller to MWW, May 4, 1923, MWW to Miller, May 5, 1923, Miller to MWW, May 5, 1923, and Harry Daugherty to Miller, May 5, 1923, file 5-647-1, box 2469, DOJ; she also interceded with Vice-President Charles Curtis to keep a woman secretary (Grace Knoeller, interview with author, Aug. 21, 1979).

94. Margaret A. Smith to Maud Wood Park, Oct. 10, 1923, and MWW to Attorney General, May 15, 1922, series 1, box 60, National League of Women Voters Papers.

95. MWW to Daugherty, Dec. 29, 1923, box 80, pt. 3, Johnson Papers; MWW

to mother, Oct. 7, 1924, MWWP. The *New York Times*, May 24, 1925, cited the $77 million figure.

96. *Herald Tribune* article cited in "The First Legal Lady of the Land"; see also *New York Times*, Sept. 20, 1929.

97. MWW to parents, Mar. 22, 1922, MWWP.

98. Ibid.

99. Frances Parkinson Keyes, "Homes of Outstanding American Women," *Better Homes and Gardens*, Mar. 1928, pp. 13–14.

100. MWW to parents, Feb. 12, 1928, MWWP. As the only woman in the subcabinet and the ranking one in the Justice Department, she was frequently the only woman at a gathering. She accepted that in business affairs but tried to avoid it on social occasions. She recounted one awkward evening at Solicitor Beck's home, when she had not noticed that the invitation had been in his, rather than Mrs. Beck's name: "I never mind that officially, but I sort of avoid it socially" (MWW to parents, Mar. 28, 1923, MWWP).

101. MWW to parents, Oct. 27, 1924, MWWP.

102. MWW to parents, Christmas 1922, Jan. 2 and Mar. 28, 1923, MWW to mother, May 13, 1923, MWW to parents, May 18, 1923 and Nov. 1927, MWWP.

103. MWW to parents, Jan. 29, 1925, Feb. 2, 1927, MWWP.

104. MWW to parents, Feb. 14, 1924, MWWP; interview with Fred Horowitz. *Polk's District of Columbia Directory* tracks the Willebrandt residences: 1922, the Chastleton Apartments; 1923, 2001 16th St. N.W. (with Winnifred Ellis); in 1924, Ellis returned to California and Willebrandt remained on 16th St.; 1925, the Hamilton; 1926, 2633 15th St. N.W. (with Louise Stanley and Annabel Matthews); 1928, 3303 18th St., N.W. (with Stanley and Matthews); in 1929, Matthews moved back to 2633 15th St.

105. MWW to parents, Mar. 19, 1925, MWWP.

106. MWW to parents, May 24, 1925, MWWP.

107. MWW to parents, Dec. 5, 1924, Mar. 22, 1922, Feb. 2, 1927, n.d. (May or June 1926), MWWP.

108. MWW to parents, Oct. 28, 1925, MWWP.

109. MWW to parents, Mar. 9, 1928, and Easter, 1929.

110. Mrs. Walker to MWW, n.d. For health concerns see Mrs. Walker to MWW, spring 1923, Nov. 24, 1929, and Nov. 22, 1924, MWWP.

111. MWW to parents, Apr. 21, 1926, MWWP.

112. D.W. Walker, journal, "My Trip," 1928, MWWP.

CHAPTER SIX

1. Don S. Kirschner, in "Conflicts and Politics in the 1920s: Historiography and Prospects," *Mid-America* 48 (Oct. 1977): 219–33, and Burl Noggle, in "The Twenties: A New Historiographical Frontier," *Journal of American History* 53 (Sept. 1966): 299–314, survey the changing interpretations of the politics of the 1920s. Frederick Lewis Allen's *Only Yesterday* (1931) analyzed the revolution of manners and morals in the 1920s and stressed the cultural changes. Don S. Kirschner, *City and Country: Rural Responses to Urbanization in the 1920s* (Westport: Greenwood

Press, 1970), effectively analyzes one aspect of cultural tension. See also Arthur S. Link, "Whatever Happened to the Progressive Movement in the 1920's?" *American Historical Review* 64 (July 1959): 833–51.

2. See Russell, *Shadow of Blooming Grove*; Murray, *Harding Era*; Chambers, *Seedtime of Reform*.

3. For speech requests see Mary Broneaugh to MWW, wire, Mar. 3, 1922, MWW to Mrs. J.O. Sylvester, Sept. 19, 1922, MWW to League of Women Voters, Sept. 29, 1922, MWW to Margaret Smith, Oct. 5, 1922, MWW to Walter Brown and MWW to W.E. Halley, Oct. 19, 1922, file 44-4-2-3-1, Mail and Files Div., DOJ; release for morning papers, Youngstown, Ohio, Oct. 31, 1922, MWWP; MWW to Senator Frank Flint, May 16, 1922, box 80, pt. 3, Johnson Papers; Hiram Johnson to Harold Ickes, Sept. 29, 1918, box 33, Ickes Papers.

4. MWW to parents, Mar. 28, 1923, MWWP.

5. MWW to parents, Mar. 28, 1923, MWWP. She noted that if she did have to campaign, she would make certain that the finances were guaranteed, since otherwise it would not be fair to her parents and the family income. She recalled that she had had to meet expenses occasionally in local campaigns, "although in retrospect I don't believe a single one was so unworthwhile that it did not net me gain in the long run."

6. Ibid. and MWW to parents, Nov. 18, 1923, MWWP.

7. MWW to parents, Nov. 18, 1923, and Mrs. Walker to MWW, Nov. 10, 1923, MWWP.

8. MWW to parents, June 30, 1924, MWWP.

9. Ibid.

10. Ibid.

11. MWW to parents, July 9 and Sept. 27, 1924; MWW to C.F.G. Austin, Oct. 9, 1924, MWWP.

12. MWW to C.F.G. Austin, Oct. 9, 1924, MWWP. Her father wrote a rare letter to her, Sept. 23, 1924, on the campaign, regretting Dawes's "cuss words" but sticking with the Republicans in spite of "Hell and Maria" candidate Charles Dawes, since "we recently furnished 300,000 young men for war corpses and cripples to make the world safe for Democracy"; his viewpoint on peace was shared by MWW.

13. MWW to parents, Sept. 23, 1924, MWWP.

14. MWW to mother, Oct. 3, 1924, MWWP; Mrs. Florence R. Buys to MWW, Oct. 4, 1922, file 44-4-2-3-1, Mail and Files Div., DOJ; *New York Times*, Oct. 25, 1924, and Oct. 28, 1924; MWW to parents, Nov. 6, 1924, MWWP.

15. MWW to parents, Mar. 4, 1925, MWWP; MWW to Annabel Matthews, June 26, 1926, box 2, Matthews Papers.

16. MWW to parents, Oct. 30, 1928, MWWP.

17. MWW to parents, Jan. 15, 1928, MWWP.

18. Ibid.

19. MWW to parents, Feb. 14, 1928, MWWP.

20. Ibid.

21. Ibid. See also MWW to parents, Mar. 9, 1928, MWWP.

22. *New York Times*, Apr. 12, 1928; *Washington Post*, Apr. 12, 1928. On May 28, MWW was back in the headlines because she was testifying before a Senate com-

mittee investigating the activities of a former prohibition agent, Frank J. Hale, who was then editing an anti-Hoover publication, *Politics*.

23. *Washington Post*, Apr. 13, 1928.

24. See press release, New York State Committee, Hoover for President, Apr. 16, 1928, box 203, Campaign and Transition, HHP.

25. *New York Times*, June 12 and 14, 1928; Morrison, "Women's Participation in the 1928 Presidential Campaign."

26. Peel and Donnelly, *The 1928 Campaign*, 90–92, 4; Burner, *Herbert Hoover*, 198–201.

27. *Washington Star*, June 12 and 13, 1928; *New York Times*, June 12 and 14, 1928, and June 13, 1928; D. W. Walker, journal, "My Trip," June 13, 1928, MWWP; *Time*, June 25, 1928. See also "The Woman Politician Arrives."

28. Post Office Inspector Report, Sept. 16, 1921, file 72-4-1-1, DOJ; William Donovan to Attorney General, June 14, 1925, file 72-4-1-2, DOJ; 69th Cong., 1st Sess., House Resolution, Mar. 9, 1926; Norris to Attorney General Sargent, Feb. 13, 1927; National Civil Service Reform League to Sargent, May 6, 1927, file 72-4-1-2, DOJ.

29. MWW memorandum to Attorney General, n.d., file 72-4-1-2, "in re Perry Howard," DOJ.

30. MWW memorandum to Marshall, July 6, 1928, file 72-4-1-2, and memorandum of conference in MWW office, Oct. 15, 1928, file 72-4-1-1, DOJ. See also *Memphis Commercial Appeal*, Sept. 6, 1928, and *Jackson (Miss.) Daily News*, Dec. 9, 1928, and Mar. 20, 1929 (clippings in file 72-4-1-5, DOJ); *New York Times*, July 13, 1928; Lichtman, *Prejudice and the Old Politics*, 182.

31. Peel and Donnelly, 40; *New York Times*, July 18, 1928; Lester G. Font to MWW, Mar. 26, 1929, MWW to Lester G. Font, Mar. 27, 1929, file 72-4-1-2, DOJ.

32. MWW to father, July 30, 1928, MWWP. See AP release in *Washington Evening Star* and *Washington Post*, July 20, 1928, on her flight to Oakland and then arrival at Seattle. The *Seattle Times* covered the arrival and speech, July 23 and July 28, 1928.

33. *New York Times*, July 8, 1928; *New York Times*, July 4, 1928; *Washington Times*, Aug. 20, 1928; *Washington Herald*, Aug. 10, 1928; *New York Times Magazine*, Sept. 2, 1928, p. 3; *New York World*, Aug. 30, 1928.

34. Mrs. Norton quoted in *Washington Evening Star*, Aug. 31, 1928; *Binghamton (New York) Press*, Sept. 1, 1928.

35. Ruth F. Lipman, Oral History, 73, box 26, HHP. At the end of August, when the U.S. attorney in Minneapolis began padlocking private homes, there was another press furor, and MWW had to deny instituting a new policy (*Washington Evening Star*, Aug. 29, 1928).

36. MWW to Hubert Work, Aug. 14, 1928, Gen. Corres., Willebrandt, box 72, Campaign and Transition, HHP.

37. Peel and Donnelly, 40, 52.

38. Smith wire quoted in Peel and Donnelly, 24. See also Smith, *Up to Now*, and Josephson and Josephson, *Al Smith*; Peel and Donnelly, 58.

39. George Akerson to Lawrence Richey, coded telegram, Aug. 20, 1928, on Borah proposal for state dispensary system (MWW code name was no. 68, and Borah was no. 31), Gen. Corres., Willebrandt, box 72, Campaign and Transition,

and Bradley Nash, Oral History, box 26, HHP; Morrison, 79; George Akerson to Henry J. Allen, Aug. 11, 1928, box 1, Henry J. Allen Papers.

40. Demand for Willebrandt as a speaker is detailed in Moore, *A Catholic Runs for President*, 175. MWW to Hubert Work, file 44-4-2-1, Mail and Files Div., DOJ. MWW had written to her parents, Aug. 21, 1928, of "the discouragement which I must not voice over this whole Republican set up" (MWWP).

41. *New York Times*, Sept. 8, 1928; the full speech is in MWW, *Inside of Prohibition*, 303–17.

42. Smith, *Up to Now*, 395–96; Josephson and Josephson, 361–62; *New York World*, Sept. 21, 1928. The linkage of the issues is the subject of Silva, *Rum, Religion and Votes*, 37. Moore, 178, Josephson and Josephson, 300, and Peel and Donnelly, 63, also discuss the speeches and issues.

43. *New York Times*, Sept. 22, 1928; the speech is included in MWW, *Inside of Prohibition*, 318–25.

44. MWW, *Inside of Prohibition*, 318–25.

45. Ibid., 326–31; see also *New York Times*, Sept. 25, 1928.

46. Summary of phone call, MWW to R.F., Sept. 24, 1928, Gen. Corres., Willebrandt, box 72, Campaign and Transition, HHP.

47. Ibid.

48. Press release, Sept. 24, 1928, box 72, Campaign and Transition, HHP.

49. *Time*, Oct. 8, 1928, p. 11; Moore, 188–89, claimed that MWW had "the goods" on Work.

50. MWW to Hubert Work, Sept. 27, 1928, box 72, Gen. Corres., Willebrandt, Campaign and Transition, HHP; MWW also recounts this in *Inside of Prohibition*.

51. *New York Times*, Sept. 27, 1928.

52. Ruth F. Lipman, Oral History, 44–46, box 26, HHP.

53. "Mrs. Willebrandt Runs Amuck," *Independent* 109 (Sept. 22, 1928): 269; *New York Times*, Sept. 27, 1928; *Daily News*, Sept. 27, 1928; *New York World*, Sept. 26, 1928; the editor of the *Nation*, Oswald Garrison Villard, wrote to Attorney General Sargent asking him whether he believed Mrs. Willebrandt's speeches befit her office and whether they damaged the reputation of the Department of Justice, Sept. 26, 1928, file 44-4-2-3-1, Mail and Files Div., DOJ.

54. *Springfield Union* and *National Enquirer* are cited in *Literary Digest*, Sept. 29, 1928, pp. 14–15; The poem on prohibition's Joan of Arc by Ed Bodin of Plainfield, N.J., file 44-4-2-3-1, Mail and Files Div., DOJ.

55. *New York Times*, Sept. 26, 30, and 22, and Oct. 6 and 12, 1928; also see Emily N. Blair, "The Case of Mrs. Willebrandt," *Woman's Journal* 14 (June 1929): 22–23.

56. *New York Times*, Oct. 4, 1928; Hill to Attorney General Sargent, Oct. 4, 1928, file 44-4-2-3-1, Mail and Files, Div., DOJ; *New York Times*, Sept. 26, 1928; "Ohio Republicans to Attorney General Sargent, n.d., file 44-4-2-3-1, Mail and Files Div., DOJ.

57. *New York Times*, Oct. 15 and 5, 1928; Stange, in "Al Smith and the Republican Party at Prayer," cites a *Milwaukee Journal* article that reported MWW's speeches as rallying "a number of German Lutherans behind Smith and probably arousing a few dry Republican Scandinavian-Lutheran voters."

58. Hiram Johnson to Harold Ickes, Sept. 29, 1928 (compare his May 22, 1926, letter to Ickes), box 33, Ickes Papers; her friend Justice Brandeis was also concerned

(Brandeis to Felix Frankfurter, Oct. 1, 1928, *Letters of Louis D. Brandeis*, vol. 5, p. 355).

59. MWW, "Inside of Prohibition," *Washington Evening Star*, Aug. 5, 1929. For details on Johnson's estrangement see Frank Doherty to Mary Connor, Aug. 19, 1929, box 34, pt. 3, Johnson Papers.

60. *Time*, Oct. 8, 1928, p. 11; news release typescript by Blakely, special for *New York Herald Tribune* in MWW file, *LAT*; a *Times* editor scribbled on it, "Don't use story, No news excuse for it. Bad politix"; Grace B. Knoeller, interview with author, Sept. 10, 1979.

61. Unsigned postcard to Attorney General Sargent, Oct. 4, 1928, and Eugene Suter to MWW, Oct. ¹, 1928, file 44-4-2-3-1, Mail and Files Div., DOJ.

62. *New York Times*, Oct. 7, 1928; Morrison, 172.

63. Speech script in speech file, MWWP.

64. Ibid.; MWW wrote to parents, Feb. 19, 1927, on the McNary-Haugen farm measure, MWWP; her addresses were covered by the *New York Times*, Oct. 9 and 10, 1928; Mrs. Verna L. Hatch, a Republican farm leader, wired MWW an offer to debate the farm issues Oct. 16, 1928 (file 44-4-2-1 Mail and Files Div., DOJ), but MWW did not accept.

65. Speech script in speech file, MWWP.

66. *New York Times*, Oct. 24 and 30, 1928; MWW had introduced Carl Lomen, the reindeer developer of Alaska, and Laura Volstead.

67. *New York Times*, Nov. 4, 1928. The speech is included in MWW, *Inside of Prohibition*, 336–37; script is in speech file, MWWP. Moore, 189–93, is critical of her indiscriminate use of quotations linking leaders to prohibition and not distinguishing between temperance, abstinence, and legal prohibition. Hayward Kendall to MWW, Oct. 8, 1928, file 44-4-2-3-1, Mail and Files Div., DOJ.

68. Script of speech in speech file, MWWP.

69. Ibid.

70. Ibid.

71. MWW, "The Republican Platform as Viewed by Mrs. Mabel Walker Willebrandt." MWW was also a participant in the League of Women Voters radio series on the issue on NBC. Both the article and radio address indicate the wide perception that she was the outstanding Republican woman in the campaign.

72. Peel and Donnelly, 52, 71; Lichtman, 41–42, 58–60, 68–70, 77, 90, 246; V.E. Simnell, "Oratory in the 1928 Presidential Campaign."

73. *New York Times*, Nov. 22, 1928; Kent, cited in *New York Times*, Dec. 31, 1928; Martin, "Mrs. Firebrand." Dry endorsements for attorney general came to Hoover, see Subject File, Campaign Endorsements, boxes 28 and 90, Campaign and Transition, HHP.

74. *Christian Herald*, n.d. (clipping in MWWP); also noted in *New York Times*, Mar. 12, 1929.

75. *Los Angeles Times*, Dec. 21, 1928. MWW sent Hoover a Thanksgiving telegram, Nov. 24, 1928, box 558, Presidential Papers, HHP; MWW to Larry Richey, Dec. 28, 1928, and MWW to Congressman Newton, Mar. 29, 1929, Gen. Corres., Willebrandt, box 72, Campaign and Transition, HHP; Herbert Hoover to H.L. Stimson, Mar. 15, 1929, box 21, Cabinet Offices—Justice, Presidential Papers, HHP. See also MWW to parents, Feb. 14, 1929, MWWP.

76. MWW to Hoover, Feb. 8, 1929, Presidential Subject— Appointments— Men Considered, HHP.

77. Ibid.

78. Ibid.

79. Ibid.

80. MWW to parents, Feb. 22, 1929, MWWP.

81. Burner, *Herbert Hoover*, 209, 390; Christian Herter to Herbert Hoover, Mar. 6, 1929, noted Donovan was in a "state of mind" box 23, Presidential Papers, HHP. Letters of support for Willebrandt are in box 90, Campaign and Transition, 1928–29, and box 27, Cabinet offices—Justice, Presidential Papers, HHP. The *New York World*, June 6, 1929, cited a crusade to name Willebrandt to the Law Enforcement Committee (clipping in box 2, Work Papers).

82. MWW to parents, Mar. 29, 1929, MWWP. Her father wrote her one of his rare letters to encourage her, Mar. 30, 1929: "The administration depends on the success of prohibition enforcement—you having that in your department become the key man of the administration. Some girl from the wind swept prairies of western Kansas, raised by Nomad parents. Success to you" (MWWP).

83. *Chicago Tribune*, June 2 and 3, 1929; Clement H. Congdon, editor, *Philadelphia Sunday Transcript* to Herbert Hoover and separate letter to MWW, Apr. 23, 1929, box 27, Cabinet Offices—Justice, Presidential Papers, HHP.

84. MWW to parents, May 8, 1929, MWWP.

85. Mrs. Walker to MWW, May 27, 1929, MWWP.

86. MWW to Herbert Hoover, May 26, 1929, box 21, Executive Departments—Justice, Presidential Papers, HHP; *Washington News*, May 27, 1929, and *Washington Herald*, May 29, 1929.

87. Herbert Hoover to MWW, May 28, 1929, box 21, Executive Departments—Justice, Presidential Papers, HHP; *New York World*, cited in "A Dry Crusader Takes to the Air," *Literary Digest*, June 8, 1929, p. 8; MWW to Herbert Hoover, May 28, 1929, Cabinet Offices—Justice, Presidential Papers, HHP; see also MWW to Larry Richey, same day. Her mother wrote a supportive letter on "her pleasanter work in a challenging field" (Mrs. Walker to MWW, June 3, 1929, MWWP).

88. *New York Times*, May 28, 1929; press response cited in *Literary Digest*, June 8, 1929; Arthur Sears Henning in *Chicago Tribune*, June 3, 1929 (see also *New York Times*, June 3, 1929); Ella A. Boole to Herbert Hoover, May 31, 1929, box 27, Cabinet Offices—Justice, Presidential Papers, HHP; Harlan Fiske Stone to MWW, May 28, 1929, box 30, Stone Papers. Telegrams of WCTU and Anti-Saloon support are in Willebrandt, box 27, Cabinet Offices—Justice, Presidential Papers, HHP.

89. Herbert Hoover to Lawrence Richey, June 3, 1929, box 21, Executive Departments—Justice, Presidential Papers, HHP.

90. MWW to parents, July 23, 1929, MWWP.

91. *New York times*, June 30, 1929.

CHAPTER SEVEN

1. Meers, "California Wine and Grape Industry and Prohibition"; see also Jos-

lyn, "A Technologist Views the California Wine Industry," 4, and Perelli-Minetti, "A Life in Wine Making," 119, CWHP; DA, FFB Minutes, Aug. 12, 1929, vol. 1, pp. 129–33.

2. DA, FFB Minutes, July 23 and Aug. 9, 1929, vol. 1, pp. 34–37, 126–29.

3. Walter Taylor, interview with author; see also Philo Biane, "Wine Making in Southern California and Recollections of Fruit Industries, Ltd." 2–4, and Leon Adams, "Revitalizing the California Wine Industry," 22, CWHP. Conn is quoted in the *Baltimore Sun*, Apr. 29, 1932.

4. Walter Taylor, interview with author. Conn had known Willebrandt since 1927 and had introduced representatives of the California Vineyardists Association who would work with her on governmental relations in September; Conn to MWW, file 44-4-2-3-3, Mail and Files Div., DOJ.

5. Walter Taylor, interview with author; see also Jacobs, "California's Pioneer Wine Families," and Adams, "Revitalizing the California Wine Industry," 22, CWHP.

6. *Baltimore Sun*, Apr. 26, 1932.

7. DA, FFB Minutes, Aug. 19 and 20, 1929, vol. 1, pp. 169–70, 174–75; see also DA, FFB Minutes, Sept. 3, 4, 17, 18, 24, and 27, 1929, vol. 1, and Oct. 15 and Dec. 14, 1929, vol. 2. In an interview with the author, Walter Taylor noted that the Fruit Industries executives asked Willebrandt to make "certain connections" and told her what they wanted to accomplish. When they went to the FFB they wanted to start off with a request for a million dollars, though they were "kind of uncertain" exactly what they would do with it. Taylor and Conn talked over the situation with Alexander Legge, who observed: "You have a lady Willebrandt. Bring her down this super woman." When Willebrandt arrived, Legge put his feet up on the table, looked at her, and said, "Are they going to do it? Are they going to win?" She replied, "They're not going to do it; the people are going to do it" (Taylor interpreted her answer to be an acknowledgment that repeal was coming).

8. DA, FFB Minutes, Feb. 1, 1930, vol. 3, p. 194. See also the discussion of Fruit Industries by the Farm Board in DA, FFB Minutes, Mar. 5 and 6, 1930, vol. 3, and Apr. 1 and May 13, 1930, vol. 4.

9. Perelli-Minetti, "A Life in Wine Making," 117, CWHP.

10. DA, FFB Minutes, May 17, 1930, and June 24, 1930, vol. 4, pp. 885–88 and 1165–66.

11. DA, FFB Minutes, July 22, 1930, vol. 5, pp. 171–76.

12. DA, FFB Minutes, Aug. 16, 1930, vol. 5, pp. 390–91, and Oct. 19, 1930, vol. 6, pp. 241–42.

13. Walter Taylor, interview with author; Biane, "Wine Making in Southern California," 8, CWHP; A.J. Day to MWW, Nov. 16, 1930, A.J. Day to MWW, press release, Nov. 13, 1930, Fruit Industries file, MWWP. Adams, in "Revitalizing the California Wine Industry," 32, observed of the Capone threats, "It's not impossible, but I'm not certain I'd believe it" (CWHP).

14. The *Chicago Tribune* editorial is in Fruit Industries file, MWWP.

15. Carlisle Bergeron, *Washington Post*, Nov. 12, 1930 (clipping in MWWP).

16. MWW to Donald Conn, Nov. 19, 1930, MWWP.

17. Copy of release in wire from Conn to MWW, Nov. 20, 1930, MWWP. In a

Nov. 19 wire to Willebrandt, Conn made his allegation of Hearst and the wet interests (MWWP).

18. Arthur J. Brown, "The Mirror," *San Bernardino Evening Telegram*, Nov. 12, 1930 (clipping in Fruit Industries file, MWWP).

19. MWW to Ralph P. Merritt, Nov. 21, 1930, Fruit Industries file, MWWP.

20. MWW memorandum to Conn, Merritt, Adams, Day, Taylor, Nov. 22, 1930, Fruit Industries file, MWWP.

21. *New York Times*, Nov. 22, 1930; *Washington Post*, Nov. 6, 1931. Brown is quoted in the *New York Times*, Dec. 10, 1930. MWW wrote of the support of Mrs. Ruth Strawbridge of Philadelphia in a letter to Conn, Nov. 29, 1930 (Fruit Industries file, MWWP).

22. E.T. Folliard covered the story in the *Washington Post*, Jan. 7, 1931; Willebrandt wrote him a letter of appreciation, Jan. 28, 1931 (Fruit Industries file, MWWP). She also wrote to the editor of the *Louisville-Courier Journal*, Dec. 22, 1932, asking for a copy of a cartoon by Pleschke, depicting Willebrandt pointing to the embarrassing grapes with the caption "Them's the Berries" (M.A. Smith to editor *Louisville-Courier Journal*, Dec. 22, 1932, MWWP).

23. H.R. Adams to MWW, Feb. 7, 1931 and MWW to Adams, Feb. 9, 1931, Fruit Industries file, MWWP. See advertisement in the *Washington Evening Star*, Mar. 11, 1931. MWW urged H.R. Adams, the public relations agent, to press the contact with a friendly editor on the *New York Herald Tribune*; he did not seem to appreciate her advice. Writing to Conn and Merritt, Mar. 18, 1931, she concluded: "I guess Mr. Adams didn't like it because I wanted him to put the ad in the *Herald Tribune*. I try not to overstep in what I know is his business, but I really think that it would be most unfortunate to have missed our opportunities with this particular set up." (Fruit Industries file, MWWP).

24. DA, FFB Minutes, Nov. 13, 1930, vol. 6, pp. 338–39. See also FFB Minutes of Mar. 11, 1931, vol. 7, pp. 402–406; May 26 and 29, 1931, vol. 8; July 28, Aug., 6, 13, 14, 15, and Sept. 17, 1931, vol. 9. *New York Times*, Aug. 10, 1931. There was a wire from a Bible class in Baltimore protesting the loan, DA, FFB Minutes, Aug. 24, 1931, vol. 9, p. 454.

25. *New York Times*, Apr. 14, 1931; Rex Collier, *Globe Democrat*, May 19, 1931; MWW to AP, May 20, 1931, and wire to Conn, May 20, 1931, Fruit Industries file, MWWP; *Washington Herald*, May 13, 1931.

26. *New York Times*, Aug. 7, 1931.

27. Will Rogers, Aug. 12, 1931 (clipping from a Tacoma, Washington paper, in Fruit Industries file, MWWP).

28. A.J. Day memorandum to MWW, Aug. 20, 1931, and MWW to Day, Aug. 24, 1931, Fruit Industries file, MWWP; *Minneapolis Sunday Tribune*, Aug. 23, 1931.

29. DA, FFB Minutes, Oct. 19, 1931, vol. 9; *New York Times*, Oct. 2, 1931; MWW to Hon. Earl Wettengel, Oct. 20, 1931, Fruit Industries file, MWWP.

30. *New York Sun*, Nov. 5, 1931, and *New York World Telegram*, Nov. 5, 1931. Walter Taylor in an interview with the author recounted receiving a telephone message: "Stop. Now. As of this minute. Stop the advertising."

31. *Washington Times*, Nov. 6, 1931.

32. *Washington Post*, Nov. 6, 1931.

33. *Baltimore Sun*, Nov. 6, 1931.

34. *Washington Daily News*, Mar. 2, 1932. The "betrayal" story was carried in the *New York Herald Tribune*, Apr. 26, 1932; *Baltimore Sun*, Apr. 28, 1932; *Washington Daily News*, Apr. 25, 1932; *Time*, May 9, 1932. The *Washington Evening Star*, Apr. 28, 1932, reported that Willebrandt would make no comment, but did quote her as saying, "My silence is not to be interpreted either as affirming or opposing the campaign for prohibition modification." Still trying to win a better press for Fruit Industries, Willebrandt sent Conn a newspaper clipping about a gift of California oranges to the needy of the District of Columbia, suggesting it would be "excellent publicity" for the grape industry (May 25, 1932, Fruit Industries file, MWWP). L.D. Adams, "Revitalizing the California Wine Industry," 28, CWHP.

35. DA, FFB Minutes, Mar. 8, 1932, vol. 12, pp. 71–72, and May 26, 1932, vol. 13, p. 237.

36. *Baltimore Sun*, Apr. 26, 1932.

37. Perrelli-Minetti, "A Life in Wine Making," 128, CWHP. Fruit Industries did succeed in converting a million gallons of the concentrate into brandy. When repeal came, Fruit Industries had the largest brandy stock in the United States. It sold under the A.R. Morrow brand. Biane, "Wine Making in Southern California and Recollections of Fruit Industries, Ltd," 25, CWHP. In an interview with the author, Walter Taylor also described Fruit Industries' success with brandy. The Federal Farm Board loans were repaid by Fruit Industries after World War II.

38. Grace Knoeller, interview with the author, July 2, 1982.

39. Hiram Johnson to Carlos McClatchy, June 17, 1929, box 9, pt. 3, Johnson Papers.

40. Herbert Hoover to C.C. Teague, June 24, 25, 26, July 1, 1929, box 32, Wilbur Papers; Alonzo E. Taylor to Lyman Wilbur, Apr. 16, 1930, and Wilbur to Taylor, Apr. 19, 1930, box 13, Wilbur Papers.

41. *Baltimore Sun*, Apr. 11, 1930.

42. H.C. Williams to author, Sept. 17, 1979.

43. Dr. Mary Ellen Collins, interview with author, July 29, 1979; *New York Times*, Mar. 8, 1925; MWW to parents, July 18, 1928, MWWP.

44. MWW to father, July 30, 1928, MWWP.

45. Ibid.

46. MWW to parents, n.d., MWWP. She ended, obviously commenting on a 1929 flight, "Haynor Hinshaw of the Aviation Corporation and I are the two men in this crowd. The others are from Boston."

47. *New York Times*, May 29, 1929.

48. Senate Special Committee on Air-Ocean Mail Contracts, 74th Cong. (hereafter referred to as Black Committee) obtained the minutes of the AVCO executive committee meetings and corporate correspondence.

49. MWW to Hinshaw, May 28, 1929, AVCO Corres., box 139, Black Committee. See also Hinshaw to G.B. Grosvener, May 27, 1929: "Mrs Willebrandt had decided. Please protect her resignation until her return," G.B. Grosvener to MWW, May 29, 1929, and MWW to G.B. Grosvener, June 7, 1929, AVCO Corres., box 139, Black Committee.

50. Komons, *Bonfires to Beacons*, 7.

51. Hinshaw to R.A. Bishop, June 24, 1929, AVCO Corres., box 139, minutes

of American Airways Executive meeting, May 6, 1930, p. 30, box 138, minutes of the Conference on Aviation Legislation, Hotel Roosevelt, N.Y., June 27, 1929, p. 15, AVCO Corres., box 139, Black Committee.

52. Komons, 78, 53, 85–86.

53. Kelly, 31–39; Komons, 67.

54. MWW to Hinshaw, July 30, 1929, AVCO Corres., box 138, Hinshaw to Lloyd B. Averill, Aug. 27, 1929, George R. Hann to C.C. Glover, Aug. 21, 1929, Hinshaw to George R. Hann, Aug. 21, 1929, AVCO Corres., box 139, Black Committee.

55. MWW to Hinshaw, Aug. 29, 1929, AVCO Corres., box 139, Black Committee.

56. Hinshaw to MWW, Sept. 12, 1929, AVCO Corres., box 139, Black Committee.

57. Kelly, 71–73.

58. Kelly, 66–67; *New York Times,* Mar. 6, 1929; Questionnaire, box 134, Black Committee; *New York Times*, Apr. 15, May 13, Mar. 21, 1929.

59. Minutes of Conference on Aviation Legislation, June 27, 1929, pp. 1–6, 9, 11, 12, AVCO Corres., box 139, Black Committee.

60. Ibid., pp. 14 and 16.

61. T.T.C. Gregory to G.B. Grosvener, Nov. 28, 1929, AVCO Corres., box 139, Black Committee.

62. Kelly, 59, 53–57, 60–64, 66–67; Komons, 67 and 199–203; Smith, *Airways,* 158.

63. MWW to G.B. Grosvener, Mar. 2, 1930, AVCO Corres., box 140, Black Committee; House Committee on the Post Office and Post Roads, *Amending the Air Mail Act*, hearing, 71st Cong., 2d sess. HR 9500, Feb. 19, 1930, pp. 38–50; Joseph W. Sabin memorandum to Office of the Executive Vice-President, Universal Aviation Corporation, Apr. 11, 1930, AVCO Corres., box 140, Black Committee.

64. Kelly, 90–91; William M. Smith to Henry Zweifel, May 12, 1930, C.R. Smith to G.B. Grosvener, May 16, 1930, Henry Zweifel to William Dewey Loucks, May 15, 1930, AVCO Corres., box 138, Black Committee.

65. Aeronautical Chamber of Commerce of America, Inc., *Aircraft Year Book, 1931*, 22.

66. Minutes of the Executive Committee, AVCO, Apr. 29, 1930, box 134, Hinshaw AVCO re Delta Airlines, AVCO Corres. Jan. 1929–Oct. 1931, box 140, Black Committee; Smith, *Airways*, 183–84; Franklyn Waltman to Raymond Henle, Oral History, 5–6, Presidential Papers, HHP.

67. Kelly, 74–75, 80–82; Komons, 202–206; Questionnaire 2, AVCO excerpts from minutes of American Airways, Oct. 3, 1930, box 134, Black Committee. Air Mail Correspondence files, American Airways folder, Jan. 1932, Post Office Department, RG 28, National Archives.

68. *Washington Herald*, Mar. 28, 1932; David, *Economics of Air Mail Transportation*, 88.

69. Komons, 228–43; Kelly, 86, 91–93; *Mobile (Alabama) Times*, Feb. 9, 1934; Air Contracts, Senatorial File, box 183, Black Papers.

70. Senate, *Investigation of Air Mail and Ocean Mail Contracts*, pt. 4, pp. 1578–79,

and pt. 6, p. 2354. See also Walter F. Brown to the President of the Senate, Air Mail Service Congressional Documents, 1933–34, Jan. 21, 1931, Post Office Department, RG 28, National Archives.

71. News release, Scottish Rite News Bureau, Jan. 22, 1931, Senatorial File, box 183, Black Papers; Kelly, 91–95; Komons, 257.

72. Komons, 266–67; Kelly, 97–99.

73. "Up from Chaos."

74. Komons, 352–56.

75. *New York Times*, May 29, 1929.

76. Komons, 47–48; Osborn and Riggs, *"Mr. Mac," William P. MacCracken, Jr.*, 146–75. For Willebrandt's cooperation with the Aeronautical Chamber of Commerce see R. W. Robbins to MWW, Aug. 13, 1929, AVCO Corres., box 138, Black Committee. Willebrandt introduced MacCracken and asked that he be allowed to speak on the committee report. *Report of the 52d Annual Meeting of the ABA, 1929*, 143; *Report of the 53rd Annual Meeting of the ABA, 1930*, 95–99 and 316–17; Komons, 50.

77. Brief of the Aviation Corporation as Amicus Curiae, *Frederick L. Swetland and Raymond H. Swetland* v. *Curtiss Airports Corporation, Ohio Air Terminals, Inc., and Curtiss Flying Service, Inc.*, nos. 5812 and 5813, U.S. 6th Circuit Court of Appeals.

78. Ibid.

79. Report of the Standing Committee on Aeronautical Law, 54th Annual Meeting of the ABA, 1931, 74; Niles, "Present Status of the Ownership of Air Space," 146.

80. *New York Times*, Feb. 16, 1931, and Aug. 16, 1931. See Aeronautical Chamber of Commerce of America, Inc., *Aircraft Year Book, 1930*, 244.

81. MWW's good friend Margaret Lambie was co-editor of the *Journal*.

82. MWW, "Comment on Uniform Aviation Liability Act."

83. MWW to Hinshaw, Sept. 23, 1929, AVCO Corres., box 138, Black Committee. Codel was an expert and frequent writer on the industry. Aeronautical and radio law were professionally paired in the *Journal of Air Law*. The firm of Cullen and Loucks, with whom Willebrandt worked in AVCO matters, was also an important firm in radio law.

84. Rosen, *Modern Stentors*, 62–66.

85. Ibid., 20–33; Schmeckebier, *Federal Radio Commission*, 4.

86. Rosen, 35–41, 59, 104–105.

87. Barnouw, *Tower in Babel*, 215.

88. Rosen, 128–44.

89. Harold A. Wheeler, *Hazeltine the Professor*, 38–54; *Hazeltine Corporation* v. *E.A. Wildermuth*, 6 U.S. Pat. Q., 221; and 35F (2d) 733; *New York Times*, July 2 and 16, 1929, May 9, 1931. See also MWW to parents, May 1932, MWWP.

90. For background of FRC allocation see Rosen, 135–38; WJKS application and hearing before the FRC, vol. 1, folder 2, box 197, docket 1156, FCC, Suitland.

91. See WJKS hearing before the FRC, vol. 1, folder 2, p. 177, box 197, docket 1156, FCC, Suitland, for example of MWW hearing difficulties.

92. 62F (2d) 854.

93. Brief for *Johnson-Kennedy Radio Corporation (Station WJKS), Intervener* v. Nelson Brothers Bond and Mortgage Co. (Station WIBO), on writ of certiorari to the Court of Appeals of the District of Columbia, nos. 659 and 660, Oct. 1932, U.S. Supreme Court (hereafter WJKS brief).

94. WJKS brief, 24–27, 28–29, 33–34.

95. Ibid., 7–9, 12–15.

96. 289 U.S. 266.

97. Rosen, 141.

98. *Yale Law Journal* 42 (June 1933), 1274–76; see also *Minnesota Law Review* 18 (Jan. 1934), 209–14, and *Columbia Law Review* 33 (May 1933), 921–22; *New York Times,* May 12, 1933.

99. Lomen, *Fifty Years in Alaska,* 154–59; the *New York Times,* Mar. 21, 1933, reviewed the claims. Also see John B. Burnham to D.C. Poole, Chief, Division of Russian Affairs, Sept. 27, 1922, 861.0144/49, Decimal File,SD.

100. Lomen, 154–60.

101. Ibid., 161–63.

102. Ibid., 166–67; MWW to parents, Mar. 19, 1925, MWWP. In the same letter, MWW wrote that she had first met Lomen in 1922 and had become quite good friends during the past year. She believed that his use of the airplane in herding his reindeer and inspecting his herds would "revolutionize Alaska." Lomen introduced her to Stefansson. Like Stefansson, she saw the value of the trans-Arctic air route. She introduced Lomen, who at one point wanted to marry her, to Laura Volstead, and Willebrandt was the matron of honor at their wedding in Oct. 1928. Decimal File 861.0144, SD, covers the Wrangel Island episodes through the 1920s.

103. MWW to parents, May 24, 1925, MWWP; MWW to Carl Lomen, Nov. 22, 1933, Lomen Papers; *New York Times,* June 29, 1933; Foreign Claims Settlement Commission of the United States, Claim No. SOV-40,944. Carl J. Lomen and Ralph Lomen to MWW in Apr. 1960 indicates the claim was settled on May 21, 1959.

104. Lomen, 206. Lomen was on the board of Alaskan Airlines, an AVCO subsidiary. Memorandum of conversations with MWW, Dec. 23, 1929; MWW wire to Stefansson, Dec. 23, 1929, Notation of Stefansson's reply on wire, Stefansson Papers.

105. Enclosure in communique from F.W.B. Coleman to the Secretary of State, from Riga, Jan. 3, 1930, and Willebrandt to Stefansson, Feb. 8, 1930, Stefansson Papers. See also Willebrandt to Lomen, Jan. 28, 1930, Lomen Papers, and Lomen, 206.

106. Lomen, 212–21; Grace Knoeller, interview with author, Nov. 12, 1979.

107. See Minutes of the Reindeer Commission, box 201, Alaska Division, Bureau of Indian Affairs, D.I. Willebrandt to Wilbur, Mar. 18, 1931, report of the hearings of the eighth meeting of the Reindeer Commission, box 202, Bureau of Indian Affairs, DI.

108. MWW to Lomen, Apr. 9, 1931, Lomen Papers; DI, Office of the Secretary, Survey of Alaskan Reindeer Service, 1931–33 (Washington, D.C., Feb. 15, 1933), 1–16.

109. MWW to Lomen, Nov. 22, 1933, Lomen Papers; Lomen, 244 and 297.

Willebrandt "assisted in rendering order out of chaos," when Lomen wrote his story, *Fifty Years in Alaska* (Lomen acknowledgments).

110. MWW, "Increasing Burden of Taxation," 64.

111. Ibid., 63.

112. Ibid., 69.

113. Ibid., 69–81.

114. *Report of the Fifty-seventh Annual Meeting of the ABA, 1934*, 612.

115. Virginia Kellogg Mortensen, telephone interview with author.

116. Judge John J. Sirica, interview with author. See *MacMillan* v. *Krist*. U.S. Court of Appeals, District of Columbia, no. 7288.

117. Willebrandt to Laura and Carl Lomen, n.d., Lomen Papers; MWW, "Women in Government" speech given to the Ebell Club, Los Angeles, Nov. 30, 1952, MWWP; DVD, interview with author, July 28, 1979; MWW to Eleanor Roosevelt, Jan. 23, 1938, box 1482, Eleanor Roosevelt Papers (hereafter ER Papers).

118. MWW, "The Creed of a Bewildered Citizen" (in a letter to her parents on June 21, 1932, MWW listed the radio stations in the West carrying her speech, MWWP.).

119. See the three Roosevelt messages in Roosevelt, *Public Papers and Addresses*, vol. 4, pp. 15–25; vol. 7, pp. 512–20; vol. 8, pp. 297–320.

120. MWW to FDR, Sept. 3, 1938, PPF, box 1986, Franklin D. Roosevelt Papers (hereafter FDR Papers).

121. MWW to FDR, May 1, 1939, ibid.

122. "Worker Willebrandt," *Time*, Oct. 8, 1928, p. 11.

123. William D. Mitchell to Mark Sullivan, July 26, 1934, box 7, Mitchell Papers; Schmidhauser, *Judges and Justices*, 19–21.

124. "A Woman on the Supreme Bench," *Christian Science Monitor*, Mar. 12, 1930; Beverly B. Cook, "The First Woman Candidate for the Supreme Court," Supreme Court Historical Society, *Yearbook, 1981*, p. 125.

125. Schmidhauser, 41–59; William D. Mitchell to Mark Sullivan, July 26, 1934, Mitchell Papers.

126. MWW to FDR, Aug. 17, 1937, OF41a, box 51, and FDR to MWW, Aug. 26, 1937, FDR Papers.

127. MWW to FDR, Feb. 16, 1939, and FDR to MWW, Mar. 21, 1939, PPF, box 1986, FDR Papers.

128. The two Phi Deltas were Sarah Perrin and Vera Mankinen; Dr. Mary Ellen Collins, interview with author.

129. Jacqueline Cochran, interview with author. See also Cochran, *Stars at Noon*.

130. Healy, *Cissy*, 145.

131. Erwin N. Griswold, interview with author, Feb. 1979. Griswold was just joining the Justice Department as Willebrandt was leaving. He noted her warmth and openness to young lawyers.

132. Judge John J. Sirica, interview with author.

133. *Christian Science Monitor*, June 15, 1939.

134. *Washington Herald*, Jan. 29, 1932 (clipping in box 2, Matthews Papers).

135. Paula Knoeller Gore, interview with author, June 1979. Mrs. Gore was

Willebrandt's secretary and long-time friend; she frequently arranged for the dinners and receptions at the Sulgrave Club.

136. Robert C. Cannom, *Van Dyke and the Mythical City, Hollywood*, 333–38.

137. *Washington Times-Herald*, Feb. 28, 1940.

138. Fred Horowitz, interview with author; the *Los Angeles Times*, Jan. 14, 1929, reported on Willebrandt's decorating assistance.

139. Fred Horowitz, interview with author.

140. MWW to mother, May 14, 1932, MWWP.

141. DVD, interview with author, July 28, 1979.

142. Mrs. Walker to MWW, Feb. 6, 1933, MWWP.

143. DVD, interview with author, July 28, 1979.

144. The *Los Angeles Times*, Jan. 26, 1934, reported the end of the association; the *Escondido Times-Advocate*, n.d., reported the sale of the 4-S ranch (clippings in MWWP).

145. Grace Knoeller, interview with author, June 1979; DVD, interview with author, July 28, 1979.

146. Mrs. Walker to MWW, Feb. 6, 1933, MWWP.

147. Grace Knoeller, interviews with author June and Sept. 1979.

148. Calvin and Mary Claggett, interview with author.

149. Sarah Perrin to Grace Knoeller, Dec. 1979, Grace Knoeller Papers; Grace Knoeller, and Paula Knoeller Gore, and Dr. Mary Ellen Collins, interviews with author.

150. DVD, interview with author, July 28, 1979.

151. David Walker to his niece, Mrs. Ed. Plumhoff, Jan. 21, 1938, MWWP; *Washington Herald*, Jan. 11, 1938, obituary for Mrs. Walker.

152. Grace Knoeller, interview with author, Sept. 1980.

153. Flyer on the Walker Fields dispersal, July 22, 1942, MWWP.

CHAPTER EIGHT

1. Gene Raymond, in an interview with the author, noted that Willebrandt's friendship with Mayer was probably significant in bringing her so many star clients.

2. MWW to parents, Feb. 19, 1927, MWWP; for MGM see Higham and Greenberg, *Hollywood in the Forties*, 8.

3. Hopper, *The Whole Truth and Nothing But* and *From under My Hat*, 225; Grace Knoeller and Paula Knoeller Gore, interview with author, Aug. 23, 1979; Marx, *Mayer and Thalberg*, 91; Hedda Hopper, "Guiding Light Lost, Says Hedda," Nov. 25, 1954, column on Ida Koverman, clipping in Individual Files, Ida Koverman, Post-Presidential Files, box 397, HHP.

4. Marx, 89–90.

5. For Julien case see W. W. Robinson, *Los Angeles*, 118; *San Francisco Daily News*, Aug. 8, 1928 (clipping in Bullock Papers); Gene Raymond, in an interview with the author, talked of friendship of Willebrandt and Koverman. Also see Allvue, *Greatest Fox of Them All*, 126; Marx, 98.

6. MWW to Wilbur J. Carr, July 3, 1930, 032, Decimal File, SD; MWW to

Secretary of State, Dec. 19, 1932; Wilbur J. Carr to MWW, Dec. 23, 1932; MWW to American consul, London, and Department of State to American consul, London, Jan. 4, 1932, 092.41/24, Decimal File, SD.

7. In a letter to Grace Knoeller, Mar. 16, 1979, Thomas N. Biddison, Jr., Baltimore attorney, wrote of the case as related to him by Judge Avrim Rifkind, who was then the assistant to Soleloff and worked with Willebrandt on the case (in the possession of Grace Knoeller).

8. MWW to father, Feb. 8, 1940, MWWP.

9. Hopper, *The Whole Truth and Nothing But*, 270–71; After the death of Willebrandt, Hopper called her Ida Koverman's "guardian angel" (*Baltimore Evening Sun*, Apr. 23, 1963).

10. Howard Strickling, MGM public relations director, stated that he did not know that Willebrandt represented Harlow but noted that everybody always asked her things and that she was helpful at the time of the suicide of Paul Bern, Harlow's husband (telephone interview with author, May 27, 1980). The list of clients was supplied by DVD. A newspaper clipping indicates that she also represented Charles Chaplin and saved him $1,025,000 (n.d., MWWP). The Willebrandt quotation on Grace Moore is from a Mason Peters story in an undated clipping, folder 23, Matthews Papers.

11. Sarris, *American Cinema*, 99–100, 87–88; Capra, 40–41; Leo McCarey, Oral History 2, interviewed by Peter Bogdanovich, 1971, American Film Institute Oral History Collection, Louis B. Mayer Film History Program. See also Kanin, *Hollywood*, 82.

12. Frank Capra, interview with author; see also Capra, *Name above the Title*, vii. Thomas, *Directors in Action*, vii–viii; Joseph Youngerman, interview with author, Nov. 7, 1979. The platform was carried in *Variety*, Sept. 21, 1938, p. 6.

13. *Variety*, Sept. 28, 1938, p. 5; Capra, 266–69; *Variety*, Feb. 22, 1939, p. 5.

14. Higham and Greenberg, 7 and 14; "Battle of Reno"; see also Reagan and Hubler, *Where's the Rest of Me*, 126, 142–46, 159.

15. *Variety*, Oct. 6, 1948.

16. Minutes of Screen Directors, Inc., Mar. 28 and June 13, 1950, in DGA office of Youngerman, Hollywood; *New York Times*, Sept. 20 and 24, 1950.

17. Joseph Youngerman, interview with author, Nov. 11, 1979, and May 28, 1980; Al Rogell, interview with author. Rogell credits Willebrandt with promoting the scholarship fund of the SDG Education and Benevolent Fund.

18. Capra, interview with author; Thomas, viii.

19. MWW to members of SDGA, Aug. 27, 1956; Joseph Youngerman, interview with author, May 5, 1980.

20. MWW note on copy of letter to SDGA, Aug. 27, 1956, sent to Grace Knoeller (in the possession of Grace Knoeller).

21. Al Rogell, interview with author.

22. Rankin cited in Ceplair and Englund, *Inquisition in Hollywood*, 54; see also Carr, *House Committee on Un-American Activities*, 55–57.

23. Barrett, Jr., *Tenny Committee*, ix, 11–13, 25–30.

24. Ceplair and Englund, 210–11.

25. *Variety*, May 14, 1947.

26. Kahn, *Hollywood on Trial*; Goodman, *Committee*, 207–209 and 302–309.

27. Carr, 55–58 and 75.

28. *Time*, Oct. 29, 1947. See House Committee on Un-American Activities, *Hearings Regarding the Communist Infiltration of the Motion Picture Industry*, 80th Cong., 1st sess., Oct. 20–30, 1947. No lawyer was cited for Wood or McCarey. Mayer was represented by Paul V. McNutt, counsel for the Motion Picture Association and Association of Motion Pictures. See also Dmytryk, *It's a Hell of a Life But Not a Bad Living*, 94.

29. Cited in Kahn, 136–37. Italics are mine.

30. *Time*, Dec. 8, 1947, 28. Kanin, 214–15, reports on the maverick Harry Cohn's interesting response. Higham and Greenberg discuss Hollywood's other actions in churning out anti-Communist films, 16–17.

31. Dmytryk, 103.

32. *Variety*, Dec., 3, 1947, 4; Ceplair and Englund, 323. Reagan and Hubler, 158–59, give the Screen Actors Guild response.

33. Barrett, 75–79, 319, and 331; Ceplair and Englund, 386; see also Navasky, *Naming Names*.

34. *Los Angeles Times*, Sept. 23, 1950; Ceplair and Englund, 349 and 362.

35. Rogell, interview with author; Ceplair and Englund, 368–69.

36. *New York Times*, Aug. 22, 1950.

37. Youngerman, interviews with author, Nov. 7, 1979 and May 27, 1980; *New York Times*, Aug. 27, 1950.

38. *New York Times*, Sept. 7, 1950.

39. Rogell, interview with author; *New York Times*, Sept. 10 and 24, 1950.

40. *New York Times*, Oct. 14, 1950; Geist, *Pictures Will Talk*, 181–83; *Variety*, Oct. 11, 1950, pp. 3 and 61.

41. *Variety*, Oct. 18, 1950, pp. 3, 22; Geist, 188–89;*New York Times*, Oct. 16, 1950; Rogell, interview with author; *Hollywood Reporter,* Oct. 17, 1950.

42. Geist, 173–79, 191, 194–95; *Hollywood Reporter,* Oct. 23, 24, 1950. *Variety*, Oct. 25, 1950, pp. 5 and 16; Rogell, interview with author.

43. *Variety*, Oct. 25, 1950, p. 3.

44. Youngerman, interview with author, July 7, 1979; Rogell, interview with author.

45. Rogell, interview with author.

46. *Time*, Apr. 23, 1951, p. 104; Capra, 428–29.

47. Capra, 428–29; Capra, interview with author.

48. Rogell, interview with author.

49. *Variety*, Nov. 17, 1954, p. 6. See also MWW to Westbrook Pegler, Nov. 30, 1945, in Subject File—Libel Suits, Quentin Reynolds, box 57, Pegler Papers.

50. MWW address, "Women and Government in Washington," Nov. 20, 1952 (in the possession of Grace Knoeller). A letter from MWW to Knoeller, Dec. 2, 1952, acknowledged that Annabel Matthews had collected much of the data for the speech (in the possession of Grace Knoeller).

51. MWW to Laura and Carl Lomen, Mar. 31, 1951, Lomen Papers.

52. MWW to the Lomens, n.d. (probably 1955), Lomen Papers.

53. "Women and Government in Washington," Knoeller Papers.

54. *Los Angeles Times*, Oct. 23, 1952.

55. Ibid., Oct. 31, 1952.

56. Ibid., Oct. 23, 1952; MWW to Grace Knoeller, Dec. 2, 1952 (in the possession of Grace Knoeller).

57. *Barbara R. Smith* v. *Walter G. Smith*, respondent's reply brief, 1st Civil 15803, District Court of Appeal, First Appellate District, California. Of counsel: Mabel Walker Willebrandt and Dwain L. Clark, Feb., 1955, 15–17, 35–41, 44–50, 88–89. MWW to Grace Knoeller, Feb. 3, 1955 (in the possession of Grace Knoeller).

58. MWW to Grace Knoeller, Feb. 3, 1955 (in the possession of Grace Knoeller).

59. For California background to 1940 Republican convention see *Los Angeles Times* series, June 23, 24, 26, 28, 1940. MWW's friend Harold Jones outlined the state's situation to Robert Taft, Sept. 29, 1939, Political File, 1940, California, box 122, Taft Papers; *Los Angeles Times*, June 28, 1940.

60. Ida Koverman to Herbert Hoover, Apr. 11, 1944, Post-Presidential File, box 397, HHP.

61. MWW to Mrs. Katharine Kennedy Brown, Sept. 5, 1947, Political File, 1948 Campaign, box 171, Taft Papers.

62. Taft to Clarence Brown, Jan. 23, 1948, box 171, Taft Papers. See also Trips 1947–48, Taft to Harold A. Jones, Aug. 18 and 25, 1947, Jones to Taft, Aug. 13, 1947, and Taft to Frank Doherty, Oct. 9, 1947, box 171, Taft Papers.

63. Frank Doherty to Clarence Brown, May 28, 1948, Political File, Campaign Miscellany, Delegates, 1947–48, box 230, Taft Papers; see also *Los Angeles Times*, June 17 and 20, 1940.

64. L. Guylay to Taft and Congressman Brown, Mar. 18, 1948; Guylay memorandum on Citizens Committee for Taft, Political File, box 171, Taft Papers.

65. *Los Angeles Times*, Oct. 28, 1948. She sent the press release to Herbert Hoover, Sept. 7, 1948, Post-Presidential File, Individual—Mabel Walker Willebrandt, box 558, HHP.

66. MWW to Herbert Hoover, Nov. 11, 1948, Post-Presidential File, box 558, HHP.

67. Ibid.

68. MWW to Robert Taft, Nov. 20, 1951; see also Taft to MWW, Feb. 7 and April 27, 1951, California, States File—W, Political File, 1952 Campaign, box 329, Taft Papers.

69. MWW to Robert Taft, Feb. 22, 1952, Political File, 1952 Campaign, box 329, Taft Papers.

70. Taft to MWW, Mar. 8, 1952, ibid.

71. MWW to Taft, March 17, 1952, MWW to Katharine Kennedy Brown, Apr. 18, 1952, ibid.

72. Frank Doherty to Taft, Mar. 3, 1952, Supporters of Taft File, box 333, Taft Papers; see also Supporters of Taft File, California Miscellany, Feb. 22, 1952, box 330, and Lawyers for Taft, Political File, box 433, Taft Papers. For Warren's campaign see Thomas Mellen, Republican Campaigns of 1950 and 1952, Earl Warren's Campaigns, vol. 2, Earl Warren Oral History Project, and Kenneth McCormac, "The Conservative Republicans of 1952," vol. 3, Earl Warren Oral History Project.

73. MWW to Robert Taft, Aug. 1952, Political File, 1952 Campaign, and Taft's response, Aug. 13, 1952, to MWW, box 329, Taft Papers.

74. MWW to Grace Knoeller, Dec. 9, 1956, and MWW to Paula Knoeller Gore, Oct. 7, 1959 (in the possession of Grace Knoeller).

75. An account of this Willebrandt speech is in the *Los Angeles Times*, "Before We Adjourn," Nov. 30, 1952 (typescript in the possession of Grace Knoeller).

76. MWW to Grace Knoeller, Nov. 3, 1960, and Nov. 14 and 15, 1962 (in the possession of Grace Knoeller).

77. MWW statement, Dec. 9, 1924, MWWP.

78. MWW to parents, Christmas 1924, MWWP.

79. Mrs. Walker to MWW, n.d. (probably autumn 1923), MWWP.

80. Grace Knoeller and Paula Knoeller Gore, interview with author, Nov. 7, 1979; Dr. Mary Ellen Collins, interview with author; *Los Angeles Times*, Sept. 11, 1935; *Newsweek*, Sept. 28, 1935, p. 26. MWW was a fast, determined driver with several speeding citations. See *Los Angeles Times*, Feb. 27, 1923, and *New York Times*, Feb. 18 and 22, 1930. As her friend Paula Knoeller Gore explained, "She just started out and drove straight ahead to where she was going" (interview with author, June 10, 1980).

81. Grace Knoeller, interview with author, Oct. 10, 1979.

82. Frank Capra, interview with author.

83. Judge John J. Sirica, interview with author.

84. MWW to Father Sylvan, Mar. 28, 1954 (copy attached to letter from MWW to Grace Knoeller, Apr. 1, 1954, in the possession of Grace Knoeller).

85. MWW to Grace Knoeller, Feb. 16, 1953 (in the possession of Grace Knoeller).

86. MWW, "Our Western Christmas Trees." *The Island Lantern*, in which this article appeared, is the publication of the U.S. Penitentiary at McNeil Island, Washington.

87. *Los Angeles Times,* July 17, 23, 24, 1940.

88. *Los Angeles Times*, July 27, 1940. MWW precipitated the action by moving to sell the house and force Maud Brown out. See MWW to father, Feb. 8, 1940, MWWP.

89. *Los Angeles Times*, July 27, 1940.

90. D.W. Walker to Laura Lomen, Jan. 2, 1942, Lomen Papers; MWW to Mrs. Anna M. Griffiths, Dec. 23, 1942, and Anna M. Griffiths to MWW, Dec. 13 and 19, 1942, MWWP. Mrs. Griffiths was the first of a series of relatives Willebrandt contacted to be with her father.

91. D.W. Walker, "Our trip to Nome Alaska and Return,"MWWP. MWW carefully checked his health before the journey (Paul A. Ferrier, M.D., to MWW, May 11, 1946, MWWP); MWW to Laura and Carl Lomen, July 24, 1947, Lomen Papers.

92. MWW to Family and Friends of D.W. Walker, Aug. 27, 1954, MWWP.

93. MWW to Grace Knoeller, Aug. 30, 1954 (in the possession of Grace Knoeller); DVD, interview with author, Oct. 1978.

94. DVD, interview with author, Oct. 1978; Hedda Hopper note in her column, June 29, 1944, *Chicago Tribune*, DVD to author, Jan. 2, 1980.

95. Hendrick and Dorothy Van Dyke, interview with author, Oct. 1978.

96. MWW to David Van Dyke, Oct. 12, 1961, May 23, July 1 and 20, 1962 (in the possession of DVD).

97. MWW to David Van Dyke, May 23, 1962 (in the possession of DVD).

98. MWW to DVD, Oct. 1, 1954, MWWP.

99. MWW to DVD, n.d. (perhaps the summer of 1946 en route to Alaska).

100. Grace Knoeller, interview with author, June 1979.

101. Calvin and Mary Claggett, interview with author, June 28, 1979.

102. Dr. Mary Ellen Collins, interview with author.

103. MWW to Grace Knoeller, Nov. 24, 1961 (in the possession of Grace Knoeller); Minnie and Mabel Wells, interview with author.

104. MWW to Grace Knoeller, Feb. 3, 1955 (in the possession of Grace Knoeller). Letters from MWW to Knoeller discuss the illness of Calvin Claggett and the sale of the Indio ranch for Federal Uranium stock. MWW moved to 9145 St. Ives Drive, Hollywood. Dr. Mary Ellen Collins, in an interview with the author, noted MWW's helpfulness to her in starting her practice and to other young professionals. MWW to DeWitt Wallace, May 2, 1960, MWW to John Allen, June 13, 1960, and Allen to MWW, Feb. 8 and July 13, 1961, MWW to Laura Lomen, Mar. 2 and July 17, 1961, Lomen Papers; MWW to Grace Knoeller, Mar. 5, 1957, Dec. 28, 1959, Mar. 4, 1958, May 6, 1959 (in the possession of Grace Knoeller).

105. Dr. Mary Ellen Collins, interview with author; MWW to Laura and Carl Lomen, Dec. 9, 1956, Lomen Papers.

106. MWW to Jan Van Dyke, Feb. 16, 1962 (in the possession of DVD).

107. MWW to Grace Knoeller, Nov. 24, 1961 (in the possession of Grace Knoeller). The *St. Louis Post Dispatch* featured her October visit in an article, "Along Came Mabel," Oct. 15, 1961.

108. MWW to Grace Knoeller, Nov. 3, 1960 (in the possession of Grace Knoeller). Her retirement card finally was sent as a New Year's greeting for 1962.

109. Dr. Mary Ellen Collins and Judge John J. Sirica, interviews with author.

110. Grace Knoeller, Oct. 1979, and Dr. Mary Ellen Collins, interviews with author.

111. Grace Knoeller, Oct. 1979, and Jacqueline Cochran, interviews with author.

112. MWW to Jan Van Dyke, Feb. 16, 1962 (in the possession of DVD); MWW to Grace Knoeller, Jan. 3, 1961, and July 1, 1961 (in the possession of Grace Knoeller).

113. MWW to Grace Knoeller, June 6, 1961 (in the possession of Grace Knoeller).

114. MWW to Grace Knoeller, Oct. 10, 1961 (in the possession of Grace Knoeller).

115. MWW to Grace Knoeller, Nov. 14 and 15, 1962 (in the possession of Grace Knoeller).

116. DVD to Father Finnerty, who said the requiem mass, Apr. 8, 1963, MWWP. The quote from Timothy is from that source and differs slightly from the King James version of the Bible. The obituary was in the *Los Angeles Times*, Apr. 7, 1963 (clipping in MWWP).

117. MWW to Grace Knoeller, July 1, 1961 (in the possession of Grace Knoeller).

Bibliography

ARCHIVES AND MANUSCRIPT COLLECTIONS

Allen, Florence E. Papers. Western Reserve Historical Society, Cleveland, and Library of Congress.

Allen, Henry J. Papers. Library of Congress.

Arizona State University. Archives. Tempe, Arizona.

Black, Hugo. Papers. Library of Congress.

Borah, William. Papers. Library of Congress.

Brandeis, Louis D. Papers. University of Louisville Library, Louisville, Ky.

Brown, Walter F. Papers. Ohio Historical Society, Columbus, Ohio.

Bullock, Georgia. Papers. University of California, Los Angeles.

Coolidge, Calvin. Papers. Library of Congress.

Daugherty, Harry M. Papers. Ohio Historical Society, Columbus, Ohio.

Dickson, Edward A. Papers. University of California, Los Angeles.

Earhart, Amelia. Papers. Schlesinger Library, Radcliffe College, Cambridge, Mass.

Edson, Katherine Philips. Papers. University of California, Los Angeles.

General Federation of Women's Clubs. Archives. GFWC Headquarters, Washington, D.C.

Harding, Warren G. Papers. Library of Congress.

Hodder, Jessie. Papers. Schlesinger Library, Radcliffe College, Cambridge, Mass.

Hoover, Herbert. Papers. Herbert Hoover Presidential Library, West Branch, Iowa.

Ickes, Harold. Papers. Library of Congress.

Johnson, Hiram. Papers. Bancroft Library, University of California, Berkeley.

Knoeller, Grace. Papers. Upper Marlboro, Md.

Lomen, Carl. Papers. University of Alaska, Fairbanks.

McCarey, Leo. Papers. American Film Institute, Los Angeles.

Matthews, Annabel. Papers. Schlesinger Library, Radcliffe College, Cambridge, Mass.

Mitchell, William D. Papers. Minnesota Historical Society, St. Paul, Minn.

National League of Women Voters. Papers. Library of Congress.

Park College. Archives. Parkville, Mo.

Pegler, Westbrook. Papers. Herbert Hoover Presidential Library, West Branch, Iowa.

Pope, James H. Papers. University of California, Los Angeles.

Roosevelt, Eleanor. Papers. Franklin D. Roosevelt Presidential Library, Hyde Park, N.Y.

Roosevelt, Franklin D. Papers. Franklin D. Roosevelt Presidential Library, Hyde Park, N.Y.

Stefansson, Vilhjalmur. Papers. Baker Memorial Library, Dartmouth College, Hanover, N.H.

Stone, Harlan Fiske. Papers. Library of Congress.

Sullivan, Mark. Papers. Hoover Institution, Stanford, Calif.

Taft, Robert. Papers. Library of Congress.

Taft, William Howard. Papers. Library of Congress.

U.S. Bureau of Prisons. Records. Record Group 129. National Archives, Washington, D.C.

U.S. Department of Agriculture. Records of the Farm Credit Administration, Federal Farm Board Minutes, vols. 1–9. Record Group 103. National Archives, Washington, D.C.

U.S. Department of the Interior. Records of the Bureau of Indian Affairs, Alaska Division, Reindeer Commission. Record Group 75. National Archives, Washington, D.C.

U.S. Department of Justice. Records. Record Group 60. National Archives, Washington, D.C., and Washington National Records Center, Suitland, Md.

U.S. Department of State. Decimal File. Record Group 59. National Archives, Washington, D.C..

U.S. Federal Communications Commission. Records. Record Group 173. Washington National Records Center, Suitland, Md.

U.S. Post Office Department. Air Mail Service, Black Committee Investigation, 1933–34. Record Group 28. National Archives, Washington, D.C.

U.S. Senate. Records of the U.S. Senate Special Committee on Air–Ocean Mail Contracts (Black Committee), 74th Congress. Record Group 46. National Archives, Washington, D.C.

University of Southern California. Archives. Los Angeles.

Van Waters, Miriam. Papers. Schlesinger Library, Radcliffe College, Cambridge, Mass.

Wilbur, Ray Lyman. Papers. Hoover Institution, Stanford, Calif.

Willebrandt, Mabel Walker. Papers. Library of Congress.

Willis, Frank B. Papers. Ohio Historical Society, Columbus, Ohio.

Women's Joint Congressional Committee. Papers. Library of Congress.

Women's Trade Union League. Papers. Library of Congress.

Work, Hubert. Papers. Hoover Institution, Stanford, Calif.

PUBLIC DOCUMENTS

Annual Report, Police Department, City of Los Angeles, for the Fiscal Year Ending June 30, 1917.

Annual Report, Police Department, City of Los Angeles, for the Fiscal Year Ending June 30, 1918.

Annual Report, U.S. Penitentiary, Atlanta, Georgia, for Fiscal Year Ending June 30, 1925. Report prepared by John W. Snook, Warden.

Annual Report, U.S. Penitentiary, Leavenworth, Kansas, for Fiscal Year Ending June 30, 1926.

Barbara R. Smith v. Walter G. Smith, 1st Civil 15803, District Court of Appeal, First Appellate District, California, respondent's reply brief. Of Counsel: Mabel Walker Willebrandt and D. Clark, Feb. 1955.

Bowers, Collector v. Kerbaugh Empire Co. 271 U.S. 170 (1926).

Cunard Steamship Co. v. *Mellon, Secretary of the Treasury.* 262 U.S. 100 (1923).

Donnelly v. *United States.* 276 U.S. 505 (1928).

Edwards v. *Chile Copper Co.* 276 U.S. 452 (1925).

Federal Radio Commission v. *Nelson Brothers Bond and Mortgage Co.*, 289 U.S. 266 (1933).

Frederick L. Swetland and Raymond H. Swetland v. *Curtiss Airports Corporation, Ohio Air Terminals, Inc., and Curtiss Flying Service, Inc.*, nos. 5812 and 5813. U.S. Circuit Court of Appeals, 6th Circuit. Brief of the Aviation Corporation as Amicus Curiae.

Hazeltine Corp. v. *E.A. Wildermuth.* 6 U.S. Pat. Q. (1930).

Heiner, Collector v. Colonial Trust Co. 275 U.S. 232 (1927).

Helmich v. *Hellman.* 276 U.S. 233 (1927).

Helmich, Collector v. *Missouri Pacific RR Co.* 273 U.S. 242 (1927).

Johnson-Kennedy Radio Corporation (Station WJKS), Intervener v. *Nelson Brothers Bond and Mortgage Co. (Station WIBO), on writs of certiorari to the Court of Appeals of the District of Columbia*, nos. 659 and 660, Oct. 1932, U.S. Supreme Court. Brief for Johnson-Kennedy Radio Corporation (Station WJKS), Intervener, Petitioner. Mabel Walker Willebrandt.

Los Angeles. City Council Records. Vols. 100–109.

Marron v. *United States.* 275 U.S. 185 (1927).

Olmstead v. *United States.* 275 U.S. 493 (1927).

Taft v. *United States.* 278 U.S. 470 (1929).

U.S. Congress. House. Committee on Un-American Activities. *Hearings Regarding the Communist Infiltration of the Motion Picture Industry. Oct. 20–30, 1947.* 80th Cong., 1st sess. Washington: GPO, 1947.

————. House. Judiciary Committee. *Hearings on H.R. 685, H.R. 2689 and H.R. 4125.* 68th Cong., 1st sess. Washington: GPO, 1924.

———. House. Judiciary Committee. *Report No. 1496*. 67th Cong., 4th sess. Washington: GPO, 1923.

———. Senate. *Investigation of Air Mail and Ocean Mail Contracts: Hearings before a Special Committee on Investigation of Air Mail and Ocean Mail Contracts*. 73d Cong. 2d sess., Jan. 9–18, 1934. Washington: GPO, 1934.

———. Senate. *Investigation of the Honorable Harry M. Daugherty*. Select Committee, 68th Cong., 1st sess. 11 vols. Washington: GPO, 1924.

U.S. Department of Justice. *Annual Report of the Attorney General of the United States*. Washington: GPO, 1922–1929.

———. *Report Submitted to President Coolidge by Attorney General H.M. Daugherty concerning Prohibition Litigation throughout the United States, Covering the Period January 16, 1920, to June 16, 1923*. Washington: GPO, 1923.

U.S. Supreme Court. *United States Reports*. Oct. 1921–Oct. 1929. Washington: GPO, 1922–30.

U.S. Treasury Department. Bureau of Prohibition. *Digest of Supreme Court Decisions Interpreting the National Prohibition Act and Willis-Campbell Act*. Washington: GPO, 1929.

INTERVIEWS AND ORAL HISTORIES

Adams, Leon. "The California Wine Industry." Oral history. California Wine Industry Oral History Project. Bancroft Library, University of California, Berkeley.

Bentley, Judge Fay L. Interview with author. Washington, D.C., Mar. 10, 1979.

Biane, Philo. "Wine Making in Southern California and Recollections of Fruit Industries, Ltd." Oral history. California Wine Industry Oral History Project. Bancroft Library, University of California, Berkeley.

Capra, Frank. Interview with author. Washington, D.C., Oct. 12, 1979.

Claggett, Calvin and Mary. Interview with author. Indio, Calif., July 25, 1979.

Cochran, Jacqueline. Interview with author. Indio, Calif., Nov. 7, 1979.

Collins, Dr. Mary Ellen. Interview with author. Oceanside, Calif., July 24, 1979.

Collins, Myra Dell. Interview with author. Alhambra, Calif., July 1978.

Foster, Louise. Interviews with author. Washington, D.C., May 1979 and Feb. 1981.

Gore, Paula Knoeller. Interviews with author. Upper Marlboro, Md., May 1978–Feb. 1982.

Griswold, Erwin N. Interview with author. Washington, D.C., Feb. 9, 1978.

Horowitz, Fred. Interview with author. Los Angeles, Calif., July 23, 1979.

Joslyn, Maynard A. "A Technologist Views the California Wine Industry." Oral history. California Wine Industry Oral History Project. Bancroft Library, University of California, Berkeley.

Knoeller, Grace B. Interviews with author. Upper Marlboro, Md., May 1978–Feb. 1982.

Lahey, Judge May. Interview with author. Los Angeles, Calif., July 1978.

Lambie, Margaret. Interview with author. Boston, Mass., Jan. 1979.

McCarey, Leo. Oral History 2. Oral History Collection. Louis B. Mayer Film History. American Film Institute. Los Angeles, Calif.

Mason, Mrs. Lowell B. (Rose d'Amore). Interview with author. Washington, D.C., Oct. 1979.

Mortensen, Virginia Kellogg. Telephone interview with author. Los Angeles, Calif., May 29, 1980.

Perelli-Minnetti, Antonio. "A Life in Wine Making." Oral history. California Wine Industry Oral History Project. Bancroft Library, University of California, Berkeley.

Raymond, Gene. Interview with author. Los Angeles, Calif., July 24, 1979.

Rogell, Albert. Interview with author. Los Angeles, Calif., May 29, 1980.

Sirica, Judge John J. Interview with author. Washington, D.C., July 8, 1978.

Taylor, Walter. Interview with author. Menlo Park, Calif., July 21, 1979.

Van Dyke, Dorothy. Interviews with author. Cannon Beach, Ore., Oct. 20, 1978, and July 28, 1979.

Van Dyke, Hendrick. Interview with author. Cannon Beach, Ore., Oct. 20, 1978.

Warren, Earl. Earl Warren Oral History Project. Bancroft Library, University of California, Berkeley.

Wells, Minnie (Mrs. Ira Wells) and Mabel. Interview with author. Fullerton, Calif., July 24, 1979.

Youngerman, Joseph. Interviews with author. Los Angeles, Calif., July 7, 1979, and May 28, 1980.

WORKS BY MABEL WALKER WILLEBRANDT

The College Student as an Immediate Citizen. New York: Citizens' Committee of One Thousand, 1924.

"Comment on Uniform Aviation Liability Act." *Journal of Air Law* 9 (Oct. 1928): 675–78.

"The Department of Justice and Some Problems of Enforcement." In *Law vs. Lawlessness*, ed. Fred B. Smith, pp. 78–91. New York: Revell, 1924.

"First Impressions." *Good Housekeeping*, May 1928, pp. 38–39, 219–29.

"Give Women a Fighting Chance!" *Smart Set*, Feb. 1930, pp. 24–26, 106–107.

"Half or Whole-Hearted Prohibition." *Woman Citizen*, Feb. 23, 1924, pp. 16–17.

"The Increasing Burden of Taxation." *Nebraska Law Bulletin* 12 (July 1933): 36–81.

"The Inns of Court." *Phi Delta Delta* 30 (Nov. 1951): 27–33.

The Inside of Prohibition. Indianapolis: Bobbs-Merrill, 1929.

"The Inside of Prohibition." *Washington Evening Star*, Aug. 1929.

"The National Prohibition Act in Its Relation to Section 3450 R.S." *Case and Comment* 34 (Jan.–Mar. 1928): 3–6.

"Our Western Christmas Trees." *Island Lantern* 5 (Jan. 1929): 21–22.

"Popular Government and Public Commissions." LL.M. thesis, Univ. of Southern California, 1917.

"The Republican Platform as Viewed by Mrs. Mabel Walker Willebrandt." *McCall's Magazine*, Nov. 1928, pp. 18 and 119.

"Smart Washington after Six O'Clock." *Ladies' Home Journal*, July 1929, pp. 10–12.

"The U.S. Department of Justice—Its Work in Prosecuting Prohibition Cases." *Congressional Digest*, Oct. 1924, p. 11.

"Will You Help Keep the Law?" *Good Housekeeping*, Apr. 1924, pp. 72–73, 235–40.

"Women—and a Decadent Jury System," *McCall's Magazine*, May 1928, pp. 30 and 113–14.

OTHER WORKS

Aeronautical Chamber of Commerce of America, Inc. *The Aircraft Year Book*. 1930–37. New York: Van Nostrand, 1930–37.

Aldrich, C. Anderson, and Mary Aldrich. *Babies Are Human Beings. An Interpretation of Growth*. New York: Macmillan, 1944.

Allen, Florence E. *To Do Justly*. Cleveland: Press of Western Reserve, 1965.

Allvue, Glendon. *The Greatest Fox of Them All*. New York: Lyle Stuart, 1969.

Arnold, Anna E. *A History of Kansas*. Topeka: State of Kansas, 1931.

Atwood, Archdeacon. "Where Friendly Help Counts." *Spirit of the Missions*, May 1909, pp. 393–94.

Banner, Lois W. *Women in Modern America: A Brief History*. New York: Harcourt Brace, 1974.

Barnouw, Erik. *A Tower in Babel: A History of Broadcasting in the United States*. Vol. 1. New York: Oxford Univ. Press, 1966.

Barrett, Edward L., Jr. *The Tenny Committee: Legislative Investigation of Subversive Activities in California*. Ithaca: Cornell Univ. Press, 1951.

Bates, Sanford. *Prisons and Beyond*. New York: Macmillan, 1936.

"Battle of Reno." *Business Week*, Oct. 7, 1944, pp. 90–94.

Bennett, James V. *I Chose Prison*. Ed. Rodney Campbell. New York: Knopf, 1970.

Blair, Emily N. "The Case of Mrs. Willebrandt." *Woman's Journal* 14 (June 1929): 22–23.

Blair, Karen J. *The Clubwoman as Feminist: True Womanhood Reformers, 1868–1914*. New York: Holmes & Meier, 1980.

Blanchard, L.H. *Conquest of Southwest Kansas*. Wichita: Eagle Press, 1931.

Brandeis, Louis D. *Letters of Louis D. Brandeis*. Ed. Melvin I. Urofsky and David W. Levy. 5 vols. Albany: State Univ. Press of New York, 1971–78.

Breckinridge, Sophonisba P. *Women in the Twentieth Century: A Study of Their Political, Social and Economic Activities*. New York: Arno Press, 1972.

Briand, Paul L., Jr. *Daughter of the Sky: The Story of Amelia Earhart*. New York: Duell, Sloan & Pearce, 1960.

Brown, Anthony C. *The Last Hero: Wild Bill Donovan*. New York: Times Books, 1982.

Brown, Dorothy M. "Mabel Walker Willebrandt." In *Notable American Women: The Modern Period*, ed. Barbara Sicherman and Carol Hurd Green. Cambridge, Mass.: Harvard Univ. Press. 1980.

Buchanan, James E., ed. *Phoenix: A Chronological and Documentary History, 1865–1976*. Dobbs Ferry, N.Y.: Oceana Publications. 1978.

Burner, David. *Herbert Hoover: A Public Life*. New York: Knopf, 1979.

———. *The Politics of Provincialism: The Democratic Party in Transition, 1918–1932*. New York: Knopf, 1967.

Burnham, J.C. "New Perspectives on the Prohibition "Experiment" of the 1920's." *Journal of Social History* 2 (Fall 1968): 51–68.

Campbell, Litta Belle Hibben. *Here I Raise Mine Ebenezer..* New York: Simon & Schuster, 1963.

———. "A Tribute to the Founders of Phi Delta Delta." *Phi Delta Delta* 51 (Nov. 1973): 8–10.

Cannon, Robert C. *Van Dyke and the Mythical City, Hollywood*. Culver City, Calif.: Murray & Gee, 1948.

Capra, Frank. *The Name above the Title: An Autobiography*. New York: Macmillan, 1971.

Carr, Robert K. *The House Committee on Un-American Activities, 1945–1950*. Ithaca: Cornell Univ. Press, 1952.

Carrington, Thomas S. "The Evolution of the Lean-to." *Survey* 22 (July 17, 1900): 553–54.

Caughey, John. *Los Angeles: Biography of a City*. Berkeley: Univ. of California Press, 1977.

Ceplair, Larry, and Steven Englund. *The Inquisition in Hollywood: Politics in the Film Community, 1930–1960* Garden City, N.Y.: Anchor Press/ Doubleday, 1980.

"A Certain Lady." *Independent Woman* 6 (July 1927): 7, 40–41.

Chafe, William H. *The American Woman: Her Changing Social, Economic, and Political Roles, 1920–1970*. New York: Oxford Univ. Press, 1972.

Chambers, Clarke A. *Seedtime of Reform: American Social Service and Social Action, 1918–1933*. Minneapolis: Univ. of Minn. Press, 1963.

"Clara Shortridge Foltz." *Women's Law Journal* 16 (July 1928): 10–11.

Cochran, Jacqueline. *The Stars at Noon*. Boston: Little, Brown, 1954.

Codel, Martin. "The New Problems Radio Brings." *Nation's Business* 17 (July 1929): 132.

Coffey, Thomas M. *The Long Thirst: Prohibition in America, 1920–1933*. New York: Norton, 1975.

Commercial Club, ed. *Kansas City Illustrated, 1901*. Kansas City: Union Bank Note Co., 1901.

Cook, A. Clyde. "A Portia of the West." *Sunset* 59 (July 1927): 43–63.

Cook, Beverly B. "The First Woman Candidate for the Supreme Court." In *Yearbook 1981*, Supreme Court Historical Society, pp. 25–30.

David, Paul T. *The Economics of Air Mail Transportation*. Washington, D.C.: Brookings Institution, 1934.

Debs, Eugene V. "Behind Prison Walls." *Century* 104 (July 1922): 362–72.

Dick, Everett. *The Sod-House Frontier, 1854–1890*. Lincoln, Neb.: Johnson, 1954.

Disque, Brice P. "Prison Progress." *Atlantic Monthly* 129 (Mar. 1922): 330–37.

Dmytryk, Edward. *It's a Hell of a Life but Not a Bad Living*. New York: Times Books, 1978.

Doherty, Sarah Patten. "Sowing the Seed of Phi Delta Delta." *Phi Delta Delta* 51 (Nov. 1973): 4–6.

Dunne, Gerald T. *Hugo Black and the Judicial Tradition*. New York: Simon & Schuster, 1977.

Eggleston, Kenneth L. *Park College Centennial Sketches*. Parkville, Mo.: Centennial Committee, 1975.

Ehrenreich, Barbara, and Deirdre English. *For Her Own Good: 150 Years of the Experts' Advice to Women*. Garden City, N.Y.: Anchor Press/ Doubleday, 1979.

Facts of Record and Editorials Concerning the Impeachment Proceedings at Washington against Hon. Harry M. Daugherty. n.p., n.d.

Farmer, Hallie. "The Economic Background of Frontier Populism." *Mississippi Valley Historical Review* 10 (Mar. 1924): 406–27.

Filo, Barbara Ann. "Reclaiming Those Poor Unfortunates: The Movement to Establish the First Federal Prison for Women." Ph.D. diss., Boston Univ., 1982.

"The First Legal Lady of the Land." *Literary Digest* 76 (Mar. 31, 1923): 41–42.

Fischer, Christine, ed. *Let Them Speak for Themselves: Women in the American West, 1849–1900*. New York: Dutton, 1978.

Flynn, Elizabeth Gurley. *The Alderson Story*. New York: International Publishers, 1963.

Fogelson, Robert M. *The Fragmented Metropolis: Los Angeles, 1850–1930*. Cambridge, Mass.: Harvard Univ. Press, 1967.

Fontaine, Joan. *No Bed of Roses*. New York: Morrow, 1978.

Freedman, Estelle. "The New Woman: Changing Views of Women in the 1920s." *Journal of American History* 61 (Sept. 1974): 372–93.

———. *Their Sisters' Keepers: Women's Prison Reform in America, 1830–1930*. Ann Arbor: Univ. of Mich. Press, 1981.

"From Wonderland." *Time*, Oct. 27, 1947, p. 25.

Garvey, Daniel E. "Secretary Hoover and the Quest for Broadcast Regulation." *Journalism History* 3 (Autumn 1976): 66–70.

The Gentleman at the Keyhole. "Where Duty Lies." *Collier's*, Oct. 27, 1928, p. 45.

Geist, Kenneth L. *Pictures Will Talk: The Life and Films of Joseph L. Mankiewicz*. New York: Scribner's, 1978.

Gibson, Helen E. "Women's Prisons: Laboratories for Penal Reform." *Wisconsin Law Review*, no. 1 (1973): 20–33.

Giglio, James N. *H.M. Daugherty and the Politics of Expediency*. Kent, Ohio: Kent State Univ. Press, 1978.

Goodman, Walter. *The Committee: The Extraordinary Career of the House Committee on Un-American Activities*. New York: Farrar, Straus & Giroux, 1968.

Gottschalk, Stephen. *The Emergence of Christian Science in American Religious Life*. Berkeley: Univ. of California Press, 1973.

Gruberg, Martin. *Women in American Politics: An Assessment and Sourcebook*. Oshkosh, Wis.: Academia Press, 1968.

Gusfield, Joseph F. *Symbolic Crusade: Status Politics and the American Temperance Movement*. Urbana: Univ. of Illinois Press, 1963.

Hamilton, Virginia V. *Hugo Black: The Alabama Years*. Baton Rouge: Louisiana State Univ. Press, 1972.

Harbaugh, William H. *Lawyer's Lawyer: The Life of John W. Davis*. New York: Oxford Univ. Press, 1973.

Hard, Anne. "America's Portia." *New York Herald Tribune*, July 1, 1928.

Harris, Barbara. *Beyond Her Sphere: Women and the Professions in American History*. Westport, Conn.: Greenwood Press, 1978.

Harris, Mary Belle. *I Knew Them in Prison*. New York: Viking Press, 1942.

Haynes, Roy A. *Prohibition Inside Out*. Garden City, N.Y.: Doubleday, 1923.

Healy, Paul F. *Cissy: The Biography of Eleanor M. "Cissy" Patterson*. Garden City, N.Y.: Doubleday, 1966.

Hewes, Leslie. *The Suitcase Farming Frontier: A Study in the Historical Geography of the Central Great Plains*. Lincoln: Univ. of Nebraska Press, 1973.

Hichborn, Frank. *The Story of the Legislative Session of the California Legislature, 1921*. San Francisco: James Barry, 1922.

Hicks, John D. *The Populist Revolt*. Lincoln: Univ. of Nebraska Press, 1959.

Higham, Charles. *Cecil B. DeMille*. New York: Scribner's, 1973.

Higham, Charles, and Joel Greenberg. *Hollywood in the Forties*. New York: Paperback Library, 1970.

History of Adair, Sullivan, Putnam, Schuyler Counties, Missouri, Chicago: Goodspeed, 1888.

History of the National Federation of Business and Professional Women's Clubs, Inc., 1919–1944. Vol. 1. Washington, D.C.: National Federation of Business and Professional Women's Clubs, 1979.

Hohman, Leslie B. *As the Twig Is Bent*. New York: Macmillan, 1944.

Holbrook, Francis X. "Amelia Earhart's Final Flight." *U.S. Naval Institute Proceedings* 97 (Feb. 1971): 48–55.

Hoover, Herbert. *The Memoirs of Herbert Hoover: The Cabinet and the Presidency, 1920–33*. New York: Macmillan, 1952.

——— *The New Day: The Campaign Speeches of Herbert Hoover*. Stanford, Calif., 1928.

Hopkins, Ernest J., and Alfred Thomas, Jr. *The Arizona State University Story*. Phoenix: Southwest, 1960.

Hopper, Hedda. *From under My Hat*. Garden City, N.Y.: Doubleday, 1952.

———. *The Whole Truth and Nothing But*. Garden City, N.Y.: Doubleday, 1963.

Hunley, Annett F. "Early History of Phi Delta Delta." *Phi Delta Delta* 51 (Nov. 1973): 6–8.

Illustrated Historical Atlas of Putnam County, Missouri. Missouri: Edwards Bros., 1877.

Ise, John. *Sod and Stubble: The Story of a Kansas Homestead* Lincoln: Univ. of Nebraska Press, 1936.

Jacobs, Julius L. "California's Pioneer Wine Families." *California Historical Quarterly* 54 (Summer 1975): 148–49.

James, Edward T., Janet Wilson James, and Paul S. Boyer, eds. *Notable American Women, 1607–1950*. Cambridge, Mass.: Harvard Univ. Press, 1971.

Jeffrey, Julia R. *Frontier Women: The Trans-Mississippi West, 1840–1880*. New York: Hill & Wang, 1979.

Jensen, Joan M. "Annette Abbott Adams, Politician." *Pacific Historical Review* 35 (May 1966): 185–201.

Johns. Dorothy. *Victims of the System: How Crime Grows in Jail and City Hall*. Los Angeles: Lind Printing Co., 1908.

Josephson, Matthew, and Hannah Josephson. *Al Smith: Hero of the Cities*. Boston: Houghton Mifflin, 1964.

Kahn, Gordon. *Hollywood on Trial: The Story of the 10 Who Were Indicted*. New York: Boni & Gaer, 1948.

Kanin, Garson. *Hollywood: Stars and Starlets, Tycoons and Flesh Peddlers, Movie Makers and Money Makers, Frauds and Geniuses, Hopefuls and Has Beens, Great Lovers and Sex Symbols*. New York: Viking Press, 1974.

Kelly, Charles J., Jr. *The Sky's the Limit: The History of the Airlines*. New York: Coward-McCann, 1963.

Keyes, Frances Parkinson. "Homes of Outstanding American Women." *Better Homes and Gardens*, Mar. 1928, pp. 11–14.

Kohler, John. *Ardent Spirits: The Rise and Fall of Prohibition*. New York: Putnam, 1973.

Komons, Nick A. *Bonfires to Beacons: Federal Civil Aviation Policy under the Air Commerce Act, 1926–1938*. Washington, D.C.: U.S. Department of Transportation, Federal Aviation Admin., 1978.

Kyvig, David E. *Repealing National Prohibition*. Chicago: Univ. of Chicago Press, 1979.

"Last Mail Contracts Awarded," *Aviation* 36 (July 1934): 220.

Lemons, J. Stanley. *The Woman Citizen: Social Feminism in the 1920's*. Urbana: Univ. of Illinois Press, 1973.

Leonard, John W., ed. *Who's Who in Finance*. New York: Joseph & Sefton, 1911.

Levin, Thomas David. *Law and Lawyers: 128 Years in the History of Los Angeles as Seen from the City Attorney's Office*. n.p., n.d.

Lewisohn, Adolph. "Prisons and Prison Labor." *Century* 106 (July 1923): 399–404.

———. "A Programme for Prison Reform" *Atlantic Monthly* 131 (Mar., 1923): 425–28.

Lichtman, Allan J. *Prejudice and the Old Politics: The Presidential Election of 1928*. Chapel Hill: Univ. of North Carolina Press, 1979.

Lomen, Carl J. *Fifty Years in Alaska*. New York: David McKay, 1954.

McAfee, Joseph E. *A Mid-West Adventure in Education*. Kansas City: Alumni Parkana Committee, 1937.

———. *College Pioneering*. Kansas City: Alumni Parkana Committee, 1938.

McCoy, Donald. *Calvin Coolidge: The Quiet President*. New York: Macmillan, 1967.

McGee, Dr. W.J. "The Desert Cure." *Independent* 59 (Dec. 1905), 669–72.

McGroarty, John S. *Los Angeles. From the Mountains to the Sea*. Vol. 2. New York: American Historical Society, 1921.

McIntire, Vice Admiral Ross. *White House Physician*. New York: Putnam, 1946.

McNeal, T.A. *When Kansas Was Young*. Topeka: Capper, 1934.

McReynolds, Edwin C. *Oklahoma: A History of the Frontier State*. Norman: Univ. of Oklahoma Press, 1954.

McWilliams, Carey. *California: The Great Exception*. Westport, Conn.: Greenwood Press, 1971.

Martin, John S. "Mrs. Firebrand." *New Yorker*, Feb. 16, 1929, pp. 23–26.

Marx, Samuel. *Mayer and Thalberg: The Make-Believe Saints*. New York: Random House, 1975.

Mason, Alpheus T. *Harlan Fiske Stone: Pillar of the Law*. New York: Viking Press, 1956.

Maxwell, Gilbert, *Helen Morgan: Her Life and Legend*. New York: Hawthorn, 1965.

Mayer, Robert, ed. *Los Angeles: A Chronological and Documentary History*. Dobbs Ferry, N.Y.: Oceana Publications, 1978.

Meers, John R. "The California Wine and Grape Industry and Prohibition." *California Historical Quarterly* 44 (Mar. 1967), 19–31.

Mennell, Robert M. "Miriam Van Waters," In *Notable American Women: The Modern Period*, ed. Barbara Sicherman and Carol Hurd Green, pp. 709–11. Cambridge, Mass.: Harvard Univ. Press, 1980.

Merz, Charles. *The Dry Decade*. Seattle: Univ. of Washington Press, 1969.

Michigan: A Guide to the Wolverine State. WPA American Guide Series. New York: Oxford Univ. Press.

Missouri: A Guide to the Show-Me State. WPA American Guide Series. New York: Duell, Sloan & Pearce, 1941.

Moore, Edmund A. *A Catholic Runs for President: The Campaign of 1928*. New York: Ronald Press, 1956.

Morrison, Glenda E. "Women's Participation in the 1928 Presidential Campaign." Ph.D. diss., Univ. of Kansas, 1978.

"Movie Pact Flops." *Business Week*, June 20, 1942, pp. 33–34.

Mowry, George E. *The California Progressives*. Chicago: Quadrangle, 1951.

"Mrs. Willebrandt Runs Amuck," *Independent* 190 (Sept. 22, 1928): 269.

"Mrs. Willebrandt's Appeal to the Methodists." *Literary Digest*, Sept. 29, 1928, pp. 14–15.

Murray, Robert F. *The Harding Era*. Minneapolis: Univ. of Minnesota Press, 1969.

Navasky, Victor. *Naming Names*. New York: Viking Press, 1980.

Niles, Emery H. "The Present Status of the Ownership of Air Space." *Air Law Review* 5 (Apr. 1934), 132–56.

O'Donnell, Jack. "Can This Woman Make America Dry?" *Collier's*, Aug. 9, 1923, p. 16.

O'Neill, William. *Divorce in the Progressive Era*. New Haven: Yale Univ. Press, 1967.

――――. *Everyone Was Brave: A History of Feminism in America*. Chicago: Quadrangle, 1971.

"Operation Hollywood." *Time*, May 7, 1951, pp. 98 and 100.

Osborn, Michael, and Joseph Riggs. *"Mr. Mac," William P. MacCracken, Jr.* Memphis: Southern College of Optometry, 1970.

Ostrander, Glenn M. *The Prohibition Movement in California, 1848–1957*. Berkeley: Univ. of California Press, 1957.

Peel, Roy V., and Thomas C. Donnelly. *The 1928 Campaign: An Analysis*. New York: Richard R. Smith, 1931.

"Pink Slips." *Time*, Dec. 8, 1947, p. 28.

Pivar, David "Cleansing the Nation: The War on Prostitution, 1917–21," *Prologue* 12 (Spring 1980): 29–40.

Plat Book of Putnam County Missouri. Missouri Publishing Co., 1897.

"Portia in Wonderland." *American Mercury*, July 1929, pp. 332–38.

"The Post Office and Air Transport." *Aviation* 29 (Oct. 1930): 194–95.

Powdermaker, Hortense. *Hollywood the Dream Factory: An Anthropologist Looks at the Movie Makers*. Boston: Little, Brown, 1950.

Powell, Lawrence C. *Arizona: A Bicentennial History*. New York: Norton, 1976.

Reagan, Ronald, and Richard Hubler. *Where's the Rest of Me?* New York: Duell, Sloan & Pearce, 1965.

Report of the Standing Committee on Aeronautical Law. 54th Annual Meeting of the American Bar Assoc. Annual Report of the American Bar Assoc. vol. 56. Balto: Lord Baltimore Press, 1931.

Riegel, Robert E. *America Moves West*. New York: Holt, 1956.

Robinson, W.W. *Lawyers of Los Angeles: A History of the Los Angeles Bar Association and of the Bar of Los Angeles County*. Los Angeles: Bar Association, 1959.

――――. *Los Angeles: A Profile*. Norman: Univ. of Oklahoma Press, 1968.

Rogin, Michael. "Progressivism and the California Electorate." *Journal of American History* 55 (Sept. 1968): 297–314.

Roosevelt, Franklin D. *Public Papers and Addresses of Franklin D. Roosevelt*. Vol. 4. New York: Random House, 1935.

――――. *Public Papers and Addresses of Franklin D. Roosevelt*. Vols. 7 and 8. New York: Macmillan, 1941.

Rosen, Philip T. *The Modern Stentors: Radio Broadcasters and the Federal Government, 1920–1934*. Westport, Conn: Greenwood Press, 1980.

Russell, Francis. *The Shadow of Blooming Grove: Warren G. Harding in His Times*. New York: McGraw-Hill, 1968.

St. Johns, Adela Rogers. *The Honeycomb*. New York: New American Library, 1969.

————. *Some Are Born Great*. Bergenfield, N.J.: New American Library, 1975.

Sarris, Andrew. *The American Cinema: Directors and Directions, 1929–1968*. New York: Dutton, 1968.

Schiesl, Martin J. "Progressive Reform in Los Angeles under Mayor Alexander, 1909–1913." *California Historical Quarterly* 54 (Spring 1975): 37–56.

Schmeckebier, Laurence F. *The Bureau of Prohibition: Its History, Activities and Organization*. Washington, D.C.: Brookings Institution, 1929.

————. *The Federal Radio Commission: Its History, Activities and Organization*. Washington, D.C.: Brookings Institution, 1932.

Schmidhauser, John R. *Judges and Justices: The Federal Appellate Judiciary*. Boston: Little, Brown, 1979.

Schweber-Koren, Claudine. "The Alderson Movement: Women and Prisons and Penal Reform in the 1920s." Paper presented to the Berkshire Conference on Women's History, June 1975.

Seaver, Mabel. *Kansas: Its Geography, History, and Government*. Boston: Allyn & Bacon, 1947.

"Second Thoughts on Air Mail Certificates." *Aviation* 28 (June 14, 1930): 1159.

Sicherman, Barbara, and Carol Hurd Green, eds. *Notable American Women: The Modern Period*. Cambridge, Mass.: Harvard Univ. Press, 1980.

Silva, Ruth C. *Rum, Religion and Votes, 1928, Re-Examined*. University Park: Pennsylvania State Univ. Press, 1962.

Simnell, V.E. "Oratory in the 1928 Presidential Campaign," *Quarterly Journal of Speech* 15 (Feb. 1929): 28–32.

Sinclair, Andrew. *Prohibition: The Era of Excess*. Boston: Little, Brown, 1962.

Sirica, John J. *To Set the Record Straight*. New York: Norton, 1979.

Smith, Alfred E. *The Campaign Addresses of Governor Alfred E. Smith*. Washington, D.C.: Democratic National Committee, 1929.

———— *Up to Now*. New York: Viking Press, 1929.

Smith, C.R. "A.A.: American Airlines since 1926." Newcomen Address. San Francisco, June 1954.

Smith, Helena Huntington. "Mrs. Willebrandt." *Outlook and Independent*, Oct. 24, 1928, pp. 105–108.

Smith, Henry Ladd. *Airways: The History of Commercial Aviation in the United States*. New York: Knopf, 1942.

Stange, Douglas C. "Al Smith and the Republican Party at Prayer: The Lutheran Vote—1928." *Review of Politics* 32 (July 1970): 347–64.

Steuart, Justin. *Wayne Wheeler, Dry Boss*. Westport, Conn.,: Greenwood Press, 1928.

The Story of the 91st Division. San Francisco: 91st Division Publications Committee, 1919.

Strakosch, Avery. "A Woman in Law." *Saturday Evening Post*, Sept. 24, 1927, pp. 17, 190–96.

Stratton, Joanna L. *Frontier Women: Voices from the Kansas Frontier*. New York: Simon & Schuster, 1981.

Stricker, Frank. "Cookbooks and Law Books: The Hidden History of Career Women In Twentieth Century America." In *A Heritage of Her Own*, ed. Nancy F. Cott and Elizabeth H. Pleck, pp. 476–92. New York: Simon & Schuster, 1979.

Tebbel, John. *The Life and Times of William Randolph Hearst*. New York: Dutton, 1952.

Thomas, Bob, ed. *Directors in Action*. Indianapolis: Bobbs-Merrill, 1973.

"Uncle Sam as a Jailer." *Review of Reviews* 72 (Dec. 1925): 645.

"U.S. Aviation & the Air Mail." *Fortune* 9 (May 1934): 85–89, 140–42.

"Up from Chaos." *Aviation* 35 (Nov. 1934): 339–44.

Upton, Harriet Taylor. *Random Recollections*. Committee for the Preservation of Ohio Suffrage Records, n.d.

Van Waters, Miriam. *Youth in Conflict*. New York: Arno Press, 1970.

Vidor, King. *A Tree Is a Tree*. New York: Harcourt, Brace, 1952.

Walker, Stanley. *The Night Club Era*. New York: Blue Ribbon Books, 1933.

Warner, Emily Smith. *The Happy Warrior: A Biography of My Father, Alfred E. Smith*. Garden City, N.Y.: Doubleday, 1956.

Wells, Mildred White. *Unity in Diversity: The History of the General Federation of Women's Clubs*. Washington, D.C.: GFWC, 1953.

Wheeler, Burton K. *Yankee from the West*. Garden City, N.Y.: Doubleday, 1962.

Wheeler, Harold A. *Hazeltine the Professor*. Greenlawn, N.Y.: Hazeltine Corp., 1978.

"Who's Who— and Why." *Saturday Evening Post*, Sept. 27, 1924, p. 74.

Wilson, Joan Hoff. *Herbert Hoover: Forgotten Progressive*. Boston: Little, Brown, 1975.

"The Woman Politician Arrives." *Outlook*, June 27, 1928, p. 326.

"Worker Willebrandt." *Time*, Oct. 8, 1928, p. 11.

NEWSPAPERS

Cleveland Plain Dealer, 1925.
Hollywood Reporter, 1950.
Kansas City Star, 1928–62 (Library files).
Los Angeles Herald-Examiner, 1915–63 (Library files).
Los Angeles Times, 1915–63 (Library files).
Louisville Courier-Journal, 1925.
Mobile Register, 1923–24.
New York Times, 1921–35.
Sacramento Union, 1919–21.
Variety, 1947–1950, 1954.

Index

Adams, Annette Abbott, 45–46
Aeronautical Chamber of Commerce, 194, 198
Alderson, West Virginia (Federal Industrial Institution for Women), 84–86, 89–90, 278n6
Allen, Florence E., 41, 216, 217
Alton, John, 4
American Airways, 195, 198
American Association of University Women, 84
American Home Economics Association, 83, 84, 86
American Prison Association, 84
Andrews, General Lincoln, 54, 75
Anthony, David, 97
Anti-Saloon League, 50, 51
Assistant Attorney General of the U.S. *See* Willebrandt, Mabel Walker
Association Against the Prohibition Amendment, 79
Atlanta, U.S. penitentiary at, 81, 92–96, 97
Atlanta Life, 94
Aviation Corporation (AVCO), 189, 192, 196

Bailey (Savannah Four family), 57
Bates, Sanford, 98–99
Baughn (Savannah Four family), 57
Beck, James, 76, 207
Benjamin, Ray, 115
Biddle (Leavenworth warden), 96
Black, Hugo: air mail contract hearings, 200; Mobile "Six" prosecutor, 62–63; Supreme Court appointment, 216
Blackwell, Oklahoma, 9
Blackwell Times, 9
Blackwell Times-Record, 10
Blair, David, 58
Blake-McKellar Act, 200–201
Bledsoe, Benjamin, 112
Boole, Mrs. Ella A., 154, 178
Bootlegging, 51
Borah, William, 56, 93, 96, 159, 210
Borland, Earl, 210
Brookhart Committee, 55, 65, 104–107, 275n51
Brookhart, Smith W., 104
Brown, Clarence, 236, 240

Brown, J. Ward, 120, 256
Brown, Maud Hubbard, 15, 110, 119–120, 136, 255–56, 285n14
Brown, Norma C., 184
Brown, Walter F., 154, 192, 195, 197, 198, 200
Bryan, William Jennings, 56, 151
Buckley, Michigan, 16
Buckley Bank, 16, 42, 271n49
Bullock, Georgia, 38, 86, 136
Bureau of Prisons, 98–99
Burns, William, 58, 102

California Fruit Exchange, 180
California grape industry, 179–89 *passim*
California Vineyardists Association, 180, 181
Camp Grant, Illinois, 90
Camp Sherman, Ohio, 91; *see also* Chillicothe
Campbell, Litta Belle Hibben, 41, 136
Capone, Al, 182–83, 294n13
Capra, Frank, 233, 234, 235, 238, 240, 241–42
Carroll, Earl, 94
Cellar, Emmanuel, 166
Chateau Marmont, 135, 221, 222
Chautauqua tours, 124, 129, 130, 148
Cherokee strip, 8–9, 267n14
Chile copper case (*Edwards* v. *Chile Copper Co.*), 100
Chillicothe, Ohio, U.S. reformatory at, 91, 280n36
Christian Church, 12, 252
Citizenship Conference, 56
Civil Aeronautics Act of 1938, 201
Civil Aeronautics Authority (CAA), 201, 203
Claggett, Calvin, 224, 259, 253, 306n104
Claggett, Mary, 224, 226, 259
Clark, James, 64
Cleveland case, 68–69, 276n65
Coast Guard, U.S., 54
Cochran, Jacqueline, 219, 259
Codel, Martin, 203–204
College of Law, University of Southern California, 30, 32
Collins, Myra Dell, 33, 136, 256
Commingore, Dorothy, 244

323

Community property law, 42, 141
Conn, Donald, 180, 181, 182, 187, 294n4
Conner, Capt. A. J., 98
Coolidge, Calvin, 55, 69, 110, 111, 112, 114
Copeland, Royal, 186
Counterattack, 238, 243
Crawley, K. T., 86, 87
Crim, John W. H., 58
Curtis, Charles, 69–70, 83, 85, 155

d'Amore, Rose (Mrs. Lowell B. Mason), 219
Daughters of the American Revolution, 84
Daugherty, Harry M: impeachment trial, 102–103; need for Willebrandt in 1924 campaign, on, 151; patronage, 46–47, 49–50; resignation, 55; support for Willebrandt judgeship, 109
Davis, Ben, 154
Davis, John, 87, 88
Davis, John W., 75, 166
Davis, Katherine B., 85, 88
Davis Amendment, 205, 208
Day, Luther, 69
Delphi, Indiana, 88
DeMille, Cecil B., 236, 238, 239, 240
Dewey, Thomas E., 248, 249
Dinwiddie, Dr. E. C., 181–82
Disney, Walt, 236
Dmytryk, Edward, 237, 238
Doherty, Frank, 46, 110, 111, 114–15, 248, 250
Doherty, Sarah Patten, 136
Donovan, William, 92, 156, 159, 174, 175
Duck Lake, Michigan, 16
Dudding, E. E., 86
Dyott, John, 71

Eaton, Cyrus, 4–5
Eaton, Thomas P., 4
Eddy, Nelson, 221
Edge, Walter, 74
Edson, Mrs. Katherine Philips, 46
Edwards, Edward I., 166
Eielson, (Colonel) Ben, 210
Eighteenth Amendment, 50, 51; *see also* Prohibition
Einstein, Izzy, 62
Eisenhower, Dwight David, 251
Ellis, Winnifred, 133, 136, 145, 222
Emery, Laura Jane, 222, 256
Escondido, California, 222
Estman, William B., 245

Farley, James P., 200
Farmer, Bradford, 22
Federal Farm Board, 180, 181, 182, 185

Federal Radio Commission (FRC), 205, 206–209
Federal Radio Commission, Johnson-Kennedy Radio Corporation, Intervener v. Nelson Brothers Bond & Mortgage Company, 207–208
Felton, J. L., 29
Ferris, W. N., 29
Fish, Hamilton, Jr., 166
"Five and Ten" law, 78
Foltz, Clara Shortridge, 41, 46
Ford, John, 241, 250
Fort Scott, Kansas, 69–70
Foster Bill, 90
Foster, Louise, 137
Freeman, Talbot, 196
Fruit Industries, Ltd., 180–89 *passim;* 295n30, 296n37

Gable, Clark, 231
Gainor, Rosa, 126, 226
Gardener, Helen H., 140
Garrett, Paul, 180, 181
General Federation of Women's Clubs (GFWC), 83, 84, 86
George, Walter, 91, 95
Girls Friendly Society, 86
Glover, Warren, 197
Goff, Guy, 86
Goldberg (Savannah Four family), 57
Good, James William, 165
Good Government League, 27, 36
Goodykoontz, Wells, 83
Goulding, Edmund, 230
Graham, George, 85, 86
Grape Stabilization Corporation, 180
Green, Colonel Ned M., 72
Gregory, T.T.G., 181, 188, 197
Grosvener, Graham, 198
Guinan, Texas, 66, 67

Haar, Willie, 57, 61
Hafford, Lida, 84, 85, 86
Halfway to Hell, 242
Hann, George, 195, 196
Harding, Warren Gamaliel, 47, 53, 104
Harlow, Jean, 231, 302n10
Harris, Mary Belle, 82, 88, 89, 90
Harris, Robert, 73
Hartman, Don, 240
Harwick, John, 4
Harwick, Susan, 4
Hawes, H. Crittenden, 85
Haynes, Major Roy, 53
Haystack massacre, 5, 266n7
Hazeltine, Louis A., 205

Hazeltine case (*Hazeltine Corp.* v. *E. A. Wildermuth*), 203, 204
Hearst, William R., 93, 230
Heindorf v. *SDGA,* 235
Helmich case (*Helmich* v. *Hellman*), 100
Henderson, Paul, 197
Henning, Arthur Sears, 177
Herter, Christian, 159
Hill, John Philip, 166
Hines, General (Director, Veterans Bureau), 91
Hinshaw, Hainer, 192, 196, 200, 203
Hodder, Jessie, 85
Holland, Rush, 62
Hollywood Ten, 237, 238
Holmes, Oliver Wendell, 65
Holzer, Harry, 216
Hoover, Herbert: declines to recommend Willebrandt for judgeship, 249; help for grape industry, 180, 187; 1920 presidential primary, 45; 1928 campaign, 165, 177, 178
Hopper, Hedda, 231, 250, 257
Horowitz, Fred: considers marriage with Willebrandt, 134, 135; consulted on adoption, 124; practice with Willebrandt, 38, 40, 221, 223–24; relations with Walkers, 118, 131
House Un-American Activities Committee (HUAC), 236–37, 241, 243
Howard Perry, 156–57
Howland, Paul, 103
Hughes, Charles Evans, 209
Hugoton, Kansas, 5

Ickes, Harold, 212
Income tax, 76–77
Indio, California, 256, 259
Inside of Prohibition, The (appeared as a series of syndicated articles and book), 78, 178

Jaffray, Julia, 84, 89
Johnson, Hiram: candidate for Republican presidential nomination, 151; critical of grape program, 188; enmity for Hoover, 153; opposition to the League of Nations, 45; patronage battles, 46–47, 73; progressive campaigns, 28; support for Willebrandt's judgeship, 110, 112, 114–15
Johnson-Kennedy Radio Corporation, 206, 207
Joint Fact-Finding Committee, 236; *see also* Tenny Committee
Jones "Five and Ten" law, 78
Jones, Wesley C., 105–106

Justice Department. *See* Willebrandt, Mabel Walker

Kansas City, Missouri, 12
Keating, Cletus, 196
Keays, Vernon, 234, 240, 241
Kellar, Oscar E., 102–103
Kellogg, Caroline, 41
Kelly, Clyde, 197
Kelly Act (Air Mail Act of 1925), 194, 195
Kenny, Elizabeth A., 41, 168
Kent, Atwater, 204, 205, 206
Kent, Frank, 173
Kingman, Kansas, 9, 10
Knoeller, Grace, 137, 224, 260, 261, 262
Koverman, Ida (Kay), 230, 231
Ku Klux Klan, 70–71

Lahey, May, 41, 136
Langley, John, 55, 68
Law Enforcement League of Philadelphia, 153
League of Women Voters, 83, 86, 140
Leavenworth, Kansas, U.S. penitentiary at, 81, 96–97, 281n59
Legge, Alexander, 180, 249n7
Lempert, Dr. Julius, 261
Lerner, Max, 237
Lever Act, 51
Lewisohn, Adolph, 98
Lincoln Park elementary school, 29–30
Linthicum, Charles, 188
Lomen, Carl, 209–11, 260
Lord, General William, 91, 98, 280n36
Loucks, William Dewey, 196
Lowden, Frank, 155
Lucerne, Missouri, 8
Lucerne Standard, 8

McAfee, John A., 14
McAfee, L. M., 14–15
McCarey, 237, 250
McCloskey, P. N., 221
McCormack, Rev. Robert, 253
McCormick, Paul, 111
MacCracken, William P., 197
MacDonald, Jeanette, 221, 231
McIntire, Admiral Ross, 214, 261
McNary-Watres Act, 197, 198, 200
McNeil Island, Washington, U.S. penitiary at, 81
Mankiewicz, Joseph, 238, 239, 240
Manual Training High School, 13–14
Marron v. *United States,* 77
Matthews, Annabel, 126, 145
Matthews, Arthur John, 22

Mayer, Louis B., 115, 229–31, 237, 250
Mayer, Rudolph, 230–31
Mellon, Andrew W., 54, 63, 104
Merritt, Ralph, 183, 184, 185
Methodist ministers, 69–70; 160–61
Metro-Goldwyn-Mayer (MGM), 179, 229, 230
Miller, White B., 58, 61
Mitchell, William D., 96, 175, 176
Mobile (Alabama) "Six," 62–63
Monahan, Florence, 85
Moore, Grace, 231–32
Moore, R. Walton, 84
Morgan, Helen, 66, 67
Morgan, Olive, 256, 262
Morrow, Dwight, 154, 194
Morrow Board, 194
Morse, Fannie French, 86–87, 88, 121
Motion Picture Alliance for the Preservation of American Ideals, 236
Mount Weather station, 83

National Aeronautic Association, 194
National Committee on Prisons and Prison Labor, 84, 90
National Congress of Mothers and Parent-Teacher Associations, 83, 84
National Consumers' League, 83
National Council of Jewish Women, 86
National Council of Women, 84, 86
National Federation of Business and Professional Women's Clubs, 83, 84
National Prohibition Act, 66; see also Volstead Act
National Women's Trade Union League, 83
Nations, Heber, 70–72
Naughty Marietta, 221
Nelson Brothers Bond & Mortgage Company, 207–208
Newton, Walter H., 160, 165
Nightclub raids, 66, 158
Norton, Mary, 158

Odlum, Floyd, 259
Olmstead v. *United States,* 77
O'Toole, Judge Mary, 87

Padlock raids, 66–67, 157
Palmer, A. Mitchell, 49
Park, Maud Wood, 83, 85
Park Academy, 14–15
Parker, John J., 175
Patterson, Cissy, 219
Perelli-Minetti, Antonio, 188
Phi Delta Delta, 32, 136
Pinchot, Gifford, 56
Pittsburgh Aviation Investors Corporation (PAIC), 194–95

Police court defenders office, 32, 34, 36
Police courts, Los Angeles, 32
Pope, James H., 34, 38, 46
Post, Carol, 234
Pound, Dean Roscoe, 137, 175
Prather, Charles, 71
Prisons: changing public attitude, 82; expansion of federal system, 83–89, 90–92; industries, 97–98; mismanagement, 92–97; need for reform, 82, 83
Prohibition: assessments of effectiveness, 79; coalition support for, 51; enforcement problems, 50–55 *passim;* lobbies in support of, 50; political influence in enforcement, 54–55; repeal drive, 79; volume of cases, 75
Prohibition unit, Treasury Department, 53
Prostitution: campaigns against in Los Angeles, 27, 39; changing public attitudes toward, 36, 82
Purity crusades, 37–38, 270n26

Radio, 204–209 *passim*
Radio Act of 1927, 204
Radio and Television Directors Guild (RTDG), 234–35
Rankin, John, 236
Raskob, John J., 158, 159
Raymond, Gene, 231
Red Channels, 238
Red Scare, 236–37
Reindeer Committee, 211–12
Remus, George, 64–65
Republican National Convention (1928), 154–55
Robinson, Sam, 5
Rogell, Al, 236, 238, 239, 240, 241, 242
Rogers, Will, 186
Roosevelt, Eleanor, 214
Roosevelt, Franklin D., 200, 215, 216, 217, 218
Roosevelt, Theodore, 25, 45
Rosebud baby case, 37–38
Rossen, Robert, 238
Rum row campaign, 56–64

St. Sure, A. F., 112
Sargent, John G., 55, 89, 100, 114, 148
Sartain, A. E., 92
Savannah, Georgia Four, 57–61, 62
Schenck, Joseph, 231
Screen Actors Guild, 233
Screen Directors Guild (SDG), 233, 234–35, 237–41
Screen Writers Guild, 233, 237
Service Star Legion, 86
Sheldon, Judge Caryl, 244
Shepherd, John, 38, 40

Sherman, Mrs. John D., 89
Shipley, Ruth, 243
Shipping Board cases, 76
Shontz, Judge Orfa Jean, 39, 41, 136
Shortridge, Samuel, 45, 46–47, 73, 109, 112, 115, 283n113
Sirica, John J., 219, 260, 277n101
Slemp, C. Bascom, 62
Smith, Alfred E., 161–62
Smith, Barbara, 245
Smith, C. R., 201
Smith, Jesse, 50, 55, 65, 69, 104
Smith, Walter, 245
Snook, John, 93, 95, 96
Snyder, Katherine, 5
Southern Pacific Railrod machine, 27, 28, 45
Springfield (Ohio) speech, 165–67
Stanley, Louise, 126, 128, 131, 213, 145
Stefansson, Vilhjalmur, 209, 211
Stephens, William, 45
Stevens, George, 241
Stinson, Roxie, 105
Stone, Harlan Fiske, 54, 55, 87–88, 261, 279n30
Straton, Rev. John Roach, 167
Sulgrave Club, 145, 221, 233, 257, 261
Swanson, Claude A., 84
Swetland case, 201

Taft, Robert, 246, 248, 250, 251
Taft, William Howard, 175
Taylor, Walter, 181, 182, 294n7
Teague, C. C., 184, 188, 189
Tempe Normal School, 22, 25
Temple City, California, 43, 119–21
Tenny, Jack B., 236
Tenny, L. S., 180
Tenny Committee, 238
Thomas, John, 96
Truman, Harry S, 249–50
Tullahoma, Tennessee, 5
Tuttle, Charles, 67

Ukiah Company, 187
United States, Justice Department. *See* Willebrandt, Mabel Walker
United States v. *Carroll*, 77
United States v. *Manly S. Sullivan*, 76–77
Upton, Harriet Taylor, 84, 109, 110, 151

Van Dyke, David, 258
Van Dyke, Rev. Hendrick, 257–58
Van Dyke, Rev. Henry, 167
Van Dyke, Jan Christopher, 258
Van Dyke, Pieter, 258
Van Dyke, Woody, 221
Van Riper, Walter, 74

Van Waters, Miriam, 39, 82
Vine-Glo (fruit concentrate), 183, 185
Vino Sano (wine brick concentrate), 186
Volstead, Laura (Mrs. Carl Lomen), 211
Volstead Act, 56, 66–68; volume of cases, 75–76, 80, 179–80, 181
Votaw, Heber, 81–82, 85, 87, 90

Waldorf-Astoria conference (1947), 238
Walker, David W.: at Republican national convention (1928), 148; death, 256–57; employment, 6, 8, 9–10, 42; personal qualities, 6; Walkers ands, living at, 256
Walker, John C., 5
Walker, Myrtle Eaton: death, 226; employment, 4, 8, 10, 13; personal qualities, 6, 42; settled in Kansas, 4
Walker family: chicken farm, 119–20; ideas on child rearing, 12; marriage of David and Myrtle Eaton, 5–6; migrations, 5–6, 6–7, 10, 12; visit to Washington (1928), 148
Walker Fields, Pennsylvania, 224, 226, 228, 256
Walkersands (family retreat), 256
Warren, Earl, 238, 246, 248
Watres Act, 198, 200
Watson, James E., 155
Wellman, William, 241
Wells, Charles, 209, 210
Wells, Mabel, 260
Wells, Minnie Hickstein (Mrs. Ira), 12, 13, 119, 259–60, 263, 268n35, 284n8
West Virginia Industrial Farm Commission, 86
Wheat, Alfred A., 100
Wheeler, Burton K., 105–106
Wheeler, Wayne, 54
White, Mrs. Edward, 84
White, Luther, 98, 146
White, Judge Thomas, 36
Whitin, Dr. E. Stagg, 97
Wilbur, Ray Lyman, 114, 189, 210, 211
Wildermuth, E. A., 203, 204
Willebrandt, Arthur F.: education, 270n18; employment, 19, 32; health, 19; marriage, and failure of marriage, 19, 168; military service, 40
Willebrandt, Dorothy Rae (Mrs. Hendrick Van Dyke): at Walker Fields, 226; debut, 257; education, 129, 222, 224, 256; family background, 123–24; grandparents, relations with, 222, 257; marriage, 257
Willebrandt, Mabel Walker
—anti-communism, 242, 243, 246
—assistant attorney general, 46–75 *passim*, 103–108 *passim*, 174–75, 283n99, 283n101
—assistant police court defender, 34–37

Willebrandt (*cont.*)
—at Democratic national convention (1924), 151–52
—aviation interests, 3, 189–90, 191–92, 196–97, 201–202
—birth, 3
—Chautauqua tours, 124, 129, 130, 148
—child rearing, ideas on, 126–28
—committee on aeronautical law, 101, 201
—courtroom teachnique, 39, 40, 68, 69, 71, 231, 235, 244–46, 260–61
—education, 13–16, 25–28, 30, 32–33, 38, 268n41
—final illness and death, 261–63
—father, admiration for, 42
—federal judgeship, hope for, 109–16, 151, 173, 216, 249
—Fruit Industries, counsel for, 181–82, 295n23, 296n36
—hearing problems, 39, 122–23, 261
—Horowitz, Fred, considered marriage with, 132, 133, 134, 136, 176–77
—Ku Klux Klan, views on, 280n37
—lawyer, decision to become, 30
—lawyers, ideas on honesty of, 38
—Lomen, Carl, friendship with, 209, 210, 260, 292n66, 299n102
—marriage and failure of marriage, 19, 30, 33–34, 40, 167–68
—Metro-Goldwyn-Mayer, counsel for, 230–31, 301n1
—money worries, 118, 121–22, 123, 289n5
—Nations libel case, 72
—personal qualities, 12, 15, 37
—plans for adoption of child, 121, 123, 124–25, 126, 128–29, 131, 257, 258–59
—political campaigns, involvement in, 150, 155–56, 160–64, 168–72, 246, 248–51, 291n53, 291n57, 291n58, 292n71
—political leaders, assessment of, 151–53, 215, 251, 263, 291n53, 291n57
—pregnancy, 25–26, 269n60
—prisons: investigations, 90–91, 92–94, 95, 96–97; lobbying for women's prison, 84, 88, 279n30; reform of, 37, 94–95, 97–98, 282n68; work for reformatory, 90–91
—private practice, early, 38–39
—progressive, 43, 44, 152, 215
—prohibition: enforcement, 53–56, 63–67, 72, 74, 78–80, 154; politics of, 53–55, 63, 68–69, 72, 74, 154; repeal, 294n7; writings and speeches on, 56–57, 72, 78, 157
—prostitution cases, 36, 37, 39–40
—radio law, 206, 207, 208
—relations with daughter, 124–25, 126, 128–29, 131, 257, 258–59
—religion, 12, 14, 15, 16, 29, 48, 96, 123, 133, 252, 253, 255
—reindeer disputes, 211–12
—Republican National Convention (1928), 155–56
—retirement, 261, 306n108
—Screen Directors Guild, counsel for, 233–39, 241
—selective service system, legal advisory board, 40
—social life, 38, 143, 145–46, 147, 148, 214, 288n100
—speeches, 3, 15, 56, 157, 160–61
—Supreme Court, arguments before, 75, 76, 77–78
—sympathy for underdog, 30, 34, 39–40
—tax issues, 56, 100–101, 212–14
—teacher and principal, 16, 28, 29, 38
—wiretapping, aversion to, 77, 277n101
—women's issues, on, 41, 42, 43, 61, 116, 137–39, 140–41, 142, 251, 287–93
—women's organizations, 41–42, 136–38
—work, attitudes toward, 43
—youth, support of, 119, 258, 260, 306n104
Willebrandt, Mrs. Rose, 30, 33
Williams, John T., 47, 75
Willkie, Wendell, 248
Wilson, Dr. Clarence True, 184
Wiretapping. *See* Olmstead case
Wise, Rabbi Stephen, 56
WJKS radio station, 206–208
Women Lawyers' Club of Los Angeles, 41
Women's Christian Temperance Union (WCTU), 50, 51, 71, 83, 84, 86, 178
Women's Committee for the Repeal of the Eighteenth Amendment, 167
Women's Joint Congressional Committee (WJCC), 83
Women's court at Los Angeles, 36
Women's Organization for Prohibition Reform, 79
Wood, Sam, 236, 237
Woodcock, (Colonel) Amos W. W., 184, 185
Woodhead, Florence, 41, 145
Woodsdale, Kansas, 4–5, 8, 70
Work, Hubert, 86, 87, 88, 159, 164
Wrangel Island, 209–10
Wyler, William, 241

Yost, Ellis A., 206, 207
Yost, Lenna (Mrs. Ellis A.), 87, 182
Youngerman, Joseph, 235, 241, 261

Zanuck, Darryl, 231

Mabel Walker Willebrandt was composed into type on the Mergenthaler Variable Input Phototypesetter in eleven-point Bembo type with two-point spacing between the lines. Centaur was selected for display. The book was designed by Jim Billingsley, typeset by Computer Composition, Inc., printed offset by Thomson-Shore, Inc., and bound by John H. Dekker & Sons. The paper on which the book is printed is designed for an effective life of at least three hundred years·

THE UNIVERSITY OF TENNESSEE PRESS : KNOXVILLE

DATE DUE

DEC 0 7 1995			